ELEMENTARY
LOGIC

ELEMENTARY LOGIC

NANCY D. SIMCO

and

GENE G. JAMES

Memphis State University

DICKENSON Publishing Company, Inc.
Encino, California
and Belmont, California

ISBN-0-8221-0156-4
Library of Congress Catalog Card Number: 75-8126

Printed in the United States of America
Printing (last digit): 9 8 7 6 5 4 3 2

Cover by Ron Rifkin

The authors acknowledge use of material from:

Clarence Darrow for the Defense, copyright 1941 by Irving Stone. Reprinted by permission of Doubleday & Co., Inc.

How To Lie With Statistics, by Darrell Huff. Pictures by Irving Geis. By permission of W. W. Norton & Company, Inc. Copyright 1954 by Darrell Huff and Irving Geis.

for JOY and BILL

TO THE INSTRUCTOR

This text is written for liberal arts students who have no training in logic and little in mathematics. In teaching students with this background, we have found that those who master formal techniques are better able to understand other topics in logic, so our first and primary objective is to present these techniques as thoroughly and briefly as possible. The procedure followed is to introduce one topic at a time, reinforcing it with numerous exercises. Although this approach can hardly be described as a pedagogical revolution, few writers of logic texts present the material this way. For example, most authors introduce a number of inference rules simultaneously, whereas we introduce them one or two at a time. The result of our approach is that the student's knowledge of natural deduction builds gradually but thoroughly.

Our goal throughout the text is pedagogical clarity rather than theoretical innovation. Standard techniques and terminology are introduced. We use the logical notation of *Principia Mathematica*, but also explain Polish notation. Indirect and conditional proof, which have become standard procedures, are discussed. Traditional logic is treated at greater length than in most recent texts, although the concepts of mood and figure are not explained since they are not necessary for understanding it. In the discussion of formal axiomatic systems, the propositional calculus serves as an example, drawing on material the student has learned in earlier chapters. The system presented is that of *Principia Mathematica*, the classic systematization of propositional logic. As is customary in logic texts, most of the examples used in discussing informal fallacies are trivial. We have found that these illustrate informal fallacies better than more interesting ones, which are likely to arouse philosophical controversy and shift the student's attention away from the central concern of a text at this level.

We agree with Harold Lee that students should *first* learn logic and *then* philosophize about it.* Thus, so far as we could, we have attempted to avoid philosophical issues. For example, our definition of the term 'proposition' is not intended to settle the dispute regarding the nature of propositions, but only to allow one to teach logic to beginners. Similarly, the chapter on language is not a treatise on the philosophy of language, but only introduces the student to certain distinctions and concepts that are useful aids to clear thinking. And we do not even mention the so-called paradox of material implication or the problem of justifying induction. This approach has the merit of leaving the instructor free to raise as many, or as few, philosophical issues as he or she wishes.

In the chapter on the predicate calculus we use language which suggests that quantification necessarily involves existential commitment. We also use language indicating that variables function as both place markers and unknowns. Our justification for this is pedagogical. The guideline we followed was to use whatever English expressions best promoted an intuitive understanding of elementary quantification theory. The rules of inference introduced in this chapter are designed to apply only to singly quantified expressions of the type found in the exercises. However, whenever possible we attempted to formulate them in such a way as to aid the student's transition to the study of inferences involving multiply quantified expressions.

Several different one-semester courses may be taught using this book. Chapters VI, VII, VIII, IX, and X have been written independently of one another, so that an instructor may teach chapters I through V and then choose one or more of these chapters to complete the course. One may also teach chapters I through V, and then select XI, XII, and XIII which may be taught as a unit. Or one may present chapters I through V, select one or more of chapters VI through X, and assign XI through XIII as parallel reading. A two-semester course may be taught by using most, or all, of the material in the text. Quarter courses may be taught by selecting chapters I through V; or chapter I, either IX or X or both, and chapters XI through XIII.

Writers of textbooks are especially indebted to the thoughts of others. In our overall approach we perhaps owe most to Howard Kahane and Irving M. Copi, whose standards of pedagogical clarity constantly challenged us. In addition to Kahane, to whom we are indebted for our

---

*Harold Newton Lee, *Symbolic Logic: An Introductory Textbook for Non-Mathematicians* (New York: Random House, 1961), p. 88.

treatment of quantification, we are indebted to the following logicians who influenced various sections of the text: Alice Ambrose and Morris Lazerowitz, formal systems and alternative notations; Frederic Fitch and Robert Neidorf, indirect and conditional proof; Lionel Ruby and William Werkmeister, fallacies; John Hospers and William Alston, language and definition. Others to whom we are indebted for specific ideas are Herbert Searles, Ernest Barker, Arthur Smullyan, William Halberstadt, Robert Olson, and Nicholas Rescher. Finally, we, and those who use this book, are indebted to our elementary logic students at Memphis State University who used earlier drafts. We also wish to thank Mrs. Amna Gardner and Mrs. Sidney Daniels for their excellent secretarial assistance.

CONTENTS

1

INTRODUCTION

Logic can be defined as the science which has as its central problem the attempt to formulate principles for appraising arguments as correct or incorrect. An **argument** is one or more propositions, called a **premise** or **premises,** which are offered as evidence for another proposition, called a **conclusion.** A **proposition** is a statement which can be evaluated as true or false. For example, 'Today is Tuesday' is a proposition but 'Please pass the salt' is not.

There are two basic types of arguments, deductive and inductive. A **deductive argument** is one in which it is claimed that if the premises are true, then the conclusion *must* be true. Deductive arguments are appraised as valid or invalid and as sound or unsound. A deductive argument is **valid** when its premises and conclusion are related in such a way that it would be impossible for the premises to be true and the conclusion false. However, the premises of a valid argument need not be true. A valid argument which has true premises is said to be **sound.** Since it is impossible for a valid argument to have true premises and a false conclusion, the conclusion of a sound argument must be true.

An **inductive argument** is one in which it is claimed that if the premises are true, then it is *probable* that the conclusion is true. Since it is not claimed that if the premises of an inductive argument are true, its conclusion must be true, inductive arguments are not appraised as valid or invalid, sound or unsound. Inductive arguments are appraised with respect to the degree of probability which their premises provide for their conclusions. All of the arguments discussed in the first nine chapters are deductive. See chapter 10 for examples of inductive arguments and principles for appraising them.

The terms 'true' and 'false' will apply here to propositions only, not to arguments. The terms 'valid' and 'invalid', 'sound' and 'unsound', will apply to deductive arguments only, not to inductive arguments or propositions. As stated above, valid arguments which have true premises, and therefore a true conclusion, are said to be sound. However, valid arguments may have both true and false premises, or only false premises. Similarly, a valid argument may have either a true or false conclusion. The only combination of propositions that cannot occur in a valid argument is one in which the premises are true and the conclusion false.

Examples of Valid Arguments

Valid arguments with true premises and true conclusions, which are, therefore, sound:

> All men are mortal.
> Socrates is a man.
> Therefore, Socrates is mortal.

> Teddy bears are both soft and cuddly.
> Therefore, teddy bears are cuddly.

A valid but unsound argument with one false premise, one true premise, and a true conclusion:

> All whales are fish.
> All fish live in water.
> Therefore, all whales live in water.

A valid but unsound argument with false premises and a true conclusion:

> All bats are birds.
> All birds can fly.
> Therefore, all bats can fly.

A valid but unsound argument with false premises and a false conclusion:

> New Orleans is north of Memphis.
> Memphis is north of St. Louis.
> St. Louis is north of Chicago.
> Therefore, New Orleans is north of Chicago.

All of the foregoing arguments are valid because their premises are related to their conclusions in such a way that it *would be impossible* for their premises to be true and their conclusions false. *If their premises were true, then their conclusions would be true.* On the other hand, the following arguments contain true propositions only, but are nevertheless invalid because it is *possible* for their premises to be true and their conclusions false:

> If anyone is from Liverpool then he is English.
> John Lennon is English.
> Therefore, John Lennon is from Liverpool.

> New York is larger than either Boston or Chicago.
> New York is the largest city in the country.

EXERCISES

1. How is logic defined above?
2. What is an argument?
3. What is a proposition?
4. What is a premise?
5. What is a conclusion?
6. What is a deductive argument and how are such arguments appraised?
7. When is a deductive argument valid?
8. When is a deductive argument sound?
9. What is an inductive argument and how are such arguments appraised?
10. Can an argument be said to be true or false?
11. Can a valid argument contain false premises?
12. Can an invalid argument contain true premises?

2

PROPOSITIONS AND PROPOSITIONAL FORMS

Since arguments are composed of propositions, we must discuss the latter before we can formulate principles for determining the validity or invalidity of arguments. Propositions are of two types, simple and compound. **Simple propositions** are those of which no part is a proposition. **Compound propositions** are those of which parts are propositions. Examples of simple propositions are:

> The pressure is increased.
> The volume is decreased.

Examples of compound propositions are:

> The pressure is increased *and* the volume
> is decreased.
>
> *Either* the pressure is increased *or* the
> volume is decreased.
>
> *If* the volume is decreased, *then* the
> pressure is increased.

Just as the letters x, y, z, etc., are used in algebra to stand for any number whatever and are known as numerical variables, so the lower case letters p through z are used in logic to stand for any proposition whatever and are called **propositional variables.**

NEGATION

Any proposition may be negated. A negation of 'The pressure is increased' is 'The pressure is not increased'. If the propositional variable p is used to stand for any proposition, then the negation of that proposition will be represented by $\sim p$.

> RULE: The negation of a true proposition is false; the negation of a false proposition is true.

This rule can also be expressed by a device known as a truth table:

p	$\sim p$
T	F
F	T

CONJUNCTION

A compound proposition composed of two propositions connected by the word 'and' is called a **conjunction,** and its component propositions are called **conjuncts.** If p and q stand for any two propositions, then the compound proposition p *and* q is symbolized as $p \cdot q$. Since $p \cdot q$ asserts that two propositions are true, it is true if and only if both p and q are true. If p is false, or q is false, or both p and q are false, then $p \cdot q$ is false.

> RULE: A conjunction is true if and only if both of its conjuncts are true.

This is also expressed by the following truth table:

p	q	$p \cdot q$
T	T	T
T	F	F
F	T	F
F	F	F

DISJUNCTION

A compound proposition composed of two propositions connected by the word 'or' is called a **disjunction,** and its component propositions are called **disjuncts.** Since the word 'or' has two different meanings, we will discuss these meanings before we construct truth tables that show the conditions under which disjunctions are true or false. Sometimes 'or' is used in an **inclusive** sense to mean 'either . . . or . . . , perhaps both'. Other times it is used in an **exclusive** sense to mean 'either . . . or . . . , but not both'. For example, consider the sentence, 'Either faculty members or the wives of faculty members are eligible for membership'. Since it is possible for someone to be either a faculty member or the wife of a faculty member, or *both,* this sentence clearly means 'either . . . or . . . , perhaps both'. Suppose, on the other hand, a menu in a restaurant states that for a certain price, one may have either salad or dessert with one's meal. This would normally be interpreted as meaning that one may have either a salad or a dessert, *but not both,* and is, therefore, an exclusive use of 'or'.

A compound proposition composed of two propositions connected by the word 'or' used in an inclusive sense will be symbolized as $p \lor q$. Because $p \lor q$ asserts that either p is true, or q is true, or both p and q are true, the following rule can be formulated:

RULE: An inclusive disjunction is true if and only if at least one of its disjuncts is true.

This rule is also expressed by the truth table:

p	q	$p \lor q$
T	T	T
T	F	T
F	T	T
F	F	F

A compound proposition composed of two propositions connected by the word 'or' used in an exclusive sense will be symbolized as $p \oslash q$. Since $p \oslash q$ asserts that either p is true, or q is true, but that it is not the case that both p and q are true, the following rule holds:

RULE: An exclusive disjunction is true if and only if one or the other, but not both, of its disjuncts is true.

As in the former cases, this rule may also be expressed by a truth table:

p	q	$p \oslash q$
T	T	F
T	F	T
F	T	T
F	F	F

TRUTH-FUNCTIONS

Logicians speak of the truth or falsity of a proposition as its **truth value.**
The truth value of the compound propositions discussed in this chapter is
a function of the truth values of their component propositions. That is to
say, whether the compound propositions are true or false depends on the
truth or falsity of their component propositions. Compound propositions
of this type are called **truth-functional propositions,** and symbols such as ~ ,
· , ∨ , and ⊗, which are used to construct truth-functional propositions, are
called **truth-functional connectives.***

EXERCISES

I

1. How do simple and compound propositions differ?
2. What is a propositional variable?
3. State the rule for negation.
4. What is a conjunction? What are the components of conjunctions called? When
   are conjunctions true, and when false?
5. What is a disjunction? What are the components of disjunctions called? How do
   inclusive and exclusive disjunctions differ? When are inclusive disjunctions true,
   and when false? When are exclusive disjunctions true, and when false?
6. What is meant by speaking of the truth value of a proposition?
7. What is meant by the term 'truth-functional proposition'?
8. What is meant by the term 'truth-functional connective'?

II

If p and q stand for true propositions and x and y for false propositions, which of the
following are true and which false?

1. $\sim p$	9. $\sim x \cdot p$	17. $\sim x \vee \sim y$
2. $\sim x$	10. $\sim y \cdot \sim p$	18. $\sim p \vee \sim q$
3. $p \cdot q$	11. $p \vee q$	19. $p \otimes q$
4. $q \cdot p$	12. $x \vee q$	20. $\sim p \otimes q$
5. $x \cdot y$	13. $x \vee y$	21. $p \otimes \sim x$
6. $p \cdot x$	14. $y \vee x$	22. $q \otimes \sim y$
7. $q \cdot \sim p$	15. $\sim x \vee p$	23. $\sim x \otimes \sim y$
8. $y \cdot \sim q$	16. $y \vee \sim q$	

*Since the symbol ~ does not, in the strict sense of the word, connect anything, some authors
refer to symbols like those above as operators rather than connective symbols.

PUNCTUATION

To express propositions without ambiguity requires special symbols called **punctuation symbols.** In natural languages such as English and French, periods, commas, semicolons, etc., serve as punctuation symbols. In specialized languages such as mathematics and logic, parentheses, brackets, and braces are often used. For example, if the expression $3 + 3 \times 4 = 24$ is unpunctuated, one cannot determine whether it is true or false. If it were punctuated $3 + (3 \times 4) = 24$, then it would express a false proposition; whereas if it were punctuated $(3 + 3) \times 4 = 24$, then it would express a true proposition. Analogously, an expression of the form $p \cdot q \vee r$ might assert a true proposition if punctuated $(p \cdot q) \vee r$, but assert a false proposition if punctuated $p \cdot (q \vee r)$.*

A truth-functional connective which represents the form of an entire compound proposition is called its **major truth-functional connective.** For example, in expressions having the form $(p \cdot q) \vee r$, the $\vee$ is the major truth-functional connective; but in those having the form $p \cdot (q \vee r)$, the $\cdot$ is the major truth-functional connective. Since the compound propositions with which we are dealing are truth-functional, one must first determine the truth value of their components before one can determine the truth value of a compound proposition represented by the major truth-functional connective. For instance, before one can ascertain whether a proposition of the form $(p \vee q) \cdot (x \vee y)$ is true or false, one must determine the truth value of $(p \vee q)$ and of $(x \vee y)$. But before one can determine the truth value of $(p \vee q)$ and $(x \vee y)$, one must determine the truth values of $p, q, x,$ and y. Thus, if p and q were both true, then $(p \vee q)$ would be true; and if x and y were both false, then $(x \vee y)$ would be false. In this case $(p \vee q) \cdot (x \vee y)$ would be false, since its major connective is a $\cdot$, and a conjunction with a false conjunct is false.

If punctuation in addition to parentheses is needed, brackets are used. For example, brackets serve to prevent ambiguity in the expression

$$[p \cdot (q \varovee r)] \vee x$$

The brackets indicate that the major truth-functional connective is the inclusive disjunction symbol. Thus the entire expression is true if either $[p \cdot (q \varovee r)]$ is true, or if x is true; it is false only if both $[p \cdot (q \varovee r)]$ and x are false.

If still more punctuation is required, then braces are used. For instance,

---

*Although one may speak of *the* form of a proposition in certain contexts, propositions cannot be said to have a unique form, but may be interpreted as having different forms in different contexts the braces in the following expression show that the second occurrence of the · is the major truth-functional connective

$$\{[p \cdot (q \otimes r)] \vee x\} \cdot y$$

If a compound proposition contains braces, then they indicate the major truth-functional connective. If braces are not present, but brackets are, the brackets indicate the major truth-functional connective. If there are neither braces nor brackets, but one or more sets of parentheses are used, then the parentheses indicate the major truth-functional connective. Thus, braces are more inclusive, or have greater scope, than brackets; and brackets are more inclusive, or have greater scope, than parentheses.

In punctuating negative propositions the following convention is adopted: If a negation symbol precedes a set of punctuation symbols, it negates the *entire* proposition within those symbols. However, if no punctuation symbols are present, then the negation symbol negates only the proposition immediately following. The negation symbol in propositions of the form $\sim p \cdot q$ negates only p, whereas the negation symbol in $\sim (p \cdot q)$ negates $p \cdot q$. Just as $\sim p$ is true when p is false, and false when p is true, so $\sim (p \cdot q)$ is true when $p \cdot q$ is false, and false when $p \cdot q$ is true. Similarly, $\sim (p \otimes q)$ is true when $p \otimes q$ is false, and false when $p \otimes q$ is true.

EXERCISES

III

1. Why are punctuation symbols required in a language?
2. What is meant by saying that a truth-functional connective is the major connective in a given proposition?
3. What punctuation symbols are used in the present text? What is their order of inclusiveness or scope?
4. State the convention regarding negation adopted in the last paragraph above.

IV

If p, q, and r stand for true propositions, and x, y, and z, for false propositions, which of the following are true and which false?

1. $\sim p \cdot q$
2. $\sim (p \cdot q)$
3. $\sim (\sim p \cdot q)$
4. $\sim (x \cdot \sim y)$
5. $\sim (p \otimes q)$
6. $\sim (\sim x \vee y)$

7. $p \cdot (q \cdot r)$
8. $(p \cdot q) \cdot x$
9. $p \cdot \sim(x \cdot r)$

10. $(p \veebar \sim y) \vee z$
11. $\sim x \vee \sim(p \vee \sim r)$
12. $\sim(x \veebar y) \vee r$

13. $p \veebar \sim(\sim q \vee \sim r)$
14. $(p \cdot q) \cdot (r \cdot \sim z)$
15. $\sim(p \cdot q) \veebar (q \cdot r)$
16. $\sim[(p \vee q) \cdot (\sim r \vee \sim x)]$
17. $\sim[(x \cdot r) \vee \sim(\sim p \cdot q)]$
18. $\sim x \cdot [(p \cdot q) \vee (r \cdot \sim z)]$
19. $[(p \vee q) \cdot (\sim r \veebar x)] \cdot (p \vee \sim x)$
20. $[(\sim x \cdot \sim r) \vee (p \cdot \sim y)] \vee [(p \vee r) \cdot \sim(r \vee x)]$
21. $\sim[(x \veebar \sim y) \cdot (r \cdot \sim z)] \cdot [(x \cdot \sim r) \vee (q \cdot \sim y)]$
22. $\{[(p \cdot r) \vee (x \cdot \sim y)] \vee \sim y\} \cdot (p \cdot q)$
23. $\sim\{[(p \cdot \sim q) \vee (r \cdot y)] \vee [(\sim x \cdot y) \veebar (\sim r \cdot q)]\}$
24. $\sim\{\sim[(r \cdot p) \vee \sim(q \cdot \sim p)] \cdot \sim[(x \cdot \sim p) \vee \sim(p \cdot \sim r)]\}$
25. $\sim\{\sim[\sim(\sim r \cdot \sim q) \veebar \sim(\sim p \cdot \sim q)] \vee \sim[\sim(r \cdot \sim p) \vee \sim(\sim q \cdot y)]\}$

SYMBOLIZING NEGATIONS, CONJUNCTIONS, AND DISJUNCTIONS

The lower case letters p through z have been taken as propositional variables to stand for any proposition whatever. Propositional variables are especially useful if we wish to talk about the forms of propositions, for example, if we wish to compare propositions having the form $\sim(p \vee q)$ with those having the form $\sim p \vee \sim q$. However, if we wish to talk about specific propositions, we need different symbols. Symbols which stand for specific propositions are called **propositional constants.** We will use the capital letters of the English alphabet for this purpose. If we let the capital letter P stand for 'Suzie is pretty' and the capital letter B stand for 'Suzie is bright', then the proposition 'Suzie is pretty but she is not bright' may be symbolized as $P \cdot \sim B$. Note that since B is used to stand for 'Suzie is bright', $\sim B$ is used to stand for 'Suzie is not bright'. Whenever we suggest notation for symbolizing propositions, we will provide symbols for affirmative assertions, leaving it to the student to add negation symbols.

Negations

Although the idea of negation is most often expressed in ordinary language by the word 'not', it may also be expressed by such phrases as 'it is false that', 'it isn't true that', 'it is not the case that', etc. And statements such as 'X is legitimate' and 'X is patriotic' may be negated by 'X is illegitimate' and 'X is unpatriotic'. However, regardless of the way negation is expressed in ordinary language, we will symbolize it by use of the $\sim$.

Conjunctions

The idea of conjunction may also be expressed in a number of ways in ordinary language. Some of the words in addition to 'and' that may be used for this purpose are: 'but', 'however', 'nevertheless', 'even though', 'whereas', 'although', 'yet', and 'still'. In some cases no word for conjunction is present at all, and only a comma or semicolon indicates that the statement is a conjunction.

Care must be taken in symbolizing the negation of conjunctions. For instance, the sentence 'It is false that Suzie is pretty and bright' is ambiguous and might be interpreted as meaning $\sim(P \cdot B)$, or $\sim P \cdot \sim B$, or possibly even $\sim P \cdot B$. The second of these expressions can be stated nonambiguously in English as 'Suzie is not pretty and she is not bright'. The third can be stated nonambiguously as 'Suzie is not pretty, but she is bright'. There is no completely nonambiguous way of stating the first expression in English. A sentence such as 'It is false both that Suzie is pretty and bright' is the least ambiguous way of stating it, although this sentence might be taken on occasion to mean $\sim P \cdot \sim B$. To avoid confusion we will always interpret expressions such as 'not both p and q' and 'It is false both that p and q' as meaning $\sim(p \cdot q)$.

It should be noted that use of the $\cdot$ is not intended as a means of symbolizing every occurrence of 'and' and related words. The $\cdot$ may be used to symbolize 'and' only when 'and' is used as a truth-functional connective. In the sentence 'The pressure is increased and the volume is decreased', the form of the sentence makes it clear that 'and' is being used as a truth-functional connective. In the sentence 'Lisa and Jennifer are watching television', the form of the sentence does not make it clear that 'and' is being used as a truth-functional connective. But, if we paraphrase this sentence as 'Lisa is watching television and Jennifer is watching television', then it is evident that 'and' is a truth-functional connective. On the other hand, the word 'and' in the sentence 'Grant and Lincoln were contemporaries' is not being used truth-functionally, for this sentence cannot be paraphrased without loss of meaning as 'Grant was a contemporary and Lincoln was a contemporary'. Similarly, the word 'and' in the sentence 'Two and two are four' is not employed truth-functionally and there is no way to paraphrase it as two statements joined by a truth-functional connective.

Disjunctions

We have used the symbol $\vee$ to express the inclusive meaning of 'or' and the symbol $\underline{\vee}$ to express its exclusive meaning. But how does one know which meaning of 'or' is intended when it is used in ordinary language? A way of making clear that an inclusive meaning is intended is to use the expression 'and/or'. A way of making clear that an exclusive meaning is intended is to use a phrase such as 'but not both' along with 'or'. Thus 'The company will pay for fire and/or water damage' is inclusive in meaning, but 'Employees who are absent may receive sick pay or vacation pay, but not both' is exclusive. Frequently, however, there are no qualifying words to indicate how 'or' is intended. In such cases the procedure we will follow is to interpret it as inclusive if there is *any possibility whatever* that both disjuncts might be intended. There are very few unqualified uses of 'or' that cannot be thus interpreted as inclusive in meaning.

The word 'unless' may also be used to assert a disjunction. For example, 'Unless you study hard you will fail' may be interpreted as meaning 'Either you study hard or you will fail'. Since it is possible for one to study hard and still fail, this proposition should be symbolized as an inclusive disjunction. On the other hand, the proposition 'You are eligible for the contest unless you are an employee' should be symbolized as an exclusive disjunction. For here it is clear that the intended meaning is that you cannot be both an employee and eligible for the contest. Our procedure for symbolizing 'unless', then, is the same as our procedure for symbolizing unqualified uses of 'or'. If there is any possibility whatever that an inclusive meaning is intended, we will interpret it inclusively. The result is that most uses of 'unless' will be symbolized as an inclusive disjunction.

The most common way of denying an inclusive disjunction in ordinary language is by using the words 'neither . . . nor . . .'. Since 'neither . . . nor . . .' denies an inclusive disjunction, it may be symbolized as $\sim(p \vee q)$. It *cannot* be symbolized as $\sim p \vee \sim q$. To say of Suzie that she is neither pretty nor bright is to deny that she is either pretty or bright, or both. Such a claim would be false, then, if she were either pretty or bright. But to describe Suzie as either not pretty or not bright does not rule out that she might be pretty or that she might be bright, although it does rule out that she might be both.

Denials of exclusive disjunctions occur infrequently in ordinary language. Their expression in English requires a phrase such as 'it is false that either p or q, but not both'; however, the denial of an exclusive disjunction can be symbolized simply as $\sim(p \underline{\vee} q)$.

Since the way of making clear that one has an exclusive 'or' in mind is to accompany 'or' with a phrase such as 'but not both', we could symbolize the exclusive use of 'or' as $(p \lor q) \cdot \sim(p \cdot q)$. However, the expression $p \otimes q$ is simpler so we will retain it for the present, although we eliminate it later.

EXERCISES

V

Symbolize the following propositions using the suggested notation:

1.   The earth is flat and the end of the world is at hand. (F, E)
2.   Either the earth is flat or the end of the world is at hand.
3.   Either the earth is flat or the end of the world is at hand, but not both.
4.   The earth is flat and/or the end of the world is at hand.
5.   The earth isn't flat, but the end of the world is at hand.
6.   The earth is flat though the end of the world is not at hand.
7.   Although it is not the case that the earth is flat, it is true that the end of the world is at hand.
8.   Unless you repent you won't be saved. (R, S)
9.   The end of the world is at hand, nevertheless you will be saved. (E, S)
10.   You haven't fallen off the earth, yet the earth is flat. (F, E)
11.   Columbus sailed and sailed; still he did not come to the end of the earth. (S, E)
12.   Columbus did not repent in spite of the fact that he sailed to the end of the earth. (R, S)
13.   Not only did he not repent, he wasn't saved. (R, S)
14.   All the while he was sailing, the end of the earth was at hand. (S, E)
15.   Columbus did not repent; however, he wished that he had. (R, W)
16.   Whereas Columbus did not fall off the earth, he thought that he was going to. (F, T)
17.   Either the game will be rained out or Charlie Brown's team will not win. (G, W)
18.   One of the following is true: Either Snoopy will play centerfield or he will play shortstop. (C, S)
19.   Only one of the following can be true: The price of grain will remain constant, or the price of breakfast cereals will fluctuate. (G, B)
20.   It is not true both that Snoopy will play centerfield and not play shortstop. (C, S)
21.   It is not the case that the president will veto the bill concerning wildlife protection; moreover, it is also not the case that the House will pass the bill. (P, H)
22.   Although it was not the case that King Ferdinand was interested in Columbus' expedition, Queen Isabella was interested. (K, Q)
23.   It is not the case that the earth is flat and that the end of the world is at hand. (F, E)
24.   It is false that either Galileo or Copernicus recanted. (G, C)
25.   Neither Galileo nor Copernicus recanted.

26. Dimitri Pestszenterzsebet is wealthy and intelligent, and he is in perfect physical condition. (*W, I, P*)

27. Either Churchy or Pogo will run for president, but not both; and Pogo will run for president. (*C, P*)

28. Pat Paulsen and Richard Nixon both ran for president; Nixon was elected. (*P, N, E*)

29. Either Arnold Ziffel is anemic or needs a transfusion, or has iron-poor blood. (*A, T, I*)

30. Hume's argument against design is correct, or St. Thomas's argument is correct and Paley's argument is correct. (*H, T, P*)

31. Either Howard Hughes likes to be photographed or he does not like to be interviewed, but he is not shy. (*P, I, S*)

32. Howard Hughes either does not like to be photographed or does like to be interviewed, but he is not shy.

33. It is not true that Howard Hughes likes to be photographed or interviewed, but he is not shy.

34. Either it is not true that Howard Hughes likes to be photographed or that he does not like to be interviewed, but he is not shy.

35. Either happiness is that at which all men aim or virtue is that at which all men aim, but not both; and Plato was right and Ross was not right. (*H, V, P, R*)

36. Either interest rates are increased and inflation will cease or interest rates will not be increased and inflation will not cease. (*R, C*)

37. Either Strawson's remarks on referring are correct and Russell's are incorrect or Strawson's remarks are incorrect and Russell's are correct, but not both. (*S, R*)

38. Neither Senator Kiles nor Judge Lumpson listed the revenue on their financial statement; although both the senator and the judge knew that *Time Magazine* knew about it. (*K, L, S, J*)

39. It is not the case both that God is omnipotent and benevolent, unless he has limited powers and is malevolent. (*O, B, L, M*)

40. Either it is not true both that the Warren Report is biased and Garrison's case is plausible, or it is not true both that Oswald was not guilty and that he was Communist inspired. (*W, P, G, C*)

41. Only one of the following holds: Either the lunar module will not lift off the moon, or it will not be the case that either the astronauts will not return to the earth or that they will not bring back lunar samples. (*L, R, B*)

42. Either it is not true that matter is dry and the world is not wholly made up of water, or it is not true that life does not start in a seminal fluid and the world is wholly made up of water. (*M, W, S*)

43. It is false that either the world is wholly made up of water or that Thales was mistaken, but not both. (*W, M*)

CONDITIONALS

Compound propositions in which the words 'if . . . then . . .' connect the component propositions are known as **conditionals** or **hypotheticals.** A conditional of the form 'If p then q' is symbolized as $p \supset q$. The proposition which precedes the $\supset$ is called the **antecedent,** the one which follows the $\supset$ is called the **consequent.** Like the other connectives introduced in this chapter, the $\supset$ is a truth-functional connective.

The only case in which a truth-functional conditional is false is when the antecedent is true and the consequent is false. For example, if we symbolize the sentence 'If I have the money, then I will take the trip' as $M \supset T$, then the only case in which $M \supset T$ is false is when M is true (i.e., when I *do* have the money) and T is false (i.e., but I do *not* take the trip). Another way of saying this is to say that $M \supset T$ is false if and only if $M \cdot \sim T$ is true. Let us construct a truth table to see the conditions under which $M \cdot \sim T$ is true.

M	T	$\sim T$	$M \cdot \sim T$
T	T	F	F
T	F	T	T
F	T	F	F
F	F	T	F

The first two columns of this table contain the four possible combinations of truth values for M and T. The third column contains the truth values for $\sim T$ in each of these four cases. Since T is true in the first and third rows, $\sim T$ is false; and since T is false in the second and fourth rows, $\sim T$ is true. The fourth column contains the truth values for the conjunction $M \cdot \sim T$. Since a conjunction is true if and only if both of its conjuncts are true, the only time that $M \cdot \sim T$ is true is in the second row, in which both M and $\sim T$ are true.

Just as the only case in which $M \supset T$ is false is when $M \cdot \sim T$ is true, the only case in which $M \supset T$ is true is when $M \cdot \sim T$ is false. Consequently, we can construct a truth table for $M \supset T$ by placing it alongside the above table for $M \cdot \sim T$, and assigning $M \supset T$ values opposite to those assigned $M \cdot \sim T$. (For the sake of simplicity, we omit the column for $\sim T$.)

M	T	$M \cdot \sim T$	$M \supset T$
T	T	F	T
T	F	T	F
F	T	F	T
F	F	F	T

Note that the only case in which $M \supset T$ is false is in Row 2, in which its antecedent is true and its consequent false; in the other cases, it is true. If we generalize this for any conditional, the following rule and truth table may be stated.

RULE: A conditional is false if and only if its antecedent is true and its consequent false; otherwise it is true.

p	q	$p \supset q$
T	T	T
T	F	F
F	T	T
F	F	T

EXERCISES

VI

If p, q, and r stand for true propositions, and x, y, and z, for false propositions, which of the following are true and which false?

1. $p \supset q$
2. $p \supset x$
3. $x \supset r$
4. $z \supset y$
5. $\sim x \supset \sim y$
6. $\sim y \supset \sim q$
7. $\sim p \supset \sim q$
8. $\sim (p \supset q)$
9. $\sim (p \supset x)$
10. $\sim (\sim z \supset \sim q)$

11. $(p \cdot q) \supset r$
12. $(p \cdot x) \supset r$
13. $\sim x \supset (x \vee y)$
14. $p \supset (r \supset \sim y)$
15. $(r \supset \sim y) \supset q$
16. $\sim (x \supset \sim r) \supset z$
17. $\sim (\sim p \otimes \sim q) \supset (\sim p \cdot x)$
18. $[(p \cdot q) \vee r] \supset \sim y$
19. $[(p \cdot \sim r) \supset y] \supset q$
20. $\sim [(r \cdot \sim y) \otimes y] \supset (q \cdot \sim y)$

21. $\sim (q \supset p) \supset \sim [(r \vee \sim y) \cdot z]$
22. $\{[(r \vee y) \cdot \sim (p \vee \sim x)] \cdot (x \cdot y)\} \supset [(r \cdot y) \vee (x \cdot \sim p)]$
23. $[(r \otimes \sim x) \otimes (p \vee \sim y)] \supset \sim \{[(r \supset q) \vee (r \supset \sim x)] \cdot (p \cdot \sim x)\}$
24. $\sim \{\sim [(y \vee x) \cdot (p \vee x)] \supset \sim [(x \otimes y) \vee (y \cdot r)]\}$
25. $\sim \{\sim [\sim (\sim z \cdot p) \cdot \sim (\sim p \cdot z)] \supset \sim [\sim (x \otimes y) \vee \sim (y \cdot \sim r)]\}$

SYMBOLIZING CONDITIONALS

There are a number of ways of asserting conditionals in English. One used frequently is a sentence containing the words 'if' and 'then', but we often leave out one or the other of these words. And we often state the antecedent after the consequent. Compare the following examples, all of which can be symbolized as $W \supset M$.

> If this is a whale, then it is a mammal.
> If this is a whale, it is a mammal.
> This is a mammal, if it is a whale.

Conditionals may also be asserted without using either the words 'if' or 'then'. The following list provides some examples and indicates how they are to be symbolized.

> Were I to put this litmus paper in acid, it
> would turn red. $L \supset R$
>
> He will get the queen's hankie, should
> he win the tournament. $T \supset H$
>
> In case he wins the tournament, he will
> get the queen's hankie. $T \supset H$
>
> Passage of this law means my taxes will
> increase. $P \supset T$
>
> Discovery of the empty container implied
> that Bill had eaten the ice cream. $D \supset B$

Although the word 'if' indicates an antecedent, the words 'only if' indicate a consequent. For example, consider the following:

> Smith is a senator only if he is over thirty
> years of age. $S \supset O$
>
> Smith is a senator if he is over thirty
> years of age. $O \supset S$

The proposition 'Smith is a senator only if he is over thirty years of age', symbolized as $S \supset O$, is likely to be true because a person must be over thirty years of age before he can be a senator. But the proposition 'Smith is a senator if he is over thirty years of age', symbolized as $O \supset S$, is likely to be false because there are many people who are over thirty years of age and who are not senators. Thus, the terms 'if . . . then . . .' and 'only if' do not have the same meaning. One can avoid confusion in symbolizing these terms if one keeps in mind the above rule that 'if' indicates an antecedent while 'only if' indicates a consequent.

In symbolizing conditionals which contain negation symbols, attention must be paid to where the negation symbols occur. For example, the negation symbol in 'If it is not true that Suzie is on time, then George will be angry' negates only the antecedent, so it should be symbolized as $\sim S \supset G$. But the negation symbol in 'It is not true that if Suzie is on time, then George will be angry' negates the entire conditional, so it should be symbolized as $\sim(S \supset G)$.

It was mentioned earlier that a word such as 'and' is not always used to assert a truth-functional relation. (p. 11). Similarly, not every use of words such as 'if . . . then . . .' is intended to express only a truth-functional relation. If someone says 'If the paper is put into the acid then it will turn red', he probably means to assert more than just that it is not the case that the paper will be put into the acid and not turn red. He may be claiming that putting the paper into the acid will *cause* it to turn red. However, if the stronger claim that putting the paper into the acid will cause it to turn red is true, then the weaker claim that it is not the case that the paper will be put into the acid and not turn red will also be true. And if the weaker claim is false, the stronger claim will be also. Consequently, symbolizing conditionals as truth-functional usually allows us to show the validity or invalidity of arguments in which they occur. If a conditional seems incorrectly symbolized by the $\supset$, one should keep in mind that the $\supset$ expresses only a truth-functional relation and, therefore, may not express all that is meant by a conditional in English.

EXERCISES

VII

Symbolize the following using the suggested notation:

1. If this is uranium, then it is dangerous. (U, D)
2. If he had won the tournament, he would have gotten the queen's hankie. (T, H)
3. Only if it is uranium is it dangerous. (U, D)
4. This is a whale only if it is a mammal. (W, M)
5. This painting is valuable if it is a Klee. (V, K)
6. If he has mononucleosis this means that he is always tired. (M, T)
7. We shall have the picnic only if it doesn't rain. (P, R)
8. The boss will fire me if he catches me. (F, C)
9. My getting caught means the boss will fire me.
10. Only if the catalyst is present, will the reaction occur. (C, R)
11. Provided that the catalyst is present, the reaction will occur.
12. If he doesn't take the antidote, he will die. (A, D)
13. In case his rich uncle dies, he will take a trip abroad. (D, T)
14. If you don't look carefully, you will miss it. (L, M)
15. If he wins the tournament and gets the queen's hankie, then he will take a trip abroad. (W, H, T)

16. If he takes a trip abroad, then he will have to have a passport and a smallpox vaccination. (*T, P, S*)

17. He will get a smallpox vaccination only if it does not hurt and is free. (*S, H, F*)

18. If it does not hurt, he will get a smallpox vaccination; but smallpox vaccinations are not free.

19. Were we to have the picnic, it would either rain or ants would be present. (*P, R, A*)

20. The catalyst was present, and when the catalyst is present the reaction occurs. (*C, R*)

21. If John gets home early, then we will eat out or we will have friends over. (*G, E, F*)

22. If John gets home early then we will eat out, or we will have friends over.

23. If either we eat out or have a party then John will drink too much. (*E, P, D*)

24. Either we will eat out or if we have a party John will drink too much.

25. If a weak force is operative between the neutral atoms or molecules, then if it arises from the interaction of the dipoles then it is a Van der Waals force. (*N, M, A, V*)

26. Had Sisyphus not been condemned to Hades, then he would not have been so avaricious and he would not have had to roll the huge stone uphill. (*S, A, R*)

27. The presence of the poltergeist implies that either the inanimate objects will behave strangely or there will be unexplained noises. (*P, I, U*)

28. If neither Kansas nor North Carolina wins, then there will be a tie or the championship will be undecided, but not both. (*K, N, T, C*)

29. It is not true that if Kansas or North Carolina wins then there will be a tie, although the championship will be undecided.

30. Had it been the case that Odysseus had not made Polyphemus drunk and had not blinded him, or had not thought of some equally clever scheme, then his companions in the cave would have been devoured at the rate of two per day. (*D, B, T, C*)

31. Odysseus could have blinded Polyphemus only if he were able to make him drunk, although Odysseus would have been able to make Polyphemus drunk only if Polyphemus could not hold his liquor. (*B, D, H*)

32. If you wish to escape purgatory then you must purchase many indulgences; and unless you have remitted for your sins and been pardoned by receiving the sacrament of penance you cannot escape purgatory. (*E, P, R, S*)

33. Either it is not the case both that the soul is mortal and we cease to exist at death or the soul is immortal and we do not cease to exist after death, though this could be the case only if there is such a thing as the soul. (*M, C, S*)

BICONDITIONALS

A compound proposition in which the words 'if and only if' are used to connect the component propositions is called a **biconditional.** As the name implies, a biconditional is the joint assertion of two conditionals. For example, to say 'He will take the trip if and only if he inherits the money' is to assert both 'He will take the trip, if he inherits the money' and 'He will take the trip, only if he inherits the money'. Consequently, this proposition can be symbolized as $(I \supset T) \cdot (T \supset I)$. However, it is useful to have a special connective for symbolizing biconditionals and we will use the symbol $\equiv$ for this purpose. Thus the foregoing proposition can be symbolized as $T \equiv I$. Since a proposition of the form $p \equiv q$ is only another way of writing $(p \supset q) \cdot (q \supset p)$, propositions having the form $p \equiv q$ are true or false in exactly the same cases as those having the form $(p \supset q) \cdot (q \supset p)$. A truth table for $(p \supset q) \cdot (q \supset p)$ shows that propositions of this form are true whenever p and q have the same truth value (both true or both false) and false whenever p and q have opposite truth values (one true, the other false). Consequently, we may state the following rule and truth table:

RULE: A biconditional is true if and only if both components have the same truth value.

p	q	$p \equiv q$
T	T	T
T	F	F
F	T	F
F	F	T

SYMBOLIZING BICONDITIONALS

Symbolization of biconditionals in which only positive propositions occur is usually rather easy, but symbolization of biconditionals containing negations can pose problems. For example, consider the propositions:

> He will not take the trip if and only if he inherits the money.

> It is false that: he will take the trip if and only if he inherits the money.

> It is false that he will take the trip if and only if he inherits the money.

The first of these propositions is relatively nonambiguous. The scope of the negation extends only to the first proposition; thus it can be symbolized as $\sim T \equiv I$. The second proposition is also relatively nonambiguous. The colon makes clear that everything that follows is to be negated, so it can be symbolized as $\sim(T \equiv I)$. The third proposition, however, is ambiguous; it is not clear whether we should symbolize it as $\sim T \equiv I$ or as $\sim(T \equiv I)$. Whenever a proposition of this type is encountered, therefore, one must simply rely on context to determine what is meant.

EXERCISES

VIII

If p, q, and r stand for true propositions, and x, y, and z, for false propositions, which of the following are true and which false?

1. $p \equiv q$
2. $x \equiv p$
3. $\sim p \equiv z$
4. $\sim x \equiv \sim y$
5. $\sim\sim x \equiv p$

6. $x \equiv (p \cdot q)$
7. $(p \oslash q) \equiv \sim x$
8. $(\sim p \vee \sim q) \equiv \sim(p \cdot q)$
9. $\sim(\sim p \vee q) \equiv (p \supset q)$
10. $\sim(\sim x \supset q) \equiv (\sim p \oslash q)$

11. $[(p \vee \sim r) \cdot \sim(z \cdot \sim q)] \equiv \sim q$
12. $\{[(p \vee q) \cdot (r \vee \sim x)] \supset (p \cdot \sim z)\} \equiv (r \supset q)$
13. $[(p \equiv \sim q) \cdot (x \equiv y)] \equiv [(p \oslash q) \cdot r]$
14. $[(p \equiv \sim r) \equiv (x \equiv p)] \cdot \sim[(p \oslash \sim r) \vee (p \oslash r)]$
15. $\sim[(p \equiv x) \equiv r] \vee [\sim r \equiv (\sim x \vee \sim y)]$
16. $[(p \cdot \sim r) \equiv r] \supset \sim(r \equiv z)$
17. $[(r \oslash y) \cdot (x \oslash \sim y)] \supset (q \equiv \sim q)$
18. $[p \supset (q \cdot r)] \equiv [(p \supset q) \supset r]$
19. $\sim[(p \cdot q) \cdot \sim r] \equiv [\sim r \supset \sim(p \cdot q)]$
20. $\sim\{[(p \equiv q) \equiv (r \equiv x)] \equiv \sim[\sim(\sim r \equiv \sim z) \equiv \sim(x \oslash y)]\}$

IX

Symbolize the following propositions using the suggested notation:
1. Bridie Murphy has been reincarnated if and only if she has undergone metempsychosis. (R, M)
2. This stock will pay dividends if and only if the market does not crash. (P, M)
3. This is not a hexagon if and only if it does not have six sides. (H, S)
4. It is false that this is a hexagon if and only if it has six sides.
5. It is false that this is a hexagon, if and only if it has six sides.
6. It is false that: Wall Street will show a steady decline in the volume index if and only if the American Exchange also shows a steady decline. (W, A)

7. The price of stock has gone up, but the market will remain at its present level if and only if wage guide lines are retained. (*P, M, W*)

8. If the wind blows this way, then we can smell the refinery if and only if it is in operation. (*W, S, O*)

9. If Wemberly enters the tennis match, he is sure to win; although he will enter if and only if the prize money exceeds five thousand dollars. (*E, W, P*)

10. Smith is a bachelor if and only if he is an unmarried male of marriageable age, and he can be an unmarried male of marriageable age and live in this state if and only if he is at least sixteen years of age. (*B, M, L, S*)

11. If it is not the case that: the pig was able to take over if and only if he was the smartest animal, then the other animals were apathetic; and if the other animals were apathetic, then the pig was the smartest animal. (*W, S, O*)

12. Either this is an intonation or it is not a Gregorian chant; however, it is not the case both that it will be played in the cathedral today and not be heard by the emperor if and only if it is heard by the emperor. (*I, G, P, H*)

TAUTOLOGICAL, CONTRADICTORY, AND CONTINGENT PROPOSITIONAL FORMS

Since expressions such as $p \supset q$ and $p \cdot (q \vee r)$ do not contain constants which stand for specific propositions but contain only variables which stand for any proposition whatever, these expressions are not propositions but propositional forms. However, if we were to replace the variables in these expressions with constants, the result would be propositions. We may define a **propositional form,** then, as an expression containing variables such that if the variables are replaced by constants the result is a proposition which may be said to have that form.

Truth-functional propositions may be classified into three types. A truth-functional proposition having a form which makes it necessarily true is called a **tautology.** A truth-functional proposition having a form which makes it necessarily false is called a **contradiction.** A truth-functional proposition having a form which permits it to be either true or false is said to be **contingent.** For example, propositions having the form $p \vee \sim p$ are tautologies. This is shown by the following truth table:

p	$\sim p$	$p \vee \sim p$
T	F	T
F	T	T

Similarly, propositions having the form $p \cdot \sim p$ are contradictions.

p	$\sim p$	$p \cdot \sim p$
T	F	F
F	T	F

Note that regardless of the value assigned to p, propositions of the form $p \vee \sim p$ are always true and propositions of the form $p \cdot \sim p$ are always false.

Most truth-functional propositions that we will consider are contingent; that is to say, they have a form such that they might be true or might be false. For example, propositions having the form $p \supset q$ are true in some cases but false in others.

It is not always apparent whether a truth-functional proposition is tautological, contradictory, or contingent. However, truth tables may be used to obtain this information. Consider the following truth table for the propositional form $p \supset (q \supset p)$:

	A	B	C	E	D
	p	q	p	$\supset$	$(q \supset p)$
1	T	T	T	T	T
2	T	F	T	T	T
3	F	T	F	T	F
4	F	F	F	T	T

In discussing this type of truth table, we will refer to vertical lines as *columns* and denote them by letters of the alphabet; we will refer to horizontal lines as *rows* and denote them by numbers. Columns A and B above show the possible truth value combinations for the variables p and q. Column C shows the possible values for the antecedent of the compound expression $p \supset (q \supset p)$. Column D shows the possible values for $q \supset p$, which is the consequent of $p \supset (q \supset p)$. Note that $q \supset p$ is false in only row 3, where q is assumed to be true and p, false. Column E shows the possible truth values for the major truth-functional connective of $p \supset (q \supset p)$. Since there is a 'T' in every row of column E, we see that regardless of the values assigned to the variables, a truth-functional proposition having the form $p \supset (q \supset p)$ is true. Thus propositions having this form are tautologies.

All the truth tables constructed up to this point, including the above, are for propositional forms containing only one or two variables. In cases in which there is one variable, two rows are required to express all possible truth values. Where there are two variables, four rows are required to express all possible truth-value combinations of the variables. If we generalize this procedure for propositional forms containing any number of variables, n, then 2^n rows will be required to express the possible truth-value combinations of the variables. For example, a truth table for the propositional form $[p \cdot (q \cdot r)] \cdot [p \supset \sim(q \cdot r)]$ which has three variables, requires 2^3, or eight, rows to express all the possible truth value combinations of the variables.

One way to be certain that a truth table contains every possible truth value combination of the variables is to systematize their arrangement in the initial columns. This may be done by assigning a value of T to the first half of the rows in the first column and a value of F to the last half of the rows in the first column. To fill out the second column, halve the number of rows that contained T's in the first column and alternate this number of T's and F's to the end of the column. Then, fill out the third column by halving the number of rows that contained T's in the second column and alternate this number of T's and F's to the end of the column. If this procedure is repeated correctly, the final column will be filled in with alternating occurrences of single T's and F's. This method was followed in the tables above and in the one following for $[p \cdot (q \cdot r)] \cdot [p \supset \sim(q \cdot r)]$.

	A	B	C	E	D	I	H	G	F
	p	q	r	$[p \cdot$	$(q \cdot r)]$	$\cdot$	$[p \supset$	$\sim(q$	$\cdot r)]$
1	T	T	T	T	T	F	F	F	T
2	T	T	F	F	F	F	T	T	F
3	T	F	T	F	F	F	T	T	F
4	T	F	F	F	F	F	T	T	F
5	F	T	T	F	T	F	T	F	T
6	F	T	F	F	F	F	T	T	F
7	F	F	T	F	F	F	T	T	F
8	F	F	F	F	F	F	T	T	F

Columns A, B, and C above, show the possible truth value combinations of the variables. Column D shows the possible values for the conjunction $q \cdot r$ and is, therefore, filled in by reference to B and C. Since column F also shows possible values for the conjunction $q \cdot r$, it is identical to column D. Column G, which represents the negation of $q \cdot r$, is filled in by reference to F. Column H results from A and G. Finally, column I shows the possible truth values of the major truth-functional connective, and is filled in by reference to E and H. Since the only values to appear in column I are F's, truth-functional propositions having the form $[p \cdot (q \cdot r)] \cdot [p \supset \sim(q \cdot r)]$ are contradictions.

The following truth table shows that truth-functional propositions of the form $p \equiv [\sim p \cdot (q \vee r)]$ are contingent. Column H contains F's in the first seven rows, but row 8 shows $p \equiv [\sim p \cdot (q \vee r)]$ to be true when all of its components are false.

	A	B	C	G	H	D	F	E
	p	q	r	p	$\equiv$	$[\sim p$	$\cdot$	$(q \vee r)]$
1	T	T	T	T	F	F	F	T
2	T	T	F	T	F	F	F	T
3	T	F	T	T	F	F	F	T
4	T	F	F	T	F	F	F	F
5	F	T	T	F	F	T	T	T
6	F	T	F	F	F	T	T	T
7	F	F	T	F	F	T	T	T
8	F	F	F	F	T	T	F	F

EXERCISES

X

Use truth tables to determine whether truth-functional propositions having the following forms are tautologies, contradictions, or contingent.

1. $[p \supset (p \supset q)] \supset q$
2. $p \supset [(p \supset q) \supset q]$
3. $(p \vee \sim p) \supset (q \cdot \sim q)$
4. $(p \oslash q) \supset (q \cdot \sim p)$
5. $(p \supset q) \equiv (\sim p \supset \sim q)$
6. $p \equiv [p \vee (p \cdot q)]$
7. $[p \supset (q \supset r)] \supset [(p \supset q) \supset (p \supset r)]$
8. $[p \supset (q \supset p)] \supset [(p \oslash \sim p) \supset (r \equiv \sim r)]$
9. $[(p \supset q) \supset r] \equiv [(q \supset p) \supset r]$
10. $\{[(p \supset q) \cdot (r \supset s)] \cdot (q \vee s)\} \supset (p \vee r)$

3

ARGUMENT FORMS
AND VALIDITY

ARGUMENT FORMS

We are now in a position to develop procedures for determining the validity or invalidity of one important type of argument. Arguments composed of propositions having truth-functional forms such that it is impossible for their premises to be true and their conclusions false have a **truth-functionally valid argument form.** For example, any argument having the form

$$p \supset q$$
$$\underline{p}$$
$$q$$

has a truth-functionally valid form. This is shown by the following truth table:

			First premise	Second premise	Conclusion
	p	q	$p \supset q$	p	q
1	T	T	T	T	T
2	T	F	F	T	F
3	F	T	T	F	T
4	F	F	T	F	F

Since it is impossible for propositions having these truth-functional forms to be related in such a way that the premises of an argument having this form could be true and the conclusion false, there is no row of the truth table in which both premises are true and the conclusion false.

Arguments composed of propositions having truth-functional forms such that it *is possible* for their premises to be true and their conclusions false have a **truth-functionally invalid argument form.** For example, any argument having the form

$$p \supset q$$
$$\underline{q}$$
$$p$$

has a truth-functionally invalid form, as is shown in the truth table below.

			First premise	Second premise	Conclusion
	p	q	$p \supset q$	q	p
1	T	T	T	T	T
2	T	F	F	F	T
3	F	T	T	T	F
4	F	F	T	F	F

Since it is possible for propositions having these truth-functional forms to be related in such a way that the premises of an argument having this form could be true and the conclusion false, there is a row of the truth table (row 3) in which both premises are true and the conclusion, false.

Truth Table for a Truth-Functionally Valid
Argument Form with One Premise

$$\frac{p \supset q}{p \supset (p \cdot q)}$$

			Premise	Conclusion
	p	q	$p \supset q$	$p \supset (p \cdot q)$
1	T	T	T	T T
2	T	F	F	F F
3	F	T	T	T F
4	F	F	T	T F

Note that there is no row in which the premise is true and the conclusion false. Hence, arguments having this form have a truth-functionally valid form.

Truth Table for a Truth-Functionally Invalid Argument Form with Three Premises

$$p \supset (p \cdot q)$$
$$p \vee r$$
$$\underline{p \cdot q}$$
$$r \oslash p$$

	p	q	r	First premise $p \supset (p \cdot q)$		Second premise $p \vee r$	Third premise $p \cdot q$	Conclusion $r \oslash p$
1	T	T	T	T	T	T	T	F
2	T	T	F	T	T	T	T	T
3	T	F	T	F	F	T	F	F
4	T	F	F	F	F	T	F	T
5	F	T	T	T	F	T	F	T
6	F	T	F	T	F	F	F	F
7	F	F	T	T	F	T	F	T
8	F	F	F	T	F	F	F	F

Note that there is a row (row 1) in which all three premises are true and the conclusion is false. Hence, arguments having this form have a truth-functionally invalid form.

The foregoing truth tables show the validity or invalidity of argument forms rather than of specific arguments. An **argument form** is a combination of symbols containing variables such that if the variables are replaced by constants, the result is a specific argument. An argument which results from an argument form in this way is said to be a **substitution instance** of that form. For example, the argument

If Smith is a senator, then he is over thirty years old.
Smith is a senator.
_____
Smith is over thirty years old.

which may be symbolized as

$$S \supset O$$
$$\underline{S}$$
$$O$$

is a substitution instance of the first truth-functionally valid argument form above.

Similarly, the argument

> If Smith is a senator, then he is over thirty years old.
> Smith is over thirty years old.
> _____
> Smith is a senator.

which may be symbolized as

$$S \supset O$$
$$\underline{O}$$
$$S$$

is a substitution instance of the first truth-functionally invalid argument form above.

Every argument that is a substitution instance of a truth-functionally valid argument form is valid. But not every argument which is a substitution instance of a truth-functionally invalid argument form is invalid, because the truth-functional relations that hold among the propositions in arguments constitute only one of the conditions that can make arguments valid. Thus an argument which is not truth-functionally valid may be valid for some other reason. We will discuss some arguments which are valid for other reasons in chapter VIII. Truth tables are an effective test for validity only if one is dealing with arguments in which truth-functional relations are the sole relevant consideration. All of the arguments discussed in this and the next four chapters are this type, so both their validity and invalidity can be shown by truth tables.

EXERCISES

I

Use truth tables to determine whether the following argument forms are truth-functionally valid or truth-functionally invalid:

1. p
   $\overline{p \lor q}$

2. p
   $\underline{q}$
   $p \cdot q$

3. $p \supset q$
   $\underline{\sim p}$
   $\sim q$

4. $\sim q \supset \sim p$
$\underline{\quad p \quad}$
$\sim q$

5. $p \supset q$
$\underline{\quad \sim q \quad}$
$\sim p$

6. $p \lor q$
$\underline{\quad \sim p \quad}$
q

7. $p \lor q$
$\underline{\quad p \quad}$
q

8. $p \supset q$
$\underline{q \supset r}$
$p \supset r$

9. $p \supset q$
$\underline{r \supset q}$
$p \supset r$

10. $(p \supset q) \cdot (r \supset s)$
$\underline{\quad p \lor r \quad}$
$q \lor s$

II

Symbolize the following arguments using the suggested notation, and use truth tables to determine whether they are substitution instances of valid or invalid truth-functional argument forms:

1. If Mark Twain had been a poor businessman, he would have had to undertake extensive lecture tours. He did undertake extensive lecture tours. Hence, he must have been a poor businessman. (*P, U*)
2. Either "The Bride of Frankenstein" or "The Mummy Under the Stairs", but not both, is playing at the Paramount. "The Mummy Under the Stairs" is not playing there. So, "The Bride of Frankenstein" must be. (*B, M*)
3. If Chuck has a pastrami on rye, then he will order a deviled egg. But he is not going to have a pastrami on rye. Hence, he will not order a deviled egg. (*P, D*)
4. If Prudence does not live in a glass house, then it is all right for her to throw stones. However, it is not all right for her to throw stones. Therefore, she does not live in a glass house. (*L, A*)
5. If the squatters settle here, then the cattlemen will be angry and there will be a fight about water rights. The squatters are going to settle here. Thus, there will be a fight about water rights. (*S, C, F*)
6. If either the butler or the maid is telling the truth, then the job was an inside one. If our lie detector is accurate, then both the butler and the maid are telling the truth. Of course, our lie detector is accurate. Consequently, the job was an inside one. (*B, M, I, A*)
7. If the poltergeist is present, that implies that either the inanimate objects will behave strangely or there will be unexplained noises. The poltergeist is present. It follows that either the inanimate objects will behave strangely or there will be unexplained noises. (*P, I, U*)
8. If I get the information, then I will send you a note by passenger pigeon if the corn has not been poisoned. Thus, if I send you a note by passenger pigeon, then the corn has not been poisoned. (*I, S, C*)
9. It is not true that: the spelunkers decided to meet at the bottom of the mountain if and only if the boulder had not slipped into the mouth of the cave during the

night. Only if the spelunkers had decided to meet at the bottom of the mountain if and only if the boulder had not slipped into the mouth of the cave during the night, will the lanterns be needed. Therefore, the lanterns will not be needed. (*S, B, L*)

10. If winter comes and the snow flies, the pass will be blocked and there will be avalanches. But it is not the case now both that the pass is blocked and that there are avalanches. Hence, it is not the case both that it is winter and that the snow is flying. (*W, S, P, A*)

PARTIAL TRUTH TABLES

Determining the validity or invalidity of argument forms with several variables by means of a complete truth table is obviously a lengthy and tedious procedure. Fortunately, however, there is a way of determining validity or invalidity without checking every possible combination of truth values for the variables. Since an invalid form is one in which the premises can be true while the conclusion is false, if an assignment of values can be made such that this is the case, then the argument form has been shown to be invalid.

Consider the argument form:

$$p \supset (q \lor r)$$
$$r \supset (s \cdot t)$$
$$\sim s$$
$$\overline{p \supset t}$$

This argument form can be shown to be invalid by assigning values to the variables so that the premises are all true while the conclusion is false.

First Premise   Second Premise

$p \supset (q \lor r)$ $r \supset (s \cdot t)$

T   T   F   F
   T   T   T
   T

Third Premise   Conclusion

$\sim s$ $p \supset t$

  F   T   F
T   F

Since the only assignment that can make a conditional false is for the antecedent to be true and the consequent false, we must assign *p* the value T and *t* the value F to make the conclusion false. But if *p* is assigned the value T, then the antecedent of the first premise is also true. In order to make the first premise true, then, we must assign a value that will make its consequent true also. This can be accomplished by assigning either q or r, or both q and r, the value T. We will assign q the value T, and r the value F. By making this assignment, rather than one of the others, we can make both the first and second premises true; the first, by making the consequent of a conditional true; the second, by making the antecedent of a conditional false. The third premise is made true by assigning s (which has not yet received a value) the value F. We have now succeeded in making all the premises true and the conclusion false, so the argument form has been shown to be invalid.

Whenever it is impossible to assign values consistently so as to make all the premises true and the conclusion false, an argument form is valid. Notice what happens if we try to proceed with the following valid argument form as we did with the above invalid form:

$$p \lor q$$
$$(p \lor r) \supset (s \cdot t)$$
$$\frac{\sim s}{q}$$

First Premise

$$p \lor q$$
$$\underset{\text{T}}{\text{T}} \quad \text{F}$$

Second Premise

$$(p \lor r) \supset (s \cdot t)$$
$$\text{T} \quad \underset{\text{T}}{\underset{\text{T}}{\text{T}}} \quad \text{T}_{\text{T}}\text{T}$$

Third Premise

$$\sim s$$
$$\underset{\text{F}}{\text{T}}$$

Conclusion

$$q$$
$$\text{F}$$

To make the conclusion false, we must assign q the value F. Then to make the first premise true, we must assign p the value T. This also renders the antecedent of the second premise true. For the second premise to be true, its consequent must now also be true. Thus both s and t must be assigned the value T. But then the third premise, $\sim s$, cannot be made true. Since it is impossible to assign values so as to make all the premises true and the conclusion false, this argument form is valid.

Partial truth tables are an effective test of validity only if *it is impossible* to assign values which will make the premises true and the conclusion false. Sometimes in testing argument forms for validity, one may have to consider two or more sets of values that would make a conclusion false or a premise true. For example, a biconditional such as $p \equiv q$ is false, both when p is true and q false, and when p is false and q true. Both of these possible value assignments must be kept in mind in testing an argument form such as the following:

$$(o \lor p) \supset q$$
$$q \supset (p \lor r)$$
$$o \supset (\sim s \supset p)$$
$$(s \supset o) \supset \sim r$$
$$\overline{p \equiv q}$$

First Premise   Second Premise

$(o \lor p) \supset q$ $q \supset (p \lor r)$

$\quad\;\; \overset{T}{} \quad F$
$\;\;T$
$\quad\;\; F$

Third Premise   Fourth Premise

$o \supset (\sim s \supset p)$ $(s \supset o) \supset \sim r$

Conclusion

$$p \equiv q$$
$$T \;\; F$$
$$F$$

If we assign p the value T and q the value F, then the conclusion is false.
But, this assignment also makes the first premise false. Thus our attempt
to show that the argument form is invalid by making the premises true and
the conclusion false seems to have failed. However, in this case we cannot
conclude that the form is valid, because there is another assignment which
will make the conclusion false, viz., the assignment in which p is false and
q is true. Given this assignment, it is possible to make all the premises true
and the conclusion false, thereby showing the argument form to be invalid.

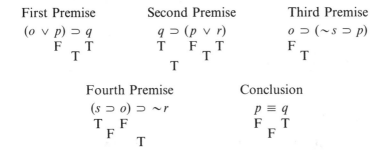

First Premise   Second Premise   Third Premise

$(o \lor p) \supset q$ $q \supset (p \lor r)$ $o \supset (\sim s \supset p)$

$\quad F \;\; T$ $T \;\; F \; T$ F
$\quad\; T$ $\;\;\; T$ $\; T$

Fourth Premise   Conclusion

$(s \supset o) \supset \sim r$ $p \equiv q$

$T \;\; F$ $F \;\; T$
$\;\; F \;\; T$ $\;\; F$

EXERCISES

III

Use partial truth tables to determine whether the following argument forms are valid
or invalid.

1. $(p \supset q) \cdot (r \supset s)$
$\underline{q \vee s}$
$p \vee r$

2. $(p \supset q) \cdot (r \supset s)$
$\underline{\sim q \vee \sim s}$
$\sim p \vee \sim r$

3. $p \supset q$
$q \supset (r \vee s)$
$\underline{(r \vee s) \ⓥ\ t}$
$p \supset t$

4. $p \supset (p \cdot q)$
$p \supset (r \cdot s)$
$(t \vee p) \supset s$
$(t \vee r) \supset q$

5. $(\sim q \cdot p) \supset (s \vee r)$
$\sim q \supset (s \supset t)$
$q \vee (r \supset u)$
$\underline{\sim q \cdot p}$
$t \vee u$

6. $\sim q \equiv \sim p$
$p \supset [r \supset (q \vee \sim r)]$
$\underline{q \supset [\sim s \supset (p \vee s)]}$
$(p \equiv q) \equiv (r \vee s)$

7. $p \equiv q$
$q \equiv (r \cdot s)$
$r \equiv (t \ⓥ\ u)$
$s \vee t$
$\underline{p \cdot (u \ⓥ\ r)}$
$q \ⓥ\ r$

8. $p \supset (q \supset r)$
$p \supset s$
$(q \supset t) \supset (r \supset u)$
$(\sim p \cdot \sim s) \supset (r \supset t)$
$\sim s$
$\underline{\sim u \vee \sim t}$
$\sim r \vee \sim q$

9. $p \supset [q \supset (r \supset s)]$
$(q \cdot r) \supset s$
$(r \vee s) \equiv (s \cdot t)$
$t \supset (q \ⓥ\ r)$
$\sim p$
$\underline{(\sim p \cdot q) \vee (q \cdot \sim s)}$
$r \ⓥ\ s$

10. $(p \vee q) \cdot r$
$[\sim s \supset \sim (r \cdot t)] \cdot [r \supset (p \supset \sim u)]$
$r \supset (t \cdot u)$
$(p \ⓥ\ q) \cdot \sim s$
$v \cdot w$
$\underline{w}$
$\sim (u \cdot \sim s)$

11. $(p \equiv q) \equiv r$
$[(p \supset q) \cdot (q \supset p)] \supset r$
$[p \supset (p \cdot q)] \cdot [q \supset (q \cdot p)]$
$(r \supset s) \cdot (s \supset t)$
$(r \vee s) \supset (t \cdot p)$
$\underline{r \equiv p}$
$r \supset (p \equiv q)$

12. $p \supset [q \supset (r \supset s)]$
$[(q \ⓥ\ r) \cdot s] \equiv t$
$[r \supset (s \supset t)] \vee u$
$(s \equiv t) \equiv v$
$[(t \vee u) \cdot (t \vee v)] \supset p$
$(t \ⓥ\ q) \cdot (t \ⓥ\ r)$
$\underline{u \supset v}$
$t \cdot s$

ARGUMENTS AND ARGUMENT FORMS
WITH INCONSISTENT PREMISES

A valid argument form is one in which it is impossible for the premises to be true and the conclusion false. It follows that any argument having premises which cannot all be true simultaneously has a valid form. Premises which cannot all be true simultaneously are said to be inconsistent.

Consider the following argument, the premises of which appear entirely irrelevant to establishing the conclusion.

> If he loves me, then he will want to marry me.
> If he wants to marry me, then he will buy me a ring.
> <u>He loves me, but he is not going to buy me a ring.</u>
> Therefore, I shall be left waiting at the church.

If we were to construct a truth table for this argument, we would not find a row in which the premises were true and the conclusion false. The reason there would not be such a row is that the conjunction of the premises is a contradiction and, therefore, it is impossible for the premises to be true simultaneously. At least one of the premises would be false in every row of the truth table. It follows that the argument is not invalid and must therefore be valid.

Suppose, however, that the conclusion were 'I shall *not* be left waiting at the church'. Once again, it is impossible to make the premises true and the conclusion false. Hence, this argument is also valid. Has something gone wrong somewhere? How can the same premises imply both that she will, and that she will not, be left waiting at the church? The fact is that any argument with inconsistent premises is valid, *regardless* of its conclusion. *Any* conclusion follows from a set of inconsistent premises. Of course, when a conclusion is shown to follow from a set of inconsistent premises, all that has been established is that those premises lead to that conclusion —not that the conclusion is true. It is important to note that although all arguments with inconsistent premises are valid, since it is impossible for their premises to be true simultaneously, they cannot be sound.*

Testing Premises for Consistency

Although complete truth tables can be used to test premises for consistency, the partial truth table method is quicker and simpler. To test a set of premises for consistency in this way, one simply *ignores the conclusion* and determines whether the premises can be true simultaneously; if they cannot, then they are inconsistent. We will illustrate this with the premises of the above argument.

$$(1) \quad L \supset M$$
$$(2) \quad M \supset R$$
$$(3) \quad L \cdot \sim R$$

Premise (3) can be true only if both L and $\sim R$ are true. If $\sim R$ is true, then R is false and the consequent of Premise (2) is false. If Premise (2) is to be

---

*All arguments with conclusions which are tautologies are also valid. Since their conclusions are necessarily true, it is impossible for them to have true premises and a false conclusion. Unlike arguments with inconsistent premises, however, this type of argument can be sound.

true, then, *M* must be false. But if *M* is false, and *L* is true as is required in Premise (3), then Premise (1) is false. Consequently, there is no way to make these propositions true simultaneously and they are therefore inconsistent.

EXERCISES

IV

1. What is meant by saying that an argument has a truth-functionally valid argument form?
2. What is meant by saying that an argument has a truth-functionally invalid argument form?
3. What is an argument form?
4. What is a substitution instance of an argument form?
5. Are all instances of truth-functionally valid argument forms valid?
6. Are all instances of truth-functionally invalid argument forms invalid?
7. Describe the procedure that must be followed for a partial truth table to be an effective test of validity for truth-functional arguments.
8. What is meant by saying that an argument has inconsistent premises?
9. Are arguments which have inconsistent premises valid or invalid?
10. Can an argument with inconsistent premises be sound?
11. Describe the procedure required to test the premises of an argument for consistency by means of a partial truth table.

V

Use partial truth tables to determine whether the premises of the following argument forms are consistent or inconsistent. For the argument forms which have consistent premises, also use a partial truth table to show whether they are valid or invalid.

1. $p \otimes q$
   $p \supset q$
   _____
   $p \cdot q$

2. $p \otimes q$
   $\sim(p \supset \sim q)$
   _____
   $p \cdot q$

3. $\sim(p \vee q)$
   $p \supset q$
   _____
   p

4. $\sim(p \vee q)$
   $\sim p \supset q$
   _____
   p

5. $p \supset (q \cdot r)$
   $(q \vee r) \supset w$
   $p \cdot \sim w$
   _____
   $\sim r$

6. $p \supset (q \cdot r)$
   $(q \vee r) \supset w$
   $\sim w$
   _____
   $\sim p$

7. $p \equiv r$
    $\sim p \supset \sim(q \vee s)$
    $\underline{\sim r \cdot s}$
    $r \vee w$

8. $(p \vee q) \equiv r$
    $\sim(q \supset r)$
    $\underline{p \vee r}$
    q

9. $p \equiv r$
    $(s \supset r) \cdot (\sim s \supset \sim z)$
    $\sim w \ \underline{\vee} \ z$
    $\sim(q \vee v) \supset w$
    $\underline{\sim q \cdot \sim v}$
    $p \vee q$

10. $s \supset [m \supset (n \cdot o)]$
    $n \vee k$
    $k \ \underline{\vee} \ (o \vee t)$
    $\underline{(o \supset r) \cdot (m \supset s)}$
    $s \cdot t$

4

FORMAL PROOF

MODUS PONENS AND
MODUS TOLLENS

At the beginning of chapter III, a truth table was used to show the
validity of the argument form

$$p \supset q$$
$$\underline{p}$$
$$q$$

Argument forms which are used frequently are often given names. This
form is called *modus ponens.* Another argument form superficially resem-
bling *modus ponens,* but which was shown at the beginning of chapter III
to be invalid, is

$$p \supset q$$
$$\underline{q}$$
$$p$$

The difference between these forms is that in *modus ponens,* the second
premise affirms the antecedent of the first premise and the conclusion affirms the consequent; while in the invalid form, the second premise affirms
the consequent of the first premise and the conclusion affirms the antecedent. Therefore, this error in logical form is called the **Fallacy of Affirming
the Consequent.**

A second valid argument form

$$p \supset q$$
$$\sim q$$
$$\overline{\sim p}$$

is called **modus tollens.** Its validity was demonstrated in number 5 of exercise I in chapter III. Once again, there is an invalid argument form which closely resembles the valid form

$$p \supset q$$
$$\sim p$$
$$\overline{\sim q}$$

In *modus tollens* the second premise denies the consequent of the first, and the conclusion denies the antecedent; but in the invalid form, the second premise denies the antecedent and the conclusion denies the consequent. The latter form, then, is known as the **Fallacy of Denying the Antecedent.** Its invalidity was demonstrated in number 3 of exercise I in chapter III.

There are too many invalid argument forms for each to be given a separate name. Thus, although the following invalid forms are similar to the Fallacies of Denying the Antecedent and Affirming the Consequent, they are less plausible and have no traditional names.

$$
\begin{array}{cccc}
p \supset q & p \supset q & p \supset q & p \supset q \\
p & \sim p & q & \sim q \\
\hline
\sim q & q & \sim p & p
\end{array}
$$

It is left for the student to show that these are invalid forms. Of the eight forms discussed, only *modus ponens* and *modus tollens* are valid.

EXERCISES

I

The following arguments are substitution instances of the eight argument forms discussed in the foregoing section. Symbolize each argument and state whether it is an instance of a valid or invalid form. If its form has a name, give that name.

1. If the sodium has been placed in the water, then it will explode. The sodium has been placed in the water. Thus, it will explode. (S, E)

2. If this is uranium, then it is dangerous. However, it is not uranium. Hence, it is not dangerous. (U, D)

3. The boss would have fired me, had he caught me. The boss has not fired me. Obviously, therefore, he has not caught me. (F, C)

4. Had she been on time, I would have had to wait an hour. I did not have to wait an hour. Therefore, she was on time. (T, W)

5. Only if the catalyst is present will the reaction occur. The catalyst is present. It follows that the reaction will occur. (C, R)

6. The presence of bones on the island implies that the cannibals ate the sailors. There are bones on the island. Therefore, the cannibals ate the sailors. (B, C)

7. If his passport was forged, then he entered the country illegally. His passport was not forged. Thus, he did not enter the country illegally. (F, E)

8. You may walk only if the light is red. But you may not walk. Therefore, the light is red. (W, R)

9. If Mae has mononucleosis, that means she will be tired all the time. Mae is tired all the time. Hence, Mae has mononucleosis. (M, T)

10. Were contemporary drama dying, today's theaters would be deserted. But to-day's theaters are not deserted. So contemporary drama is not dying. (C, T)

Complex Substitution Instances

We may define *modus ponens* as an argument form composed of two premises, one a conditional and the other an affirmation of the conditional's antecedent, with a conclusion which affirms the conditional's consequent. Similarly, the Fallacy of Affirming the Consequent may be defined as an argument form composed of two premises, one of which is a conditional and the other an affirmation of its consequent, with a conclusion affirming its antecedent. It follows from these definitions that the arguments listed below are substitution instances of *modus ponens* and the Fallacy of Affirming the Consequent.

Complex Substitution Instances of Modus Ponens

$$A \supset {\sim}B$$
$$A$$
$$\overline{{\sim}B}$$

$$\sim A \supset B$$
$$\sim A$$
$$\overline{B}$$

$$\sim A \supset {\sim}B$$
$$\sim A$$
$$\overline{{\sim}B}$$

$$(A \cdot B) \supset C$$
$$A \cdot B$$
$$\overline{C}$$

$$A \supset {\sim}(A \vee B)$$
$$A$$
$$\overline{{\sim}(A \vee B)}$$

$$(R \equiv {\sim}S) \supset Q$$
$$R \equiv {\sim}S$$
$$\overline{Q}$$

Complex Substitution Instances of the Fallacy of Affirming the Consequent

$$A \supset {\sim}B$$
$$\sim B$$
$$\overline{A}$$

$$\sim A \supset B$$
$$B$$
$$\overline{{\sim}A}$$

$$\sim A \supset {\sim}B$$
$$\sim B$$
$$\overline{{\sim}A}$$

$$(A \cdot B) \supset C$$
$$C$$
$$\overline{A \cdot B}$$

$$A \supset {\sim}(A \vee B)$$
$$\sim(A \vee B)$$
$$\overline{A}$$

$$(R \equiv {\sim}S) \supset Q$$
$$Q$$
$$\overline{R \equiv {\sim}S}$$

Since *modus tollens* and the Fallacy of Denying the Antecedent may be defined in a manner paralleling the definitions of *modus ponens* and the Fallacy of Affirming the Consequent, the following are substitution instances of these forms:

Complex Substitution Instances of Modus Tollens

$$\frac{\begin{array}{l} \sim A \supset B \\ \sim B \end{array}}{\sim \sim A} \qquad \frac{\begin{array}{l} A \supset (A \otimes B) \\ \sim (A \otimes B) \end{array}}{\sim A} \qquad \frac{\begin{array}{l} (R \equiv \, \sim S) \supset \, \sim Q \\ \sim \sim Q \end{array}}{\sim (R \equiv \, \sim S)}$$

Complex Substitution Instances of the Fallacy of Denying the Antecedent

$$\frac{\begin{array}{l} A \supset \, \sim B \\ \sim A \end{array}}{\sim \sim B} \qquad \frac{\begin{array}{l} A \supset (A \otimes B) \\ \sim A \end{array}}{\sim (A \otimes B)} \qquad \frac{\begin{array}{l} (R \equiv \, \sim S) \supset Q \\ \sim (R \equiv \, \sim S) \end{array}}{\sim Q}$$

EXERCISES

II

The following argument forms are complex substitution instances of *modus ponens, modus tollens*, the Fallacy of Affirming the Consequent, and the Fallacy of Denying the Antecedent. State the argument form which each exemplifies.

1. $$\frac{\begin{array}{l} [(p \equiv \, \sim q) \vee r] \supset s \\ (p = \, \sim q) \vee r \end{array}}{s}$$

2. $$\frac{\begin{array}{l} (p \otimes r) \supset (s \cdot t) \\ \sim (s \cdot t) \end{array}}{\sim (p \otimes r)}$$

3. $$\frac{\begin{array}{l} (p \otimes r) \supset (s \supset t) \\ \sim (p \otimes r) \end{array}}{\sim (s \supset t)}$$

4. $$\frac{\begin{array}{l} (s \supset t) \supset [p \equiv (s \vee r)] \\ p \equiv (s \vee r) \end{array}}{s \supset t}$$

5. $$\frac{\begin{array}{l} (p \vee s) \supset \, \sim (q \vee r) \\ \sim \sim (q \vee r \end{array}}{\sim (p \vee s)}$$

6. $$\frac{\begin{array}{l} \sim (p \cdot r) \supset [(s \equiv t) \cdot \sim q] \\ \sim (p \cdot r) \end{array}}{(s \equiv t) \cdot \sim q}$$

7. $$\frac{\begin{array}{l} (p \otimes r) \supset \, \sim (s \cdot t) \\ \sim (s \cdot t) \end{array}}{p \otimes r}$$

8. $$\frac{\begin{array}{l} \{[(p \otimes r) \supset (s \supset t)] \cdot (q \vee r)\} \supset [(p \equiv \, \sim r) \otimes (s \equiv \, \sim t)] \\ [(p \otimes r) \supset (s \supset t)] \cdot (q \vee r) \end{array}}{(p \equiv \, \sim r) \otimes (s \equiv \, \sim t)}$$

PROOF

Truth tables provide a completely mechanical procedure of applying certain rules for determining in every case the validity or invalidity of truth-functional argument forms. However, there are important areas of logic and mathematics in which such mechanical procedures are not applicable. One method used to show the validity of arguments in these areas is to deduce the conclusion from the premises. The result of this procedure is known as formal proof. A **formal proof of validity** for an argument is a series of propositions, each of which is either a premise or a proposition that follows from previous propositions by an elementary valid argument form. The last proposition in the series is the conclusion. An **elementary valid argument form** is an argument form, such as *modus ponens* or *modus tollens,* whose validity is relatively easy to demonstrate. When used to justify steps in formal proofs, elementary valid argument forms are called **rules of inference.**

An example of a formal proof is provided by the following deduction of the conclusion $\sim s$ from the premises $p \supset q,\ q \supset \sim r,\ s \supset r$ and p.

$$
\begin{array}{lll}
(1) & p \supset q & \qquad \big|\ \sim s \\
(2) & q \supset \sim r & \\
(3) & s \supset r & \\
(4) & p & \\
\hline
(5) & q & \text{1, 4 } M.\ P. \\
(6) & \sim r & \text{2, 5 } M.\ P. \\
(7) & \sim s & \text{3, 6 } M.\ T.
\end{array}
$$

The conclusion to be proven is written to the right of the premises for convenient reference. The line between (4) and (5) indicates that (1) through (4) are premises and (5) through (7) are propositions which follow from previous propositions. The last proposition in the proof is the conclusion. Proposition (5) is deduced from (1) and (4) by *modus ponens*. This is to say that (1) and (4) have the form of the premises of the elementary valid argument form *modus ponens:* Premise (1) is a conditional and (4) asserts its antecedent; since the conclusion of *modus ponens* is the consequent of the conditional, the consequent of the conditional in (1) can be stated as a conclusion at step (5). The reason, or justification, for the deduction of (5) is indicated to its right, and cites the numbers of the two previous premises which have the form of the premises of *modus ponens* and an abbreviation (*M.P.*) of the name, *modus ponens*. Similarly, (2) is a conditional and (5) is its antecedent, so the consequent of this conditional can be asserted at step (6). Premise (3) is also a conditional and its consequent is denied in (6), so (3) and (6) have the form of the premises of *modus tollens;* thus a conclusion of the form of a *modus tollens* (*M.T.*) conclusion, which is the denial of the antecedent of the conditional, can be asserted at step (7).

EXERCISES

III

State the justification for each line that is not a premise in the following proofs of validity:

1.   (1) $p \supset q$ $| \; q$
     (2) p
     (3) q

2.   (1) $p \supset q$ $| \sim p$
     (2) $\sim q$
     (3) $\sim p$

3.   (1) $p \supset q$ $| \; r$
     (2) p
     (3) $q \supset r$
     (4) q
     (5) r

4.   (1) $p \supset q$ $| \; t$
     (2) $q \supset r$
     (3) $\sim p \supset s$
     (4) $s \supset t$
     (5) $\sim r$
     (6) $\sim q$
     (7) $\sim p$
     (8) s
     (9) t

5.   (1) $p \supset q$ $| \sim p$
     (2) $q \supset \sim r$
     (3) $\sim \sim r$
     (4) $\sim q$
     (5) $\sim p$

6.   (1) $(p \cdot q) \supset r$ $| \sim (p \cdot q)$
     (2) $\sim r$
     (3) $\sim (p \cdot q)$

7.   (1) $(p \oslash q) \supset \sim s$ $| \sim s$
     (2) $\sim (t \vee w) \supset (p \oslash q)$
     (3) $(t \vee w) \supset (r \equiv \sim s)$
     (4) $\sim (r \equiv \sim s)$
     (5) $\sim (t \vee w)$
     (6) $p \oslash q$
     (7) $\sim s$

8.   (1) $[(r \equiv s) \vee (w \equiv \sim t)] \supset \sim (p \oslash q)$ $| \sim [(r \cdot s) \vee t]$
     (2) $[(u \supset v) \cdot (x \vee y)] \supset [(r \equiv s) \vee (w \equiv \sim t)]$
     (3) $(u \supset v) \cdot (x \vee y)$
     (4) $[(r \cdot s) \vee t] \supset (p \oslash q)$
     (5) $(r \equiv s) \vee (w \equiv \sim t)$
     (6) $\sim (p \oslash q)$
     (7) $\sim [(r \cdot s) \vee t]$

IV

Symbolize the following arguments and construct formal proofs of their validity:

1. If he had thought monism were true, then Empedocles would have held that reality is composed of only one kind of substance. But Empedocles did not hold that reality is composed of only one kind of substance. Empedocles could have held that there are four basic elements if he did not think that monism were true. Hence, Empedocles could indeed have held that there are four basic elements. (*M, R, F*)

2. American foreign policy is realistic only if the administration does not commit us to points all over the globe. It is not true that the administration has not committed us to points all over the globe. But if the Senator's analysis is correct, then American foreign policy is realistic. The Senator's analysis is incorrect only if his committee lacked relevant information. Therefore his committee did lack relevant information. (*A, C, S, L*)

3. If the committee members have all the relevant information and are nonpartisan, their report will be valuable. Their report will be valuable only if the political situations in their home states are stable. If it is near election time, then the political situations in their home states will not be stable. It is near election time. Thus, the committee members cannot both have all the relevant information and be nonpartisan. (*R, N, V, S, E*)

4. If the population increases geometrically while the food supply increases arithmetically, then mass poverty is inevitable and the human race will cease to exist. The population increases geometrically while the food supply increases arithmetically, if Thomas Malthus was correct. If the population explosion can be checked if and only if prudential means of checking it are put into operation immediately, then Thomas Malthus was correct. The population explosion can be checked if and only if prudential means of checking it are put into operation immediately. Therefore, mass poverty is inevitable and the human race will cease to exist. (*P, F, M, H, T, E, C*)

5. If the principle of simplicity can be used to decide between opposing scientific theories, then the heliocentric theory is correct and the geocentric theory is incorrect. Copernicus' arguments are sound if the heliocentric theory is correct and the geocentric theory is incorrect. Of course, Copernicus' arguments are sound only if Ptolemy's arguments are unsound. If epicycles are necessary, then Ptolemy's arguments are not unsound. Epicycles are necessary. So the principle of simplicity cannot be used to decide between opposing scientific theories. (*S, H, G, C, P, E*)

HYPOTHETICAL SYLLOGISM

The elementary valid argument form

$$p \supset q$$
$$\underline{q \supset r}$$
$$p \supset r$$

is known as **hypothetical syllogism** and is abbreviated as H. S. Its validity was demonstrated in number 8 of exercise I in chapter III. Hypothetical syllogisms are sometimes called "chain arguments" because their basic form can be expanded to any number of variables, as in:

$$p \supset q$$
$$q \supset r$$
$$r \supset s$$
$$\underline{s \supset t}$$
$$p \supset t$$

The term 'hypothetical syllogism', however, is usually reserved for arguments of the first type which have two premises, and we will adopt only this type as a rule of inference. Given hypothetical syllogism as a rule of inference, the following alternative proof for the argument we used to illustrate formal proofs is possible:

(1) $p \supset q$ $\big|\, {\sim} s$
(2) $q \supset {\sim} r$
(3) $s \supset r$
(4) $\underline{p}$
(5) $p \supset {\sim} r$ 1, 2 H. S.
(6) ${\sim} r$ 4, 5 *M. P.*
(7) ${\sim} s$ 3, 6 *M. T.*

EXERCISES

V

1. Use partial truth tables to show that:
   (a) the following forms are invalid:

$p \supset q$	$p \supset q$
$r \supset q$	$r \supset s$
$p \supset r$	$q \supset s$

   (b) a chain argument with four propositional variables and three premises can be valid.

2. Give alternative proofs of validity using hypothetical syllogism for 3, 4, and 5 in exercise III above.

3. Give alternative proofs of validity using hypothetical syllogism for 2, 3, 4, and 5 in exercise IV above.

EXERCISES

VI

Symbolize the following arguments and construct formal proofs of their validity.

1. If minds and bodies are so defined that interaction is impossible, then there is a temptation to think of persons as ghosts in machines. If there is a temptation to think of persons as ghosts in machines, there is definitely a mind-body problem. Hence, if minds and bodies are so defined that interaction is impossible, there is definitely a mind-body problem. (D, T, P)

2. Democracy can survive only if people can be taught to work for the public good rather than for their own narrow self-interest. People can be taught to work for the public good rather than for their own narrow self-interest only if the theory of psychological egoism is false. Therefore, democracy can survive only if the theory of psychological egoism is false. (D, P, T)

3. If the earth is surrounded by a "sea of air," then objects in this sea are subject to air pressure. If these objects are subject to air pressure, then a simple suction pump can raise water approximately 34 feet. And if a simple suction pump can raise water approximately 34 feet, then such a pump will be able to raise a liquid heavier than water a distance proportionate to its weight in comparison with the weight of water. If a pump can raise a liquid heavier than water a distance proportionate to its weight in comparison with the weight of water, then it can raise mercury about $^{34}/_{14}$ the height it raises water. Thus we can conclude that if the earth is surrounded by a "sea of air," a simple suction pump can raise mercury about $^{34}/_{14}$ the height it raises water. (E, O, S, D, M)

4. If Skinner's position in *Beyond Freedom and Dignity* is correct, then if we wish to avoid the predicted results we should look carefully for the factors leading to those results. If deterministic and teleological explanations are incompatible, then Skinner's position is correct. But if Skinner's position rests on confused presuppositions about the nature of man, then it is not the case that if we wish to avoid predicted results we should look carefully for the factors leading to those results. Skinner's position does rest on confused presuppositions about the nature of man. Therefore, deterministic and teleological explanations are not incompatible. (S, W, L, I, R)

5. If the classical certainty theory of knowledge as held by Descartes and Spinoza is correct, then one knows if and only if one is certain. But if one knows if and only if one is certain, then one cannot discover at a later time that something one was certain about is in error. It is false that one cannot discover at a later time that something one was certain about is in error. Hence, the classical certainty theory of knowledge as held by Descartes and Spinoza is incorrect. (T, K, C, D)

6. Great Britain's reduction in armament was reasonable only if Chamberlain's policy of appeasement made sense. Chamberlain's policy of appeasement made sense only if Hitler could be trusted to keep his promise of 1936 that Germany did not desire any European territory. Hitler could be trusted to keep his promise of 1936 only if either Germany was too weak to seize territory or she had no allies. If Germany signed a treaty with Italy and increased the strength of the Luftwaffe, then she was neither too weak to seize territory nor had no allies. She did sign a treaty with Italy and she also increased the strength of the Luftwaffe. Therefore, Great Britain's reduction in armament was unreasonable. (*R, C, H, W, A, S, I*)

7. Dialectical materialism is true if and only if economic determinism is true. If dialectical materialism is true if and only if economic determinism is true, then both nature as a whole and economic conditions contain opposing forces. If nature as a whole and economic conditions contain opposing forces, these forces can be expressed as laws. Given that such forces can be expressed as laws, their formulation may be discovered by observing history. Their formulation may be discovered by observing history only if there is progress in history and enough time has elapsed for the pattern to be observable. Hence, as Marx claimed, there is progress in history and enough time has elapsed for the pattern to be evident. (*D, E, N, C, L, F, P, T*)

8. If either rolling stones gather no moss or a stitch in time saves nine, then the early bird gets the worm. But the early bird came home without a worm. If it is false that either rolling stones gather no moss or a stitch in time saves nine, it is true that the worm has turned. Since the worm has turned, we must walk softly and carry a big stick. Walking softly and carrying a big stick implies that you won't have to shoot until you see the white of their eyes or that you will get there firstest with the mostest. Either you won't have to shoot until you see the white of their eyes or you will get there firstest with the mostest, implies that the meek inherit the earth. So, we conclude by coining the phrase, the meek will inherit the earth. (*R, S, E, T, W, C, U, F, M*)

9. If either Colonel Mustard or Professor Plum committed the murder, then it took place in the billiard room. If it took place in the billiard room, then it was done with the lead pipe or candlestick. It was done with the lead pipe or the candlestick only if Mrs. White was not in the kitchen. It is false that Mrs. White was not in the kitchen. If neither Colonel Mustard nor Professor Plum committed the murder, then Miss Scarlet was in the dining room and Mr. Green was in the study. If Miss Scarlet was in the dining room and Mr. Green was in the study, then the murder was committed in the kitchen. If it was committed in the kitchen, then Mrs. White is the assassin. Therefore Mrs. White is the assassin. (*M, P, B, L, C, W, S, G, K, A*)

10. If Dr. Pangloss is right, then this is the best of all possible worlds. Of course, this is the best of all possible worlds only if the evils it contains are necessary evils. If the evils it contains are necessary evils, this implies the truth of the Principle of Sufficient Reason—i.e., that there is good reason for everything being as it is and not otherwise. If there is good reason for everything being as it is and not otherwise, then there must be a good reason for Candide having

been kicked out by the baron and for the earthquake having destroyed Lisbon. And if either Candide had not been involved in the Inquisition or had not desired Lady Cunegonde, then either he would not have wandered over America on foot or he would not have lost the sheep from Eldorado. If he had not wandered over America on foot or had not lost the sheep from Eldorado, then some principle other than the Principle of Sufficient Reason would be required to explain what happens in this world. And no principle other than the Principle of Sufficient Reason is required to explain what happens in this world. If it were not true that either Candide had not been involved in the Inquisition or that he had not desired Lady Cunegonde, then it still would be true that Dr. Pangloss is right. Therefore, there must be a good reason for Candide having been kicked out by the baron and for the earthquake having destroyed Lisbon. (*P*, *B*, *E*, *R*, *C*, *L*, *I*, *D*, *W*, *S*, *O*)

DISJUNCTIVE SYLLOGISMS

Arguments of the forms

$$
\begin{array}{cccc}
p \lor q & p \lor q & p \oslash q & p \oslash q \\
\sim p & \sim q & \sim p & \sim q \\
\hline
q & p & q & p
\end{array}
$$

are called disjunctive syllogisms (abbreviated as D. S.). The first two forms are **inclusive disjunctive syllogisms;** the last two are **exclusive disjunctive syllogisms.** All four forms are valid. Although the first premise of an inclusive disjunctive syllogism asserts that both of its disjuncts might be true, and the first premise of an exclusive disjunctive syllogism asserts that exactly one of its disjuncts is true, both assert that *at least one* of their disjuncts is true. Since the second premise in each case states that one of the disjuncts is not true, we must conclude that the other is true. We will adopt disjunctive syllogisms as additional rules of inference. As with *modus ponens, modus tollens,* and hypothetical syllogism, one justifies a step in a formal proof using disjunctive syllogism by citing the numbers of the propositions from which that step follows, along with the abbreviation, D. S. Disjunctive syllogism is used twice in the following proof:

$$
\begin{array}{lll}
(1) & p \lor q & \quad \lfloor \sim s \\
(2) & \sim q & \\
(3) & p \supset \sim r & \\
(4) & r \lor \sim s & \\
\hline
(5) & p & \quad 1, 2 \text{ D. S.} \\
(6) & \sim r & \quad 3, 5 \text{ M. P.} \\
(7) & \sim s & \quad 4, 6 \text{ D. S.}
\end{array}
$$

EXERCISES

VII

1. The following argument forms are not instances of disjunctive syllogisms and will not be used in proofs. However, they appear superficially similar to D. S. Use partial truth tables to show that:
   (a) The following forms are invalid:

$$\begin{array}{ccc}
p \lor q & p \lor q & p \lor q \\
\underline{p} & \underline{p} & \underline{q} \\
q & \sim q & p
\end{array}$$

$$\begin{array}{ccc}
p \lor q & p \otimes q & p \otimes q \\
\underline{q} & \underline{p} & \underline{q} \\
\sim p & q & p
\end{array}$$

   (b) The following forms are valid:

$$\begin{array}{cc}
p \otimes q & p \otimes q \\
\underline{p} & \underline{q} \\
\sim q & \sim p
\end{array}$$

2. Explain why the argument forms in (a) above are invalid, but those in (b) are valid.

VIII

Symbolize the following arguments and construct formal proofs of their validity:

1. Unless we employ effective devices to prevent the dumping of industrial wastes into our streams and rivers, pollution will continue to increase dangerously. Obviously we are not going to employ effective devices to prevent the dumping of wastes into streams and rivers. Hence, pollution will continue to increase dangerously. (*E*, *I*)

2. If the wind velocity increases again, then either this was the eye of the storm or the storm has passed. If the storm has passed, we would have heard an all-clear signal. We have not heard an all-clear signal. The wind velocity is increasing again. Therefore, this was the eye of the storm. (*W*, *E*, *P*, *H*)

3. If "The Purple People-Eater" is playing at the Capri, then it is either an art film or pornographic or both. If it is pornographic, then the vice squad will raid the theater. If the vice squad raids the theater, then the manager will be held without bond. "The Purple People-Eater" is playing at the Capri. However, it is not an art film. Therefore, the manager will be held without bond. (*C*, *A*, *P*, *V*, *M*)

4. If the ether exists, then every interstice of space is filled with matter or ether. But if every interstice of space is filled with matter or ether, then the earth travels through ether in its revolution on its axis and in its orbital movements. Either the speed of a beam of light varies according to whether it travels with, against, or across the stream of ether caused by the movement of the earth, or the earth

does not travel through ether during its revolutionary and orbital movements. On the other hand, if the speed of a beam of light varies according to whether it travels with, against, or across the stream of ether caused by the earth's movement, then a beam of light that is split and sent off at right angles should travel at different velocities. As the Michelson-Morley experiment proved, a beam of light split into two and sent off at right angles does not travel at different velocities. Hence, the ether does not exist.   (*E, F, T, S, D*)

5.   If we accept the traditional view, then the ancestor of Darwin's finches was a true finch. Now, if a warblerlike bird can evolve from a finch, then a finchlike bird can evolve from a warbler. Most Geospiza are finchlike. That most Geospiza are finchlike implies that either a warblerlike bird can evolve from a finch or that there were more vacant niches in the Galapagos for finches than warblers, but not both. If the ancestor of Darwin's finches was a true finch, then it is not true that a finchlike bird can evolve from a warbler. We do accept the traditional view. Therefore, there were more vacant niches in the Galapagos for finches than warblers.   (*A, T, W, F, G, V*)

6.   Capital punishment is justifiable only if it serves as a deterrent. Unless most homicides are premeditated, capital punishment could not serve as a deterrent. If either most homicides are due to negligence or are crimes of passion, then they are not premeditated. Most homicides are due to negligence or are crimes of passion, if human action is often habitual or the result of stimulus-response. Either man has achieved control over his unconscious or human action is often habitual or the result of stimulus-response. But as Freud has pointed out, man has not achieved control over his unconscious. Consequently, capital punishment is not justifiable.   (*J, S, P, N, C, H, D, A*)

7.   Either stories about UFOs manned by men from Mars are to be believed only if there are trained scientific observers, or if large numbers of people are convinced that they saw men from Mars then one must conclude that there are men from Mars. It is not true that if large numbers of people are convinced that they saw men from Mars then one must conclude that there are men from Mars. There are men from Mars only if that planet will support life and beings from that planet have the technical capability for interplanetary travel. Either all the data we have concerning Mars is erroneous or it is false both that Mars will support life and that beings from that planet have the technical capability for interplanetary travel, but not both. It is not the case that all the data we have concerning Mars is erroneous. Either there are men from Mars or there are no trained scientific observers. Therefore, stories about UFOs manned by men from Mars are not to be believed.   (*S, T, L, C, M, P, B, D*)

8.   If I take your bishop, then you will take my pawn and my queen will be in danger. If you take my pawn and endanger my queen, then you will not be able to castle. But either you will be able to castle or you can avoid being put in check if and only if you lose your knight. If you can avoid being put in check if and only if you lose your knight, you will put me in check with your next move. Either I am going to take your bishop or I will sacrifice my own bishop. But I will not sacrifice my bishop. So it appears that you will put me in check with your next move. (*B, P, Q, C, A, K, N, S*)

9. If there is a strike then the company will have to recognize the union, or, if there is no strike then they will continue their present hiring policies. If no strike means that the present hiring policies are to be continued, then there will be violence. If there is violence, there will be a public outcry and the Governor will send in the National Guard. If there is a public outcry and the Governor sends in the National Guard, then the NLRB will intervene. If the NLRB intervenes, then the company will have to pay a penalty and will lose money. If the officers of the company act in their own best interest, then they will not allow a situation to occur in which the company has to pay a penalty and loses money. Of course, the officers of the company will act in their own best interest. Thus, if there is a strike the company will have to recognize the union. (*S, R, H, V, P, G, N, C, L, O*)

10. Either the money and jewels are missing or the captain and the detective are wrong. If the captain and the detective are wrong, then the evidence will be re-evaluated. Should the evidence be reevaluated, either the statement of the up-stairs maid would be checked for consistency or the plumber would be interrogated again. It is not the case that both the money and jewels are missing. If it were not the case that the valuables had been hidden, then the upstairs maid's statement would not be checked for consistency. But if they were hidden, it could be the case that there was only an attempted robbery if and only if the robbery report is misleading. And it is false that: there was just an attempted robbery if and only if the robbery report is misleading. So, the plumber will be interrogated again. (*M, J, C, D, E, U, P, H, A, R*)

DILEMMAS

The following valid argument forms are known as dilemmas:

$$(p \supset q) \cdot (r \supset s)$$
$$\underline{p \vee r}$$
$$q \vee s$$

$$(p \supset q) \cdot (r \supset s)$$
$$\underline{p \,\underline{\vee}\, r}$$
$$q \vee s$$

$$(p \supset q) \cdot (r \supset s)$$
$$\underline{\sim q \vee \sim s}$$
$$\sim p \vee \sim r$$

$$(p \supset q) \cdot (r \supset s)$$
$$\underline{\sim q \,\underline{\vee}\, \sim s}$$
$$\sim p \vee \sim r$$

The first two forms are **constructive dilemmas** (C. D.); the last two are **destructive dilemmas** (D. D.). The validity of all four is easily demonstrated by means of partial truth tables, and we will adopt them as additional rules of inference. Notice that all these forms have an inclusive disjunction as a conclusion; none of the dilemmas which we adopt as inference rules has an exclusive disjunction as a conclusion. For further discussion of dilemmas, see chapter XIII.

EXERCISES

IX

Use partial truth tables to show that:

(a)   The following forms are invalid:

$$(p \supset q) \cdot (\sim p \supset s)$$
$$\underline{p \ \otimes \ \sim p}$$
$$q \ \otimes \ s$$

$$(p \supset q) \cdot (r \supset s)$$
$$\underline{p \ \otimes \ r}$$
$$q \ \otimes \ s$$

$$(p \supset q) \cdot (r \supset s)$$
$$\underline{\sim q \ \otimes \ \sim s}$$
$$\sim p \ \otimes \ \sim r$$

$$(p \supset q) \cdot (r \supset s)$$
$$\underline{p \ \vee \ r}$$
$$q \ \otimes \ s$$

(b)   The following forms are valid:

$$(p \supset q) \cdot (\sim p \supset s)$$
$$\underline{p \ \otimes \ \sim p}$$
$$q \ \vee \ s$$

$$(p \supset q) \cdot (r \supset \sim q)$$
$$\underline{\sim q \ \otimes \ q}$$
$$\sim p \ \vee \ \sim r$$

$$(p \supset q) \cdot (r \supset q)$$
$$\underline{p \ \vee \ r}$$
$$q$$

$$(p \supset q) \cdot (p \supset r)$$
$$\underline{\sim q \ \vee \ \sim r}$$
$$\sim p$$

X

Symbolize the following arguments and construct formal proofs of their validity:

1. If the sun shines, the tourists will be happy; whereas if the sun does not shine, the farmers will be happy. The sun will either shine or not shine. Hence, either the tourists or the farmers will be happy. (S, T, F)

2. If the bill under deliberation by the Senate furthers the interests of the majority, there will be pressure on the Senate to pass it; however, if it attempts to protect minority rights, then the majority will feel threatened by its passage. Either there will not be pressure on the Senate to pass it or the majority will not feel threatened by its passage. Therefore, the bill under deliberation either does not further the interests of the majority or does not attempt to protect minority rights. (F, P, A, T)

3. If the books in the library agree with the Koran, then they are useless; and if they disagree with the Koran, then they are pernicious. If a book is either useless or pernicious, then it should be destroyed. The books in the library must either agree or disagree with the Koran. Therefore, they should be destroyed. (A, U, P, D)

4. If the Stoics are correct, then the good life is a life of duty; but if the Hedonists are correct, then the good life is a life of immediate pleasure. The good life is not a life of immediate pleasure unless pleasures are never followed by pain. But it is false that pleasures are never followed by pain. Either the Stoics or the Hedonists are correct. Thus, the good life is a life of duty. (S, D, H, I, N)

5. The inspector will sign the form only if the building code is being followed; and if the building code is not being followed, the foreman will be reprimanded. If the contract requires that action be taken today, it will be the case either that the building code is not being followed or that the foreman will not be reprimanded. The contract does require that action be taken today. Therefore, either the inspector will not sign the form or it is not the case that the building code is not being followed.   (*I, B, F, C*)

6. If the World Trade Organization is successful, then communication among all countries will be established; and we can hope for a workable procedure for settling international disputes only if there is a common ground for understanding among nations. If diplomats from all countries do not meet to discuss mutual problems, then communication among all countries will not be established; and if it is not seen that our problems have a common basis, then there will not be a common ground for understanding among nations. Either diplomats from all countries will not meet to discuss mutual problems or it has not been seen that our problems have a common basis. Therefore, either the World Trade Organization will not be successful or we cannot hope for a workable procedure for settling international disputes.   (*W, C, P, G, D, S*)

7. If the arms race is continued, then all nations will eventually have nuclear weapons; and world peace can be achieved only if the threat of nuclear warfare is diminished. Either all nations will attain a realistic view of the world situation, or every nation will continue to attempt to spend more money on armament than any other nation. If all nations attain a realistic view of the world situation, then either the arms race will continue or world peace will be achieved. But it is not the case that every nation will continue to attempt to spend more money on armament than any other nation. Hence, either all nations will eventually have nuclear weapons or the threat of nuclear warfare will diminish.   (*A, N, W, D, R, S*)

8. That men are held responsible for their actions implies that the thesis of strict determinism is not true; but if physiological causes account for all human behavior, then the thesis of strict determinism is true. Either it is false that the thesis of strict determinism is not true, or it is simply not true. It is not the case that men are not held responsible for their actions. Therefore, physiological causes do not account for all human behavior.   (*H, S, P*)

9. Either time is real or it cannot be measured, or either time is unreal or it can be measured. If time is real, then we must ask whether it is eternal; and if time cannot be measured, we must ask how we can properly refer to it and how we can come to know about it. If it is true that either time is unreal or can be measured, then we can doubt whether it has natural divisions. If we can doubt whether it has natural divisions, then we are clear about what a unit of time is. But we are not clear about what a unit of time is. Hence we must ask whether time is eternal or must ask how we can properly refer to it and how we can come to know about it.   (*R, M, E, P, K, N, C*)

10. I shall eat the cake only if it is like the other things I have eaten in this place. If it is like the other things I have eaten in this place, then it will either make me grow larger or grow smaller. If I eat the cake, then were I to grow larger I could

reach the key and were I to grow smaller I could creep under the door. If I reach the key or creep under the door, then I shall get into the garden. I shall eat the cake. Therefore, I shall get into the garden. (*E, O, L, S, R, C, G*)

11. If the earth does not rotate on its axis and does not revolve around the sun, then an object dropped from a tower will fall directly beneath the point from which it is dropped; and if the earth does rotate on its axis and does revolve around the sun, then an object dropped from a tower will hit the ground at a point which differs from the point beneath which it was dropped in proportion to the speed at which the earth is turning. Either the earth does not rotate on its axis and does not revolve around the sun, or the earth does rotate on its axis and does revolve around the sun. An object dropped from a tower will not hit the ground at a point which differs from the point beneath which it was dropped in proportion to the speed at which the earth is turning. An object dropped from a tower will fall directly beneath the point from which it is dropped only if there is either no wind or the object is heavy. If there is no wind or the object is heavy, then this procedure will not count as a demonstration that the earth moves. Therefore, this procedure will not count as a demonstration that the earth moves. (*A, S, O, D, W, H, C*)

12. Either Congress reduces spending or the national debt will continue to increase. If Congress reduces spending, then no additional funds will be spent on existing programs; while, if the national debt continues to increase, there will be a severe recession. If Congress reduces spending, then the farm price support program will be eliminated; and if the national debt continues to increase there will be a money shortage. Were either the farm support program eliminated or a money shortage to occur, large numbers of rural families would move to the city. Of course, if large numbers of rural families move to the city, then more money will be spent on welfare programs. If more money is spent on welfare programs, then it is false that no additional funds will be spent on existing programs. Therefore, there will be a severe recession. (*R, N, A, S, F, M, L, W*)

13. If there are Comanches in this area, we will soon see signs of their activity; and if they are still angry, they will burn our wagons. If we hear more bird calls than usual, then there are Comanches in this area; and, if the cavalry is still pursuing them, they are still angry. They will hide in the trees provided that it is a cloudy night and there is enough wind to cover the noise of their movements. If they are hiding in the trees, then either we will hear more bird calls than usual or the cavalry is still pursuing them. It is a cloudy night and there is enough wind to cover the noise of their movements. Therefore, either we will soon see signs of their activity or they will burn our wagons. (*C, S, A, B, H, P, T, N, W*)

14. That men are held responsible for their actions implies that the thesis of strict determinism is not true; but if physiological causes account for all human behavior, then the thesis of strict determinism is true. Either it is false that the thesis of strict determinism is not true, or it simply is not true. If physiological causes do not account for all human behavior, then it can be demonstrated that some particular action has no physiological cause or that the physiological account does not offer a complete explanation. If it can be demonstrated either that some particular action has no physiological cause or that the physiological

account does not offer a complete explanation, then the word 'cause' is used more narrowly than in ordinary discourse. But the word 'cause' is not used more narrowly than in ordinary discourse. Therefore, men are not to be held responsible for their actions.   (*H, S, P, A, E, C*)

15. If Dimitri bicycles across Europe he will travel lightly, and if he walks across Europe he will wear his track shoes. If either he does not bicycle across Europe or does not walk across Europe, then he will sail his yacht along the southern coast. If he sails his yacht along the southern coast, then he will either take his friends or his horses. If he takes either his friends or his horses, he will have the appropriate accessories. And if he has the appropriate accessories, he will have his saxophone or wear his cowboy boots. He will not have his saxophone. Also, he will not travel lightly unless he does not wear his track shoes. Therefore, Dimitri will wear his cowboy boots.   (*B, L, W, T, Y, F, H, A, S, C*)

CONJUNCTION AND SIMPLIFICATION

Two elementary valid argument forms which are used as rules of inference follow from the definition of conjunction. Any two propositions that have been asserted in an argument may be conjoined. Thus we have the following form known as **conjunction** (Conj.):

$$\frac{\begin{array}{c} p \\ q \end{array}}{p \cdot q}$$

From the assertion of a conjunction, the assertion of either of its conjuncts follows. Therefore, we have the following forms known as **simplification** (Simp.):

$$\frac{p \cdot q}{p} \qquad \frac{p \cdot q}{q}$$

EXERCISES

XI

Symbolize the following arguments and construct formal proofs of their validity:

1. The stock is being sold and the chairman of the board is being replaced. If the stock is being sold, the company must be in financial difficulty. It follows that the company is in financial difficulty.   (*S, C, F*)

2. If the villagers were awake then they could have heard the volcano erupting, although they could not have seen it. Either they could have seen it or they could not have heard it. Therefore the villagers were not awake.   (*A, H, S*)

3. F is a commutative ring with more than one element and having a unity. Every nonzero element of F has a multiplicative inverse in F. If F is a commutative ring with more than one element and having a unity, and every nonzero element of F has a multiplicative inverse in F, then F is a field. Therefore, F is a field. (*C, U, N, F*)

4. If you can travel during the week, then you will pay the cheaper fare; and if you pay the cheaper fare, then you will have some money to spend in New York. If you have some money to spend in New York, you will want to go to Sam Goodie's. So, if you can travel during the week, you will want to go to Sam Goodie's. (*T, P, M, S*)

5. If the world is in a continual state of flux, then one cannot step into the same river twice. One cannot step into the same river twice only if the forces of love and strife keep all the elements moving on their upward and downward paths, but if the world is a plenum then there is no change. Either the world is in a continual state of flux or it is a plenum. Thus either the forces of love and strife keep all the elements moving on their upward and downward paths or there is no change. (*W, R, F, P, C*)

6. Either pleasures differ only quantitatively or they also differ in kind, and either Bentham is correct or Mill is correct. If poetry gives one a different kind of pleasure than pushpin, then one may be said to be higher than the other, and if one may be said to be higher than the other then Bentham is not correct. Poetry does give one a different kind of pleasure than pushpin, and pleasures do not differ only quantitatively. Therefore, Mill is correct and pleasures also differ in kind. (*Q, K, B, M, P, H*)

7. If the prisoners ate polished rice, they developed beriberi; but if they ate unpolished rice, they did not develop beriberi. Furthermore, if the chickens were fed polished rice they developed a nervous paralysis similar to beriberi, although if they were given unpolished rice to eat they did not develop such a nervous paralysis. If the prisoners' eating polished rice resulted in their developing beriberi and if the chickens' being fed polished rice resulted in their developing a nervous paralysis similar to beriberi, while if the prisoners' eating unpolished rice meant that they did not develop beriberi and if the chickens' being given unpolished rice to eat meant that they did not develop a nervous paralysis similar to beriberi, this implies that some substance in the husk removed from the rice can prevent beriberi from developing. If there is some substance in the husk removed from rice which can prevent beriberi from developing and this substance can be isolated in the laboratory, then such a discovery would constitute the beginning of the development of the science of nutrition. Such a substance was isolated in the laboratory. Consequently, that discovery constituted the beginning of the development of the science of nutrition. (*P, D, U, F, N, G, S, I, C*)

8. If the fact that the airship *Albatross* had powerful weapons meant it could destroy objects on the ground, and its capability of destroying objects on the ground meant that its captain could enforce his will over all the earth, then the captain either had good motives for controlling the world or his motives were evil. The airship *Albatross* had powerful weapons only if its captain had more advanced scientific knowledge than his contemporaries; and if the captain

had more advanced scientific knowledge than his contemporaries, then the *Albatross* could destroy objects on the ground. It is either the case that if the *Albatross* could destroy objects on the ground its captain could enforce his will over all the earth, or it is the case that if he attempted to blow up the British vessel then his passengers would recognize the hoax. It is not the case that his attempt to blow up the British vessel resulted in his passengers' recognizing a hoax. Furthermore, the captain's motives for controlling the world were not evil. Therefore, his motives were good.   (*A, D, W, G, E, S, B, P*)

9. If either the trees discontinue their production of auxin or there is a drought, then the leaves will change color. If the number of chloroplasts in the leaves is maintained and the volume of water in the cells remains the same, then the leaves will not change color. It will not be the case that either the trees discontinue their production of auxin or that there will be a drought, only if there is not an unseasonal variation in the weather. If the current proportions in the production of plant hormones are maintained, then the number of chloroplasts in the leaves will be maintained. Unless the transmission of water in the xylem is interrupted, the volume of water in the cells will remain the same. The current proportions in the production of plant hormones are being maintained and there has been no interruption in the transmission of water in the xylem. Thus, there is no indication of an unseasonal variation in the weather.   (*A, D, C, N, V, U, P, I*)

10. Con Edison had a power failure only if their supply of carrots ran out and the goats refused to work the treadmills. Their supply of carrots ran out only if the rabbit population increased greatly, and the rabbit population increased greatly only if the fox population decreased greatly. Only if there were more fox hunters this year than last would the fox population decrease greatly. If the goats refused to work the treadmills, then the officials of Con Edison will have some absurd explanation. Either they will not have some absurd explanation or there were not more fox hunters this year than last. If either the goats did not refuse to work the treadmills or Con Edison's supply of carrots did not run out, then it is false both that the supply of carrots did run out and that the goats refused to work. Obviously, therefore, Con Edison did not have a power failure.   (*P, S, G, R, F, H, A*)

ADDITION AND ABSORPTION

The validity of the argument form, **addition** (Add.),

$$\frac{p}{p \lor q}$$

may not be immediately obvious, but its validity is easily demonstrated by means of a truth table, or by reflection on the meaning of $\lor$. Propositions containing a $\lor$ assert only that at least one of their disjuncts must be true. So, given the assertion of any proposition, the assertion of that proposition in an inclusive disjunction with *any* other proposition follows.

The validity of the elementary argument form called **absorption** (Abs.) was demonstrated on page 27. We will also adopt it as a rule.

$$\frac{p \supset q}{p \supset (p \cdot q)}$$

EXERCISES

XII

1. If either the butler or the caretaker was lying, then the maid did not commit the murder. The butler was lying. Therefore the maid did not commit the murder. (*B*, *C*, *M*)

2. If factories continue to dump wastes into Lake Erie, then the pollution will become so great that it will be a fire hazard. If factories continue to dump wastes into Lake Erie and the pollution becomes so great that it is a fire hazard, then people in Cleveland will be able to get firewater from their kitchen taps. Therefore, if factories continue to dump wastes into Lake Erie, people in Cleveland will be able to get firewater from their kitchen taps. (*C*, *P*, *F*)

3. If either Lee or Jackson arrived before him, Grant would be cut off and the Confederacy would win the day's battle. If the Confederacy won either that day's battle or the next, then the end of the war would be delayed for six months. Lee did arrive before Grant. Hence, the end of the war was delayed for six months. (*L*, *J*, *G*, *C*, *N*, *D*)

4. If the particles introduced into the tube are negative, then either their path will be curved toward the top of the screen or they will strike the center of the screen. If the particles introduced into the tube are negative and either their path is curved toward the top of the screen or they strike the center of the screen, then we will be able to determine the nature of the field across the tube. We cannot determine the nature of the field across the tube. Therefore, the particles introduced into the tube were not negative. (*N*, *T*, *C*, *F*)

5. If Tylor is correct, then later religions may be explained as modifications of a more primitive animism. On the other hand, if Muller is correct then the concept of *mana* is even more basic than the concept of the soul upon which the doctrine of animism is based. Of course, later religions may be explained as modifications of a more primitive animism only if a genetic-evolutionary model is adequate to explain religion. But a genetic-evolutionary model is inadequate to explain religion. Therefore, either Tylor or Muller, or both, are incorrect. (*T*, *L*, *M*, *C*, *G*)

6. If either the shortstop or third baseman has been thrown out of the game, then Snoopy will be moved to the infield. If either Snoopy is moved to the infield or the third baseman has been thrown out of the game, then if the shortstop has been thrown out of the game then Pig Pen will come into the game if and only if he can be the catcher. The shortstop has been thrown out and Pig Pen is coming in. So, Pig Pen is coming into the game if and only if he can be the catcher. (*S*, *T*, *M*, *P*, *C*)

7. Beard's economic interpretation of the Constitution is plausible only if he is correct in maintaining that most of the support for ratification came from the financial-mercantile and landowning classes and most of the opposition to ratification came from the farmer and debtor classes. He is correct in maintaining that most of the support for ratification came from the financial-mercantile and landowning classes and most of the opposition came from the farmer and debtor classes only if the predominantly agricultural states were much slower to ratify the Constitution than the other states. In fact though, not only did the predominantly argicultural states not ratify the Constitution more slowly, but they ratified it by a larger majority. If the predominantly agricultural states either did not ratify the Constitution more slowly or ratified it by a larger majority, then the people of those states apparently did not find the Constitution adverse to their interests. Had the Constitution contained rigid property qualifications or special class privileges, the people of those states would have found it adverse to their interests. If the Constitution contains neither rigid property qualifications nor special class privileges, then only a biased interpretation could make it appear above all an economic document. If only a biased interpretation could make the Constitution appear above all an economic document, Beard failed in his aim to present history as a study of real forces rather than as political propaganda. Therefore, Beard's economic interpretation of the Constitution is not plausible and he failed in his attempt to present history as a study of real forces rather than as political propaganda.   (*E, S, O, P, L, A, R, C, B, F*)

8. If the soul is the harmony of the body, then it is not prior to the body. If the soul is the harmony of the body and is not prior to the body, then the soul is mortal. It is not the case that the soul is both the harmony of the body and is mortal. Therefore, the soul is not the harmony of the body.   (*H, P, M*)

9. If Dimitri escorts Gina Lollobrigida to the ball, then Elizabeth Taylor will be hurt. And if his escorting Gina Lollobrigida means that Brigitte Bardot will be upset, then he will either escort Suzanne Pleshette or Raquel Welch. If he escorts Gina Lollobrigida and Elizabeth Taylor is hurt, then Brigitte Bardot will also be upset. Dimitri will not escort Suzanne Pleshette. So, he will escort Raquel Welch.   (*G, E, B, S, R*)

10. If Cleanthes accepts the argument from design, then he believes in the existence of a deity. If he accepts the argument from design and believes in the existence of a deity, then he believes that unalterable and immutable laws govern the universe; although if he accepts the argument from miracles, then he believes in divine intervention. Either he does not believe that unalterable and immutable laws govern the universe or he does not believe in divine intervention. It is false that he does not accept the argument from miracles. Consequently, he does not accept the argument from design.   (*D, E, U, M, I*)

11. The OEO has approved the housing project but no funds have been allocated. If either the OEO or HEW has approved the project, then if the local officials have been informed they are looking for a site. If the local officials are looking for a site, then the neighborhood action committees will be alarmed. Either funds have been allocated, or if there was no publicity then the neighborhood action committees do not know that the project was planned. Either there was

no publicity or the local officials have been informed. Therefore, either the neighborhood action committees do not know that the project was planned or they will be alarmed. (*O, F, H, I, L, A, P, K*)

12. If either the Cubs and White Sox win the pennants or the Mets and Yankees win the pennants, the World Series will be played wholly in one city. If the World Series is played wholly in one city, that city will be Chicago, Illinois, or New York City. If the World Series is played in Chicago, Illinois, and the weekday games are scheduled for Wrigley Field, then the baseball fans will be annoyed. The baseball fans will be annoyed only if they can expect to see just the weekend games; and if they can expect to see just the weekend games, they will hope the Series goes beyond five games. The Cubs and White Sox have clinched the pennants. The World Series will not be played in New York, and the weekday games are scheduled for Wrigley Field. Therefore, the baseball fans will hope the Series goes beyond five games. (*C, W, M, Y, P, I, N, F, B, E, H*)

13. If it is true that 2 + 2 = 4 is a necessary truth if and only if it is capable of being established *a priori,* then it is also true that it is capable of being established *a priori* if and only if it is an analytic proposition. The fact that 2 + 2 = 4 is a necessary truth if and only if it is capable of being established *a priori* and it is capable of being established *a priori* if and only if it is an analytic proposition, implies that 2 + 2 = 4 is a necessary truth if and only if it is an analytic proposition. It is not the case, however, that 2 + 2 = 4 is a necessary truth if and only if it is an analytic proposition. Therefore it is not true that 2 + 2 = 4 is a necessary truth if and only if it is capable of being established *a priori.* (*N, C, A*)

14. If light travels in straight lines, then it is not subject to gravitation; whereas if it is subject to gravitation, then it does not travel in straight lines. Either it is false both that it travels in straight lines and is not subject to gravitation, or it is false both that it is subject to gravitation and does not travel in straight lines. If either light does not travel in straight lines or is not subject to gravitation, then either classical or modern physicists are mistaken. Therefore, either classical or modern physicists are mistaken. (*S, G, C, M*)

15. Scotland Yard is working around the clock, but they have not yet caught the cat burglar. If the cat burglar was an amateur, then they will have many clues. If M. Lestrade is in charge, then there will be a very efficient investigation. If Scotland Yard is working around the clock, then either they do not have many clues or their investigation is not very efficient. If either the cat burglar was not an amateur or M. Lestrade is not in charge then they must know the identity of the cat burglar. If they know his identity, then either they have caught him or they will catch him soon. If they catch him soon, then the newspapers will praise them highly. Therefore, either they will catch him soon and the newspapers will praise them highly or they will have to call in Sherlock Holmes. (*W, C, A, M, L, V, K, S, N, H*)

5

TRUTH-FUNCTIONAL EQUIVALENCES

DOUBLE NEGATION

There are many valid arguments composed of truth-functional propositions the validity of which cannot be demonstrated by the rules of inference we have introduced. For example, although arguments having the following form are valid, we have no rule that will allow us to deduce the conclusion from the premises.

$$
\begin{array}{ll}
(1) \ r \supset \sim p & \left\lfloor \sim r \right. \\
(2) \ p
\end{array}
$$

However, if we were to replace the second premise p with $\sim \sim p$, then we could deduce the conclusion by *modus tollens*.

$$
\begin{array}{lll}
(1) \ r \supset \sim p & \left\lfloor \sim r \right. \\
(2) \ p & \\
(3) \ \sim \sim p & \text{Replacement of 2 by 3} \\
(4) \ \sim r & 1, \ 3 \ M. \ T.
\end{array}
$$

How can such replacement be justified? Note that any two propositions of the forms p and $\sim \sim p$ have the same truth value. Whenever two propositions have the same truth value because of their truth-functional forms, they are said to be **truth-functionally equivalent.** Two propositions are truth-functionally equivalent if and only if a compound proposition in which they are connected by a biconditional symbol is a tautology. The following truth table shows that propositions having the forms p and $\sim \sim p$ are truth-functionally equivalent. The propositional form $p \equiv \sim \sim p$ is known as the law of **double negation** (D.N.).

$$p \equiv \; \sim \sim p$$

T T	T	F
F T	F	T

If all, or any part, of a truth-functional proposition is replaced by an expression that is truth-functionally equivalent, the resulting expression is equivalent in truth value to the original. It follows that the substitution of truth-functionally equivalent expressions for one another does not alter the validity or invalidity of truth-functional arguments. Hence, we may adopt the following rule:

RULE: Any truth-functional expression may be substituted for a truth-functionally equivalent expression.

In making substitutions one cites the number of the original proposition and an abbreviation of the law which justifies the substitution. A justification for the above proof then is

(1) $r \supset \sim p$ $\big| \sim r$
(2) p
(3) $\sim \sim p$ 2, D. N.
(4) $\sim r$ 1, 3 M. T.

Since substitution may be made for part of, as well as for an entire, expression, so long as the expression substituted is equivalent to the original, the following proof is also correct:

(1) $\sim \sim p \supset q$ $\big| q$
(2) p
(3) $p \supset q$ 1, D. N.
(4) q 2, 3 M. P.

COMMUTATION AND ASSOCIATION

The laws of **commutation** (Comm.) and **association** (Assoc.), like the law of double negation, are easily seen to be truth-functionally equivalent forms.

Commutation

$$(p \cdot q) \equiv (q \cdot p)$$
$$(p \lor q) \equiv (q \lor p)$$

The idea underlying the law of commutation is that the order in which conjunctions and disjunctions are written is irrelevant to their truth value.

Association

$$[(p \cdot q) \cdot r] \equiv [p \cdot (q \cdot r)]$$
$$[(p \lor q) \lor r] \equiv [p \lor (q \lor r)]$$

Similarly, the idea which underlies the law of association is that the grouping of components in conjunctions or disjunctions is irrelevant to their truth value.

Neither commutation nor association holds for conditionals. The order of the components in conditionals is important because $p \supset q$ is *not* truth-functionally equivalent to $q \supset p$. Thus, these two expressions cannot be substituted for one another in every context without a change of truth value. The grouping of the components in conditionals also affects their truth value. The expression $[(p \supset q) \supset r]$ is *not* truth-functionally equivalent to $[p \supset (q \supset r)]$. Hence, their substitution for one another is not permissible.

Commutation and association do hold for exclusive disjunctions and biconditionals, but we will not adopt them as substitution rules.

Example of the Use of Double Negation, Commutation, and Association in a Proof

(1) $(p \lor q) \supset \sim \sim s$		$w \lor (r \lor q)$
(2) $q \lor p$		
(3) $s \supset [r \lor (q \lor w)]$		
(4) $p \lor q$	2, Comm.	
(5) $\sim \sim s$	1, 4 *M. P.*	
(6) s	5, D. N.	
(7) $r \lor (q \lor w)$	3, 6 *M. P.*	
(8) $(r \lor q) \lor w$	7, Assoc.	
(9) $w \lor (r \lor q)$	8, Comm.	

EXERCISES

I

Use truth tables to determine whether propositions having the following forms are truth-functional equivalences:

1. $(p \supset q) \equiv (\sim p \vee q)$
2. $(p \supset q) \equiv (\sim q \supset \sim p)$
3. $(p \supset q) \equiv (\sim q \vee p)$
4. $(p \supset q) \equiv (\sim p \supset \sim q)$
5. $\sim (p \cdot q) \equiv (\sim p \vee \sim q)$
6. $\sim (p \cdot q) \equiv (\sim p \cdot \sim q)$
7. $[(p \cdot q) \supset r] \equiv [p \supset (q \supset r)]$
8. $[p \vee (q \cdot r)] \equiv [(p \vee q) \cdot (p \vee r)]$
9. $p \equiv (p \vee p)$
10. $(p \equiv q) \equiv [(p \supset q) \cdot (q \supset p)]$

II

Symbolize the following arguments and construct formal proofs of their validity:

1. The current has ceased to flow only if the switch is not closed. If the current is flowing, then the motor will start. The switch is closed. Therefore, the motor will start. *(F, C, M)*

2. Either Professor Learned, or perhaps Professor Staff or Professor Pedantic will teach the course. If either Professor Learned or Professor Pedantic teaches the course, then it will not be an easy one. Professor Staff will not teach the course. Hence, it will not be an easy course. *(L, S, P, E)*

3. If either laws are not sufficiently clear in the state of nature or some injured parties in the state of nature are not strong enough to execute the laws justly, and men in the state of nature are capable of being unbiased judges if and only if they have no personal stake in disputes, then men will enter into a social contract. If Locke is correct, then it follows both that men in the state of nature are capable of being unbiased judges if and only if they have no personal stake in disputes and either laws are not sufficiently clear in the state of nature or some injured parties in the state of nature are not strong enough to execute the laws justly. Thus Locke is correct only if men will enter into a social contract. *(L, I, J, P, S, C)*

4. If Dr. Lieberatten is not a behaviorist, then he does not have any white rats; whereas if he is a behaviorist and has white rats, then he is hostile toward clinical psychologists and considers them to be unscientific. If Dr. Lieberatten is hostile toward clinical psychologists or considers them to be unscientific, then there is going to be a departmental feud. Dr. Lieberatten definitely has some white rats. Hence, there is going to be a departmental feud. *(B, W, H, C, F)*

5. If Fermat's Last Theorem can be proved, then there are not four natural numbers greater than 2 which satisfy the equation: $x^n + y^n = z^n$. Unless there are four natural numbers greater than 2 which satisfy the equation: $x^n + y^n = z^n$

we should be able to prove the theorem, or we are not entitled to say that we know the theorem is true. If either the intuitionists are correct or Kant is correct, then neither should we be able to prove the theorem nor are we not entitled to say that we know the theorem is true. We should adopt puritanical standards of logical rigor only if Kant or the intuitionists are correct. We should adopt puritanical standards of logical rigor. Therefore, Fermat's Last Theorem cannot be proved. (*F, N, A, E, I, K, P*)

6. If neither Allied Steel nor Bethlehem Steel withdraws its price increase, then Chrysler Corporation and General Motors will have to increase prices on this year's models. If Chrysler Corporation and General Motors have to increase prices on their current models, then the economy as a whole will advance. Either the economy as a whole will not advance and the prices of all manufactured goods will be stabilized, or there will be a general trend toward recession. Inflation will continue only if there is not a general trend toward recession. It is obvious that inflation will continue. Therefore, either Allied Steel or Bethlehem Steel will withdraw its price increase. (*A, B, C, G, E, P, R, I*)

7. If the capital is moved, the populace will be demoralized. If the populace is demoralized and the capital is moved, then there will be little support for the new regime; although if the military continues to support the regime, internal order will be maintained. Should the capital not be moved, the revolutionary groups will not combine to ensure the success of a coup. But the revolutionary groups are combining to ensure the success of a coup. Hence, there will be little support for the new regime unless internal order is maintained. (*C, P, L, M, I, R*)

8. If the circus folds, then the animals will be sold to the zoo; and the lion tamer will be able to find another job only if the zoo will hire him. Either it is the case that if the animals are sold to the zoo the lion tamer will be able to find another job, or the zoo will hire the lion tamer only if he doesn't mind selling peanuts on the side. If the zoo will hire the lion tamer only if he doesn't mind selling peanuts, then neither will the lion tamer be able to find another job nor will the zoo have a new peanut vendor. Either the lion tamer will be able to find another job or the zoo will have a new peanut vendor. So, if the circus folds, the zoo will hire the lion tamer. (*F, S, L, H, M, N*)

9. Fly-by-Night Airlines serves Pittsburgh, and also New York and Boston. If Fly-by-Night serves either Washington or New York and I have to take a regularly scheduled flight, then I will be delayed while the plane circles the airport waiting for landing instructions. I will get the Confederated Nonsense account only if I am not delayed while the plane circles the airport waiting for landing instructions, but I will have to take a regularly scheduled flight. Therefore, I will not get the Confederated Nonsense account. (*P, N, B, W, T, D, C*)

10. If the concept of causality cannot be adequately understood in terms of experience alone, then the entailment theory is correct; although the entailment theory is correct only if there are synthetic *a priori* connections. If Hume is correct and causality is only constant conjunction, and can be adequately understood in terms of experience alone, then causal reasoning can never be more than probable. It is not true both that the entailment theory is correct and that there are synthetic *a priori* connections; moreover, causality is only constant conjunc-

tion and Hume is correct. Therefore, causal reasoning can never be more than probable. (*A, E, S, H, C, R*)

11. If I am thinking at this moment, then if consciousness exists, we must find a way to account for it; and, if I am not sleeping and not dreaming, then I am thinking at this moment. Either I am not sleeping or I only think that I am conscious, and either I am not dreaming or this is a very vivid dream. If I am being deceived, then it is not the case that I only think that I am conscious; but if I am not being deceived, then I can conclude that there is a thinking substance. Either I am being deceived or I am not being deceived. I cannot conclude that there is a thinking substance, although I can conclude that there is a thinking process and it is true that this is not a very vivid dream. Therefore, if consciousness exists, then consciousness exists and we must find a way to account for it. (*I, C, W, S, D, O, V, B, T, P*)

12. If there is neither widespread nor highly organized opposition, the city council will vote to begin fluoridation. On the other hand, if there is either widespread or highly organized opposition, the city council will either vote to table the issue or they will vote to authorize a further study. There will be highly organized opposition only if the John Birch Society opposes the recommendation. If there is no widespread and no highly organized opposition, then it will not be the case that the city council will either vote to authorize a further study or to table the issue. If there is highly organized opposition and the John Birch Society opposes the recommendation, then the newspaper will not come out in its favor. However, if the newspaper does come out in its favor, then there will not be widespread opposition. The newspaper is definitely going to come out in favor of the recommendation. Thus, the city council will vote to begin fluoridation. (*W, H, B, T, F, J, N*)

13. If Dimitri Pestszenterzsebet inherited the Pestszenterzsebet lands, he lives in a castle; and if he inherited the Pestszenterzsebet lands, then he also inherited the family fortune. Either he inherited the Pestszenterzsebet lands, or he either inherited the family fortune or acquired his wealth some other way. If he inherited the family fortune, then he has either maintained it or has increased its value; and if he were his father's only son then he inherited the family fortune. Either Dimitri is not an astute financier or he did not acquire his wealth some other way, and he is an astute financier. If Dimitri has either maintained the family fortune or has increased its value, he lives in a villa. So, Dimitri either lives in a castle or a villa. (*L, C, F, W, M, I, O, A, V*)

14. If either we buy a new computer or get a grant, then our programmer will have to learn FORTRAN or we cannot use all of our data. We are going to buy a new computer and expand our entire operation, but we cannot do this with the funds now available. If we expand our entire operation, this will mean the addition of new personnel and will allow us to use all of our data. Our programmer will have to learn FORTRAN only if either we get all the money we have asked for or at least get enough money to buy the model we want. If Jones is still chairman of the board, then the board will be skeptical about our proposal; and if the board is skeptical about our proposal, we will not get all the money we asked for. And if Thompson is not allowed to present our case at the meeting then we will not even get enough money to buy the model we want. So we may conclude that either Jones cannot still be chairman of the board or Thompson

will have to be allowed to present our case at the board meeting. (*B, G, P, D, E, F, A, M, L, J, S, T*)

15. Either Tolstoy or Chekhov wrote *The Brothers Karamazov,* or else either Dostoevski or Pasternak wrote it. If this novel contains a development of Kierkegaardian projects and attempts to describe rather than evaluate them, then Tolstoy did not write it. If it attempts to describe rather than evaluate those projects but describes them wholly from an existentialist viewpoint, then Chekhov did not write it. This novel does contain a development of Kierkegaardian projects and attempts to describe rather than evaluate them, and it describes them wholly from an existentialist viewpoint. Pasternak wrote *The Brothers Karamazov* only if its themes do not have religious implications, and this novel does not contain a development of Kierkegaardian projects unless its themes have religious implications. Therefore, Dostoevski wrote *The Brothers Karamazov.* (*T, C, D, P, K, A, E, R*)

DE MORGAN'S THEOREMS

The following pair of laws, abbreviated as D.M., is named for one of the first men to formulate them, the nineteenth century mathematician and logician, Augustus De Morgan. They are especially useful in that they allow substitution of disjunctions for conjunctions, and vice versa.

$$\sim(p \cdot q) \equiv (\sim p \vee \sim q)$$
$$\sim(p \vee q) \equiv (\sim p \cdot \sim q)$$

The first law allows substitution of a negated conjunction for a disjunction in which the values of the components have been changed. (The value of a component has been changed when a positive component has been negated, or when a negative component has been made positive.) The second law permits substitution of a negated disjunction for a conjunction in which the values of the components have been changed. Of course, since these are equivalences, substitution may also be carried out in the opposite direction, i.e., a disjunction in which the values of the components have been changed may be substituted for a negated conjunction, and a conjunction in which the values of the components have been changed may be substituted for a negated disjunction. Careful study of the foregoing remarks will show that the following are instances of De Morgan's laws:

$$\sim(\sim p \cdot q) \equiv (p \vee \sim q)$$
$$\sim(p \cdot \sim q) \equiv (\sim p \vee q)$$
$$\sim(\sim p \cdot \sim q) \equiv (p \vee q)$$
$$\sim(\sim p \vee q) \equiv (p \cdot \sim q)$$
$$\sim(p \vee \sim q) \equiv (\sim p \cdot q)$$
$$\sim(\sim p \vee \sim q) \equiv (p \cdot q)$$

EXERCISES

III

Symbolize the following arguments and construct formal proofs of their validity:

1. Had I paid both the principal and the interest, I would have received a letter stating that my account is in order. On the other hand, if I did not pay the principal or did not pay the interest, then they have probably issued a warrant for my arrest. I have not received a letter stating that my account is in order. Hence, they have probably issued a warrant for my arrest. (*P*, *I*, *L*, *W*)

2. If God is omnipotent, then he is able to prevent evil; and if he is benevolent, then he is willing to prevent evil. Evil can exist only if God is either not able or not willing to prevent it. If God exists, then he must be both omnipotent and benevolent. Evil does exist. Therefore, God does not exist. (*O*, *A*, *B*, *W*, *E*, *G*)

3. If he is either not male or not single, then Jones is ineligible to join the Y.M.C.A. If he is both male and single, then he is a bachelor; though of course he is a bachelor only if he is not married. Either he is married or he is happy, but not both. Jones is not happy. Therefore, he is ineligible to join the Y.M.C.A. (*M*, *S*, *I*, *B*, *R*, *H*)

4. The patient has typhoid or paratyphoid fever only if the Widal test turns out positive. The Widal test will not turn out positive unless the culture is prepared with a salt solution and allowed to incubate at 98° for an hour. If it is not the case either that the culture is not prepared with a salt solution or not allowed to incubate at 98° for an hour, then the Widal test is not an effective test for typhoid and paratyphoid fever. If the patient has not been vaccinated for typhoid fever then the Widal test will be an effective test for typhoid and paratyphoid fever. The patient has not been vaccinated for typhoid fever. Therefore, he has neither typhoid nor paratyphoid fever. (*T*, *P*, *W*, *S*, *I*, *E*, *V*)

5. The government should spend more money on job corps training only if it is false both that although skilled workers are turned out, they cannot find jobs. Either the government should spend more money on job corps training, or the current economic level can be maintained if and only if there is a permanent class of unemployed. If it is true that the current economic level can be maintained if and only if there is a permanent class of unemployed, then our economy is similar to the one described in Galbraith's *Affluent Society*. On the other hand, if we have not yet eliminated ghettos and poverty, then we have a long way to go before we achieve an affluent society. Only one of the following holds: Either we do not have a long way to go before we achieve an affluent society, or our economy is not similar to the one described in Galbraith's *Affluent Society*. However, it is true that we have not yet eliminated ghettos and poverty. Therefore, either job corps training is not turning out skilled workers or they can find jobs. (*M*, *S*, *F*, *C*, *P*, *A*, *E*, *L*)

6. If it is false both that the difference between ancient and modern science is that ancient scientists did not experiment and that they did not have the same purpose in mind as modern scientists, then if modern science is unique it is the result of cultural differences. Of course, ancient scientists did experiment, and their attempt to "save the appearances" implies that they had the same purpose

in mind as modern scientists. It is false both that modern science is unique and is the result of cultural differences. If either modern science is not unique or differs from ancient science only in technology, then those historians who stress the novelty of modern science are mistaken. I conclude, then, that those historians who stress the novelty of modern science are mistaken.   (E, P, U, C, A, T, H)

7. If man has been responsible for a number of rapid evolutionary changes, then even if he knows the causes of these changes then he still knows little about their long-range effects. Man is not responsible for a number of rapid evolutionary changes only if he does not know the causes of these changes. Neither organophosphates nor DDT have been shown not to have long-range effects on insect populations. If DDT and cyclodienes have been shown to have long-range effects on insect populations, then man does know the causes of these rapid evolutionary changes. It is not the case that DDT has been shown to have long-range effects on insect populations, unless either cyclodienes have also not been shown to have long-range effects or there is not an adequate explanation for insecticide resistance in over one hundred species. Either cyclodienes have been shown to have long-range effects on insect populations, or it has been shown both that cyclodienes have long-range effects and that there is an adequate explanation for insecticide resistance in over one hundred species. Therefore, little is known about the long-range effects of rapid evolutionary changes produced by man. (R, K, L, O, D, C, I)

8. If the polls had shown that the people of his district were in favor of the bill to prevent campus disorders, then the Senator would not have voted against it; while if the polls had shown that the people of his district do not wish scholarships given to campus rebels, then he would have supported the bill to cut off funds to anyone found guilty of participating in a campus riot. If it is false both that the polls showed that the people of his district favor the bill to prevent campus disorders and that they do not wish scholarships given to campus rebels, then the people of his district must be much more liberal than the general populace. It is false that the Senator both supported the bill to cut off funds to anyone found guilty of participating in a campus riot and did not vote against the bill to prevent campus disorders. Therefore, the people of his district must be much more liberal than the general populace.   (F, V, W, S, L)

9. If he makes a good impression in spring training, then he will be taken north; and if the regular catcher is traded, he has a good chance of staying with the team all season. However, it is not the case that he will both be taken north and has a good chance of staying with the team all season. If he lives up to the scout's expectations and doesn't have any injuries, he will make a good impression in spring training. If he either does not live up to the scout's expectations or is injured, then he is sure to start the season with a minor league club. Either he is not sure to start the season with a minor league club and will be working just to keep a place on the parent club's roster, or he will not be competing for the position of their regular catcher. He will be competing for the regular catcher's position. So, the regular catcher will not be traded.   (S, N, R, G, L, I, M, W, C)

10. If the automotive industry were not so excessively concerned with profits or were sincere about its avowed claim to promote public safety, then it would build

automobiles which are more easily repaired and would equip them with more effective safety devices. Obviously, however, the automobile industry is neither going to build automobiles which are more easily repaired, nor which are equipped with more effective safety devices. If the automotive industry is not sincere about its avowed claim to promote public safety, then Congress should pass laws that will force it to fulfill its obligation to the public. It follows then that Congress should pass laws that will force the automotive industry to fulfill its obligation to the public. (*C, S, R, E, P*)

MATERIAL IMPLICATION AND TRANSPOSITION

Two propositional forms which are truth-functionally equivalent to $p \supset q$ are especially useful

$$(p \supset q) \equiv (\sim p \lor q)$$
$$(p \supset q) \equiv (\sim q \supset \sim p)$$

The first is the law of **material implication** (M. I.); the second is the law of **transposition** (Trans.). Material implication allows conditionals and disjunctions to be substituted for one another. Transposition allows the antecedents and consequents of conditionals to be interchanged. *Note carefully, however, the changes in the values of the components.* The following instances of material implication and transposition, respectively, follow the same pattern:

$$(\sim p \supset q) \equiv (p \lor q)$$
$$(p \supset \sim q) \equiv (\sim p \lor \sim q)$$
$$(\sim p \supset \sim q) \equiv (p \lor \sim q)$$

$$(\sim p \supset q) \equiv (\sim q \supset p)$$
$$(p \supset \sim q) \equiv (q \supset \sim p)$$
$$(\sim p \supset \sim q) \equiv (q \supset p)$$

EXERCISES

IV

1. Either the book club did not receive my reply or I forgot to send it. Had I forgotten to send it, I would have received this month's selection. Therefore, it cannot be the case both that the book club received my reply and that I did not receive this month's selection. (*B, F, R*)
2. Either many adults do not understand the lyrics of certain contemporary rock tunes or they would protest their being on the air. If they were to protest their

being on the air then they would probably be removed. Hence the fact that they are not removed implies that many adults do not understand the lyrics of certain contemporary rock tunes. (*U, P, R*)

3. If magic and science are merely the result of man's desire to control his environment, then chemists and alchemists share the same ultimate end. But, if it is false that magic and science are merely the result of man's desire to control his environment, then Aristotle's claim that disinterested curiosity is one of the motivations for science could be correct. Of course, Aristotle's claim that disinterested curiosity is one of the motivations for science could not be correct unless Bacon is in error in holding that knowledge is valued for its utility alone. Therefore, if Bacon is correct in holding that knowledge is valued for its utility alone, then chemists and alchemists share the same ultimate end. (*M, U, A, B*)

4. It could not be the case both that he is a senior and that he does not have eighty-five hours credit. Either he must have gone to summer school or he does not have eighty-five hours credit. Therefore, if he did not go to summer school, then he is not a senior. (*S, E, G*)

5. John Stuart Mill's philosophy of mathematics is adequate only if mathematical statements are empirical generalizations. Of course, if either numericals do not denote observable objects or mathematical relations do not stand for relations among observable objects, then mathematical statements are not empirical generalizations. If Frege's arguments are conclusive, then it cannot be the case both that numericals denote observable objects and that mathematical relations stand for relations among observable objects. Either Mill's philosophy of mathematics is adequate or Frege was justified in making fun of it by calling it a pebble and biscuit theory. Thus, if Frege's arguments are conclusive, he was justified in making fun of Mill's philosophy of mathematics by calling it a pebble and biscuit theory. (*M, E, N, R, C, J*)

6. If Hobbes' theory of human nature is correct, then men will cooperate with one another if and only if they think it in their interest to do so. But if Butler's theory of human nature is correct, then it is false that men will cooperate with one another if and only if it is in their interest to do so. Either Butler's theory of human nature is correct or men have neither particular passions directed toward the good of others nor a general propensity toward benevolence. It follows, therefore, that if Hobbes' theory of human nature is correct, then men do not have a general propensity toward benevolence and do not have particular passions directed toward the good of others. (*H, C, T, B, P, G*)

7. If the tightrope walker joined the circus in Brussels, then he is the man Scotland Yard is looking for. If the fat lady is not lying, then he is not the man Scotland Yard is looking for, and either the fat lady is telling the truth or the sword swallower is lying. If the sword swallower's not lying implies that the tightrope walker did not join the circus in Brussels, then it is not the case that both the lion tamer is protecting someone and the horse trainer is not telling all he knows. Therefore, if the lion tamer is protecting someone, the horse trainer is telling all he knows. (*T, M, F, S, L, H*)

8. The vaccine will be effective if it can be disseminated quickly, but even so it will be effective only if it is administered properly. If it cannot be disseminated quickly, then the epidemic will be unavoidable. If there are not a large number

of trained volunteer workers, the hospital personnel will not have time to train an adequate number of novices. The vaccine will not be administered properly unless the hospital personnel does have time to train an adequate number of novices. Therefore, the epidemic will be unavoidable unless there are a large number of trained volunteer workers. (*V, D, A, E, T, H*)

9. If Thoreau's thesis in his essay on civil disobedience is correct and government is at best only an expedient, then the best form of government is either that which governs least or does not govern at all. If the best form of government is that which does not govern at all, then government is not justifiable; although if it is false that the best form of government is that which governs least, then government is justifiable. If government is desirable at all, then the best form of government cannot be that which governs least. Government is desirable but it is true that it is at best only an expedient. Consequently, Thoreau's thesis in his essay on civil disobedience is incorrect. (*T, E, L, A, J, D*)

10. James McCosh's narration of David Hume's death was put forth in good faith only if he believed that hearsay is acceptable evidence. Had McCosh been motivated by the same dispassionate desire for truth as Hume, then he would have subscribed to only those beliefs that it is possible to verify; but had he subscribed to only those beliefs that it is possible to verify, then he would not have believed that hearsay is acceptable evidence. If it is false both that McCosh's narration of Hume's death was put forth in good faith and that he was motivated by the same dispassionate desire for truth as Hume, then he did Hume a great injustice. Therefore, McCosh did Hume a great injustice. (*N, B, M, S, H*)

11. Either Oceania has set out to win the war and destroy the enemies with which she continually struggles, or there will be a permanent state of war and its sole purpose will be to use up the products of industry. Oceania will not destroy the enemies with which she continually struggles. If the war creates a strong feeling of nationalism but does not enhance the loyalty of the citizens to the state, then it cannot be both a permanent state and have using up the products of industry as its sole purpose. Therefore, if the war creates a strong feeling of nationalism, then it will enhance the loyalty of the citizens to the state. (*O, D, P, S, C, E*)

12. If Dimitri entered the winter Olympics, then he entered all the skiing events for men. Either he did not enter the winter Olympics or he did not enter all the skiing events for men. If Dimitri's entering the winter Olympics implies that he won all the events he entered, then he is the world's greatest skier. So, Dimitri is the world's greatest skier. (*E, S, W, G*)

13. The U. S. either offers other nations foreign aid with no strings attached or she expects something in return, or her motives are the improvement of the conditions of life for all people and a stable peace. It is not the case both that the U. S. offers other nations foreign aid with no strings attached and that she does not try to influence their internal affairs. The U. S. does not offer other nations foreign aid with no strings attached if she tries to influence their internal affairs. The current U. S. policies toward unindustrialized countries will be changed unless she does not expect something in return. The current U. S. policies toward unindustrialized countries are not being changed, but foreign aid funds are being reduced. It follows, nevertheless, that the motives of the U. S. are the

improvement of the conditions of life for all people and a stable peace.   (*O, E, L, S, I, P, R*)

14. If the information that the man at the service station gave us is correct, then the guidebook is incorrect and we are hopelessly lost. If the guidebook is correct, then this is our destination and that dumpy-looking hotel is where we are going to spend the night. Either the guide book is correct or you lied to me and brought me to this dumpy-looking hotel on purpose. But if you either lied to me or brought me to this dumpy-looking hotel on purpose, then you do not love me and I am going home to mother. It is not true that if this is our destination then that dumpy-looking hotel is where *we* are going to spend the night. Obviously, therefore you do not love me.   (*I, G, H, D, S, L, B, A, M*)

15. If necessary statements are reports of linguistic usage, then they are factual claims. It is either not the case that they are either factual claims or are not reports of linguistic usage, or they are prescriptive statements. If they are prescriptive statements and have no truth value, then they are not amenable to a purely logical analysis. Therefore, if necessary statements have no truth value, they are not amenable to a purely logical analysis.   (*R, F, P, T, A*)

DISTRIBUTION

In logic, as in mathematics, it is possible to "distribute" an expression across a parenthesis as long as the resultant expression is equivalent to the original. The **distribution laws** (Dist.) which permit truth-functional substitutions are

$$[p \cdot (q \lor r)] \equiv [(p \cdot q) \lor (p \cdot r)]$$
$$[p \lor (q \cdot r)] \equiv [(p \lor q) \cdot (p \lor r)].$$

A convenient way to remember the distribution laws is to note that the same logical connective appears first in both the original expression and in its logical equivalent.

EXERCISES

V

Symbolize the following arguments and construct formal proofs of their validity:

1. According to his agent, Dimitri was booked for Atlanta and either Memphis or Houston. According to Dimitri, he was not booked for both Atlanta and Memphis. If Dimitri was booked for both Atlanta and Houston, then the police in these cities should be alerted so that they may control the crowds. Therefore, the police in those cities should be alerted so that they may control the crowds. (*A, M, H, P*)

2. Either the car was hit while parked on Main Street, or you backed into the sign and are not admitting that you are responsible for the dent. Thus it follows that if the car was not hit while parked on Main Street, then you are not admitting that you are responsible for the dent. (*H, B, A*)

3. Either termites are eating the foundation of your house, or the lumber is decaying and the supports are crumbling. If either termites are eating your foundation or the lumber is decaying, then the floor will soon start to sag. It is false that both the floor will soon start to sag and that you can get the price you are asking for the house. Therefore, you cannot get the price you are asking for the house. (*T, L, S, F, P*)

4. Either there are many activities which directly display qualities of mind and which are not themselves intellectual operations, or there are many activities which directly display qualities of mind and which are not effects of intellectual operations. If there are many activities which directly display qualities of mind, then either intelligent practice is a stepchild of theory or theorizing is one practice amongst others. Intelligent practice is neither a stepchild of theory nor are adjectives like 'intelligent' and 'stupid' inapplicable to theorizing. Therefore, theorizing is one practice amongst others. (*M, I, E, P, T, A*)

5. Cooper was the greatest American novelist only if his novels are both typical of American experience during the time about which he wrote and have universal philosophical significance. If Mark Twain is correct, then Cooper's romanticism and inaccuracy of observation imply that his novels were not typical of American experience during the time of which he wrote. Not only is Mark Twain correct, but Copper's novels certainly do not have universal philosophical significance. Thus, Ccoper was not the greatest American novelist. (*G, T, U, M, R, I*)

6. The situation on the Senate floor was tense, and either the Senator from Maine or the Senator from Washington left the chamber in a huff. If the situation on the Senate floor was tense and the Senator from Maine left the chamber in a huff, then the bill will not be passed this afternoon and there will be a filibuster. If the situation on the Senate floor was tense and the Senator from Washington left in a huff, then the bill already has enough support to pass. Therefore, if it is false both that the bill will not be passed this afternoon and that there will be a filibuster, then the bill already has enough support to pass. (*S, M, W, B, F, E*)

7. Either North Carolina or Wake Forest will win; although if North Carolina does not win then there will not be a play-off. Now the A.C.C. will have a team in the N.C.A.A. tournament only if North Carolina does not win. It is not true both that Wake Forest will win and that there will not be a play-off. A team from the A.C.C. can win the N.C.A.A. tournament this year only if the A.C.C. has a team in the tournament and they did not participate in a play-off. Therefore, no team from the A.C.C. can win the N.C.A.A. tournament this year. (*N, W, P, H, T*)

8. If there are regularities in nature, then we can make predictions and control the course of events. If we can control the course of events, then either we are not exercising our ability to control them or we do not consider the consequences when we take advantage of the regularities in nature. We are exercising our ability to control the course of events and the results are disastrous. Therefore,

if there are regularities in nature, then we do not consider the consequences when we take advantage of these regularities. (R, P, C, E, A, D)

9. If Dimitri's grape harvest matches its precedent, then if the world's finest wineries send representatives to his villa, then he will get the best price ever paid for grapes although the grapes would have to be transported a great distance. If Dimitri's grape harvest matches its own precedent, and the world's finest wineries send representatives to his villa but the grapes have to be transported a great distance, then Dimitri will use the entire crop in the family winery and not endanger the reputation of the family vineyards by risking deterioration in shipping. Therefore, if Dimitri's grape harvest matches its precedent, then if the world's finest wineries send representatives to his villa then he will not endanger the reputation of the family vineyards by risking deterioration in shipping. (G, W, B, T, U, E)

10. If the fishing vessel either sailed out of international waters or was swamped by the storm, then if it was either captured by the country into whose waters it sailed or now rests on the ocean floor then the country into whose waters it sailed is not friendly with the U.S. and the storm was more severe than predicted. If the country into whose waters it sailed is either not friendly with the U.S. or is not averse to capturing fishing vessels for propaganda purposes, then there will be an international incident. Therefore, if the fishing vessel sailed out of international waters and was captured by the country into whose waters it sailed, then there will be an international incident. (W, S, C, R, F, M, A, I)

MATERIAL EQUIVALENCE

The following two laws allow substitution for propositions having the form $p \equiv q$:

$$(p \equiv q) \equiv [(p \supset q) \cdot (q \supset p)]$$
$$(p \equiv q) \equiv [(p \cdot q) \vee (\sim p \cdot \sim q)]$$

The first law can be seen to hold by recalling that when the biconditional symbol was introduced, it was said to be equivalent to the joint assertion of two conditionals. The second law can be seen to hold by reflecting on the truth table for biconditionals. Since $p \equiv q$ is true if and only if either both p and q are true, or both p and q are false, to assert an expression of the form $(p \cdot q) \vee (\sim p \cdot \sim q)$ is equivalent to asserting $p \equiv q$. Both forms are referred to as the law of **material equivalence** (M. E.).

EXERCISES

VI

Symbolize the following arguments and construct formal proofs of their validity:

1. Either the civil engineers are wrong, or the proposed building will sink three

feet before the third story is complete. If the proposed building sinks three feet before the third story is complete, then the geological report is in error. Either the geological report is not in error or the civil engineers are correct. Therefore, the civil engineers are correct if and only if the proposed building sinks three feet before the third story is complete.   (C, P, G)

2. If the city council approves the new park, then they will budget money only if its cost does not exceed a million dollars. If Smith is still chairman, then if the cost does not exceed a million dollars, they will budget the money. If it is true that they will budget the money if and only if the cost does not exceed a million dollars, then the new park will be built. The city council will approve the new park and Smith is still chairman. Therefore the new park will be built.   (A, B, C, S, W)

3. If the railroads continue to operate, then they will either rely on a large volume of passenger traffic or they must successfully compete with trucking companies. If they successfully compete with trucking companies, then they will also rely on a large volume of passenger traffic. But they will not rely on a large volume of passenger traffic. So, the railroads will continue to operate if and only if they successfully compete with trucking companies.   (R, L, S)

4. He will be sued if and only if he did not secure permission from the publisher. Either he will not be sued or he did secure permission from the publisher. Therefore, he will not be sued.   (S, P)

5. Had Warren G. Harding been a good judge of character, he would have chosen his friends and advisers with greater care; and had he chosen his friends and advisers with greater care, then he would not have surrounded himself with corrupt and inept subordinates. One thing is certain, either Harding was a good judge of character or he surrounded himself with corrupt and inept subordinates, although both could be the case. If it is true that Harding was a good judge of character if and only if he did not surround himself with corrupt and inept advisers, then if he was not a good judge of character, he should not have been elected president. Therefore, if Harding was not a good judge of character, he should not have been elected president.   (G, C, S, E)

6. The universe is heliocentric if and only if it is not geocentric. If the universe is heliocentric, then neither Ptolemy nor Aristotle is correct. Either the universe is not geocentric or Copernicus is not correct. Therefore, if either Ptolemy is correct or Aristotle is correct, then Copernicus is not correct.   (H, G, P, A, C)

7. Russell's argument in *The Principles of Mathematics* is sound if and only if Being belongs to every conceivable term and every possible object of thought. Being belongs to every conceivable term and every possible object of thought if and only if everything that can occur in a proposition and propositions themselves have Being. It cannot be true both that everything that occurs in a proposition and propositions themselves have Being, unless to say that something does not exist is either false or meaningless. Of course, if it is either false or meaningless to say that something does not exist, then the statement 'A is not' implies that A must exist. Either it is false that the statement 'A is not' implies that A must exist or it is not the case both that something is wrong with Russell's

analysis and the robust sense of reality that underlies ordinary language has been ignored. If the robust sense of reality underlying ordinary language has been ignored, then there is something wrong with Russell's analysis. Therefore, if the robust sense of reality that underlies ordinary language has been ignored, then Russell's argument in *The Principles of Mathematics* is not sound.   (*S, T, O, E, P, F, M, A, W, R*)

8. It is not the case that either the currency is in danger of being devalued or that austerity measures will be introduced. If the currency is in danger of being devalued if and only if austerity measures are introduced, then the economy is stable. Therefore, the economy is stable.   (*C, A, E*)

9. If the insurance company paid the claim, then there must have been either fire damage or water damage. Of course, there was water damage if and only if there was fire damage. If there were both fire damage and water damage, then the fire department must be rather inefficient. The insurance company did pay the claim. Hence, the fire department must be rather inefficient.   (*P, F, W, I*)

10. Ponti's new movie is very long, and either boring or thoroughly absorbing. If Ponti's new movie is very long and thoroughly absorbing, then neither the critics in London nor the critics in New York understood it. If either the critics in London did not understand it or the critics in New York did not understand it, then it is not the case both that Ponti's new movie is very long and is boring. Therefore, the critics in London understood it if and only if the critics in New York understood it.   (*P, B, T, L, N*)

TAUTOLOGY AND EXPORTATION

Two laws remain to be discussed. These are **tautology** (Taut.), and **exportation** (Exp.).

Tautology

$$p \equiv (p \lor p)$$
$$p \equiv (p \cdot p)$$

Exportation

$$[(p \cdot q) \supset r] \equiv [p \supset (q \supset r)]$$

The law of tautology can be seen to hold by reflecting on the truth conditions for disjunctions and conjunctions. The law of exportation can be seen to hold by noting that $(p \cdot q) \supset r$ and $p \supset (q \supset r)$ both assert that p and q are antecedents of r.

EXERCISES

VII

1. If James is still enrolled as a student, then if he has paid the entrance fee, he entered the racket ball tournament. But if James enters the racket ball tournament, he is sure to win. Therefore, if James is still enrolled as a student and has paid the entrance fee, then he is sure to win the tournament. (*J, P, E, S*)

2. Had Ben Franklin gone to bed early, then he would have had the virtues of being healthy, wealthy, and wise. If Franklin had the virtues of being healthy, wealthy, and wise, then he would have been involved in business and community affairs. But he would have been involved in business and community affairs only if he did not go to bed early. Therefore, Franklin did not go to bed early. (*B, V, I*)

3. If Engel's theory is correct, then men ultimately derive their moral ideas from the practical relations on which their class position is based, i.e., the economic modes of production and exchange. But Engel's theory is correct only if his condemnation of class morality is not itself class-bound. Either men do not ultimately derive their moral ideas from the practical relations on which their class position is based, or Engel's condemnation of class morality is itself class-bound. Therefore, Engel's theory is incorrect. (*E, P, C*)

4. If the princess kissed the frog and he turned into a prince, then the magician was right. If the frog turned into a prince then the magician was right, if and only if either he was no ordinary frog to begin with or the witch had put a curse on him. He was an ordinary frog to begin with and the witch had not put a curse on him. Therefore, the princess did not kiss the frog. (*P, T, M, O, W*)

5. Dimitri received a letter from the alumni association asking for money and either one asking for money or one asking for stock, if and only if he is both wealthy and famous. Dimitri either received a letter asking for money or he both received one asking for money and one asking for stock. Therefore, Dimitri is both wealthy and famous. (*M, S, W, F*)

6. If it is true that W. C. Fields is alive and drunk in San Francisco only if he is well, then he is living under a pseudonym and the rumor that he is dead has been greatly exaggerated. If he is living under a pseudonym, then there are people who know his real identity only if the rumor that he is dead has not been greatly exaggerated. There are people who know his real identity and he is well. Therefore, W. C. Fields is alive and drunk in San Francisco. (*A, D, W, P, R, K*)

7. If it is a sine curve, then it is not the case that our original interpretation of the data implies that it is a sine curve. If it is not a sine curve, then our hypothesis is correct. If it is not a sine curve and our hypothesis is correct, then we have made a mistake in our calculations. Therefore, we have made a mistake in our calculations. (*S, D, H, M*)

8. If the universe is an illusion, then I am always deceived. If I am always deceived, then I am deceived each time I am thinking; but if I know what 'illusion' means, then I am not deceived each time I am thinking. It is false both that I do not know what 'illusion' means and that the universe is an illusion. Therefore, the universe is not an illusion. (*U, A, T, K*)

9. If the Bolshevik revolution can be called a proletarian revolution, then its being called a proletarian revolution implies that the Russian peasants were not its driving force. But the Bolshevik revolution can truly be called a proletarian revolution if and only if the Russian peasants were in fact its driving force. Therefore, the Bolshevik revolution cannot be called a proletarian revolution and the Russian peasants were not its driving force. (*B, R*)

10. If the newspaper story was accurate, then the university laboratory staff has discovered a way to arrest the disease temporarily but they have not found a permanent cure for it. If they have discovered a way to arrest the disease temporarily, then if they have new information about its nature, they will have ideas about how it can be combatted. So, if the newspaper story was accurate and they have new information about the nature of the disease, then they will have ideas about how it can be combatted. (*N, T, P, I, C*)

11. Either the Zambian ambassador or both the Zambian ambassador and the Prime Minister will attend the conference. If the Zambian ambassador attends the conference, then neither the Tanzanian ambassador nor the Kenyan ambassador will attend. If the Tanzanian ambassador does not attend then, if the refugee problem is discussed, it will be settled only if the Kenyan ambassador attends. Therefore, if the refugee problem is discussed, then it will not be settled. (*Z, P, T, K, R, S*)

12. If I go to Europe, then if I go to Paris, I shall go to the Louvre; and if I go to the Louvre and am disappointed in it, then I shall go to the Folies. If the Louvre is full of tourists, then I shall be disappointed in it; and if the Folies is very expensive, then I shall not go. Of course, the Louvre is always full of tourists and the Folies is very expensive. Either I shall go to Europe and to Paris, or it is false both that the Folies is very expensive and either I won't spend the money to get into the Folies or no amount of money is too much to spend to see the Folies. Therefore, I shall spend the money to get into the Folies. (*E, P, L, D, F, T, V, S, N*)

13. If the structure of the world can be explained as Leibnitz explains it, then individuals are monads. If monads have no windows, then they are not influenced by anything external to themselves. If monads are not influenced by anything external to themselves, then individuals are monads only if monads are influenced by something external to themselves. Either the structure of the world cannot be explained as Leibnitz explains it or monads have windows, if and only if the Doctrine of Preestablished Harmony is inadequate and God is something other than a master mathematician. Therefore either the Doctrine of Preestablished Harmony is inadequate or monads are influenced by something external to themselves. (*S, I, W, E, D, G*)

14. If I pay my taxes, then I will be supporting an unjust war; and if I support an unjust war, then I am immoral. If either I am insensitive to the lot of my fellow man or I am immoral, then I can treat myself as a person if and only if I can live in self-deception. Either I cannot treat myself as a person or if I can treat myself as a person then I cannot live in self-deception. If I accept my obligations and paying taxes is an obligation, then if I am not immoral then I will pay my taxes. I do accept my obligations and paying taxes is an obligation. I conclude that I can not live in self-deception. (*P, U, I, L, T, S, A, O*)

15. Ratification of the treaty implies that the smaller countries will form a coalition, if and only if the fact that the treaty is signed implies that if the larger countries vote together, then the rights of the smaller countries will be imperiled. Therefore, if the larger countries vote together and the treaty is signed, then it will fail to be ratified only if the rights of the smaller countries are imperiled.   (R, F, S, L, I)

INTERDEFINITION OF TRUTH-FUNCTIONAL CONNECTIVES

Truth-functional equivalences allow us to replace an expression in which a given truth-functional connective occurs with an equivalent expression in which that connective does not occur. For example, M.E. allows us to replace $p \equiv q$ with $(p \supset q) \cdot (q \supset p)$. Reflection on this raises the question whether the symbol $\equiv$ might not be eliminated. All that is required to eliminate this symbol is for us to symbolize phrases such as 'p if and only if q' as $(p \supset q) \cdot (q \supset p)$. This raises another question, viz., whether it might not be possible to eliminate all except one or two of the connectives we have introduced by defining some in terms of others. In fact, such interdefinition is not very difficult. The following set of definitions, in which '= df.' signifies 'equals by definition', illustrates this in terms of the $\sim$ and $\cdot$ symbols.

$$
\begin{array}{ll}
1. & (p \supset q) = \text{df.}\ \sim(p \cdot \sim q) \\
2. & (p \equiv q) = \text{df.}\ \sim(p \cdot \sim q) \cdot \sim(q \cdot \sim p) \\
3. & (p \vee q) = \text{df.}\ \sim(\sim p \cdot \sim q) \\
4. & (p \otimes q) = \text{df.}\ \sim(\sim p \cdot \sim q) \cdot \sim(p \cdot q)
\end{array}
$$

Definitions (1) and (3) require very little explanation. The expression $\sim(p \cdot \sim q)$ was shown to be equivalent to $p \supset q$ when we introduced the $\supset$ symbol. And $p \vee q$ is equivalent to $\sim(\sim p \cdot \sim q)$ by De Morgan. Definition (2) also requires minimal explanation. Since $p \equiv q$ is equivalent to $(p \supset q) \cdot (q \supset p)$, and $p \supset q$ is equivalent to $\sim(p \cdot \sim q)$, and $q \supset p$ is equivalent to $\sim(q \cdot \sim p)$, it follows that $p \equiv q$ is equivalent to $\sim(p \cdot \sim q) \cdot \sim(q \cdot \sim p)$. Only definition (4) requires more extended explanation. A comparison of the truth tables for the $\vee$ and $\otimes$ shows that they differ only in row 1. That is to say, propositions of the forms $p \vee q$ and $p \otimes q$ are both true or both false under exactly the same conditions, except that $p \otimes q$ is false, and $p \vee q$ true, when both p and q are true. Thus, if we jointly assert $p \vee q$ and $\sim(p \cdot q)$, we have asserted an expression equivalent to $p \otimes q$.

We need not have chosen the $\sim$ and $\cdot$ symbols as the basis for defining the other symbols. We could have chosen $\sim$ and $\vee$, or $\sim$ and $\supset$. Proof of this is left to the student as an exercise.

EXERCISES

VIII

1. Define each of the other truth-functional connectives in terms of $\sim$ and $\vee$.
2. Define each of the other truth-functional connectives in terms of $\sim$ and $\supset$.
3. Rewrite each of the following using only $\sim$ and $\cdot$. (Eliminate double negations.)

    a) $(\sim q \supset \sim p) \vee r$
    b) $(p \supset q) \supset r$
    c) $p \equiv \sim q$
    d) $\sim[p \supset (q \vee r)]$
    e) $\sim(p \supset q) \equiv \sim r$

4. Rewrite each of the following using only $\sim$ and $\vee$. (Eliminate double negations.)

    a) $p \supset (q \cdot r)$
    b) $p \equiv (q \equiv r)$
    c) $(p \cdot \sim q) \supset \sim r$
    d) $p \supset [(q \otimes r) \cdot s]$
    e) $[(p \supset q) \cdot (q \supset r)] \supset (p \supset r)$

5. Rewrite each of the following using only $\sim$ and $\supset$. (Eliminate double negations.)

    a) $p \cdot (q \vee r)$
    b) $p \cdot (q \otimes r)$
    c) $p \vee (\sim q \cdot r)$
    d) $\sim[(p \cdot q) \cdot (q \cdot \sim r)]$
    e) $p \equiv (q \vee r)$

SUGGESTED READINGS

Copi, Irving M., *Symbolic Logic*. 4th ed. New York: Macmillan, 1973.

Kahane, Howard, *Logic and Philosophy*. 2nd ed. Belmont, Calif.: Wadsworth, 1973.

Lambert, Karel and Bas C. van Fraassen, *Derivation and Counterexample*. Encino, Calif.: Dickenson Publishing Co., Inc., 1972.

Quine, W. V., *Methods of Logic*. 3rd ed. New York: Holt, Rinehart and Winston, Inc., 1972.

Smullyan, Arthur, *Fundamentals of Logic*. Englewood Cliffs, N. J.: Prentice-Hall, Inc., 1962.

6

FORMAL AXIOMATIC
SYSTEMS

At the beginning of chapter I, we defined logic as the science which has as its central problem the attempt to formulate principles for appraising the correctness or incorrectness of arguments. We have now formulated a number of such principles and in the remainder of the book will formulate a number of others. A mere listing of principles, however, no matter how extensive, is not a science. A body of knowledge is not a science unless it is organized in such a way that, given information about some of its concepts and propositions, one may deduce information about others. For example, the science of physics is so structured that, given information about force and mass, one may deduce information about acceleration.

A body of knowledge is said to be **axiomatized** or to be an **axiomatic system** when certain propositions, called **axioms,** are selected as a starting point and the other propositions, called **theorems,** are shown to follow from the axioms. An axiomatic system is said to be **formalized** or a **formal axiomatic system** when both the elements which compose it and all the logical operations permitted within it are explicitly stated. We will illustrate the nature of a formal axiomatic system by constructing one for the logical principles which we have introduced. The system which we will present is a modification of the one developed by Bertrand Russell and Alfred North Whitehead in *Principia Mathematica.*

PRIMITIVE SYMBOLS

A **primitive symbol** is one which is undefined within a system. It might be thought that all the symbols in a system could be defined within the system, but such a belief is mistaken. Symbols can only be defined within a system by means of other symbols, and if all the symbols in a system were defined within it, then either an infinite regress of definitions would be required or the definitions would be circular. The ideal sought in a formal axiomatic system, then, is not to define every symbol, but rather to reduce the number of undefined symbols to a useful minimum.

The fact that a symbol is taken as undefined within a system does not mean that it cannot be defined. It may be defined within some other system. It may also be given some extrasystematic interpretation. For example, since the system we are constructing is intended to systematize the principles introduced earlier, its variables are propositional variables. If some other subject matter were being systematized, then the variables would be given a different interpretation. They might be taken, e.g., to refer to classes or electric circuits. The symbols which we will use as propositional variables are those introduced earlier, the lower case letters p through z.

In addition to variables, formal axiomatic systems must contain connective symbols. The two symbols we will adopt as primitive connectives are the truth-functional connectives $\sim$ and $\vee$. It was shown in the previous chapter that the other truth-functional connectives which we introduced can be defined in terms of these two connectives. It should be apparent also from the discussion there that alternative systems can be constructed using either the $\sim$ and $\cdot$, or the $\sim$ and $\supset$ as primitive connectives.

The third type of primitive symbol required in a formal axiomatic system is punctuation symbols. Although we have previously used parentheses, brackets, and braces as punctuation symbols, parentheses alone will suffice. For reasons of economy, we will use only parentheses in the system being constructed. The conventions regarding scope of punctuation symbols adopted earlier will be retained.

OBJECT LANGUAGE AND
METALANGUAGE

The only symbols we have adopted as primitive symbols are: p, q, r, etc., (,), $\sim$ and $\vee$. These symbols constitute the elements of the language of the system we are constructing. However, we have used other symbols in discussing these symbols. Our discussion of the symbols which occur in the system is obviously not a part of the system. It takes place in English, not in the language being systematized. A language used to talk about another language is called a **metalanguage,** and the language being talked about is called an **object language.** In our case, then, English is the metalanguage and the logical language being systematized is the object language. The rules and definitions taken up in the following sections are part of the metalanguage, not of the object language.

FORMATION RULES

In addition to primitive symbols, a formal axiomatic system must have rules for combining symbols in meaningful ways. Rules specifying which combinations of symbols are meaningful and which are not are called **formation rules.** Any combination of symbols in a system is a formula of that system, but only a combination which satisfies the formation rules is a **well-formed formula** (*wff*). For instance, $p \lor {\sim} \lor$) is a formula containing primitive symbols, but it is not a *wff*. Stating what constitutes a *wff* within a system is equivalent to stating formation rules for that system. If we let the symbols A and B stand for any *wff* whatever, then the formation rules in the system we are constructing may be stated as follows:

1. Any propositional variable is a *wff*.
2. If any formula A is a *wff*, then ${\sim}A$ is also a *wff*.
3. If any two formulae A and B are *wffs*, then $A \lor B$ is a *wff*.
4. Only formulae which satisfy conditions 1–3, or which are definitionally equivalent to expressions satisfying 1–3, are *wffs*.

DEFINITIONS

Although all the formulae of the system can be stated using only the primitive connectives ${\sim}$ and $\lor$, this results in unnecessarily cumbersome expressions when there are much simpler equivalent expressions. Introducing the symbols $\cdot$, $\supset$, and $\equiv$ by definition, adds nothing theoretically to the system, but it facilitates expression within the system. Consequently, we adopt the following definitions:

D1. '$p \supset q$' = df. '${\sim}p \lor q$'
D2. '$p \cdot q$' = df. '${\sim}({\sim}p \lor {\sim}q)$'
D3. '$p \equiv q$' = df. '$(p \supset q) \cdot (q \supset p)$'

It should be noted that definitions and statements of truth-functional equivalence are not the same. For example, the expression

'$p \supset q$' = df. '${\sim}p \lor q$'

is a statement in the metalanguage which mentions '$p \supset q$', telling us that it is equivalent by definition to '${\sim}p \lor q$'.

The expression

$$(p \supset q) \equiv (\sim p \vee q)$$

on the other hand, is a statement in the object language in which the expression $p \supset q$ is used to assert a truth-functional equivalence.

AXIOMS

An **axiom** or **postulate** is a proposition assumed for the purpose of organizing a set of propositions into an axiomatic system. Just as it is impossible to define all the symbols within a system, so it is impossible to prove all the propositions within a system. No proposition can be proved unless some other proposition is assumed. To try to prove all propositions within a system, then, would lead to either circular proofs or an infinite regress. Thus, the ideal sought in an axiomatic system is not to prove every proposition, but only to reduce the number of unproved propositions to a useful minimum.

It was once believed that axioms had to be "self-evident," i.e., they had to be such that anyone who reflected on them would come to see their truth. Unfortunately, many propositions once thought to be self-evident are now known to be false. Self-evidence is, therefore, no longer taken as a requirement of axioms. The *basic* or *most fundamental requirement of a set of axioms* is simply that it serve as a basis for organizing the system, i.e., that it be such that the other propositions or theorems can be deduced from it. Thus, the truth of axioms is often less "evident" than the truth of the theorems. In fact, as will be shown in the discussion of uninterpreted systems, the truth or falsity of axioms is not a logical consideration at all.

The only other requirements usually imposed on a set of axioms is that it be *consistent, independent,* and *complete.* An axiom set is **consistent** if no axiom or combination of axioms contradicts any other axiom.* An axiom set is **independent** if it is impossible to deduce any axiom from any other axiom or combination of axioms. Independence is not as important a requirement as consistency, for to show that one axiom follows as a theorem from some other axiom or axioms is to show only that the system contains more axioms than is needed. Furthermore, it may be easier to derive theorems if the axioms are not independent. But since economy is also one of

---

*More specifically, an axiom set is consistent with respect to a given set of transformation rules if it is impossible to deduce contradictory formulae by means of those rules. Thus, an axiom set may be consistent with respect to one set of transformation rules, but inconsistent with respect to another. See below for a discussion of transformation rules.

the features desired in an axiomatic system, independence is usually sought to the extent that it is practical. (The axiom set we adopt below is not independent; axiom 5 can be deduced from the others.)

An axiom set is **expressively complete** with respect to a given subject matter when it is possible to interpret the primitive terms in such a way that every proposition (true or false) about the subject matter can be expressed as a *wff* of the system. For example, an axiom set for Euclidean geometry is expressively complete if it is possible to formulate all the statements of Euclidean geometry within the system. Thus, an axiom set for Euclidean geometry which did not provide a way of talking about circles would be expressively incomplete.

Expressive completeness is an extrasystematic consideration. It involves what can be said in the system, not what can be proved. However, there is another kind of completeness, deductive completeness, which involves what can be proved in the system. An axiom set is **deductively complete** when all the formulae one wishes to prove can be proved within the system. (Since both consistency and completeness are desirable, one normally wishes to be able to deduce either a formula or its negation, but not both.)

Before proceeding further, we need to discuss the nature of the logical principles introduced in the previous chapters. It will be recalled that they are of two types, elementary valid argument forms and truth-functional equivalences. It has been pointed out that truth-functional equivalences have a tautological form, but it has not been shown that elementary valid argument forms may also be written so that they have a tautological form. For example, if the elementary valid argument form H.S. is written as a conditional, it has the tautological form $[(p \supset q) \cdot (q \supset r)] \supset (p \supset r)$. And if the elementary valid argument form D. S. is written as a conditional, it has the tautological form $[(p \vee q) \cdot \sim p] \supset q$. Every valid argument form may be written similarly as a conditional with a tautological form.

Since one of the purposes of the formal axiomatic system constructed in this chapter is to axiomatize the principles introduced in the previous chapters, its axiom set will be complete if all of those principles can be deduced from it. In fact, however, the axiom set chosen is more powerful than this. It is complete in the sense that any truth-functional expression that is tautological in form can be deduced from it. (Proof that this is the case requires a proof about the system, rather than a proof within the system. Proofs *about*, rather than *within* a system, are called **metaproofs.** A discussion of metaproofs, however, is beyond the scope of our treatment of axiomatic systems.) Because of space limitations, not all of the principles introduced in the previous chapters will be deduced, although completeness proofs have been given for the system showing that they could be deduced because they are all tautological in form. (For a discussion of completeness see Irving M. Copi, *Symbolic Logic,* Chapters 7 and 8.)

The axiom set which we adopt is

A1. $\sim(p \lor p) \lor p$
A2. $\sim q \lor (p \lor q)$
A3. $\sim(p \lor q) \lor (q \lor p)$
A4. $\sim(p \lor (q \lor r)) \lor (q \lor (p \lor r))$
A5. $\sim(\sim q \lor r) \lor (\sim(p \lor q) \lor (p \lor r))$

TRANSFORMATION RULES

Rules must now be stated for deriving theorems from the axioms. These are called **transformation rules** and are of two types: **substitution rules** and **rules of inference.**

Two kinds of substitution are permissible within the system. The first is **substitution for variables.** Given any tautology such as Axiom 1

$$\sim(p \lor p) \lor p$$

any variable may be substituted for p, provided the substitution is complete. Substitution is *complete* only if the same substitution is made for every occurrence of the variable being replaced. If r is substituted for p in Axiom 1, the result is

$$\sim(r \lor r) \lor r$$

Any *wff* also may be substituted for a variable, provided the substitution is complete. For example, if $p \supset q$ is substituted for p in Axiom 1, the result is

$$\sim((p \supset q) \lor (p \supset q)) \lor (p \supset q)$$

The reason for the restriction that substitution must be complete is that incomplete substitution does not always preserve the truth value of the original expression. All the axioms and theorems of our system are tautological in form, but expressions which result from incomplete substitution are not necessarily tautological in form. The following substitution of $q \lor r$ for p in Axiom 1 is incomplete and, therefore, is not permissible:

$$\sim((q \lor r) \lor p) \lor (q \lor r)$$

Stated formally as a rule for derivation within the system, the rule of substitution for variables is:

TRANSFORMATION RULE 1:   Any variable in any axiom or theorem may be replaced by any other variable or *wff*, provided replacement is complete.

Transformation Rule 1 *does not permit substitution for complex expressions,*
but only for variables. For example, substitution of p for $\sim p$ in $p \vee \sim p$ is
not permitted because the result is not a tautology. Although Transformation Rule 1 does not permit substitution for complex expressions, we can
formulate a rule which does permit such substitution and at the same time
ensures that the result will be a tautology. This is the **Rule of Definitional
Substitution.**

TRANSFORMATION RULE 2:   Any expression may be replaced by an expression
which is definitionally equivalent to it in any axiom or theorem.

Because substitution of expressions that are definitionally equivalent does
not alter truth value, it does not have to be carried out completely. Thus,
the following replacement of $\sim p \vee q$ for $p \supset q$ in $(p \supset q) \supset (p \supset q)$ is
permissible:

$$(\sim p \vee q) \supset (p \supset q)$$

It should be remembered from the discussion of definition that definitions
are not the same as truth-functional equivalences. Substitution of expressions that are definitionally equivalent is permitted by Transformation
Rule 2, but substitution of truth-functionally equivalent expressions is not.

The second type of transformation rule is **rules of inference.** The only
rule of inference we will use is the **Rule of Detachment.**

TRANSFORMATION RULE 3:   Given any axioms or proved theorems, A and
$A \supset B$, we may infer B.

The purpose of the Rule of Detachment is to allow us to state separately
theorems which are logical consequences of the axioms. Notice the difference between the Rule of Detachment, which is a rule of inference stated
in the metalanguage, and $(p \cdot (p \supset q)) \supset q$, which is a theorem within the
system. The consequent of the latter expression cannot be detached from
its antecedent except when we are given the antecedent, and then it can
be detached only by use of the Rule of Detachment.

THEOREMS

We are now ready to derive theorems from the axiom set. For con-
venience in reference the axioms, definitions, and transformation rules of
the system are listed here.

A1. $\sim(p \vee p) \vee p$
A2. $\sim q \vee (p \vee q)$
A3. $\sim(p \vee q) \vee (q \vee p)$
A4. $\sim(p \vee (q \vee r)) \vee (q \vee (p \vee r))$
A5. $\sim(\sim q \vee r) \vee (\sim(p \vee q) \vee (p \vee r))$

D1. $(p \supset q) = \mathrm{df.} \sim p \vee q$
D2. $(p \cdot q) = \mathrm{df.} \sim(\sim p \vee \sim q)$
D3. $(p \equiv q) = \mathrm{df.} (p \supset q) \cdot (q \supset p)$

TR1:   Any variable in any axiom or theorem may be replaced by any other variable or *wff*, provided replacement is complete.

TR2:   Any expression may be replaced by an expression which is definitionally equivalent to it in any axiom or theorem.

TR3:   Given any axioms or proved theorems, A and $A \supset B$, we may infer B.

Theorems are numbered consecutively and the theorem to be proved is stated first. The justification for each step in the proof is written to the right and cites the axiom, theorem, definition, or transformation rule used.

T1. $(p \vee p) \supset p$

   Proof:
   1) $\sim(p \vee p) \vee p$ A1
   2) $(p \vee p) \supset p$ D1

Theorem 1 is proved by assuming Axiom 1 and then rewriting it by definitional substitution. When any theorem has been proved, it may then be used in succeeding proofs in the same way that axioms are used.

T2. $p \supset (p \vee p)$

   Proof:
   1) $\sim q \vee (p \vee q)$ A2
   2) $q \supset (p \vee q)$ D1
   3) $p \supset (p \vee p)$ TR1 p/q

TR1, which permits substitution of variables or *wffs* for another variable, is used for the first time in proving Theorem 2. The result of using TR1 to substitute a variable or *wff* for another variable is indicated by writing the expression replacing the variable followed by a slash and the variable being replaced. Thus, p/q indicates that p is being substituted for q.

T3. $(p \supset \sim q) \supset (q \supset \sim p)$

Proof:

1) $\sim(p \vee q) \vee (q \vee p)$ A3
2) $\sim(\sim p \vee \sim q) \vee (\sim q \vee \sim p)$ TR1 $\sim p/p$, $\sim q/q$
3) $(p \supset \sim q) \supset (q \supset \sim p)$ D1

The connection between T3 and the law of transposition should be noted. The law of transposition asserts that $p \supset q$ and $\sim q \supset \sim p$ are truth-functionally equivalent. T3 makes a weaker assertion but shows that part of the stronger assertion is deducible from the axioms.

T4. $(q \supset r) \supset ((p \supset q) \supset (p \supset r))$

Proof:

1) $\sim(\sim q \vee r) \vee (\sim(p \vee q) \vee (p \vee r))$ A5
2) $\sim(\sim q \vee r) \vee (\sim(\sim p \vee q) \vee (\sim p \vee r))$ TR1 $\sim p/p$
3) $(q \supset r) \supset ((p \supset q) \supset (p \supset r))$ D1

T5. $p \supset p$

Proof:

1) $(q \supset r) \supset ((p \supset q) \supset (p \supset r))$ T4
2) $((p \vee p) \supset p) \supset ((p \supset (p \vee p)) \supset (p \supset p))$ TR1 $p \vee p/q$, p/r
3) $(p \vee p) \supset p$ T1
4) $(p \supset (p \vee p)) \supset (p \supset p)$ TR3 2, 3
5) $p \supset (p \vee p)$ T2
6) $p \supset p$ TR3 4, 5

Three previously proven theorems are used in the proof of T5. It is unnecessary to deduce every theorem directly from the axioms, since if the theorem to be proved is deducible from other theorems which were deduced from the axioms, it is always possible to trace its deduction back to the axioms. The Rule of Detachment is also used for the first time in the proof of T5. Justification for its use cites the number of the rule (TR3) and the numbers of the relevant lines in the proof.

T6. $\sim p \vee p$

Proof of T6 is simple and is left to the reader.

T7. $p \lor \sim p$

    Proof:
1) $\sim(p \lor q) \lor (q \lor p)$ A3
2) $\sim(\sim p \lor p) \lor (p \lor \sim p)$ TR1 $\sim p/p, p/q$
3) $(\sim p \lor p) \supset (p \lor \sim p)$ D1
4) $\sim p \lor p$ T6
5) $p \lor \sim p$ TR3 3, 4

T8. $p \supset \sim\sim p$

Proof of T8 is left to the reader.

T9. $\sim\sim p \supset p$

    Proof:
1) $p \supset \sim\sim p$ T8
2) $\sim p \supset \sim\sim\sim p$ TR1 $\sim p/p$
3) $\sim(\sim q \lor r) \lor (\sim(p \lor q) \lor (p \lor r))$ A5
4) $(q \supset r) \supset ((p \lor q) \supset (p \lor r))$ D1
5) $(\sim p \supset \sim\sim\sim p) \supset ((p \lor \sim p) \supset$ TR1 $\sim p/q,$
       $(p \lor \sim\sim\sim p))$ $\sim\sim\sim p/r$
6) $(p \lor \sim p) \supset (p \lor \sim\sim\sim p)$ TR3 2, 5
7) $p \lor \sim p$ T7
8) $p \lor \sim\sim\sim p$ TR3 6, 7
9) $\sim(p \lor q) \lor (q \lor p)$ A3
10) $(p \lor q) \supset (q \lor p)$ D1
11) $(p \lor \sim\sim\sim p) \supset (\sim\sim\sim p \lor p)$ TR1 $\sim\sim\sim p/q$
12) $\sim\sim\sim p \lor p$ TR3 8, 11
13) $\sim\sim p \supset p$ D1

T10. $(q \lor p) \supset (p \lor q)$

Proof of T10 is left to the reader. Note the connection between T10 and commutativity.

T11. $(\sim p \supset q) \supset (\sim q \supset p)$

    Proof:
1) $(q \supset r) \supset ((p \supset q) \supset (p \supset r))$ T4
2) $(q \supset \sim\sim q) \supset ((\sim p \supset q) \supset (\sim p \supset \sim\sim q))$ TR1 $\sim p/p, \sim\sim q/r$

3) $p \supset \sim\sim p$ T8

4) $q \supset \sim\sim q$ TR1 q/p

5) $(\sim p \supset q) \supset (\sim p \supset \sim\sim q)$ TR3 2, 4

6) $(p \supset \sim q) \supset (q \supset \sim p)$ T3

7) $(\sim p \supset \sim\sim q) \supset (\sim q \supset \sim\sim p)$ TR1 $\sim p/p,\ \sim q/q$

8) $(\sim\sim p \supset p) \supset ((\sim q \supset \sim\sim p) \supset (\sim q \supset p))$ 1, TR1 $\sim q/p,$
$\sim\sim p/q,\ p/r$

9) $\sim\sim p \supset p$ T9

10) $(\sim q \supset \sim\sim p) \supset (\sim q \supset p)$ TR3 8, 9

11) $((\sim p \supset \sim\sim q) \supset (\sim q \supset \sim\sim p)) \supset$ 1, TR1 $\sim p \supset q/p,$
$(((\sim p \supset q) \supset (\sim p \supset \sim\sim q)) \supset$ $\sim p \supset \sim\sim q/q,$
$((\sim p \supset q) \supset (\sim q \supset \sim\sim p)))$ $\sim q \supset \sim\sim p/r$

12) $((\sim p \supset q) \supset (\sim p \supset \sim\sim q)) \supset$ TR3 7, 11
$((\sim p \supset q) \supset (\sim q \supset \sim\sim p))$

13) $(\sim p \supset q) \supset (\sim q \supset \sim\sim p)$ TR3 5, 12

14) $((\sim q \supset \sim\sim p) \supset (\sim q \supset p)) \supset$ 1, TR1 $\sim p \supset q/p,$
$(((\sim p \supset q) \supset (\sim q \supset \sim\sim p)) \supset$ $\sim q \supset \sim\sim p/q,$
$((\sim p \supset q) \supset (\sim q \supset p)))$ $\sim q \supset p/r$

15) $((\sim p \supset q) \supset (\sim q \supset \sim\sim p)) \supset$ TR3 10, 14
$((\sim p \supset q) \supset (\sim q \supset p))$

16) $(\sim p \supset q) \supset (\sim q \supset p)$ TR3 13, 15

T11 is another part of the law of transposition. Note that in the justification of steps 8, 11, and 14, a number appears before the citation of TR1. This convention has been adopted to show which previous step of a proof yields a substitution instance when it does not come from the step directly preceding it. Steps 8, 11, and 14 all result by substitution from T4, which is the first assumption in the proof. If step 8 had been a substitution instance of step 7, no number would have been cited before citing the transformation rule.

T12. $p \supset (q \lor p)$

Proof of T12 is left to the reader.

T13. $p \supset (p \lor q)$ `

Proof:

1) $(q \lor p) \supset (p \lor q)$ T10

2) $(q \supset r) \supset ((p \supset q) \supset (p \supset r))$ T4

3) $((q \lor p) \supset (p \lor q)) \supset ((p \supset (q \lor p)) \supset$ TR1 $q \lor p/q,\ p \lor q/r$
$(p \supset (p \lor q)))$

4) $(p \supset (q \lor p)) \supset (p \supset (p \lor q))$ TR3 1, 3

5) $p \supset (q \vee p)$ T12
6) $p \supset (p \vee q)$ TR3 4, 5

The connection between T13 and the elementary valid argument form, addition, should be noted.

T14. $(p \cdot q) \supset p$

Proof:
1) $p \supset (p \vee q)$ T13
2) $\sim p \supset (\sim p \vee \sim q)$ TR1 $\sim p/p$, $\sim q/q$
3) $(\sim p \supset q) \supset (\sim q \supset p)$ T11
4) $(\sim p \supset (\sim p \vee \sim q)) \supset (\sim(\sim p \vee \sim q) \supset p))$ TR1 $\sim p \vee \sim q/q$
5) $\sim(\sim p \vee \sim q) \supset p$ TR3 2, 4
6) $(p \cdot q) \supset p$ D2

T14 demonstrates the conditional form of the elementary valid argument form, simplification.

T15. $(p \supset (q \supset r)) \supset (q \supset (p \supset r))$

Proof of T15 is left to the reader.

T16. $(p \supset q) \supset ((q \supset r) \supset (p \supset r))$

Proof:
1) $(p \supset (q \supset r)) \supset (q \supset (p \supset r))$ T15
2) $((q \supset r) \supset ((p \supset q) \supset (p \supset r))) \supset$ TR1 $q \supset r/p$,
    $((p \supset q) \supset ((q \supset r) \supset (p \supset r)))$ $p \supset q/q$, $p \supset r/r$
3) $(q \supset r) \supset ((p \supset q) \supset (p \supset r))$ T4
4) $(p \supset q) \supset ((q \supset r) \supset (p \supset r))$ TR3 2, 3

T17. $(q \supset r) \supset ((p \vee q) \supset (r \vee p))$

Proof of T17 is left to the reader.

T18. $(p \vee q) \supset (\sim p \supset q)$

Proof:
1) $p \supset \sim\sim p$ T8
2) $(q \supset r) \supset ((p \vee q) \supset (r \vee p))$ T17
3) $(p \supset \sim\sim p) \supset ((q \vee p) \supset (\sim\sim p \vee q))$ TR1 p/q, $\sim\sim p/r$, q/p
4) $(q \vee p) \supset (\sim\sim p \vee q)$ TR3 1, 4
5) $\sim(p \vee q) \vee (q \vee p)$ A3
6) $(p \vee q) \supset (q \vee p)$ D1
7) $(p \supset q) \supset ((q \supset r) \supset (p \supset r))$ T16

8) $((p \vee q) \supset (q \vee p)) \supset (((q \vee p) \supset$
$(\sim\sim p \vee q)) \supset ((p \vee q) \supset (\sim\sim p \vee q)))$ TR1 $p \vee q/p,\ q \vee p/q,$
               $\sim\sim p \vee q/r$

9) $((q \vee p) \supset (\sim\sim p \vee q)) \supset$
$((p \vee q) \supset (\sim\sim p \vee q))$ TR3   6, 8

10) $(p \vee q) \supset (\sim\sim p \vee q)$ TR3   4, 9

11) $(p \vee q) \supset (\sim p \supset q)$ D1

T19. $(p \vee (q \vee r)) \supset (p \vee (r \vee q))$

Proof:

1) $(q \vee p) \supset (p \vee q)$ T10
2) $(q \vee r) \supset (r \vee q)$ TR1 r/p
3) $\sim(\sim q \vee r) \vee (\sim(p \vee q) \vee (p \vee r))$ A5
4) $\sim(\sim p \vee q) \vee (\sim(r \vee p) \vee (r \vee q))$ TR1 $r/p,\ p/q,\ q/r$
5) $(p \supset q) \supset ((r \vee p) \supset (r \vee q))$ D1
6) $((q \vee r) \supset (r \vee q)) \supset$
$(((p \vee (q \vee r)) \supset (p \vee (r \vee q)))$ TR1 $q \vee r/p,$
               $r \vee q/q,\ p/r$
7) $(p \vee (q \vee r)) \supset (p \vee (r \vee q))$ TR3   2, 6

T19 is part of the law of commutativity.

T20. $(p \vee (q \vee r)) \supset ((p \vee q) \vee r)$

Proof:

1) $(p \vee (q \vee r)) \supset (p \vee (r \vee q))$ T19
2) $\sim(p \vee (q \vee r)) \vee (q \vee (p \vee r))$ A4
3) $(p \vee (q \vee r)) \supset (q \vee (p \vee r))$ D1
4) $(p \vee (r \vee q)) \supset (r \vee (p \vee q))$ TR1 $r/q,\ q/r$
5) $(p \supset q) \supset ((q \supset r) \supset (p \supset r))$ T16
6) $((p \vee (q \vee r)) \supset (p \vee (r \vee q))) \supset$
$(((p \vee (r \vee q)) \supset (r \vee (p \vee q)) \supset$
$((p \vee (q \vee r)) \supset (r \vee (p \vee q)))$ TR1 $p \vee (q \vee r)/p,$
               $p \vee (r \vee q)/q,$
               $r \vee (p \vee q)/r$
7) $((p \vee (r \vee q)) \supset (r \vee (p \vee q))) \supset$
$((p \vee (q \vee r)) \supset (r \vee (p \vee q)))$ TR3   1, 6
8) $(p \vee (q \vee r)) \supset (r \vee (p \vee q))$ TR3   4, 7
9) $(q \vee p) \supset (p \vee q)$ T10
10) $(r \vee (p \vee q)) \supset ((p \vee q) \vee r)$ TR1 $r/q,\ p \vee q/p$
11) $((p \vee (q \vee r)) \supset (r \vee (p \vee q))) \supset$
$(((r \vee (p \vee q)) \supset ((p \vee q) \vee r)) \supset$
$((p \vee (q \vee r)) \supset ((p \vee q) \vee r)))$ 5, TR1 $p \vee (q \vee r)/p,$
               $r \vee (p \vee q)/q,$
               $(p \vee q) \vee r/r$
12) $((r \vee (p \vee q)) \supset ((p \vee q) \vee r)) \supset$
$((p \vee (q \vee r)) \supset ((p \vee q) \vee r))$ TR3   8, 11
13) $(p \vee (q \vee r)) \supset ((p \vee q) \vee r)$ TR3   10, 12

T20 is part of the law of association.

T21. $(p \supset (q \supset r)) \supset ((p \cdot q) \supset r)$

Proof:

1) $p \supset p$ T5
2) $(p \supset (q \supset r)) \supset (p \supset (q \supset r))$ .... TR1 $p \supset (q \supset r)/p$
3) $(p \supset (q \supset r)) \supset (\sim p \vee (\sim q \vee r))$ D1
4) $(p \vee (q \vee r)) \supset ((p \vee q) \vee r)$ T20
5) $(\sim p \vee (\sim q \vee r)) \supset ((\sim p \vee \sim q) \vee r)$ ...... TR1 $\sim p/p,\ \sim q/q$
6) $(p \supset q) \supset ((q \supset r) \supset (p \supset r))$ T16
7) $((p \supset (q \supset r)) \supset (\sim p \vee (\sim q \vee r))) \supset$ .... TR1 $p \supset (q \supset r)/p,$
   $((((\sim p \vee (\sim q \vee r)) \supset ((\sim p \vee \sim q) \vee r)) \supset$ .... $\sim p \vee (\sim q \vee r)/q,$
   $((p \supset (q \supset r)) \supset ((\sim p \vee \sim q) \vee r)))$ .... $(\sim p \vee \sim q) \vee r/r$
8) $((\sim p \vee (\sim q \vee r)) \supset ((\sim p \vee \sim q) \vee r)) \supset$ TR3 3, 7
   $((p \supset (q \supset r)) \supset ((\sim p \vee \sim q) \vee r))$
9) $(p \supset (q \supset r)) \supset ((\sim p \vee \sim q) \vee r)$ TR3 5, 8
10) $(p \vee q) \supset (\sim p \supset q)$ T20
11) $((\sim p \vee \sim q) \vee r) \supset (\sim (\sim p \vee \sim q) \supset r)$ .... TR1 $\sim p \vee \sim q/p,\ r/q$
12) $((p \supset (q \supset r)) \supset ((\sim p \vee \sim q) \vee r)) \supset$ .... 6, TR3 $p \supset (q \supset r)/p,$
    $((((\sim p \vee \sim q) \vee r) \supset (\sim (\sim p \vee \sim q) \supset r)) \supset$ .... $(\sim p \vee \sim q) \vee r/q,$
    $((p \supset (q \supset r)) \supset (\sim (\sim p \vee \sim q) \supset r)))$ .... $\sim (\sim p \vee \sim q) \supset r/r$
13) $(((\sim p \vee \sim q) \vee r) \supset (\sim (\sim p \vee \sim q) \supset r)) \supset$ TR3 9, 12
    $((p \supset (q \supset r)) \supset (\sim (\sim p \vee \sim q) \supset r))$
14) $(p \supset (q \supset r)) \supset (\sim (\sim p \vee \sim q) \supset r)$ TR3 11, 13
15) $(p \supset (q \supset r)) \supset ((p \cdot q) \supset r)$ D2

T21 is part of the law of exportation.

T22. $((p \supset q) \cdot (q \supset r)) \supset (p \supset r)$

Proof:

1) $(p \supset (q \supset r)) \supset ((p \cdot q) \supset r)$ T21
2) $((p \supset q) \supset ((q \supset r) \supset (p \supset r))) \supset$ .... TR1 $p \supset q/p,\ q \supset r/q,$
   $(((p \supset q) \cdot (q \supset r)) \supset (p \supset r))$ .... $p \supset r/r$
3) $(p \supset q) \supset ((q \supset r) \supset (p \supset r))$ T16
4) $((p \supset q) \cdot (q \supset r)) \supset (p \supset r)$ TR3 2, 3

T22 should be recognized as the conditional form of the elementary valid argument form, hypothetical syllogism.

T23. $p \vee ((p \vee q) \supset q)$

Proof:

1) $\sim p \vee p$ T6
2) $\sim (p \vee q) \vee (p \vee q)$ .... TR1 $p \vee q/p$
3) $\sim (p \vee (q \vee r)) \vee (q \vee (p \vee r))$ A4

4) $(p \lor (q \lor r)) \supset (q \lor (p \lor r))$ D1

5) $(\sim(p \lor q) \lor (p \lor q)) \supset$ TR1 $\sim(p \lor q)/p$,
$(p \lor (\sim(p \lor q) \lor q))$ $p/q,\ q/r$

6) $p \lor (\sim(p \lor q) \lor q)$ TR3 2, 5

7) $p \lor ((p \lor q) \supset q)$ D1

T24. $(p \cdot (p \supset q)) \supset q$

Proof:

1) $p \lor ((p \lor q) \supset q)$ T23

2) $\sim p \lor ((\sim p \lor q) \supset q)$ TR1 $\sim p/p$

3) $p \supset ((p \supset q) \supset q)$ D1

4) $(p \supset (q \supset r)) \supset ((p \cdot q) \supset r)$ T21

5) $(p \supset ((p \supset q) \supset q)) \supset ((p \cdot (p \supset q)) \supset q)$ TR1 $p \supset q/q,\ q/r$

6) $(p \cdot (p \supset q)) \supset q$ TR3 3, 5

T24 is the conditional form of the elementary valid argument form, *modus ponens*.

T25. $((p \lor q) \lor r) \supset (p \lor (q \lor r))$

Proof:

1) $(q \lor p) \supset (p \lor q)$ T10

2) $((p \lor q) \lor r) \supset (r \lor (p \lor q))$ TR1 $p \lor q/q,\ r/p$

3) $\sim(p \lor (q \lor r)) \lor (q \lor (p \lor r))$ A4

4) $\sim(r \lor (p \lor q)) \lor (p \lor (r \lor q))$ TR1 $r/p,\ p/q,\ q/r$

5) $(r \lor (p \lor q)) \supset (p \lor (r \lor q))$ D1

6) $(p \supset q) \supset ((q \supset r) \supset (p \supset r))$ T16

7) $(((p \lor q) \lor r) \supset (r \lor (p \lor q))) \supset$ TR1 $(p \lor q) \lor r/p$,
$(((r \lor (p \lor q)) \supset (p \lor (r \lor q))) \supset$ $r \lor (p \lor q)/q$,
$((p \lor q) \lor r) \supset (p \lor (r \lor q)))$ $p \lor (r \lor q)/r$

8) $((r \lor (p \lor q)) \supset (p \lor (r \lor q))) \supset$ TR3 2, 7
$(((p \lor q) \lor r) \supset (p \lor (r \lor q)))$

9) $((p \lor q) \lor r) \supset (p \lor (r \lor q))$ TR3 5, 8

10) $(p \lor (q \lor r)) \supset (p \lor (r \lor q))$ T19

11) $(p \lor (r \lor q)) \supset (p \lor (q \lor r))$ TR1 $r/q,\ q/r$

12) $(p \supset q) \supset ((q \supset r) \supset (p \supset r))$ T16

13) $(((p \lor q) \lor r) \supset (p \lor (r \lor q))) \supset$ TR1 $(p \lor q) \lor r/p$,
$(((p \lor (r \lor q)) \supset (p \lor (q \lor r))) \supset$ $p \lor (r \lor q)/q$,
$((p \lor q) \lor r) \supset (p \lor (q \lor r)))$ $p \lor (q \lor r)/r$

14) $((p \lor (r \lor q)) \supset (p \lor (q \lor r))) \supset$ TR3 9, 13
$(((p \lor q) \lor r) \supset (p \lor (q \lor r)))$

15) $((p \lor q) \lor r) \supset (p \lor (q \lor r))$ TR3 11, 14

T25 should be recognized as another part of the law of association.

T26. $p \supset (q \supset (p \cdot q))$

Proof:

1) $p \vee \sim p$	T7
2) $(\sim p \vee \sim q) \vee \sim(\sim p \vee \sim q)$	TR1 $\sim p \vee \sim q/p$
3) $(\sim p \vee \sim q) \vee (p \cdot q)$	D2
4) $((p \vee q) \vee r) \supset (p \vee (q \vee r))$	T25
5) $((\sim p \vee \sim q) \vee (p \cdot q)) \supset$	TR1 $\sim p/p, \sim q/q,$
$(\sim p \vee (\sim q \vee (p \cdot q)))$	$p \cdot q/r$
6) $\sim p \vee (\sim q \vee (p \cdot q))$	TR3 3, 5
7) $p \supset (q \supset (p \cdot q))$	D1

DERIVED RULES OF INFERENCE

If an axiomatic system contains only one rule of inference, proofs are repetitious and lengthy. For example, in the proof of T25, premises (2) and (5) have the form of hypothetical syllogism; but we could not immediately deduce a conclusion of the form hypothetical syllogism, since our only rule of inference is the Rule of Detachment. Thus, to deduce the conclusion that we wanted, we stated T16, $(p \supset q) \supset ((q \supset r) \supset (p \supset r))$, and made the appropriate substitutions. The same strategy occurs in other proofs. For, given any two theorems of the forms $p \supset q$ and $q \supset r$ and T16, $(p \supset q) \supset ((q \supset r) \supset (p \supset r))$, it is obvious that one can always conclude that an expression of the form $p \supset r$ is a theorem. But though a conclusion of this type can always be deduced, its actual derivation is rather tedious. Consequently, to prevent unnecessary steps, we will adopt as an additional rule of inference the principle

DRI-1:   Given any axioms or theorems $A \supset B$ and $B \supset C$, we may infer $A \supset C$.

Since our justification for adopting DRI-1 is that it allows us to omit unnecessary steps which could be justified by use of T16, DRI-1 may be spoken of as a **derived rule of inference.** Note, however, that DRI-1 and T16 are not the same rule. DRI-1 is an inference rule formulated in the metalanguage, whereas T16 is a theorem within the system.

We will also adopt the following as a derived rule of inference:

DRI-2:   Given any axioms or theorems A and B, we may infer $A \cdot B$.

The justification for adopting DRI-2 as a derived rule of inference is that given T26, $p \supset (q \supset (p \cdot q))$ and any two theorems p and q, we can always deduce their conjunction $p \cdot q$. DRI-2 is especially useful in proving equivalences since it permits us to conjoin theorems having the forms $p \supset q$ and

$q \supset p$ to obtain $(p \supset q) \cdot (q \supset p)$. Given a theorem having this form and D3, we can deduce that expressions having the form $p \equiv q$ are theorems.

EQUIVALENCE THEOREMS

Thus far none of the truth-functional equivalences used earlier has been derived as a theorem. In this section we will derive some of them, making use of the derived rules of inference. The first one we will derive is one of De Morgan's theorems.

T27. $\sim(p \cdot q) \equiv (\sim p \vee \sim q)$

Proof:

1) $p \vee \sim p$	T7
2) $(p \cdot q) \vee \sim(p \cdot q)$	TR1 $p \cdot q/p$
3) $\sim(\sim p \vee \sim q) \vee \sim(p \cdot q)$	D2
4) $(\sim p \vee \sim q) \supset \sim(p \cdot q)$	D1
5) $p \supset p$	T5
6) $(p \cdot q) \supset (p \cdot q)$	TR1 $p \cdot q/p$
7) $\sim(\sim p \vee \sim q) \supset (p \cdot q)$	D2
8) $(\sim p \supset q) \supset (\sim q \supset p)$	T11
9) $(\sim(\sim p \vee \sim q) \supset (p \cdot q)) \supset (\sim(p \cdot q) \supset$ $(\sim p \vee \sim q))$	TR1 $\sim p \vee \sim q/p$, $p \cdot q/q$
10) $\sim(p \cdot q) \supset (\sim p \vee \sim q)$	TR3 7, 9
11) $(\sim(p \cdot q) \supset (\sim p \vee \sim q)) \cdot ((\sim p \vee \sim q) \supset$ $\sim(p \cdot q))$	DRI-2 4, 10
12) $\sim(p \cdot q) \equiv (\sim p \vee \sim q)$	D3

T28. $(p \supset q) \equiv (\sim q \supset \sim p)$

Proof:

1) $(q \vee p) \supset (p \vee q)$	T10
2) $(\sim p \vee q) \supset (q \vee \sim p)$	TR1 $\sim p/q$, q/p
3) $(p \supset q) \supset (q \vee \sim p)$	D1
4) $(p \vee q) \supset (\sim p \supset q)$	T18
5) $(q \vee \sim p) \supset (\sim q \supset \sim p)$	TR1 q/p, $\sim p/q$
6) $(p \supset q) \supset (\sim q \supset \sim p)$	DRI-1 3, 5
7) $(p \supset \sim q) \supset (q \supset \sim p)$	T3
8) $(\sim q \supset \sim p) \supset (p \supset \sim \sim q)$	TR1 $\sim q/p$, p/q
9) $\sim \sim p \supset p$	T9
10) $\sim \sim q \supset q$	TR1 q/p
11) $(q \supset r) \supset ((p \supset q) \supset (p \supset r))$	T4
12) $(\sim \sim q \supset q) \supset ((p \supset \sim \sim q) \supset (p \supset q))$	TR1 $\sim \sim q/q$, q/r

13) $(p \supset \sim \sim q) \supset (p \supset q)$	TR3 10, 12
14) $(\sim q \supset \sim p) \supset (p \supset q)$	DRI-1 8, 13
15) $((p \supset q) \supset (\sim q \supset \sim p)) \cdot$	DRI-2 6, 14
$\qquad ((\sim q \supset \sim p) \supset (p \supset q))$	
16) $(p \supset q) \equiv (\sim q \supset \sim p)$	D3

T28 is the equivalence known as transposition.

T29. $(p \cdot q) \equiv (q \cdot p)$

Proof:

1) $(q \vee p) \supset (p \vee q)$	T10
2) $(\sim p \vee \sim q) \supset (\sim q \vee \sim p)$	TR1 $\sim p/q$, $\sim q/p$
3) $(p \supset q) \equiv (\sim q \supset \sim p)$	T28
4) $((p \supset q) \supset (\sim q \supset \sim p)) \cdot$	D3
$\qquad ((\sim q \supset \sim p) \supset (p \supset q))$	
5) $(p \cdot q) \supset p$	T14
6) $(((p \supset q) \supset (\sim q \supset \sim p)) \cdot$	TR1 $(p \supset q) \supset$
$\qquad ((\sim q \supset \sim p) \supset (p \supset q))) \supset$	$\quad (\sim q \supset \sim p)/p$,
$\qquad ((p \supset q) \supset (\sim q \supset \sim p))$	$\quad (\sim q \supset \sim p) \supset$
	$\quad (p \supset q)/q$
7) $(p \supset q) \supset (\sim q \supset \sim p)$	TR3 4, 6
8) $((\sim p \vee \sim q) \supset (\sim q \vee \sim p)) \supset$	TR1 $\sim p \vee \sim q/p$,
$\qquad (\sim(\sim q \vee \sim p) \supset \sim(\sim p \vee \sim q))$	$\quad \sim q \vee \sim p/q$
9) $\sim(\sim q \vee \sim p) \supset \sim(\sim p \vee \sim q)$	TR3 2, 8
10) $(q \cdot p) \supset (p \cdot q)$	D2
11) $(\sim q \vee \sim p) \supset (\sim p \vee \sim q)$	1, TR1 $\sim q/q$, $\sim p/p$
12) $((\sim q \vee \sim p) \supset (\sim p \vee \sim q)) \supset$	7, TR1 $\sim q \vee \sim p/p$,
$\qquad (\sim(\sim p \vee \sim q) \supset \sim(\sim q \vee \sim p))$	$\quad \sim p \vee \sim q/q$
13) $\sim(\sim p \vee \sim q) \supset \sim(\sim q \vee \sim p)$	TR3 11, 12
14) $(p \cdot q) \supset (q \cdot p)$	D2
15) $((p \cdot q) \supset (q \cdot p)) \cdot ((q \cdot p) \supset (p \cdot q))$	DRI-2 10, 14
16) $(p \cdot q) \equiv (q \cdot p)$	D3

T29 is the commutative law for conjunction.

T30. $p \equiv (p \cdot p)$

Proof:

1) $(p \cdot q) \supset p$	T14
2) $(p \cdot p) \supset p$	TR1 p/q
3) $(p \vee p) \supset p$	T1
4) $(\sim p \vee \sim p) \supset \sim p$	TR1 $\sim p/p$
5) $(p \supset \sim q) \supset (q \supset \sim p)$	T3
6) $((\sim p \vee \sim p) \supset \sim p) \supset (p \supset \sim(\sim p \vee \sim p))$	TR1 $\sim p \vee \sim p/p$, p/q

7) $p \supset \sim(\sim p \vee \sim p)$ TR3 4, 6

8) $p \supset (p \cdot p)$ D2

9) $(p \supset (p \cdot p)) \cdot ((p \cdot p) \supset p)$ DRI-2 2, 8

10) $p \equiv (p \cdot p)$ D3

T30 is one of the laws of tautology.

Proof of the six following theorems is left to the reader. T31 is the second principle of tautology discussed in chapter V; T32 is double negation; T33 is association for the $\vee$; T34 is commutativity for the $\vee$; T35 is material implication; and, T36 is material equivalence.

T31. $p \equiv (p \vee p)$

T32. $p \equiv \sim \sim p$

T33. $(p \vee (q \vee r)) \equiv ((p \vee q) \vee r)$

T34. $(p \vee q) \equiv (q \vee p)$

T35. $(p \supset q) \equiv (\sim p \vee q)$

T36. $(p \equiv q) \equiv ((p \supset q) \cdot (q \supset p))$

INTERPRETED AND UNINTERPRETED SYSTEMS

The formal axiomatic system we have constructed is an **interpreted system,** i.e., although its primitive symbols have not been defined, they have been given a specific interpretation. The variables have been interpreted as propositional variables and the connectives as truth-functional connectives. An interpreted system is often spoken of as a **calculus.** Thus a system such as the one we have constructed, in which the variables are interpreted as propositional variables, is referred to as a **propositional calculus.**

Whenever a system is constructed with some specific interpretation in mind, that interpretation is said to be the **primary interpretation** of that system. Thus, the propositional calculus is the primary interpretation of the system we have constructed. However, formal axiomatic systems may be interpreted in various ways to yield calculi for dealing with a variety of data. For example, the variables of the system we have developed might be interpreted as class variables and the connectives $\sim$ and $\vee$ might be interpreted as referring to relations among classes. This interpretation of the system would yield a **class calculus.** (Some modifications to the system would be required to obtain an adequate class calculus.)

Since every formal system can be interpreted in more than one way, it is obvious that no formal system is identical to any of its interpretations. A system considered abstractly, apart from any of its interpretations, is said to be uninterpreted. An **uninterpreted system** is one in which the primitive symbols are not only not defined within the system but are given no specific interpretation whatsoever. Since no interpretation is given to the primitive symbols, the axioms of an uninterpreted system cannot be said to be true or false. This consideration is quite irrelevant, however, since our purpose in constructing and studying uninterpreted systems is to analyze their structure. If we conceive a formal system as analogous to an extended deductive argument, then it can be said that our concern is with validity only, not with soundness. In both cases the ultimate goal is the same—to achieve greater rigor of reasoning by excluding content.

It is this type of consideration which led Bertrand Russell to comment that logic and mathematics are sciences in which we do not know what we are talking about or whether what we are saying is true or false. It is also this type of consideration, however, which leads to the great utility of formal systems.

SUGGESTED READINGS

BLANCHÉ, ROBERT, *Axiomatics*. New York: Free Press of Glencoe, 1962.

COPI, IRVING M., *Symbolic Logic*. 4th ed. New York: Macmillan, 1973.

KAHANE, HOWARD, *Logic and Philosophy*. 2nd ed. Belmont, Calif.: Wadsworth, 1973.

KLEENE, STEPHEN C., *Mathematical Logic*. New York: John Wiley, 1967.

WHITEHEAD, ALFRED NORTH and BERTRAND RUSSELL, *Principia Mathematica*. Cambridge: Cambridge University Press, 1962.

7

OTHER METHODS
OF PROOF AND
NOTATION

The methods of proof introduced in chapters IV and V are sufficient to show the validity of any truth-functionally valid argument. However, other methods of proof are sometimes simpler or more useful for particular purposes. And there are alternative notations for truth-functional connectives and punctuation symbols. In this chapter we introduce some of these other methods of proof and notation.

CONDITIONAL PROOF

One of the most useful and frequently used methods of proof, *conditional proof*, can be justified as follows: Suppose we write a conditional whose antecedent is the conjunction of the premises of a valid argument and whose consequent is the argument's conclusion. Since it is impossible for the premises of a valid argument to be true and its conclusion false, a conditional of this type is a tautology. For example, if *modus ponens* is written this way, the result is the tautology

$$[(p \supset q) \cdot p] \supset q$$

The converse also holds, i.e., any conditional which is a tautology can be written as a valid argument. For example, if the tautology

$$[(p \supset q) \cdot (q \supset r)] \supset (p \supset r)$$

is written as an argument, then it has the form H. S.

Suppose that we have an argument of the form

$$\frac{p}{q \supset r}$$

If an argument having this form were valid, then the corresponding conditional $p \supset (q \supset r)$ would be a tautology. Now $p \supset (q \supset r)$ is equivalent by exportation to $(p \cdot q) \supset r$, so if $p \supset (q \supset r)$ were a tautology, then $(p \cdot q) \supset r$ would be a tautology also. And if $(p \cdot q) \supset r$ were a tautology, then an argument of the form

$$\begin{array}{c} p \\ q \\ \hline r \end{array}$$

would be valid. Furthermore, by the same reasoning, if an argument of the form

$$\begin{array}{c} p \\ q \\ \hline r \end{array}$$

were valid, then one of the form

$$\frac{p}{q \supset r}$$

would also be valid. Thus, if we prove that an argument having either of these forms is valid, then we will have proven that an argument having the other form is valid, too. It follows that if we have an argument of the form

$$\frac{p}{q \supset r}$$

and assume q as an additional premise so as to obtain an argument of the form

$$\begin{array}{c} p \\ q \\ \hline r \end{array}$$

and succeed in showing that the latter is valid, then we will have succeeded in showing that the former is valid also.

Conditional proof is used in the following manner:

$$\begin{array}{lll}
(1) & p \supset (q \cdot r) & \quad\lfloor p \supset z \\
(2) & r \supset s & \\
(3) & s \supset z & \\
\hline
(4) & \lvert\ p & \text{C.P.} \\
(5) & \lvert\ q \cdot r & 1, 4\ \textit{M.P.} \\
(6) & \lvert\ r & 5,\ \text{Simp.} \\
(7) & \lvert\ s & 2, 6\ \textit{M.P.} \\
(8) & \lvert\ z & 3, 7\ \textit{M.P.} \\
(9) & p \supset z & 4\text{--}8\ \text{C.P.}
\end{array}$$

The assumption of p, the antecedent of the conclusion, as an additional premise is indicated by the abbreviation C.P. in step (4). The vertical line from step (4) through step (8) indicates that these steps fall within the scope of the conditional proof. The only kind of assertion which can follow a vertical line is a conditional whose antecedent is the assumption on which the conditional proof is based and whose consequent is the last step within the scope of the conditional proof.

Conditional proof can be used whenever we wish to establish a conclusion having the form of a conditional. There is no need for the conditional to be the last step in a proof.

$$\begin{array}{lll}
(1) & p \supset (q \cdot r) & \quad\lfloor y \\
(2) & (q \vee s) \supset t & \\
(3) & (t \supset u) \cdot w & \\
(4) & (\sim p \vee t) \supset y & \\
\hline
(5) & \lvert\ p & \text{C.P.} \\
(6) & \lvert\ q \cdot r & 1, 5\ \textit{M.P.} \\
(7) & \lvert\ q & 6,\ \text{Simp.} \\
(8) & \lvert\ q \vee s & 7,\ \text{Add.} \\
(9) & \lvert\ t & 2, 8\ \textit{M.P.} \\
(10) & p \supset t & 5\text{--}9\ \text{C.P.} \\
(11) & \sim p \vee t & 10\ \text{M.I.} \\
(12) & y & 4, 11\ \textit{M.P.}
\end{array}$$

Nor is there any need for conditional proof to be the first step in a proof. The following proof is also legitimate:

$$\begin{array}{ll}
(1) & \sim p \vee (q \cdot r) \qquad\lfloor w \\
(2) & \sim(q \vee s) \\
(3) & [\sim p \cdot (t \supset u)] \supset w \\
(4) & \sim t \vee x \\
(5) & (x \cdot \sim s) \supset u
\end{array}$$

(6)	$(\sim p \vee q) \cdot (\sim p \vee r)$	1, Dist.
(7)	$\sim p \vee q$	6, Simp.
(8)	$\sim q \cdot \sim s$	2, D.M.
(9)	$\sim q$	8, Simp.
(10)	$\sim p$	7, 9 D.S.
(11)	$\quad t$	C.P.
(12)	$\quad t \supset x$	4, M.I.
(13)	$\quad x$	11, 12 M.P.
(14)	$\quad \sim s$	8, Simp.
(15)	$\quad x \cdot \sim s$	13, 14 Conj.
(16)	$\quad u$	5, 15 M.P.
(17)	$t \supset u$	11–16 C.P.
(18)	$\sim p \cdot (t \supset u)$	10, 17 Conj.
(19)	w	3, 18 M.P.

In the proofs presented in earlier chapters, any previous step could be cited at any point in a proof. However, once a conditional proof has been concluded, steps within its scope cannot be appealed to in subsequent steps. For example, the following proof is incorrect:

(1) $p \supset (q \cdot r)$		$\underline{\quad u}$
(2) $(q \vee s) \supset t$		
(3) $(t \supset u) \cdot w$		
(4) $[(p \supset t) \cdot w] \supset y$		
(5) $\quad p$	C.P.	
(6) $\quad q \cdot r$	1, 5 M.P.	
(7) $\quad q$	6, Simp.	
(8) $\quad q \vee s$	7, Add.	
(9) $\quad t$	2, 8 M.P.	
(10) $p \supset t$	5–9 C.P.	
(11) $t \supset u$	3, Simp.	
(12) u	9, 11 M.P.	

The mistake here occurs in step (12). Citing step (9) as evidence for this step is illegitimate because t has not been established; t has been proven only on the assumption that p is the case. Thus, we may legitimately conclude in step (10) that t is the case *if* p holds, but we cannot conclude that t by itself is the case. Mistakes of this type can be avoided if one thinks of steps within the scope of a conditional proof as "sealed off" from the rest of the proof by means of the vertical line.

Conditional proof may be used more than once in a proof.

(1) $(p \lor q) \supset r$		z
(2) $(r \supset s) \cdot u$		
(3) $u \supset [t \supset (u \cdot w)]$		
(4) $[(p \supset s) \cdot (t \supset w)] \supset z$		
(5) $r \supset s$	2, Simp.	
(6) u	2, Simp.	
(7) $(p \lor q) \supset s$	1, 5 H.S.	
(8) p	C.P.	
(9) $p \lor q$	8, Add.	
(10) s	7, 9 M.P.	
(11) $p \supset s$	8–10 C.P.	
(12) t	C.P.	
(13) $t \supset (u \cdot w)$	3, 6 M.P.	
(14) $u \cdot w$	12, 13 M.P.	
(15) w	14, Simp.	
(16) $t \supset w$	12–15 C.P.	
(17) $(p \supset s) \cdot (t \supset w)$	11, 16 Conj.	
(18) z	4, 17 M.P.	

Note that one of the steps in the second conditional proof, step (13), depends upon steps which occur prior to the first conditional proof. This is legitimate because any previous step may be cited, provided that it does not occur within the scope of a conditional proof. Thus, any step other than (8), (9), and (10), which are sealed off, can be appealed to in the second conditional proof. The same principle holds for subsequent steps. Steps (12) through (15) cannot be appealed to after the conditional proof in which they occur has been closed.

Finally, conditional proofs can occur within conditional proofs. For example

(1) $(p \lor q) \supset [(r \lor s) \supset (t \cdot u)]$		$p \supset (r \supset w)$
(2) $(t \cdot u) \supset w$		
(3) p	C.P.	
(4) r	C.P.	
(5) $p \lor q$	3, Add.	
(6) $(r \lor s) \supset (t \cdot u)$	1, 5 M.P.	
(7) $r \lor s$	4, Add.	
(8) $t \cdot u$	6, 7 M.P.	
(9) w	2, 8 M.P.	
(10) $r \supset w$	4–9 C.P.	
(11) $p \supset (r \supset w)$	3–10 C.P.	

Note that in giving the inner conditional proof, it is legitimate to cite steps which occur in the outer conditional proof. This is done in step (5). However, in giving the outer conditional proof, no appeal can be made to steps that occur within the scope of the inner conditional proof. Thus in step (11) one may cite step (10), which is the conclusion of the inner conditional proof; but one may not cite steps (4) through (9) which are sealed off from the rest of the argument.

EXERCISES

I

Construct proofs for the following argument forms using the method of conditional proof:

1. (1) $(p \cdot q) \supset (r \cdot s)$ $\quad\lfloor p \supset \sim t$
    (2) $q \cdot (r \supset \sim t)$

2. (1) $(p \vee q) \supset (r \cdot s)$ $\quad\lfloor p \supset t$
    (2) $\sim t \supset (\sim r \cdot u)$

3. (1) $q \supset (\sim r \vee s)$ $\quad\lfloor p \supset (q \supset \sim r)$
    (2) $\sim p \vee \sim s$

4. (1) $(s \vee q) \supset (m \cdot w)$ $\quad\lfloor r \supset [(s \cdot p) \supset t]$
    (2) $(m \cdot r) \supset t$

5. (1) $s \supset [\sim t \supset (u \cdot v)]$ $\quad\lfloor s \equiv u$
    (2) $\sim t \cdot \sim r$
    (3) $(u \vee p) \supset [\sim r \supset (s \cdot p)]$

6. (1) $\{[(p \vee q) \cdot (p \vee r)] \cdot (p \cdot r)\} \supset t$ $\quad\lfloor p \supset (r \supset t)$

7. (1) $(p \vee r) \cdot (p \vee s)$ $\quad\lfloor t \supset (s \vee r)$
    (2) $(\sim p \supset r) \supset (q \cdot s)$

8. Number 8, page 74.

9. Number 9, page 75.

10. Number 10, page 75.

INDIRECT PROOF

A second method of proof, *indirect* or *reductio ad absurdum proof,* can be justified as follows: Suppose we assume that a proposition, p, is true and then conjoin p and another proposition, $\sim q$. Suppose further that we are able to deduce a false conclusion from $p \cdot \sim q$. Suppose, in particular, that we are able to deduce a contradiction. Since we have assumed that p is true, it follows that $\sim q$ must be false or we could not have deduced a false conclusion from $p \cdot \sim q$. But if $\sim q$ is false, then q must be true. Consequently, we have shown that if p is true, then q must be true also. Now, assume that p represents the premises of an argument and q represents its conclusion. Since we have shown that if p is true, then q must be true also, we have shown that the argument is valid. This may be summed up as follows: If the negation of an argument's conclusion is assumed as an additional premise and a contradiction is derived, then the argument is valid.

Suppose we had an argument of the form

$$
\begin{array}{ll}
(1)\ p \supset (q \cdot r) & \quad \lfloor s \\
(2)\ (q \vee r) \supset s & \\
(3)\ \sim r \supset (p \cdot s) &
\end{array}
$$

The conclusion to be proven is s. Thus we assume $\sim s$ as an additional premise, citing as our justification the rule of indirect proof (I.P.). Since, as shown below, this allows us to deduce a contradiction, the initial argument is valid.

$$
\begin{array}{lll}
(1)\ p \supset (q \cdot r) & \quad \lfloor s & \\
(2)\ (q \vee r) \supset s & & \\
(3)\ \sim r \supset (p \cdot s) & & \\
(4)\ \sim s & & \text{I.P.} \\
(5)\ \sim(q \vee r) & & 2,\,4\ M.T. \\
(6)\ \sim q \cdot \sim r & & 5,\ D.M. \\
(7)\ \sim r & & 6,\ \text{Simp.} \\
(8)\ p \cdot s & & 3,\,7\ M.P. \\
(9)\ s & & 8,\ \text{Simp.} \\
(10)\ s \cdot \sim s & & 4,\,9\ \text{Conj.}
\end{array}
$$

In this particular case, the contradiction obtained is a conjunction of the original conclusion and its negation. However, the deduction of any contradiction whatever is sufficient to show that the original argument is valid. Hence, we might have proceeded in the following fashion:

$$
\begin{array}{lll}
(1)\ p \supset (q \cdot r) & \quad \lfloor s & \\
(2)\ (q \vee r) \supset s & & \\
(3)\ \sim r \supset (p \cdot s) & & \\
(4)\ \sim s & & \text{I.P.} \\
(5)\ \sim(q \vee r) & & 2,\,4\ M.T. \\
(6)\ \sim q \cdot \sim r & & 5,\ D.M. \\
(7)\ \sim r & & 6,\ \text{Simp.} \\
(8)\ p \cdot s & & 3,\,7\ M.P. \\
(9)\ p & & 8,\ \text{Simp.} \\
(10)\ q \cdot r & & 1,\,9\ M.P. \\
(11)\ r & & 10,\ \text{Simp.} \\
(12)\ r \cdot \sim r & & 7,\,11\ \text{Conj.}
\end{array}
$$

Once a contradiction is obtained, the original conclusion can always be deduced by use of addition and disjunctive syllogism. For example, from line (11) above one can deduce $r \lor s$ by addition, and from this statement and line (7) one can deduce s by disjunctive syllogism. Some logicians do not consider a *reductio ad absurdum* proof complete unless the original conclusion is deduced in this manner. In practice, however, one may stop after having deduced a contradiction since it is obvious that the original conclusion can always be deduced if one so desires.

EXERCISES

II

Use indirect proof to demonstrate the validity of the following argument forms:

1. (1) $(p \supset q) \cdot (r \supset s)$ $\vert \sim(p \lor r)$
   (2) $(q \lor s) \supset t$
   (3) $\sim t$

2. (1) $q \supset (r \supset s)$ $\vert \sim r$
   (2) $\sim s$
   (3) $(q \supset \sim r) \supset s$

3. (1) $(r \lor s) \supset (t \cdot u)$ $\vert \sim x$
   (2) $(t \lor w) \supset (\sim x \cdot y)$
   (3) $(x \lor z) \supset (r \cdot p)$

4. (1) $u \supset (v \supset p)$ $\vert q \lor p$
   (2) $\sim q \supset (u \lor p)$
   (3) $u \supset v$

5. (1) $(p \supset q) \supset (r \cdot s)$ $\vert p$
   (2) $(r \lor t) \supset (s \supset p)$

6. (1) $(p \supset \sim r) \cdot (q \supset s)$ $\vert \sim x \cdot y$
   (2) $(\sim r \supset t) \cdot (s \supset \sim u)$
   (3) $(t \supset \sim x) \cdot (\sim u \supset y)$
   (4) $p \cdot q$

7. Number 14, page 60.
8. Number 9, page 72.
9. Number 7, page 74.
10. Number 8, page 78.

Conditional and Indirect Proof
Applied to Tautologies

Conditional and indirect proof can also be used to demonstrate that propositions have a tautological form. Indirect proof can be applied to any proposition, but conditional proof can only be applied to conditionals. To show that a conditional has a tautological form, one needs to show that if the antecedent is true, then the consequent must be true. To demonstrate this by conditional proof, one assumes as many antecedents as are needed and then deduces the consequents. For example, to show that $(p \supset q) \supset [p \supset (p \cdot q)]$ has a tautological form, one needs to make two assumptions

		$\underline{\;(p \supset q) \supset [p \supset (p \cdot q)]\;}$
(1)	$p \supset q$	C.P.
(2)	p	C.P.
(3)	q	1, 2 M.P.
(4)	$p \cdot q$	2, 3 Conj.
(5)	$p \supset (p \cdot q)$	2–4 C.P.
(6) $(p \supset q) \supset [p \supset (p \cdot q)]$		1–5 C.P.

To demonstrate by indirect proof that a proposition has a tautological form, one shows that its negation entails a contradiction. The following proof shows that $[(p \supset q) \cdot p] \supset q$ has a tautological form:

	$\underline{\;[(p \supset q) \cdot p] \supset q\;}$
(1) $\sim\{[(p \supset q) \cdot p] \supset q\}$	I.P.
(2) $\sim\{\sim[(p \supset q) \cdot p] \vee q\}$	1, M.I.
(3) $[(p \supset q) \cdot p] \cdot \sim q$	2, D.M.
(4) $(p \supset q) \cdot p$	3, Simp.
(5) $p \supset q$	4, Simp.
(6) p	4, Simp.
(7) q	5, 6 M.P.
(8) $\sim q$	3, Simp.
(9) $q \cdot \sim q$	7, 8 Conj.

EXERCISES

III

Show that the following have tautological forms by using either conditional or indirect proof:

1. $\sim(p \vee q) \supset (\sim p \cdot \sim q)$
2. $\sim p \vee (q \vee p)$
3. $[(p \supset q) \cdot (q \supset r)] \supset (p \supset r)$
4. $\sim(p \cdot \sim p) \vee (q \cdot \sim q)$
5. $(p \equiv q) \vee [(p \cdot \sim q) \vee (q \cdot \sim p)]$
6. $[p \supset (q \supset r)] \supset [(p \supset q) \supset (p \supset r)]$

ALTERNATIVE NOTATIONS

The logical notation of *Principia Mathematica* (*P.M.*) is used throughout this text. In the following sections we will introduce some alternative notations for truth-functional connectives and punctuation symbols. These are not the only notational devices which have been used, but they are the most widely adopted alternatives to *P.M.* notation, and mastery of them will enable one to read most works dealing with truth-functional logic.

Polish Notation

One of the most frequently adopted sets of symbols for expressing truth-functional connectives was developed by Jan Lukasiewicz, and is called the Polish notation. The following table correlates this notation with the one we have been using:

$\sim p$	Np
$p \vee q$	Apq
$p \cdot q$	Kpq
$p \supset q$	Cpq

The symbols for variables in the Polish notation are the same as those we have used. But connectives are represented by capital letters immediately preceding expressions which fall within their scope. One advantage of this notation is that it eliminates the need for punctuation symbols. Another practical consideration is that the symbols appear on any standard typewriter keyboard.

The way in which these symbols may be combined to form more complicated expressions is shown by the following table:

$p \supset (q \supset r)$	$CpCqr$
$(p \supset q) \supset r$	$CCpqr$
$p \vee (q \cdot r)$	$ApKqr$
$p \supset (\sim q \vee p)$	$CpANqp$
$\sim(p \vee q)$	$NApq$
$\sim(p \supset q) \cdot (\sim r \cdot s)$	$KNCpqKNrs$

EXERCISES

IV

Rewrite the following using Polish notation:

1. $\sim p \cdot r$
2. $r \vee \sim q$
3. $\sim p \supset \sim q$
4. $\sim(p \supset \sim q)$
5. $(p \supset q) \supset r$
6. $(p \vee q) \cdot r$

7. $\sim p \lor (q \lor \sim r)$
8. $\sim(p \cdot q) \cdot \sim r$
9. $(p \lor q) \cdot (q \lor r)$
10. $\sim(p \cdot \sim q) \lor \sim(q \cdot \sim p)$

Dot Notation

Another commonly used notation differs from the one we have been using by employing dots as punctuation symbols. When dot notation is adopted, the expression

$$(p \supset q) \supset (p \supset r)$$

is punctuated as

$$p \supset q \,.\supset.\, p \supset r$$

Parentheses, brackets, and braces occur in pairs, and the occurrence of one member of a pair indicates the direction of the symbol's operation. That is, (, [, and { operate to the right, while),], and } operate to the left. But dots are single symbols, and call for a different convention. The convention adopted is that dots operate away from the connective to which they are adjacent. Notice that the dots in our example above both occur adjacent to the major connective. The first dot operates away from that connective to indicate that $p \supset q$ is a compound expression; the second dot operates away from that connective to indicate that $p \supset r$ is a compound expression.

Since dots operate away from adjacent connectives, there is no danger of mistaking a dot used as a punctuation symbol for one serving as a conjunction symbol.

The expression

$$(p \supset q) \cdot (q \supset r)$$

could be rendered in the dot notation as

$$p \supset q \,.\,\cdot\,.\, q \supset r$$

However, since three dots together appear redundant, most logicians who adopt the dot notation would represent this as simply

$$p \supset q . q \supset r$$

Just as more than one set of parentheses, brackets, or braces may be needed to punctuate an expression, additional dots may be required to punctuate an expression. Double dots have greater scope than single dots, triple dots have greater scope than double, etc. Thus

$$p \supset [q \supset (r \supset s)]$$

becomes

$$p \supset : q \supset . r \supset s$$

The following provide additional illustrations:

$\sim(p \equiv q) \vee (p \cdot \sim q)$ $\sim .p \equiv q : \vee : p \sim q$

$p \supset [(p \vee q) \vee (p \vee \sim q)]$ $p \supset : p \vee q . \vee . p \vee \sim q$

$p \vee \{r \equiv [q \supset (p \cdot r)]\}$ $p \vee : r \equiv . q \supset . p r$

$[p \vee (q \vee r)] \equiv [(p \vee q) \vee r]$ $p \vee . q \vee r : \equiv : p \vee q . \vee r$

$(p \supset q) \supset \{q \supset [r \supset (s \vee p)]\}$ $p \supset q . \supset : . q \supset : r \supset .s \vee p$

Dots may also be combined with parentheses, brackets, and braces. This is the system used by Russell and Whitehead in *Principia Mathematica.* For example

$$[\sim(p \cdot q) \supset (\sim p \vee \sim q)] \equiv [\sim(\sim p \vee \sim q) \supset (p \cdot q)]$$

may be written as

$$\sim(p \cdot q). \supset \sim p \vee \sim q : \equiv : \sim(\sim p \vee \sim q) \supset .p \cdot q$$

EXERCISES

V

Rewrite the following using dot notation:

1. $\sim(p \supset \sim q)$
2. $(p \vee q) \cdot (p \vee r)$
3. $[(p \vee q) \cdot p] \vee r$
4. $(p \vee q) \cdot [(n \equiv s) \cdot \sim q]$
5. $\{[(p \equiv q) \cdot s] \supset (p \vee r)\} \supset (\sim p \cdot q)$

The Stroke and Slash Notations

We have shown that logical systems can be constructed using only two truth-functional connectives as primitive terms. A logical system using $\sim$

and ∨ was constructed in chapter VI, and the section on interdefinitions in chapter V shows that comparable systems can be constructed using the ∼ and · or the ∼ and ⊃ as primitives. However, one can build even more economical systems. The stroke and the slash are connectives which allow systems to be constructed using only one primitive connective.

The stroke symbol, $p|q$, asserts that at least one of its components is false. Hence, the following truth table defines the stroke:

p	q	$p|q$
T	T	F
T	F	T
F	T	T
F	F	T

Using dot notation, other connectives can be defined by means of the stroke as follows:

$$\sim p = \text{df. } p|p$$
$$p \cdot q = \text{df. } p|q.|.p|q$$
$$p \vee q = \text{df. } p|p.|.q|q$$
$$p \supset q = \text{df. } p.|.q|q$$

It can be shown by truth tables that these definitions preserve the usual truth-functional interpretations of the connectives. For example

p	q	$p \supset q$	$p.|.q|q$
T	T	T	T F
T	F	F	F T
F	T	T	T F
F	F	T	T T

Demonstration that other definitions preserve the usual interpretation of the connectives is left as an exercise for the reader.

The slash symbol, p/q, asserts that both of its components are false, so its truth table definition is

p	q	p/q
T	T	F
T	F	F
F	T	F
F	F	T

The other connectives can be defined by means of the slash as follows:

$$\sim p = \text{df. } p/p$$
$$p \cdot q = \text{df. } p/p./.q/q$$
$$p \vee q = \text{df. } p/q./.p/q$$
$$p \supset q = \text{df. } p/p./q:/:p/.p/q$$

Logical systems can be constructed using either the slash or the stroke as the only primitive connective. To illustrate this, we will outline the construction of a system which adopts the stroke as its only primitive. This system, called the Nicod system, is named for its originator, J. C. P. Nicod. The primitive symbols in the Nicod System are letters for propositional variables, subscripts on the variables, dots (as punctuation symbols), and |. *Wffs* in the system are defined exclusively as follows:

(1) p, q, r . . . are *wffs*.
(2)   If A and B are *wffs*, then $A|B$ is a *wff*.

The only axiom of the Nicod System is

$$p.|.q|r:|::t.|.t|t:.|:.s|q:|:p|s.|.p|s$$

The only rules of inference are a substitution rule and the rule that given p and $p.|.r|q$ one may infer q.

Although the Nicod System offers considerable gain in economy, derivations in this system are extremely tedious. To see why, one need only consider the formulation of $(p \supset q) \supset [(r \vee p) \supset (r \vee q)]$ in this system:

$$p|p.|.p|p:|:q|q:.|:.\ p|p.|.p|p:|:q|q::|:::p|p.|.p|p:|:q|q:.|$$
$$:.p|p.|.p|p:|:q|q:::|:::r|r.|.p|p:|:r|r.|.p|p:.|:.r|r.|.p|p:|$$
$$:r|r.|.p|p::|:::r|r.|.q|q:|:r|r.|.q|q::.|:::r|r.|.p|p:|$$
$$:r|r.|.p|p:.|:.r|r.|.p|p:|:r|r.|.p|p::|:::r|r.|.q|q:|:r|r.|.q|q$$

The Nicod System demonstrates that all tautologies can be derived using only one axiom, two rules of inference, and one connective—given enough time and patience!

SUGGESTED READINGS

AMBROSE, ALICE and MORRIS LAZEROWITZ, *Fundamentals of Symbolic Logic*. Rev. ed. New York: Holt, Rinehart and Winston, 1962.

COPI, IRVING M., *Symbolic Logic*. 4th ed. New York: Macmillan, 1973.

KRETZMANN, NORMAN, *Elements of Formal Logic*. Indianapolis: The Bobbs-Merrill Co., Inc., 1965.

8

THE PREDICATE CALCULUS

QUANTIFICATION

All the arguments we have considered can be shown to be valid or invalid using the techniques and principles of the propositional calculus.* However, there are many valid arguments whose validity cannot be shown by the propositional calculus. For example

> If anyone is at home, then he will hear us knock.
> Bob is at home.
> Bob will hear us knock.

If we were to attempt to symbolize this argument using our previous techniques, it might seem to have the form

$$p \supset q$$
$$r$$
$$s$$

This symbolization fails to exhibit the formal structure which makes this argument valid. To exhibit its structure and show its validity, we need additional techniques of symbolization and additional logical principles. These techniques and principles include symbols for individuals as well as symbols for predicates, and the system resulting from their addition to the

---

*See page 100 for a definition of the term 'propositional calculus'.

propositional calculus is known as the **predicate calculus.** By an **individual** we mean here anything that can be treated as a unit for the purpose of discourse. For example, not only a single stone but also a pile of stones can be regarded as an individual. By a **predicate** we mean a term which stands for a property or characteristic of an individual.

Singular Propositions

Bob is at home.
Bob is not at home.
If Bob is at home, then he will hear us knock.
The Memphis State team won.
That tree is not an oak; it is a beech.
If the Queen Mary arrives today, then she will
    dock at either New York or Boston.

The foregoing are **singular propositions,** that is, they are propositions which assert something about particular individuals. The first asserts that the property, *is at home,* belongs to the individual named by the word 'Bob'. If we let the capital letter H stand for the property, *is at home,* and the lower-case letter b stand for the individual Bob, then this proposition, which is an affirmative singular proposition, may be symbolized as

$$Hb$$

and the second proposition above, which is a negative singular proposition, may be symbolized as

$$\sim Hb$$

If we let K stand for the property, *will hear us knock,* then the third proposition above may be symbolized as

$$Hb \supset Kb$$

The other propositions in the list may be symbolized similarly:

$$Wm$$

$$\sim Ot \cdot Bt$$

$$Aq \supset (Nq \vee Bq)$$

Lower case letters such as b, m, and q which stand for particular individuals are called **individual constants,** while capital letters such as H, K, and B which stand for particular properties are called **predicate constants.**

In addition to individual and predicate constants, we need individual and predicate variables. Just as we used the lower case letters p, q, r, . . . as propositional variables to stand for any given proposition, we will now use the lower case letters x, y, z, . . . as **individual variables** to stand for any given individual, and the Greek letters ϕ and ψ as **predicate variables** to stand for any given property.

General Propositions

1. Some things are destructible.
2. Some things are not destructible.
3. Several of the players wept after the game.
4. A few of the players were either too excited or did not get enough sleep.

5. Everything is destructible.
6. Nothing is destructible.
7. If anyone is at home, then he will hear us knock.
8. All oak trees have acorns, but no beech trees have acorns.
9. People are eligible for the contest if and only if they do not work for the company.

The foregoing are examples of **general propositions,** that is, they are propositions which assert something about some or all individuals of a certain kind. The last five are **universal propositions:** they assert that *all* individuals of a certain kind do, or do not, have certain properties. The first four are **existential propositions:** they assert that *some* individuals of a certain kind do, or do not, have certain properties. Every existential proposition may be interpreted as asserting that *at least one individual exists.* However, unlike singular propositions, they do not single out particular individuals.

Existential Quantification

The symbol used to assert the existence of at least one individual ($\exists x$) is called the **existential quantifier.** It may be used to symbolize any term, such as 'some', 'several', 'a few', 'most', and 'many', which indicates less than all of some class of individuals. Note that though these words do not indicate precise quantities, they all indicate 'at least one'.*

---

*Just as the symbolization of conditionals in ordinary language by means of the '$\supset$' often results in weaker assertions than the original, so use of the existential quantifier to symbolize such terms as 'several', 'a few' and 'many' results in weaker claims than the original. However, since the weaker claims are true whenever the stronger ones are, and the stronger claims false whenever the weaker ones are, this procedure usually allows us to show the validity or invalidity of arguments in ordinary language.

If we let D stand for the property, *destructible,* then the proposition 'Some things are destructible', which is an affirmative existential proposition, may be symbolized as

$$(\exists x)Dx$$

and the proposition 'Some things are not destructible', which is a negative existential proposition, may be symbolized as

$$(\exists x) \sim Dx$$

The first of these expressions may be read as 'There exists at least one individual x, such that x is destructible', or more simply as 'There exists at least one x such that x is destructible'. The second expression may be read similarly as 'There exists at least one x such that x is not destructible'.

The individuals referred to in the foregoing propositions may be of any type whatever; but in the proposition 'Several of the players wept after the game', it is clear, although implicitly understood, that the class of individuals referred to is human beings. Consequently, if we let H stand for, *is a human being, P* stand for, *is a player,* and W stand for, *wept after the game,* the proposition may be symbolized as

$$(\exists x)[Hx \cdot (Px \cdot Wx)]$$

However, since it is clear that the class of individuals referred to is human beings, this proposition may also be symbolized more simply as

$$(\exists x)(Px \cdot Wx)$$

As a rule it is not necessary to symbolize implicitly understood properties such as, *is a human being,* to determine the validity of arguments, but sometimes it is.

The remaining example of an existential proposition, 'A few of the players were either too excited or did not get enough sleep', may be symbolized as

$$(\exists x)[Px \cdot (Tx \vee \sim Gx)]$$

Universal Quantification

The proposition 'Everything is destructible' asserts that every individual in the universe is destructible. Hence, it may be paraphrased as 'Given any individual whatever, that individual is destructible'. To symbolize this proposition, we need a symbol to stand for the idea 'given any individual whatever'. The symbol adopted (x) is called the **universal quantifier.**

If we again let D stand for, *is destructible,* then the proposition 'Everything is destructible', which is an affirmative universal proposition, may be symbolized as

$$(x)Dx$$

and the proposition 'Nothing is destructible', which is a negative universal proposition, may be symbolized as

$$(x) \sim Dx$$

The first expression may be read as 'Given any individual whatever, that individual is destructible' or as 'Given any individual x, x is destructible' or yet more simply as 'Given any x, x is destructible'. The second expression may be read similarly as 'Given any x, x is not destructible'.

If we let H stand for, *is at home,* and K stand for, *will hear us knock,* then the proposition 'If anyone is at home, then he will hear us knock' may be symbolized as

$$(x)(Hx \supset Kx)$$

This may be read as 'Given any x, if x is at home, then x will hear us knock'. Note that this proposition could *not* have been symbolized as $(x)(Hx \cdot Kx)$. This expression says that given any person whatever, that person is both at home and will hear us knock. But the proposition we are symbolizing does not say that all people are at home; it states only that *if* anyone is at home, then he will hear us knock.

Similarly, the proposition 'All oak trees have acorns' cannot be symbolized as $(x)(Ox \cdot Ax)$, but must be symbolized as $(x)(Ox \supset Ax)$. And the proposition 'No beech trees have acorns' cannot be symbolized as $(x)(Bx \cdot \sim Ax)$, but must be symbolized as $(x)(Bx \supset \sim Ax)$. The eighth proposition in the above list, therefore, may be symbolized as $(x)(Ox \supset Ax) \cdot (x)(Bx \supset \sim Ax)$. The ninth proposition, 'People are eligible for the contest if and only if they do not work for the company', may be symbolized as $(x)(Ex \equiv \sim Wx)$.

Close attention must be given to propositions containing the words 'a', 'an', and 'the'. For instance, 'A budget revision is needed' is an existential proposition which may be symbolized as $(\exists x)(Bx \cdot Nx)$, but 'A banana peel is slippery' is a universal proposition which may be symbolized as $(x)(Bx \supset Sx)$. Similarly, 'An abalone is not a fur-bearing animal' is a universal proposition which may be symbolized as $(x)(Ax \supset \sim Fx)$, but 'An apple fell' is an existential proposition which may be symbolized as $(\exists x)$ $(Ax \cdot Fx)$. The universal proposition 'The albatross is a web-footed sea bird' may be symbolized as $(x)[Ax \supset (Wx \cdot Sx)]$, but 'The old man is stubborn' may be interpreted as an existential proposition symbolized as $(\exists x)(Ox \cdot Sx)$.

Some propositions containing the word 'and' are more conveniently symbolized using the $\vee$ than the $\cdot$. For example, the proposition 'Zebras and tigers are striped' can be symbolized as $(x)(Zx \supset Sx) \cdot (x)(Tx \supset Sx)$, but it is usually more convenient to symbolize it as $(x)[(Zx \vee Tx) \supset Sx]$. It *cannot* be symbolized as $(x)[(Zx \cdot Tx) \supset Sx]$, for this expression says that if anything is *both* a zebra and a tiger then it is striped, whereas the original clearly means that anything which is *either* a zebra or a tiger is striped.

Finally, propositions such as 'Some dogs have fleas' *cannot* be symbolized as $(\exists x)(Dx \supset Fx)$, but must be symbolized as $(\exists x)(Dx \cdot Fx)$. The former expression says that there exists at least one thing; and *if* that thing is a dog, then it has fleas. This claim would be true if anything whatever were to exist provided that it were not a dog. The latter expression says that there exists at least one thing and that thing is a dog which has fleas. This claim could be true only if there is at least one dog with fleas. Thus it, and not the former expression, is the correct symbolization of 'Some dogs have fleas'.

EXERCISES

I

Symbolize the following propositions using the suggested notation.

1. Ralph is a card shark. (C, r)
2. ° Sadie is a belly dancer. (B, s)
3. Merlin is a magician and Stanley is a taxman. (M, T, m, s)
4. If Bruce is an empiricist, then Carl is a mystic. (E, M, b, c)
5. Nixon is president if and only if Paulsen is not. (P, n, p)
6. Either Tom lost his watch or he forgot the date and will miss the meeting. (L, F, M, t)
7. If Donald had the tickets, Ed will be able to get in; but if Ed had the tickets, then he will have left them at home. (H, G, L, d, e)
8. All triangles are polygons. (Tx, Px)
9. Chickens are all bipeds. (Cx, Bx)
10. Some chickens are roosters. (Cx, Rx)
11. Some chickens are hens. (Cx, Hx)

12. Any chicken is either a rooster or a hen. (*Cx, Rx, Hx*)
13. Everything is extended. (*Ex*)
14. All things are either in motion or at rest. (*Mx, Rx*)
15. Several things were lost. (*Lx*)
16. If anything is a dragon, it breathes fire. (*Dx, Bx*)
17. If anything breathes fire, then it is not a whale. (*Bx, Wx*)
18. Some politicians are either conservative or liberal. (*Px, Cx, Lx*)
19. There are politicians who are neither conservative nor liberal. (*Px, Cx, Lx*)
20. A penny saved is a penny earned. (*Px, Sx, Ex*)
21. A tiger escaped from the zoo. (*Tx, Ex*)
22. The claim is false. (*Cx, Fx*)
23. Freshmen and sophomores are not eligible. (*Fx, Sx, Ex*)
24. The tiger is a carnivore. (*Tx, Cx*)
25. All passengers must have a ticket or they will not be allowed to board. (*Px, Mx, Ax*)
26. Passengers can ride free if and only if they either have an employee identification card or a pass issued by the president. (*Px, Rx, Ex, Ix*)
27. No employee identification card or pass issued by the president will be honored if it is more than a year old. (*Ex, Px, Hx, Mx*)
28. Police officers and fire fighters are dedicated public servants and should make more money. (*Px, Fx, Dx, Sx*)
29. If Popoff commits either an intentional or a technical foul, then he will be removed from the game and sent to the dressing room. (*I, T, R, S, p*)
30. If anyone is at home and is bothered by a salesman, then he is apt to lose his temper; but if he is at the office and a salesman calls on him, then he does not mind unless, of course, it is his lunch hour. (*Hx, Bx, Ax, Ox, Sx, Mx, Lx*)

FREE AND BOUND VARIABLES

The **scope of a quantifier,** like the scope of a negative symbol, extends only to expressions which immediately follow. For example, in $(\exists x)(Fx \cdot Gx)$ both Fx and Gx are within the scope of the quantifier $(\exists x)$, but in $(\exists x)Fx \cdot Gx$ only Fx is within the scope of the quantifier. If a variable occurs outside the scope of a quantifier, or if it occurs within its scope but is not the same variable as the quantifier variable, then that variable is **free** with respect to that quantifier. If a variable occurs within the scope of a quantifier and is the same variable as the quantifier variable, then that variable is **bound** by the quantifier. For example, all three variables are bound by the quantifier in $(x)[(Fx \cdot Gx) \supset Hx]$, but only the first two are bound by the quantifier in $(x)(Fx \cdot Gx) \supset Hx$ because the third is outside the scope of (x). And in $(x)(Fx \supset Gx)$ both variables are bound by (x), but in $(x)(Fx \supset Gy)$ only the first variable is bound because the second variable is not the same as the quantifier variable.

EXERCISES

II

Which of the following variables are bound and which free?

1. $(x)[(Fx \supset Gx) \vee Hx]$
2. $(x)[(Fx \supset Gx) \vee Hy]$
3. $(x)(Fx \supset Gx) \vee Hx$
4. $(\exists x)[(Fx \vee Gy) \cdot Hy]$
5. $(\exists x)[(Fx \vee Gy) \cdot Hx]$

PROOF

The scope of the quantifier in $(x)Fx \supset Ga$ is limited to the antecedent, but the scope of the quantifier in $(x)(Fx \supset Gx)$ extends over the entire conditional. Consequently, the expression $(x)Fx \supset Ga$ has the form $p \supset q$, but the expression $(x)(Fx \supset Ga)$ does not have this form. If expressions in the predicate calculus have the same form as expressions in the propositional calculus, then any principle applicable in the propositional calculus will also apply in the predicate calculus. For example, since $(x)Fx \supset Ga$ has the form $p \supset q$, the following proof is legitimate:

(1) $(x)Fx \supset Ga$ Ga
(2) $(x)Fx$
(3) Ga 1, 2 *M.P.*

But, since $(x)(Fx \supset Ga)$ does not have the form $p \supset q$, the following proof is *not* legitimate:

(1) $(x)(Fx \supset Ga)$
(2) $(x)Fx$
(3) Ga

The following proof is also legitimate:

(1) $(x)(Fx \supset Gx)$ $(x) \sim (Fx \cdot \sim Gx)$
(2) $(x)(\sim Fx \vee Gx)$ 1, M.I.
(3) $(x) \sim (Fx \cdot \sim Gx)$ 2, D.M.

because M.I. and D.M. are applied to units within the quantified expressions which have the same form as expressions in the propositional calculus. But the following proof is *not* legitimate:

$$\frac{(1) \sim (x)(Fx \supset Gx)}{(2) \ (x)(Fx \lor Gx)}$$

because the expression $\sim (x)(Fx \supset Gx)$ does not have the form of an expression in the propositional calculus. The negation symbol in $\sim (x)(Fx \supset Gx)$ negates the entire quantified expression, not the expression $Fx \supset Gx$, so one cannot change $\sim (x)(Fx \supset Gx)$ to $(x)(Fx \lor Gx)$ by use of M.I.

As stated at the beginning of the chapter, additional logical principles are required to show validity in the predicate calculus. Four of these principles are stated below, and a fifth is stated in the next section.

Universal Instantiation

Universal propositions having the form $(x)\phi x$ are true if and only if every individual has the property ϕ. Thus, given $(x)\phi x$ one may infer that any individual has the property ϕ. For example, one may infer ϕa, ϕb, ϕc, etc. One may also infer ϕx, ϕy, ϕz, etc. The only difference in these sets of inferences is that in the former case the symbols a, b, and c are constants which stand for particular individuals, whereas in the latter case the symbols x, y, and z are variables which stand for any given individual. Since in both cases we are deducing that some instance of a universal proposition holds, the rule permitting these inferences is known as **universal instantiation** (U.I.).

The following argument forms illustrate the correct use of U.I.:

$$\frac{(x)Fx}{Fa} \qquad \frac{(x)Fx}{Fy} \qquad \frac{(x)(Fx \supset Gx)}{Fb \supset Gb}$$

$$\frac{(x)(Fx \lor Gy)}{Fz \lor Gy} \qquad \frac{(x)[Fx \cdot (Gx \lor Hx)]}{Fx \cdot (Gx \lor Hx)}$$

Note that every instance of the variable being instantiated has been replaced by instances of a single variable or a single constant. For example in the argument form

$$\frac{(x)(Fx \supset Gx)}{Fb \supset Gb}$$

every instance of x in $Fx \supset Gx$ has been replaced by the constant b. And in the argument form

$$\frac{(x)(Fx \lor Gx)}{Fz \lor Gz}$$

every instance of x in $Fx \lor Gx$ has been replaced by z.

The following argument forms are *invalid* and are *not* instances of U.I.:

$$\frac{(x)(Fx \supset Gx)}{Fb \supset Gx} \qquad \frac{(x)(Fx \lor Gx)}{Fz \lor Gx} \qquad \frac{(x)[Fx \cdot (Gx \lor Hx)]}{Fz \cdot (Gy \lor Hy)}$$

The invalidity of the first form may be seen as follows. Suppose that $(x)(Fx \supset Gx)$ were to represent the proposition 'If anything is a fish, then it has gills' and $Fb \supset Gx$ were to represent the false proposition 'If b is a fish, then some arbitrarily selected individual x has gills'. If that were the case, then an argument having the first form would be invalid because it would have a true premise and a false conclusion. Similar reflection will show that arguments with the second and third forms are also invalid. To avoid this kind of erroneous reasoning, *every* instance of the variable being instantiated must be replaced by instances of a *single* variable or a *single* constant. If we build this restriction into the rule, U.I. may be formulated as follows:

> **From $(x)\phi x$ one may infer either ϕa or ϕy, provided that every x in ϕx is replaced by a corresponding a in ϕa or a corresponding y in ϕy.**

Use of U.I. and *modus ponens* allows us to demonstrate the validity of the argument that served as an example at the beginning of the chapter.

> If anyone is at home, then he will hear us knock.
> Bob is at home.
> _____
> Bob will hear us knock.

(1) $(x)(Hx \supset Kx)$	Kb	
(2) Hb		
(3) $Hb \supset Kb$	1, U.I.	
(4) Kb	2, 3 *M.P.*	

Universal Generalization

If something is true of any individual whatever, then it is true of all individuals. For example, if something is true of any given triangle, then it is true of all triangles. Thus, given expressions such as ϕx, ϕy, ϕz, etc., where x, y, and z stand for any given individual, one may infer a proposition of the form $(x)\phi x$. Since inferences of this type involve generalization from an arbitrarily selected individual to all individuals, the rule which permits them is known as **universal generalization** (U.G.).

The following argument forms illustrate the correct use of U.G.:

$$\frac{Fy}{(x)Fx} \qquad \frac{Fx}{(x)Fx} \qquad \frac{(Fx \lor Gx) \supset Hz}{(x)[(Fx \lor Gx) \supset Hz]}$$

$$\frac{Fx \cdot Ga}{(x)(Fx \cdot Ga)} \qquad \frac{Fz \cdot Gy}{(x)(Fx \cdot Gy)}$$

Note that in each case the expression generalized is a variable and not a constant. Given an expression of the form ϕy, one may validly deduce an expression of the form $(x)\phi x$. But given an expression of the form ϕa, one may *not* validly deduce one of the form $(x)\phi x$. The reason for this is that lower-case letters such as a are constants denoting particular individuals; and from the fact that some particular individual has a certain property, it obviously does not follow that all individuals have that property.

Note also that only instances of one variable have been generalized. For example, in

$$\frac{Fz \cdot Gy}{(x)(Fx \cdot Gy)}$$

only z has been generalized, and in

$$\frac{(Fx \lor Gx) \supset Hz}{(x)[(Fx \lor Gx) \supset Hz]}$$

only x has been generalized. Generalizing instances of two variables at the same time results in invalid arguments. For example, the following form in which both z and x are generalized is invalid:

$$\frac{Fz \cdot Gx}{(x)(Fx \cdot Gx)}$$

The invalidity of this form may be made intuitive by supposing that Fz represents 'z is flat' and Gx represents 'x is green'. If that were the case, then from 'z is flat' and 'x is green' we could deduce the false proposition 'Everything is both flat and green'.

The mistake in this argument is the result of binding two different variables at once. In generalizing from $Fz \cdot Gx$ to $(x)(Fx \cdot Gx)$, we have used the quantifier (x) to bind both z and x. This inference is fallacious because we have no way of ensuring that x and z refer to the same individual. One way to avoid mistakes of this type in using U.G. is to use a different variable from any contained in the premise. For example, if we were to use y

rather than x in generalizing from the above premise so as to obtain

$$\frac{Fz \cdot Gx}{(y)(Fy \cdot Gx)}$$

there would be little likelihood of inadvertently binding two variables. (Although we have previously used only the variable x in writing quantifiers, since variables stand for any individual whatever, any variable may be used in writing a quantifier.)

Since y in ϕy represents a variable rather than a constant, both of the restrictions we have discussed can be built into U.G. by formulating it as follows:

From ϕy one may infer $(x)\phi x$, provided that every y, and only y, in ϕy is replaced by a corresponding x in ϕx.

The following argument form illustrates use of U.I. and U.G. in the same proof.

(1) $(x)(Fx \supset Gx)$	$\lfloor (x)(Fx \supset Hx)$	
(2) $(x)(Gx \supset Hx)$		
(3) $Fy \supset Gy$	1, U.I.	
(4) $Gy \supset Hy$	2, U.I.	
(5) $Fy \supset Hy$	3, 4 H.S.	
(6) $(x)(Fx \supset Hx)$	5, U.G.	

Existential Generalization

A proposition of the form $(\exists x)\phi x$ is true if and only if there is at least one individual with the property ϕ. It follows that given an expression of either the form ϕa or one of the form ϕx, one may infer one of the form $(\exists x)\phi x$. The rule allowing us to draw these inferences is called **existential generalization** (E.G.).

The correct use of E.G. is illustrated by the following argument forms:

$$\frac{Fa}{(\exists x)Fx} \qquad \frac{\sim Gz}{(\exists x)\sim Gx} \qquad \frac{Kd \supset (Md \vee Nd)}{(\exists x)[Kx \supset (Mx \vee Nx)]}$$

$$\frac{Fy \cdot (Gy \cdot Hy)}{(\exists x)[Fx \cdot (Gx \cdot Hx)]} \qquad \frac{Ga \cdot Fb}{(\exists x)(Gx \cdot Fb)}$$

A restriction similar to the second restriction placed on U.G. must also be placed on E.G. Consider the following *invalid* argument form:

$$\frac{Px \cdot Ba}{(\exists x)(Px \cdot Bx)}$$

The invalidity of this argument form may be seen as follows. Suppose that Px represents 'x is purple' and Ba represents 'Abraham Lincoln had a beard'. If we were to allow the inference that this argument form incorporates, then from 'x is purple' and 'Abraham Lincoln had a beard' we could fallaciously deduce that there is something which is both purple and has a beard. A similar mistake occurs in arguments of the form

$$\frac{Px \cdot By}{(\exists x)(Px \cdot Bx)}$$

We can avoid mistakes of this kind if we use E.G. to replace only one constant or one variable at a time. Thus E.G. may be formulated as follows:

> **From ϕa or ϕy one may infer $(\exists x)\phi x$, provided that every a, and only a, in ϕa, or every y, and only y, in ϕy, is replaced by a corresponding x in ϕx.**

The following argument form illustrates use of both U.I. and E.G. in the same proof:

(1) $(x)(Fx \cdot Gx)$ | $(\exists x)Fx$
(2) $Fx \cdot Gx$ 1, U.I.
(3) Fx 2, Simp.
(4) $(\exists x)Fx$ 3, E.G.

Existential Instantiation

Since existentially quantified propositions of the form $(\exists x)\phi x$ are true if and only if there is at least one individual with the property ϕ, it follows that, given an expression of the form $(\exists x)\phi x$, one may infer an expression of the form ϕy.

The following argument forms illustrate the correct use of E.I.:

$$\frac{(\exists x)Gx}{Gy} \qquad \frac{(\exists x)(Gx \supset Fx)}{Gz \supset Fz} \qquad \frac{(\exists x)[Gx \equiv \sim(Fx \vee Hx)]}{Gy \equiv \sim(Fy \vee Hy)}$$

Whenever we use E.I. to infer an expression of the form ϕy from one of the form $(\exists x)\phi x$, y must be a variable and not a constant. From the fact that there is at least one individual having the property ϕ, one can deduce that some individual or other has that property; but from that fact alone one *cannot* deduce that some particular individual has that property. If we were to ignore this restriction, the following *invalid* argument form would be possible:

$$\frac{(\exists x)Bx}{Bn}$$

The invalidity of this form may be seen by supposing that $(\exists x)Bx$ represents 'There exists something which is black' and Bn represents 'Richard Nixon is black'. If this argument form were permitted, then from the true proposition 'There exists something which is black' we could infer the false proposition 'Richard Nixon is black'.

E.I. also cannot be used to deduce ϕy from $(\exists x)\phi x$ if y has a previous free occurrence. If we were to allow such an inference, the following *invalid* proof would be possible:

(1) $(\exists x)Rx$ $(\exists x)(Rx \cdot Sx)$
(2) $(\exists x)Sx$
(3) Ry 1, E.I.
(4) Sy 2, E.I. (invalid)
(5) $Ry \cdot Sy$ 3, 4 Conj.
(6) $(\exists x)(Rx \cdot Sx)$ 5, E.G.

Suppose that $(\exists x)Rx$ represents 'There exists something which is round' and $(\exists x)Sx$ represents 'There exists something which is square'. In that case, step· (3)—that something-or-other is round—follows validly from step (1). And *if* we were to use a different variable, say z, then step (4)— that something-or-other is square—would also follow validly. But using y in step (4) involves the unwarranted assumption that the round something-or-other is the *same* something-or-other which is square. If we were to permit this inference, then from it, conjunction, and E.G. we could deduce the false conclusion that something exists which is both round and square. To avoid this type of erroneous inference, we must not use E.I. to deduce ϕy from $(\exists x)\phi x$ if y has any previous free occurrence.

A third restriction, one similar to the one placed on U.I., must be placed on E.I. In instantiating by E.I., one must replace every instance of the variable being instantiated by occurrences of a single variable. If we were to disregard this restriction, the following *invalid* proof would be possible:

$$\frac{(\exists x)(Sx \cdot Cx)}{Sy \cdot Cx}$$

The invalidity of this argument form may be seen in the following way. Suppose that $(\exists x)(Sx \cdot Cx)$ represents 'There exists something which is both the sun and the center of our solar system', Sy represents 'y is the sun' and Cx represents 'x is the center of our solar system'. Then, from 'There exists something which is both the sun and the center of our solar system', one could deduce 'y is the sun' and 'x is the center of our solar system'. Since it is possible for x and y to refer to different individuals, we have begun with a premise about a single individual and reached a conclusion which might hold of two individuals. To avoid inferences of this type, we must replace every instance of the variable being instantiated by instances of a single variable.

We may now formulate E.I. as follows:

From $(\exists x)\phi x$ one may infer ϕy, provided that every x in ϕx is replaced by a corresponding y in ϕy and y has no previous free occurrence.

Additional Restrictions

When both E.I. and U.G. are used in the same proof, an additional restriction must be imposed. This restriction might be worded so as to apply to either E.I. or U.G. *One may not universally generalize on a variable in a line inferred by E.I.* If this restriction were ignored, the following *invalid* proof would be possible:

$$
\begin{array}{lll}
(1) & (\exists x)Fx & \quad\mid (x)Fx \\
(2) & Fy & 1, \text{E.I.} \\
(3) & (x)Fx & 2, \text{U.G. (invalid)}
\end{array}
$$

Suppose that $(\exists x)Fx$ represents 'There is something which is capable of flying' and $(x)Fx$ represents 'Everything is capable of flying'. If we were to allow this inference, then, from 'There is something which is capable of flying', we could deduce 'Everything is capable of flying'. To block this inference we must not apply U.G. to a variable in a line inferred by E.I.

Finally, the restriction must be added that *all four rules apply only to whole lines in proofs.* They function in this respect like rules of inference such as *modus ponens* rather than like equivalences such as D.M. For example, in the argument form

$$
\begin{array}{lll}
(1) & (\exists x)Px \cdot Ba & \quad\mid Px \\
(2) & (\exists x)Px & 1, \text{Simp.} \\
(3) & Px & 2, \text{E.I.}
\end{array}
$$

E.I. could not have been used on (1) because the scope of the quantifier does not include the entire expression. One may use E.I. on (2), however, because the scope of the quantifier does extend to the entire expression.

The following proof is invalid for similar reasons:

(1) $(x)(Fx \supset Hx)$
(2) $(x)(Hx \supset Ga)$
(3) $Fx \supset Hx$ 1, U.I.
(4) $Hx \supset Ga$ 2, U.I.
(5) $Fx \supset Ga$ 3, 4 H.S.
(6) $(x)Fx \supset Ga$ 5, U.G. (invalid)

The mistake in this proof occurs at step (6). This inference is invalid because the scope of the quantifier includes only the antecedent, not the whole line. A legitimate use of U.G. from (5) to (6) would yield $(x)(Fx \supset Ga)$.

The following argument form illustrates the correct use of all four rules in the same proof. Note that since a variable instantiated by E.I. cannot have a previous free occurrence, E.I. has been used *before* U.I. Note also that the second premise cannot be instantiated because it does not contain a quantifier whose scope extends over the entire premise.

(1) $(x)(Fx \supset Gx)$ $(y) \sim Ky$
(2) $(\exists x)(Gx \vee Hb) \supset \sim Ja$
(3) $(\exists x)Fx$
(4) $Ja \vee (y)My$
(5) $(x)(Mx \supset \sim Kx)$
(6) Fx 3, E.I.
(7) $Fx \supset Gx$ 1, U.I.
(8) Gx 6, 7 *M.P.*
(9) $Gx \vee Hb$ 8, Add.
(10) $(\exists x)(Gx \vee Hb)$ 9, E.G.
(11) $\sim Ja$ 2, 10 *M.P.*
(12) $(y)My$ 4, 11 D.S.
(13) My 12, U.I.
(14) $My \supset \sim Ky$ 5, U.I.
(15) $\sim Ky$ 13, 14 *M.P.*
(16) $(y) \sim Ky$ 15, U.G.

EXERCISES

III

In each of the following invalid proofs, mark each step that is an illegitimate inference and explain why the inference is illegitimate:

1. (1) $(\exists x)(Fx \cdot Gx)$ | Jy
    (2) $(x)(Fx \supset Jx)$
    (3) $Fx \supset Jy$ 2, U.I.
    (4) $Fx \cdot Gx$ 1, E.I.
    (5) Fx 4, Simp.
    (6) Jy 3, 5 *M.P.*

2. (1) $(\exists x)(Fx \lor Gx)$ | $(x)Fx$
    (2) $\sim Ga$
    (3) $Fa \lor Ga$ 1, E.I.
    (4) Fa 2, 3 D.S.
    (5) $(x)Fx$ 4, U.G.

3. (1) $(\exists x)(Fx \cdot Gx)$ | $(x)(Hx \cdot Ix)$
    (2) $(x)(Gx \supset Hx)$
    (3) $(y)Iy$
    (4) $Fx \cdot Gy$ 1, E.I.
    (5) $Gy \supset Hy$ 2, U.I.
    (6) Gy 4, Simp.
    (7) Hy 5, 6 *M.P.*
    (8) Iz 3, U.I.
    (9) $Hy \cdot Iz$ 7, 8 Conj.
  (10) $(x)(Hx \cdot Ix)$ 9, U.G.

4. (1) $Pt \lor Qt$ | $\sim Qt$
    (2) $(\exists x)(\sim Qx \lor \sim Qb)$
    (3) $(x)Qx$
    (4) $\sim Qt \lor \sim Qb$ 2, E.I.
    (5) Qb 3, U.I.
    (6) $\sim Qt$ 4, 5 D.S.

5. (1) $(\exists x)Px$ | $(y)Sy$
    (2) $Pb \supset (\exists y)(Ry \lor Sy)$
    (3) $(y)(\sim Ry \cdot \sim Sb)$
    (4) Pb 1, E.I.
    (5) $(\exists y)(Ry \lor Sy)$ 2, 4 *M.P.*
    (6) $\sim Ry \cdot \sim Sy$ 3, U.I.
    (7) $Ry \lor Sy$ 5, E.I.
    (8) $\sim Ry$ 6, Simp.
    (9) Sy 7, 8 D.S.
  (10) $(y)Sy$ 9, U.G.

6. (1) $(x)(\sim Px \lor Tx)$ | $(x)Tx$
    (2) $(\exists y)(Py \cdot Sy)$
    (3) $(x)(Px \supset Tx)$ 1, M.I.
    (4) $Px \supset Tx$ 3, U.I.
    (5) $Px \cdot Sx$ 2, E.I.
    (6) Px 5, Simp.
    (7) Tx 4, 6 *M.P.*
    (8) $(x)Tx$ 7, U.G.

7. (1) $(\exists x)Fx \cdot Ga$ $\mid (\exists x)(Gx \cdot Hx)$
    (2) $Hc \cdot Mc$
    (3) $Fx \cdot Ga$ 1, E.I.
    (4) Hc 2, Simp.
    (5) Ga 3, Simp.
    (6) $Ga \cdot Hc$ 4, 5 Conj.
    (7) $(\exists x)(Gx \cdot Hx)$ 6, E.G.

8. (1) $(x)[(Fx \vee Bx) \supset Gx]$ $\mid (x) \sim Fx$
    (2) $\sim Gd$
    (3) $(Fd \vee Bd) \supset Gd$ 1, U.I.
    (4) $\sim (Fd \vee Bd)$ 2, 3 M.T.
    (5) $\sim Fd \cdot \sim Bd$ 4, D.M.
    (6) $\sim Fd$ 5, Simp.
    (7) $(x) \sim Fx$ 6, U.G.

9. (1) $(\exists x)(Fx \cdot Cx)$ $\mid (\exists x)(Fx \cdot Rx)$
    (2) $(x)Cx \supset Ry$
    (3) $Fx \cdot Cx$ 1, E.I.
    (4) Cx 3, Simp.
    (5) $Cx \supset Ry$ 2, U.I.
    (6) Ry 4, 5 M.P.
    (7) Fx 3, Simp.
    (8) $Fx \cdot Ry$ 6, 7 Conj.
    (9) $(\exists x)(Fx \cdot Rx)$ 8, E.G.

10. (1) $Ca \supset Jb$ $\mid Ca \supset (x)Fx$
    (2) $(y)(Jy \supset Ny)$
    (3) $(x)(Nb \supset Fx)$
    (4) $Jb \supset Nb$ 2, U.I.
    (5) $Ca \supset Nb$ 1, 4 H.S.
    (6) $Nb \supset Fx$ 3, U.I.
    (7) $Ca \supset Fx$ 5, 6 H.S.
    (8) $Ca \supset (x)Fx$ 7, U.G.

11. (1) $(x)(Fx \cdot Gy)$ $\mid (x)(Ax \cdot By)$
    (2) $(x)(Fx \cdot Gx) \supset (Ha \cdot Ia)$
    (3) $(\exists x)(Hx \cdot Ia) \supset Ja$
    (4) $Ja \supset (\exists x)(Av \cdot Bx)$
    (5) $Fx \cdot Gy$ 1, U.I.
    (6) $(x)(Fx \cdot Gx)$ 5, U.G.
    (7) $Ha \cdot Ia$ 2, 6 M.P.
    (8) $(\exists x)(Hx \cdot Ia)$ 7, E.G.
    (9) Ja 3, 8 M.P.
    (10) $(\exists x)(Ax \cdot Bx)$ 4, 9 M.P.
    (11) $Ax \cdot By$ 10, E.I.
    (12) $(x)(Ax \cdot By)$ 11, U.G.

12. (1) $(x)(Fx \lor Wx)$ | $(\exists x)(Kx \cdot Pa)$
     (2) $(Fa \lor Wb) \supset (x)Hx$
     (3) $(\exists y)Jy \cdot Pa$
     (4) $(x)(Hx \cdot Jx) \supset Ka$
     (5) $Fa \lor Wb$ 1, U.I.
     (6) $(x)Hx$ 2, 5 M.P.
     (7) $(\exists y)Jy$ 3, Simp.
     (8) Jy 7, E.I.
     (9) Hx 6, U.I.
    (10) $Hx \cdot Jy$ 8, 9 Conj.
    (11) $(x)(Hx \cdot Jx)$ 10, U.G.
    (12) Ka 4, 11 M.P.
    (13) Pa 3, Simp.
    (14) $Ka \cdot Pa$ 12, 13 Conj.
    (15) $(\exists x)(Kx \cdot Pa)$ 14, E.G.

IV

Construct proofs for each of the following argument forms:

1. (1) $(x)(Hx \lor Jx)$ | Ja
    (2) $\sim Ha$

2. (1) $(x)(Ax \supset Bx)$ | $(x) \sim Ax$
    (2) $(x)(Bx \supset Cx)$
    (3) $(x) \sim Cx$

3. (1) $(\exists x)(Fx \cdot \sim Gx)$ | $(\exists x) \sim Jx$
    (2) $(x)(Jx \supset Gx)$

4. (1) $(x)[(\sim Ax \cdot Bx) \lor Cx]$ | $(x)(Ax \supset Cx)$

5. (1) $(\exists x)[Bx \cdot (Cx \lor Dx)]$ | $(\exists x)(Bx \cdot Dx)$
    (2) $(x) \sim Cx$

6. (1) $(x)[(Px \cdot Tx) \supset \sim Jx]$ | $\sim Pa$
    (2) $Ta \cdot Ja$

7. (1) $(x)\{Dx \supset [Fx \supset (Gx \cdot Hx)]\}$ | $(\exists x)(Fx \supset Hx)$
    (2) $(\exists x)Dx$

8. (1) $(x)[Ax \supset (Bx \cdot Lx)]$ | $(x)\{Ax \supset [Kx \supset (Lx \lor Mx)]\}$

9. (1) $(\exists x) \sim (Px \lor Qx)$ | $(\exists x) \sim (Rx \cdot Sx)$
    (2) $(x)[(Rx \equiv Sx) \supset Px]$

10. (1) $(x)[(Lx \lor Nx) \supset Kx]$ | $(x)(Sx \cdot Tx)$
     (2) $(x)(\sim Kx \cdot Mx)$
     (3) $(x)\{\sim Lx \supset [\sim Nx \supset (Sx \cdot Tx)]\}$

V

Symbolize the following arguments using the suggested notation and give a formal proof of their validity:

1. All humans are mortal. Socrates is a human. Therefore, Socrates is mortal. (*Hx*, *Mx*, *s*)

2. Anyone who can beat this full house will win the pot. And anyone who wins the pot will take my ranch. So, anyone who can beat this full house will take my ranch. (*Bx*, *Wx*, *Rx*)

3. Brazilian vessels must pay a tariff. However, there are some vessels which do not pay a tariff. Therefore, some of the vessels are not Brazilian vessels. (*Bx*, *Vx*, *Tx*)

4. Some rubber plants grow well with little water. Whatever grows well with little water will be suitable for the experiment. But nothing that either has thick leaves or a high chlorophyl content will be suitable for the experiment. All rubber plants have thick leaves and a high chlorophyl content. So, some rubber plants will not be suitable for the experiment. (*Rx*, *Gx*, *Sx*, *Tx*, *Hx*)

5. Anything is a koala bear if and only if it eats eucalyptus leaves. There is something which is either a koala bear or eats eucalyptus leaves. If anything is a koala bear and eats eucalyptus leaves, then it lives in Australia. Therefore there is something that lives in Australia. (*Kx*, *Ex*, *Ax*)

6. All proponents of Social Darwinism were either intellectuals or wealthy. Those proponents of Social Darwinism who were intellectuals saw the theory as a key to understanding the structure of society. Those proponents of Social Darwinism who were wealthy used the theory as a justification for their own wealth. All those who used the theory as a justification for their own wealth were sincere in their philanthropic endeavors. Anyone who either uses the theory to justify his own wealth and is sincere in his philanthropic endeavors or who operates as though the theory were true does see the theory as a key to understanding the structure of society. Andrew Carnegie was both wealthy and a proponent of Social Darwinism. Therefore, Carnegie both used the theory as a justification for his wealth and saw it as a key to understanding the structure of society; and he was sincere in his philanthropic endeavors. (*Px*, *Ix*, *Wx*, *Kx*, *Jx*, *Sx*, *Ox*, *c*)

7. No camel can go through the eye of a needle. Anyone who can go through the eye of a needle can get into heaven easily. No rich man can get into heaven easily. Therefore, if anything goes through the eye of a needle, it is neither a camel nor a rich man. (*Cx*, *Nx*, *Hx*, *Rx*)

8. If anyone is either obnoxious or disliked, then he will have difficulty securing approval of legislation he favors. Therefore, if anyone is a senator, then if he is both relentless and disliked, he will have difficulty securing approval of legislation he favors. (*Ox*, *Lx*, *Dx*, *Sx*, *Rx*)

9. If a person has a real or fanciful character defect, then he will develop an inferiority complex. If anyone develops an inferiority complex, he will either become obsequious and ingratiating or he will have a tyrannical personality. If anyone has a tyrannical personality then he will not have many friends. Were anyone to have a severely traumatic childhood experience, then he would have a real

character defect. If a person were named 'Foster Phobia', then he would have had a severely traumatic childhood experience. Foster Phobia is named 'Foster Phobia', and he is neither obsequious nor ingratiating. Therefore, Foster Phobia does not have very many friends. $(Rx, Fx, Dx, Ox, Ix, Tx, Mx, Sx, Nx, p)$

10. Every monarch must follow the advice of Machiavelli. If a monarch follows the advice of Machiavelli, then he will be both feared and loved. If any monarch is loved, then his subjects will be bound to him by a sense of obligation. And if any monarch is feared, then his subjects will be bound to him by the threat of punishment. If anyone is a monarch whose subjects are bound to him by both a sense of obligation and the threat of punishment, then if he is not hated he must be benevolent. Any monarch who is benevolent will be loved. Therefore, if anyone is a monarch, then if he is not hated he will be loved. $(Mx, Ax, Fx, Lx, Ox, Tx, Hx, Bx)$

QUANTIFIER NEGATION

Propositions having the forms $(x)\phi x$ and $(\exists x) \sim \phi x$ are contradictories, that is, they are related such that they always have opposite truth values. For example, if 'Everything is destructible' is true (false), then 'There is at least one thing which is not destructible' is false (true); and if 'There is at least one thing which is not destructible' is true (false) then 'Everything is destructible' is false (true). Since propositions of the form $(x)\phi x$ and $(\exists x) \sim \phi x$ always have opposite truth values, it follows that the negation of one is equivalent to the other. This can be expressed symbolically as

$$\sim(x)\phi x \equiv (\exists x) \sim \phi x$$
$$\sim(\exists x) \sim \phi x \equiv (x)\phi x$$

Propositions having the forms $(x) \sim \phi x$ and $(\exists x)\phi x$ are also contradictories. Hence by the same reasoning as above, the following equivalences hold:

$$\sim(x) \sim \phi x \equiv (\exists x)\phi x$$
$$\sim(\exists x)\phi x \equiv (x) \sim \phi x$$

These four equivalences may be used as rules of replacement in the predicate calculus and are called **quantifier negation** (Q.N.).

Q.N. allows us to rewrite universally quantified propositions as existentially quantified and vice versa. Taken in conjunction with equivalences such as De Morgan's Theorem and Material Implication, Q.N. allows us to show that alternative symbolizations of propositions are equivalent. For example, the proposition 'Not all dragons breathe fire' can be symbolized as either $\sim(x)(Dx \supset Bx)$ or $(\exists x)(Dx \cdot \sim Bx)$. That these two expressions are equivalent can be shown as follows:

$$
\begin{array}{ll}
(1) \sim(x)(Dx \supset Bx) & \lvert\, (\exists x)(Dx \,\cdot\, \sim Bx) \\
\hline
(2) (\exists x)\sim(Dx \supset Bx) & 1, \text{Q.N.} \\
(3) (\exists x)\sim(\sim Dx \lor Bx) & 2, \text{M.I.} \\
(4) (\exists x)(Dx \,\cdot\, \sim Bx) & 3, \text{D.M.}
\end{array}
$$

$$
\begin{array}{ll}
(1) (\exists x)(Dx \,\cdot\, \sim Bx) & \lvert\, \sim(x)(Dx \supset Bx) \\
\hline
(2) \sim(x)\sim(Dx \,\cdot\, \sim Bx) & 1, \text{Q.N.} \\
(3) \sim(x)(\sim Dx \lor Bx) & 2, \text{D.M.} \\
(4) \sim(x)(Dx \supset Bx) & 3, \text{M.I.}
\end{array}
$$

Since we have demonstrated that if $\sim(x)(Dx \supset Bx)$ is assumed, then $(\exists x)(Dx \,\cdot\, \sim Bx)$ can be deduced, and if $(\exists x)(Dx \,\cdot\, \sim Bx)$ is assumed then $\sim(x)(Dx \supset Bx)$ can be deduced, it follows that $\sim(x)(Dx \supset Bx) \equiv (\exists x)(Dx \,\cdot\, \sim Bx)$.

EXERCISES

VI

Symbolize the following propositions using a universal quantifier; then write an equivalent expression using an existential quantifier:

1. Everything changes. (Cx)
2. Nothing changes. (Cx)
3. All dogs have fleas. (Dx, Fx)
4. A boy scout is trustworthy. (Bx, Tx)
5. Not all of the players were in the fight. (Px, Fx)
6. Not any of the councilmen were present. (Cx, Px)

Symbolize the following propositions using an existential quantifier; then write an equivalent expression using a universal quantifier:

1. There are no utopias. (Ux)
2. Some things are not blue. (Bx)
3. A lady is present. (Lx, Px)
4. None of the passengers survived. (Px, Sx)
5. Some of the errors were not detected. (Ex, Dx)

VII

Construct proofs for each of the following:

1. $(x)(Fx \supset \sim Gx)$ $\quad\lvert\, \sim(\exists x)(Fx \,\cdot\, Gx)$

2. $\sim (x)Fx$ $\underline{\,(\exists x)(Fx \supset Gx)}$

3. (1) $(x)[(Fx \lor Gx) \supset Hx]$ $\underline{\,(\exists z)Hz}$
   (2) $\sim (y)(Jy \lor \sim Fy)$

4. (1) $\sim (\exists x)[Hx \cdot (\sim Rx \lor \sim Sx)]$ $\underline{\,\sim (x)\sim (Hx \supset Wx)}$
   (2) $\sim (x)Rx$

5. (1) $\sim (x)(Gx \supset Jx)$ $\underline{\,(\exists y)(\sim Fy \lor Jy)}$
   (2) $\sim (y)[Fy \cdot (Gy \lor Hy)]$
   (3) $\sim (\exists x)[(Fx \cdot \sim Gx) \cdot \sim Jx]$

6. If anyone stole the Marobe Diamond from the museum and got it out of the country, then he will still have difficulty getting cash for it. Therefore, it is not the case that there is someone who stole the Marobe Diamond from the museum, and who got it out of the country and is not having difficulty getting cash for it. (Sx, Cx, Dx)

7. All prime ministers of England live at Number 10, Downing Street. It is not the case that there is a person who both lives at Number 10, Downing Street, and is a brickmason and who does not like cigars. If anyone is a member of the brickmason's union, then he is a brickmason. Winston Churchill was both prime minister of England and a member of the brickmason's union. Therefore, Churchill liked cigars. (Px, Lx, Bx, Cx, Ux, c)

8. It is false that there exists a bank clerk who is not timid. If anyone is timid, then he is not going to attempt to stop a holdup. Were anyone a good citizen and present when a holdup occurred, then he would attempt to stop it. If anyone were in the 12th Street Bank at 10:00 a.m. yesterday, then he was present when a bank holdup occurred. Johnson was in the 12th Street Bank at 10:00 a.m. yesterday. Therefore, there is someone who is not both a good citizen and a bank clerk. $(Bx, Tx, Ax, Gx, Px, Yx, j)$

9. It is not true of everyone that he is either offering sincere social criticism or well-researched alternative solutions to our problems, or that he is not offering sincere social criticism and is capitalizing on the political mistakes of others. However, there are individuals who are not politically ambitious, and who are conscientious and offer well-researched alternative solutions to our problems. If anyone wishes to become president, he must capitalize on the political mistakes of others. Therefore, it is not true that everyone wishes to become president. (Sx, Wx, Mx, Px, Cx, Bx)

10. Nothing exists which is both a great work of art and is unfinished. Of course, it is false that all things are both finished and great works of art. If a work of art is not great, then it will be purchased by a museum if and only if it is typical of some school of painting. It is not the case that there is a work of art which both will be purchased by a museum if and only if it is typical of some school of painting and which has not been both widely discussed by art critics and is available at a reasonable price. Therefore, there are works of art which have been both widely discussed by art critics and are available at a reasonable price. (Gx, Fx, Px, Tx, Wx, Ax)

INDIRECT AND CONDITIONAL PROOF

Indirect and conditional proof may also be used in the predicate calculus. Indirect proof is used in precisely the same manner as in the propositional calculus. One assumes the denial of the conclusion and attempts to deduce a contradiction.

(1)	$(x)[Dx \supset (Lx \cdot Mx)]$	$\lfloor (\exists x) \sim Dx$
(2)	$(y)(My \supset \sim Dy)$	
(3)	$\sim(\exists x) \sim Dx$	I.P.
(4)	$(x)Dx$	3, Q.N.
(5)	Dx	4, U.I.
(6)	$Dx \supset (Lx \cdot Mx)$	1, U.I.
(7)	$Lx \cdot Mx$	5, 6 $M.P.$
(8)	Mx	7, Simp.
(9)	$Mx \supset \sim Dx$	2, U.I.
(10)	$\sim Dx$	8, 9 $M.P.$
(11)	$Dx \cdot \sim Dx$	5, 10 Conj.

In using conditional proof in the predicate calculus, it is often useful to assume an unquantified expression. For example

(1)	$(x)(Fx \supset Gx)$	$\lfloor (x)[Fx \supset (Gx \cdot Hx)]$
(2)	$(x)(Gx \supset Hx)$	
(3)	$\lvert\ Fx$	C.P.
(4)	$\lvert\ Fx \supset Gx$	1, U.I.
(5)	$\lvert\ Gx$	3, 4 $M.P'$
(6)	$\lvert\ Gx \supset Hx$	2, U.I.
(7)	$\lvert\ Hx$	5, 6 $M.P.$
(8)	$\lvert\ Gx \cdot Hx$	5, 7 Conj.
(9)	$Fx \supset (Gx \cdot Hx)$	3–8 C.P.
(10)	$(x)[Fx \supset (Gx \cdot Hx)]$	9 U.G.

The expression $Fx \supset (Gx \cdot Hx)$ is established in step (9), and then U.G. is applied to obtain the desired conclusion.

An additional restriction must be placed on U.G. when indirect and conditional proof is used. An expression of the form $(x)\phi x$ cannot be inferred from one of the form ϕy, if the inference takes place within the scope of an indirect or conditional proof based on an assumption in which y is free.

If we were to ignore this restriction, the following *invalid* proof would be possible:

$$\begin{array}{ll} & \boxed{Fy \supset (x)Fx} \\ (1) \quad | \ Fy & \text{C.P.} \\ (2) \quad | \ (x)Fx & \text{1, U.G.} \\ (3) \ Fy \supset (x)Fx & \text{1–2 C.P.} \end{array}$$

Suppose that F stands for the property, *is fat*. Then from the assertion that something-or-other is fat, we would have inferred that if something-or-other is fat, then everything is fat.

EXERCISES

VIII

Construct conditional proofs for argument forms 7 and 8 of exercise IV, page 135, arguments 8 and 10 of exercise V, pages 136–137, and argument form 5 of exercise VII, page 139.

Construct indirect proofs for argument forms 1 and 7 of exercise IV, page 135, arguments 3 and 5 of exercise V, page 136, and argument 6 of exercise VII, page 139.

INVALIDITY

In this section we show how the method of partial truth tables, which was used in chapter III to show the invalidity of arguments in the propositional calculus, can be modified to show the invalidity of arguments in the predicate calculus.

Since universal propositions make assertions about *all* individuals, it is not possible to examine everything to which they refer. Suppose, however, that there were only one individual in the universe. Let us call this individual a. If this were the case, then a proposition of the form $(x)(Px \supset Qx)$ would be equivalent to one of the form $Pa \supset Qa$. Similarly, a proposition of the form $(x)(\sim Px \lor \sim Rx)$ would be equivalent to one of the form $\sim Pa \lor \sim Ra$. Now, consider the argument

$$\begin{array}{ll} (x)(Px \supset Qx) & \boxed{(x)(Qx \lor Rx)} \\ (x)(\sim Px \lor \sim Rx) \end{array}$$

In our one-member universe, this argument would be equivalent to

$$\begin{array}{ll} Pa \supset Qa & \boxed{Qa \lor Ra} \\ \sim Pa \lor \sim Ra \end{array}$$

Suppose that we proceed as we did in the propositional calculus by applying a partial truth table to this argument. To make the conclusion false we
must assign both disjuncts the value, false. This assignment makes both
premises true, the first because it is a conditional with a false antecedent,
the second because it is a disjunction with a true disjunct.

$$
\begin{array}{ccc}
Pa \supset Qa & \sim Pa \lor \sim Ra & \left| \; Qa \lor Ra \right. \\
\text{F} \quad \text{F} & \text{T} \qquad \text{T} & \text{F} \quad \text{F} \\
\text{T} & \text{T} & \text{F}
\end{array}
$$

Since these assignments show that it is possible for the premises to be true
and the conclusion false, this argument is invalid in a one-member universe.

Suppose, next, that we wish to show that the following argument is
invalid:

$$
\begin{array}{ll}
(x)(Px \supset Qx) & \left| \; (x)(Px \supset \sim Qx) \right. \\
(\exists x)(Qx \cdot Rx) & \\
(\exists x)(\sim Qx \lor \sim Rx) &
\end{array}
$$

Again, we assume a one-member universe, and call that member a. In this
one-member universe, the above argument is equivalent to

$$
\begin{array}{ll}
Pa \supset Qa & \left| \; Pa \supset \sim Qa \right. \\
Qa \cdot Ra & \\
\sim Qa \lor \sim Ra &
\end{array}
$$

It is impossible to assign values so as to make the premises of this argument
true and its conclusion false. If this situation were to occur in the propositional calculus, we could conclude that the argument was valid. But in the
present case we must take further account of the fact that the argument
contains quantified expressions. We do this by assuming another hypothetical universe, one containing only two members, a and b.

The first premise of the argument contains a universal quantifier, so it
makes an assertion about everything in the universe. Since a and b are
everything in the universe we are now considering, the first premise asserts

$$
(Pa \supset Qa) \cdot (Pb \supset Qb)
$$

The second and third premises contain existential quantifiers, so they only
make assertions about at least one individual. Since the universe we are
considering contains two and only two members, a and b, the second and
third premises must assert something about either a or b. Thus the second
premise is equivalent to

$$
(Qa \cdot Ra) \lor (Qb \cdot Rb)
$$

and the third is equivalent to

$$(\sim Qa \lor \sim Ra) \lor (\sim Qb \lor \sim Rb)$$

Finally, the conclusion is equivalent to

$$(Pa \supset \sim Qa) \cdot (Pb \supset \sim Qb)$$

We can now construct a partial truth table for this argument which shows it to be invalid in a two-member universe.

$$(Pa \supset Qa) \cdot (Pb \supset Qb)$$
    T   T   F
       T   T
          T

$$(Qa \cdot Ra) \lor (Qb \cdot Rb)$$
    T   T   F
       T   F
             T

$$(\sim Qa \lor \sim Ra) \lor (\sim Qb \lor \sim Rb)$$
    F   F   T
       F   T
          T

$$(Pa \supset \sim Qa) \cdot (Pb \supset \sim Qb)$$
    T   F   T
       F   T
          F

If we had been unable to show this argument to be invalid in a two-member universe, we would have had to consider a three-member universe. And if we had been unable to show it invalid in a three-member universe, we would have had to consider a four-member universe, and so forth.

At this point a question arises about how many possible universes one has to consider in order to determine whether an argument is valid. The answer is that before one can be certain by this method that an argument is valid, one has to show that an argument containing n number of predicates is valid for all universes up to and including those which contain 2^n members. However, as a rule it is not necessary to consider this many possibilities. For if one has shown that an argument is valid for several possible universes, one can often see that it will also be valid for more extensive universes.

EXERCISES

IX

Use partial truth tables to determine whether the following argument forms are valid or invalid. The argument forms have been selected so that if they are invalid, their invalidity can be shown in a universe containing no more than three members.

1. (1) $(x)[Fx \supset (Gx \supset Hx)]$ $(\exists x)Hx$
     (2) $(\exists x)Gx$

2. (1) $(\exists x)(Fx \lor Gx)$ $\lfloor (\exists x)(\sim Fx \lor \sim Gx)$
    (2) $(\exists x)[(\sim Fx \equiv Gx) \cdot (Fx \equiv \sim Gx)]$

3. (1) $(\exists y)[(Py \lor Qy) \cdot Ry]$ $\lfloor (x)(Px \supset Rx)$
    (2) $(x)[(Px \cdot Qx) \supset Sx]$

4. (1) $(x)(Px \supset Rx)$ $\lfloor (\exists x)(Qx \cdot \sim Px)$
    (2) $(\exists x)(\sim Rx \cdot Qx)$

5. (1) $(\exists x)(Px \cdot Qx)$ $\lfloor (x)(Rx \supset Px)$
    (2) $(\exists x)(Px \cdot \sim Qx)$

6. (1) $(x)[Px \supset (Sx \supset Tx)]$ $\lfloor (x)(Px \supset Wx)$
    (2) $(\exists x)[(Rx \cdot Tx) \lor Sx]$
    (3) $(x)[Sx \supset (Ux \cdot Wx)]$
    (4) $(x)(Px \supset Ux)$

7. (1) $(x)[(Px \lor Qx) \supset Rx]$ $\lfloor (\exists x)(Px \cdot \sim Tx)$
    (2) $(y)[Ry \supset \sim(Sy \cdot Ty)]$
    (3) $(\exists x)[Qx \cdot (Sx \cdot \sim Ux)]$
    (4) $(\exists y)(Py \cdot Uy)$

8. (1) $(x)[(Px \lor Qx) \supset Rx]$ $\lfloor (\exists x)(Px \cdot Tx)$
    (2) $(y)[Ry \supset \sim(Sy \lor Ty)]$
    (3) $(\exists x)[Qx \cdot (Sx \cdot \sim Ux)]$
    (4) $(\exists y)(Py \cdot Uy)$

9. (1) $(x)[Sx \supset (Tx \lor Rx)]$ $\lfloor (\exists y)[(Py \cdot Sy) \supset Ry]$
    (2) $(\exists y)[Ty \supset (Ky \cdot Ay)]$
    (3) $(\exists y)[Ky \supset (Py \lor Zy)]$
    (4) $(\exists x)[(Sx \cdot Ax) \supset (Tx \supset Rx)]$

10. (1) $(x)[Px \supset (Fx \lor Gx)]$ $\lfloor (\exists x)\sim Rx$
    (2) $(x)\{Gx \supset [Hx \supset (Ix \equiv Jx)]\}$
    (3) $(x)[Px \lor (Hx \cdot Ix)]$
    (4) $(\exists x)Ix$
    (5) $(x)[Rx \supset (Px \cdot Hx)]$

MULTIPLE QUANTIFICATION

All of the propositions symbolized in this chapter have been symbolized using a single quantifier. However, more than one, or **multiple quantifiers,** may be needed to symbolize propositions adequately. For example, the proposition 'Everyone has a father' may be symbolized as $(x)(\exists y)Fyx$. This may be read as 'Given any x, there exists a y such that y is the father of x'. In addition to having more than one quantifier, this expression differs from those previously considered because it contains a two-place predicate Fyx. A **two-place predicate** is one which indicates a relation between two individuals. Three-place predicates, four-place predicates, etc., may also be needed to symbolize propositions adequately. If multiple quantifiers and many-place predicates are added to the predicate calculus, then the rules of inference which we have introduced require other restrictions to ensure that all valid, and only valid, inferences are permitted. Discussion of multiple quantification can be found in the suggested readings for this chapter.

SUGGESTED READINGS

CHURCH, ALONZO, *Introduction to Mathematical Logic*. Vol. I. Princeton, N. J.: Princeton University Press, 1956.

COPI, IRVING M., *Symbolic Logic*. 4th ed. New York: Macmillan, 1973.

KAHANE, HOWARD, *Logic and Philosophy*. 2nd ed. Belmont, Calif.: Wadsworth, 1973.

QUINE, W. V., *Methods of Logic*. 3rd ed. New York: Holt, Rinehart and Winston, Inc., 1972.

9

TRADITIONAL LOGIC

The propositional and predicate logic discussed in the previous chapters was developed primarily in the late nineteenth and early twentieth centuries and is often called "symbolic," or "modern," logic. However, logic has been studied for over two thousand years, ever since the time of Aristotle. The logic developed during this long period is known as "Aristotelian" or "traditional" logic. Modern logic is not totally different in kind from its predecessor, but is an extension and development of traditional logic. Hence, all the arguments which can be shown to be valid in traditional logic can also be shown to be valid in modern logic. But since modern logic is an extension of traditional logic, there are some arguments which can be shown to be valid in modern logic which cannot be shown to be valid in traditional logic. Nevertheless, traditional logic is worth studying both for its historical importance and because the symbolic forms it employs are more similar to ordinary language expressions and sometimes provide a more convenient method of analyzing arguments in ordinary language.

CATEGORICAL PROPOSITIONS

Traditional logicians interpret all propositions as **categorical,** i.e., as asserting that a relation of inclusion or exclusion holds between two classes.* Only four types of propositions are recognized and all other propositions must be translated into one of these types. A standard way

*The word 'categorical' also conveys the idea of holding without exception or qualification.

146

of writing the four types of propositions is also adopted. Only propositions that have one of the following forms are said to be in **standard form:**

> *All S is P*
> *No S is P*
> *Some S is P*
> *Some S is not P*

Analysis of Categorical Propositions

The first class term of a categorical proposition, represented above by the letter *S*, is known as the **subject term.** The second class term, represented above by the letter *P*, is known as the **predicate term.** The word 'is', which is used to connect the subject and predicate terms, is known as the **copula.** The words 'all', 'no', and 'some' indicate the quantity or number (all or part) of the members of the subject class referred to, and are called **quanti-fiers.** Categorical propositions are also said to be **affirmative or negative in quality** depending upon whether they assert a relation of inclusion or exclusion.

The Four Basic Types of Categorical Propositions

Because they assert that the subject class is totally included within the predicate class, propositions of the form *All S is P* are called **universal affirmatives.** Similarly, propositions of the form *No S is P*, which assert that the subject class is totally excluded from the predicate class, are called **universal negatives.** Propositions of the form *Some S is P,* which assert that the subject class is partially included within the predicate class, are called **particular affirmatives.** And propositions of the form *Some S is not P,* which assert that the subject class is partially excluded from the predi-cate class, are called **particular negatives.** To avoid constant use of the cumbersome expressions 'universal affirmative', 'universal negative', 'partic-ular affirmative', and 'particular negative', traditional logicians also refer to propositions with these forms as **A, E, I,** and **O** propositions, respectively. (Use of these letters is said to come from the Latin words *AFFIRMO* and *NEGO* which mean 'I affirm' and 'I deny'.)

Translating Categorical Propositions Into Standard Form

Copulas: Categorical propositions may be expressed in a variety of ways in ordinary language. For instance, not only the word 'is' but also such words as 'are', 'was', 'were', 'has', and 'have' may be used as copulas. And in some cases the copula may be omitted entirely. The propositions listed below and their translation into standard form illustrate these points. Note that regardless of the tense of the English verb, the word 'is' is used in stating propositions in standard form.

All socialists are pacifists.	*All S is P*
No freshman was a member of the glee club.	*No F is M*
Some dinosaurs were twenty feet tall.	*Some D is T*
No aardvark has a pouch.	*No A is P*
All kangaroos have pouches.	*All K is P*
All babies cry a great deal.	*All B is C*
Some birds do not fly south for the winter.	*Some B is not F*
Some birds will spend the winter in the north.	*Some B is S*
All who live by the sword shall die by the sword.	*All L is D*

The meaning of most of the symbols used to symbolize the subject and predicate terms above should be apparent. For example, in the first proposition *S* stands for the class *socialists* and *P* stands for the class *pacifists*. However, the meaning of some of the symbols may not be apparent. Consider the last proposition. Since the classes referred to in this proposition contain only people as members, it can be reformulated as 'All people who live by the sword are people who shall die by the sword'. Taking the letter *L* to stand for the class of people who live by the sword, and the letter *D* to stand for the class of people who shall die by the sword, it can be symbolized as *All L is D*.

Parameters: A word such as 'people', which is introduced in both the subject and predicate terms of a categorical proposition so that it can be reformulated in standard form, is known as a **parameter.** Other words often used as parameters are 'things', 'objects', 'animals', 'places', and 'times'. Further illustration of the use of parameters is provided by the following examples: 'A thing of beauty is a joy forever' may be reformulated as 'All things that are beautiful are things that are a joy forever', and may be symbolized as *All B is J*. 'Everywhere he goes, she goes' may be reformulated as 'All places he goes are places she goes', and symbolized as *All H is S*. 'Bears usually hibernate in the winter' may be reformulated as 'All animals which are bears are animals which usually hibernate in the winter', and stated symbolically as *All B is H*. 'It always rains at picnics' is a bit more complicated than the previous examples; it does not mean that all times are times when it is raining at picnics. Instead it means 'All times at which picnics occur are times at which it rains', which may be symbolized as *All P is R*.

Quantifiers: The propositions used as examples in the foregoing section also illustrate that there are many ways of quantifying categorical propositions in ordinary language and that quantifiers may be missing altogether. Whenever quantifiers are omitted in ordinary language, the rule adopted by traditional logicians is that all propositions are to be interpreted as universal unless the context makes it clear that the proposition is particular. Thus, the proposition 'Bears usually hibernate in the winter' is put into standard form as an **A** rather than as an **I** proposition.

The list below shows some of the ways in which categorical propositions may be quantified in ordinary language and gives a translation into standard form. Note that the articles 'a', 'an', and 'the' may quantify either a universal or a particular proposition. Note, also, that while the words 'any' and 'every' mean the same, the words 'not any' and 'not every' do not mean the same. Finally, note that the word 'some' refers to an indefinite quantity and may replace any word that refers to at least one, but less than all, of the members of a class.

A Propositions

Every scientist is a philosopher.	*All S is P*
Any baby cries a great deal.	*All B is C*
Each candidate was defeated.	*All C is D*
Whoever holds his tongue is wise.	*All H is W*
Whatever one sows, one reaps.	*All S is R*
Everybody at the party was drunk.	*All P is D*
Anybody who is ruthless will succeed.	*All R is S*
Everything that is a mammal is a vertebrate.	*All M is V*
Anything that goes up must come down.	*All U is D*
An aardvark is a mammal.	*All A is M*
A boy scout is trustworthy.	*All B is T*
The lion is a carnivore.	*All L is C*
Babies cry a great deal.	*All B is C*
Cats like milk.	*All C is L*

E Propositions

None of the candidates was defeated.	*No C is D*
Nothing worthwhile is easy.	*No W is E*
Nobody at the party was drunk.	*No P is D*
No one who is ruthless will succeed.	*No R is S*
Not any of the students passed.	*No S is P*
He who holds his tongue is not wise.	*No H is W*
Aardvarks are not mammals.	*No A is M*
The baboon is not a carnivore.	*No B is C*
Babies do not cry a great deal.	*No B is C*
It never rains at picnics.	*No P is R*

I Propositions

At least one of the new students is a girl.	*Some N is G*
One of the students who took the test failed.	*Some S is F*
Two of the books he gave me were on chemistry.	*Some B is C*
Sixteen of the zoo's swans were black.	*Some Z is B*
Twenty percent of the workers were sick.	*Some W is S*
A few of the books he gave me were easy to read.	*Some B is E*
Several of the books were very thick.	*Some B is V*
Many of the students were freshmen.	*Some S is F*
Most of the books he gave me were easy to read.	*Some B is E*
There are Martians who are green.	*Some M is G*

O Propositions

At least one member of the glee club is not a student.	*Some M is not S*
Two of the books were not found.	*Some B is not F*
A few of the candidates were not elected.	*Some C is not E*
There were several of the new employees who were not at work.	*Some N is not W*
Nine of the swans were not black.	*Some S is not B*
Not all socialists are pacifists.	*Some S is not P*
There are socialists who aren't pacifists.	*Some S is not P*
Not every bear hibernates.	*Some B is not H*

Exclusive Propositions: Propositions such as 'None but faculty may park here' and 'Only males are professional football players' are known as exclusive propositions. They assert that only members of the subject class are included in the predicate class, that is, *all other things are excluded* from the predicate class. To formulate exclusive propositions in standard form, interchange the subject and predicate terms and prefix the word 'all'. The result of applying this procedure to the above propositions is: 'All who may park here are faculty' *(All P is F)* and 'All professional football players are male' *(All P is M)*. At first sight these symbolizations may not seem correct, but a moment's reflection will show that they are. For example, 'Only males are professional football players' clearly means 'All professional football players are male' and not 'All males are professional football players'.

Exceptive Propositions: Propositions such as 'All except employees are eligible' and 'Only some of the soldiers returned alive' are known as exceptive propositions. They do not make one claim but two. The first asserts both 'No employees are eligible' and 'All nonemployees are eligible'. Similarly, the second asserts both 'Some soldiers returned alive' and 'Some soldiers did not return alive'. Some other words which may be used to assert exceptives are: 'almost all', 'nearly everybody', 'almost everyone', 'not quite all', 'all but a few', and 'only a few'. Although such expressions *may* express two propositions, they do not always do so, and very slight differences in wording may determine whether one or two propositions are being asserted. For example, an expression such as 'A few of the apples were rotten' would usually be interpreted as asserting only an **I** proposition, *Some A is R*. But one such as 'Few of the apples were rotten' would usually be interpreted as asserting both an **I,** *Some A is R,* and an **O,** *Some A is not R.* The fact that some expressions may assert two propositions must be borne in mind in testing arguments for validity. For if such propositions are taken to have a single meaning, then arguments which are valid may appear invalid, and vice versa.

Singular Propositions: Since traditional logicians interpret all propositions as asserting a relation of inclusion or exclusion between two classes, propositions that do not seem to be assertions about classes must be reinterpreted before they can be expressed as **A, E, I,** and **O** propositions. Consider the following **singular propositions:** 'This sheet of paper is white' and 'Socrates was not a coward'. These propositions do not assert or deny that one class is included within another, but assert or deny that a specific individual is a member of some class. However, traditional logicians interpret these propositions as equivalent to 'All members of the class which contains only this sheet of paper are white' and 'No member of the class containing only Socrates is a coward'. If we let *P* stand for the class which contains only this sheet of paper as a member, and *W* stand for the class of white things, then the first proposition may be symbolized as *All P is W.* And if we let *S* stand for the class which contains only Socrates as a member, and *C* stand for the class *cowards,* then the second proposition may be symbolized as *No S is C.* Although this procedure is rather cumbersome, it allows one to express all singular propositions as either an **A** or an **E** proposition.

One last comment regarding symbolization: Since ordinary language is sometimes vague and ambiguous, one may occasionally encounter expressions such that it is not clear how they are to be symbolized. For example, an expression such as 'It is false that boy scouts are trustworthy' might be taken in one context as asserting an **E** proposition, but be taken in another context as asserting an **O**. Also, note that in addition to the exceptive propositions discussed above, almost any **I** or **O** proposition may function as an exceptive in some contexts. In the ultimate analysis, then, one must simply rely on reflection as to what is meant as a guide in symbolizing.

EXERCISES

I

1. What is meant by the term 'traditional logic'?
2. How is modern logic related to traditional logic?
3. What is a categorical proposition?
4. Into what five factors may categorical propositions be analyzed? Describe each of these.
5. Name the four basic types of categorical propositions. How do they differ? What letters are used as abbreviations for their names?
6. What is a parameter?
7. How do traditional logicians interpret propositions lacking quantifiers?
8. To what quantity does the word 'some' refer?
9. What is an exceptive proposition?
10. What is an exclusive proposition?
11. What is a singular proposition?

II

Symbolize the following propositions in standard form using the suggested notation.
1. No dinosaurs were twenty feet tall. (D, T)
2. Dogs can't climb trees. (D, C)
3. Some abecedarians are not yet three years old. (A, T)
4. Katharine Hepburn is an actress. (K, A)
5. Fools never learn. (F, L)
6. One of the books is lost. (B, L)
7. Dolly Madison made pies. (D, P)
8. It always rains on weekends. (R, W)
9. Only people who are at least eighteen years of age will be admitted. (L, A)
10. Most of the seats were taken. (S, T)
11. Tyrannosaurus Rex is extinct. (T, E)
12. Nearly everybody at the party was drunk. (P, D)
13. I wasn't drunk. (I, D)
14. It is false that marijuana is a weed. (M, W)
15. At least one thing he did was wrong. (T, W)
16. Peanut butter sandwiches are the only kind he will eat. (P, E)
17. Dimitri can speak Greek. (D, G)
18. Elephants never forget. (E, F)
19. Only chemistry professors were eligible for the grant. (C, E)
20. Whoever lies, his nose grows longer. (L, N)
21. Anybody with a long nose is a liar. (N, L)
22. Baboons are not shy. (B, S)
23. Expert scuba divers are the only ones who can reach the wreck. (S, R)
24. Not any of the crates were damaged. (C, D)

25. None of the Indians except the Hopi had a rain god. (H, R)
26. Only some students attended the lecture. (S, A)
27. An abalone is a gastropod. (A, G)
28. Almost all dogs have fleas. (D, F)
29. My dog doesn't have fleas. (M, F)
30. Twelve boy scouts were missing. (B, M)
31. None but tenors can sing that part. (T, S)
32. The meek shall inherit the earth. (M, I)
33. Only a few dictators are benevolent. (D, B)
34. Not every oyster contains a pearl. (O, C)
35. None of the strikers lost his job. (S, L)
36. All but a few cats like milk. (C, L)
37. There are oysters that don't contain pearls. (O, C)
38. Everything green is extended. (G, E)
39. Several of the soldiers were missing in battle. (S, B)
40. All who have completed this exercise should go out and get a beer. (C, B)

THE SQUARE OF OPPOSITION

Two standard form categorical propositions having the same subject and predicate terms may differ in quantity or quality or both. To express these differences traditional logicians use the word 'opposition'. This use of 'opposition' is not synonymous with the use of 'disagreement' in ordinary language. Given two propositions with the same subject and predicate terms which differ in quantity but not in quality (e.g., *All S is P* and *Some S is P*), we might or might not say in ordinary language that they disagree. But in the traditional logician's sense of 'opposition', they are opposed.

The relationships among opposed propositions can be shown by placing them on a square:

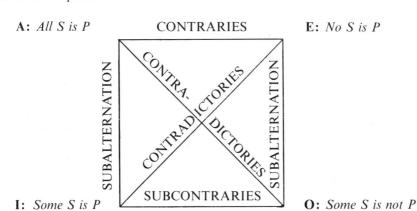

A: *All S is P*   CONTRARIES   **E:** *No S is P*

I: *Some S is P*   SUBCONTRARIES   **O:** *Some S is not P*

The propositions which are diagonally opposed (**A** and **O**, **E** and **I**) differ in both quantity and quality and are called **contradictories**. Calling them contradictories indicates that one member of each pair is the denial of the other. If one member of a pair of contradictories is true, then the other member must be false and vice versa. Thus it is impossible for both to be true, or both false. If we know, e.g., that an **I** proposition is true, then we can infer that an **E** proposition with the same subject and predicate is false.

A and **E** propositions differ only in quality and are called **contraries**. They cannot both be true, although they can both be false. So if we know that an **A** or **E** is true, we can infer that its contrary is false; but if we know that an **A** or **E** is false, we cannot infer the truth value of its contrary. In this case the truth value of the contrary is said to be indeterminate.

I and **O** propositions also differ only in quality and are called **subcontraries**. They cannot both be false, although they can both be true. Hence knowing that an **I** or **O** is false allows us to infer that its subcontrary is true; but knowing that an **I** or **O** is true does not yield any information about its subcontrary. Its value is indeterminate.

The vertical relationship on the square between the **A** and **I**, the **E** and **O**, is known as subalternation. The universal propositions are called **superalterns**, and the particular propositions are called **subalterns**. If a superaltern is true, then its subaltern is also true; but if a superaltern is false, the truth value of its subaltern is indeterminate. On the other hand, if a subaltern is false, then its superaltern is also false; but if a subaltern is true, then the truth value of its superaltern is indeterminate.

If one knows the truth value of a standard form categorical proposition, it is sometimes possible to deduce the truth value of all three of its opposing propositions. For instance, given that an **A** proposition is true, we can infer that its contradictory, **O**, is false; its contrary, **E**, is false; and its subaltern, **I**, is true. However, knowing the truth value of a standard form categorical proposition does not always yield this much information. Thus, given that an **A** proposition is false, we can infer only that its contradictory, **O**, is true. The truth value of its contrary, **E**, and its subaltern, **I**, are indeterminate. In saying that the truth values of the **E** and **I** are indeterminate, we mean that *none* of the relationships on the square of opposition allows us to infer their truth values. The reasons that no information can be deduced about an **E** by assuming that an **A** is false are: (1) the value of **E** does not follow from its contradictory **I**, because the value of **I** cannot be deduced when its subaltern **A** is false, (2) the value of **E** does not follow from its contrary **A**, since in knowing that **A** and **E** are contraries we know only that both cannot be true, (3) **E** is a universal proposition, so it does not have a subcontrary, and (4) since **A** is false we can deduce that **O**, the subaltern of **E**, is true; but we cannot deduce the value of **E** because the value of a superaltern does not follow from the truth of its subaltern.

EXERCISES

III

Fill in each of the following blanks with either the word 'similar' or the word 'different':

a) Contradictories are _____ quantitatively
   and _____ qualitatively.

b) Contraries are _____ quantitatively
   and _____ qualitatively.

c) Subcontraries are _____ quantitatively
   and _____ qualitatively.

d) Super- and subalterns are _____
   quantitatively and _____ qualitatively.

IV

Complete the following table by writing 'true', 'false', or 'indeterminate' in each of the blanks.

If A is true, then	E is false	I is true	O is false
If E is true, then	A is _____	I is _____	O is _____
If I is true, then	A is _____	E is _____	O is _____
If O is true, then	A is _____	E is _____	I is _____
If A is false, then	E is indeterminate	I is indeterminate	O is true
If E is false, then	A is _____	I is _____	O is _____
If I is false, then	A is _____	E is _____	O is _____
If O is false, then	A is _____	E is _____	I is _____

DISTRIBUTION

When all members of a class are referred to, the term standing for that class is said to be **distributed**; whereas when only some members of a class are referred to, the term standing for that class is said to be **undistributed**. For example, since an **A** proposition, *All S is P,* makes an assertion about all *S*'s but not about all *P*'s, its subject, but not its predicate term, is distributed. However, both the subject and predicate terms of an **E** proposition are distributed. This is because *No S is P* asserts that *no* member of *S* is among *any* of the members of *P*. Since *Some S is P* obviously does not assert anything about all of either *S* or *P*, neither the subject nor the predicate term of an **I** proposition is distributed. Finally, although the subject term of an **O** proposition is undistributed, the predicate term is distributed. For while *Some S is not P* does not make an assertion about all members of *S*, it does make an assertion about all members of *P*, viz., that there are some members of *S* that are not among *any* of the members of *P*. The following table summarizes this:

		SUBJECT	PREDICATE
A	*All S is P*	Distributed	Undistributed
E	*No S is P*	Distributed	Distributed
I	*Some S is P*	Undistributed	Undistributed
O	*Some S is not P*	Undistributed	Distributed

OTHER INFERENCES

Inferences represented on the square of opposition are not the only inferences permissible within traditional logic. In this section we will discuss two others: conversion and obversion.

Conversion

Conversion consists of interchanging or converting subject and predicate terms. Conversion of an **E** or **I** yields a valid inference, but conversion of an **A** or **O** does not. For example, from 'No socialists are pacifists', it follows that 'No pacifists are socialists', and from 'Some socialists are pacifists', it follows that 'Some pacifists are socialists'. But from 'All socialists are pacifists', it does not follow that 'All pacifists are socialists', and from 'Some socialists are not pacifists', it does not follow that 'Some pacifists are not socialists'.

The reason that inferences from *All S is P* to *All P is S* and from *Some S is not P* to *Some P is not S* are invalid should be clear from our discussion of distribution. In each case there is a term which is undistributed in the first proposition, but distributed in the second. Thus, the invalidity results from attempting to infer that something must be true of all members of a class because it is true of some members.

The inference from *All S is P* to *Some P is S* is valid. This may be seen by reflecting on the fact that *Some P is S* follows from *Some S is P* by conversion, and *Some S is P* follows from *All S is P* by subalternation. Thus if we convert the subject and predicate terms of an **A** proposition and *at the same time replace the word 'all' with 'some'*, a valid inference will result. This procedure is known as partial conversion, or **conversion by**

limitation, to distinguish it from full conversion, in which the subject and predicate terms are interchanged, but no change is made in quantifiers.

The following table lists the inferences that may be made by conversion:

	ORIGINAL	CONVERSE
A	*All S is P*	*Some P is S* (by limitation)
E	*No S is P*	*No P is S*
I	*Some S is P*	*Some P is S*
O	*Some S is not P*	No converse

Obversion

A second type of inference, known as **obversion,** results from replacing the predicate term of a categorical proposition with its class complement and then changing the quality of the proposition. The **complement** of a class is the class of all things that are *not* members of that class. (The complement of *c* is *non-c,* the complement of *non-c* is *c.*) To change the quality of an affirmative proposition, make it negative; to change the quality of a negative proposition, make it affirmative. The following table shows the outcome of obverting the four standard types of categorical propositions. In each case the resulting proposition, or obverse, is equivalent to the original. The reader should obvert each of the original propositions to assure himself that the table is accurate.

	ORIGINAL	OBVERSE
A	*All S is P*	*No S is non-P*
E	*No S is P*	*All S is non-P*
I	*Some S is P*	*Some S is not non-P*
O	*Some S is not P*	*Some S is non-P*

COMBINING INFERENCES

Contraposition

Conversion and obversion may be combined to yield other inferences. One especially useful combination, known as **contraposition,** consists of obverting, then converting, and then obverting again. For example, to derive the contrapositive of an **A** proposition, *All S is P*, obvert to obtain *No S is non-P;* then convert this to *No non-P is S*, and obvert again to obtain *All non-P is non-S*. To obtain the contrapositive of an **E**, *No S is P*, we obvert to obtain *All S is non-P*. Next we convert; but since we now have an **A** proposition, we can only convert by limitation to *Some non-P is S*. Then obverting this we get *Some non-P is not non-S*. The following table summarizes this and gives the contrapositive of the remaining propositions:

	ORIGINAL	CONTRAPOSITIVE
A	*All S is P*	*All non-P is non-S*
E	*No S is P*	*Some non-P is not non-S* (by limitation)
I	*Some S is P*	No contrapositive
O	*Some S is not P*	*Some non-P is not non-S*

Other Combinations

Conversion, obversion, and contraposition may also be combined with inferences from the square of opposition to yield more information than either of these sets of inferences yields alone. For example, suppose we are given that *All S is P* is true and wish to deduce the value of *Some non-P is non-S*. First we note that if *All S is P* is true, then its contrapositive, *All non-P is non-S,* is true also. Next we note that *Some non-P is non-S* is the subaltern of *All non-P is non-S* and thus, if *All non-P is non-S* is true, then *Some non-P is non-S* must be true also. Given that *Some non-P is non-S* is true, we can then go on to deduce additional information, for example, that its contradictory, *No non-P is non-S,* is false.

EXERCISES

V

1. What is meant by saying that two propositions are opposed?
2. Define the following terms: 'contradictory', 'contrary', 'subcontrary', 'subaltern', and 'superaltern'.
3. What is meant by saying that a proposition's truth value is indeterminate?
4. What is meant by the term 'distribution'?
5. Why is the inference from *Some S is not P* to *Some P is not S* invalid?
6. What must one do to convert a categorical proposition? What is partial conversion? In what cases is conversion valid, and in what cases invalid?

7. What must one do to obvert a categorical proposition? In what cases is it valid, and in what cases invalid?

8. What is meant by the term 'class complement'?

9. What must one do to contrapose a categorical proposition? In what cases is it valid, and what cases invalid?

VI

Give, where possible, the converse, obverse, and contrapositive of each of the following propositions:

1. All wombats are gentle.

2. No hedgehog reads the *Times*.

3. Some of Dolly Madison's pies were tasty.

4. Dimitri's mother is a feminist.

5. Some feminists' arguments are not nonvalid.

6. All nonreckless drivers are nonaccident prone.

7. No follower of Ayn Rand is a nonobjectivist.

8. Some nonreligious people attend church.

VII

If the proposition 'All officers are soldiers' is true, what can be inferred about the truth value of each of the following? What can be inferred if 'All officers are soldiers' is false?

1. All nonsoldiers are nonofficers.

2. No nonsoldiers are nonofficers.

3. Some nonofficers are nonsoldiers.

4. Some nonsoldiers are not nonofficers.

5. No nonofficers are soldiers.

6. No nonsoldiers are officers.

7. All nonofficers are soldiers.

8. Some soldiers are nonofficers.

9. Some nonofficers are not nonsoldiers.

10. No officers are nonsoldiers.

VIII

If the proposition 'No enlisted men are officers' is true, what can be inferred about the truth value of each of the following? What can be inferred if 'No enlisted men are officers' is false?

1. No nonofficers are enlisted men.

2. No enlisted men are nonofficers.

3. Some officers are enlisted men.
4. Some enlisted men are not nonofficers.
5. No nonenlisted men are officers.
6. Some officers are not nonenlisted men.
7. All nonofficers are nonenlisted men.
8. All nonenlisted men are nonofficers.
9. All officers are nonenlisted men.
10. Some nonenlisted men are not nonofficers.

CATEGORICAL SYLLOGISMS

Categorical syllogisms are arguments containing three categorical propositions, two of which are premises and one, the conclusion. Every categorical syllogism contains three class terms, each of which occurs twice, although not in the same proposition. In the syllogism

> All felines are carnivores.
> All tigers are felines.
> _____
> All tigers are carnivores.

the three terms are 'felines', 'carnivores', and 'tigers'. The term which occurs twice in the premises is called the **middle term** ('feline' in the above example). The predicate term of the conclusion is called the **major term.** When a categorical syllogism is in standard form, the premise containing the major term is stated first and is called the **major premise.** The subject term of the conclusion is called the **minor term,** and the premise in which it occurs is called the **minor premise.** In the above syllogism, 'carnivores' is the major term and 'tigers' the minor term.

Determining Validity by Traditional Rules

Only arguments which satisfy the following six rules were traditionally considered to be valid categorical syllogisms.

Rules Defining Categorical Syllogisms

1. Every categorical syllogism must contain three and only three categorical propositions.

2. Every categorical syllogism must contain three and only three class terms, each of which occurs twice, but not in the same proposition.

Rules of Quantity

3. The middle term must be distributed at least once.

4. If a term is distributed in the conclusion, then it must be distributed in a premise.

Rules of Quality

5. If the conclusion is negative, one and only one premise must be negative.

6. If the conclusion is affirmative, then both premises must be affirmative.

Any argument which violates one or more of these rules is either not a syllogism or is invalid. Violation of Rule 3 is known as the *Fallacy of Undistributed Middle*. If the major term is distributed in the conclusion, but not in a premise, then violation of Rule 4 is known as the *Fallacy of Illicit Major;* if the minor term is distributed in the conclusion, but not in a premise, then violation of Rule 4 is called the *Fallacy of Illicit Minor*. Violation of Rule 5 is known as the *Fallacy of Illicit Exclusion;* violation of Rule 6, the *Fallacy of Illicit Inclusion*.

Examples of Invalid Syllogisms

All contemporary philosophers should take account of
recent advances in symbolic logic.
Plato and Parmenides were contemporary philosophers.

Plato and Parmenides should take account of recent
advances in symbolic logic.

Since this syllogism contains three and only three categorical propositions, it satisfies Rule 1. However, it violates Rule 2 because, though it appears to have three and only three class terms, the phrase 'contemporary philosophers' does not have the same meaning in both of its occurrences. In the major premise it means 'philosophers living today', while in the minor premise it means 'philosophers living at the same time'. Consequently, the argument contains four terms and is not a categorical syllogism. (Some authors prefer to say that it is a categorical syllogism, but is invalid because it commits the *Fallacy of Four Terms*.)

No abominable snowmen are introverts.
Some introverts are timid.

Some abominable snowmen are not timid.

This syllogism also consists of three and only three categorical propositions. And it contains three and only three class terms, each of which occurs twice, but not in the same proposition. Thus, it satisfies both Rules 1 and 2. Since the middle term, 'introverts', is distributed in the first premise, it also satisfies Rule 3. However, the predicate term, 'timid', is distributed in the conclusion, but not in a premise, so it violates Rule 4.

Example of a Valid Syllogism

No abominable snowmen are introverts.
Some introverts are timid.
Some timid people are not abominable snowmen.

This syllogism also satisfies both Rules 1 and 2. And since the middle term, 'introverts', is distributed in the first premise, it satisfies Rule 3. The only term distributed in the conclusion is 'abominable snowmen', and it is distributed in the first premise, so it satisfies Rule 4. The conclusion is negative, but the syllogism contains one and only one negative premise, so it satisfies Rule 5. Finally, since the conclusion is negative rather than positive, Rule 6 does not apply and the syllogism is valid.

EXERCISES

IX

Test each of the following syllogisms for validity by means of the traditional rules. In each case in which the syllogism is invalid, state the rules violated.

1. Only people who take vitamins are healthy.
    John always takes vitamins.
    John is healthy.

2. Some clumsy people are not very smart.
    No cat burglars are clumsy.
    Some cat burglars are very smart.

3. All who repent will be saved.
    None who are saved will roast in Hell.
    Some who repent will not roast in Hell.

4. Some skillful rhetoricians are not politicians.
    Some actors are not skillful rhetoricians.
    Some actors are not politicians.

5. Some eggheads are intellectuals.
    Humpty Dumpty was an egghead.
    Humpty Dumpty was an intellectual.

6. All egg factories are employers of hens.
   No employers of hens are respectable establishments.
   No respectable establishments are egg factories.

7. Only those wearing ties will be admitted, although those wearing loud
   ties will not be admitted.
   John is wearing a loud tie.
   John will not be admitted.

8. No good citizen hates the police.
   Some hippies hate the police.
   No hippie is a good citizen.

9. No hippies subscribe to the slogan, "America, Love it or Leave it."
   Mayor Loeb subscribes to the slogan, "America, Love it or Leave it."
   Mayor Loeb is not a hippie.

10. All who are saved go to Heaven.
    Some who go to Heaven will play harps.
    Some who are saved will play harps.

Syllogisms Containing Class Complements

Syllogisms containing class complements often appear to be invalid by traditional rules even though they are valid. For example, the syllogism

> All vain people are egotistical.
> No actors are nonvain.
> All actors are egotistical.

appears to violate both the rule that a syllogism can contain three and only three class terms and the rule that if the conclusion is affirmative, then both premises must be affirmative. But if we obvert the second premise to obtain the equivalent proposition 'All actors are vain people', and re-formulate the syllogism as

> All vain people are egotistical.
> All actors are vain people.
> All actors are egotistical.

it then satisfies all the traditional rules for validity.

The foregoing is not the only reformulation which can be given for the above syllogism. For example, instead of replacing the second premise with its obverse, we can replace the first premise with its contrapositive and the conclusion with its obverse:

> All nonegotistical people are nonvain.
> No actors are nonvain.
> _____
> No actors are nonegotistical.

This syllogism also satisfies all the traditional rules for validity.

In general a syllogism containing four terms can be reformulated as one containing only three, provided that one of the four terms is a complement of one of the others. A syllogism containing five terms can be reformulated as one containing only three provided that two of the five terms are complements of two others. And a syllogism containing six terms can be reformulated as one containing only three provided that three of the six are complements of three others. For example, consider the following syllogism, which contains six terms, three of which are complements of the other three:

> All nonfattening foods are nonstarchy.
> No high protein food is fattening.
> _____
> All starchy foods are non-high protein.

If we replace the first premise of this argument with its contrapositive and the conclusion with its obverse, we obtain the valid syllogism:

> All starchy foods are fattening.
> No high protein food is fattening.
> _____
> No starchy foods are high protein.

EXERCISES

X

Reformulate the following syllogisms so that they contain three and only three class terms, and test for validity using the traditional rules.

1. All laws that are constitutional should be obeyed.
   No unconstitutional law will be upheld by the Supreme Court.
   _____
   All laws that are upheld by the Supreme Court should be obeyed.

2. All gems are expensive.
   Some things that are not gems are stones.
   _____
   Some stones are inexpensive.

3. No sound argument has inconsistent premises.
   Some valid arguments have inconsistent premises.
   Some unsound arguments are not invalid.

4. Many Patagonians are toothless.
   Only people with teeth can eat treacle.
   Some non-Patagonians are non-treacle eaters.

5. Most nonalcoholic beverages are carbonated.
   No soft drink is an alcoholic beverage.
   Some non-soft drinks are uncarbonated.

ENTHYMEMES

An argument with an implicitly understood premise or conclusion such that its explicit statement results in a syllogism is known as an **enthymeme.** Since in arguing people often assume that certain propositions are implicitly understood by their hearers or readers, most syllogistic reasoning in ordinary language is enthymematic. For example, consider the argument 'Dimitri made 95 on the test, so he received an A'. As it stands this argument is not a syllogism, but it can be put into syllogistic form if we supply the implicitly understood premise 'All people who made 95 on the test received an A'.

> All people who made 95 on the test received an A.
> Dimitri made 95 on the test.
> Dimitri received an A.

Not only a premise, but also the conclusion of a syllogism may be missing. Suppose, for example, that an official of the U.S. State Department has just announced that diplomatic relations will be broken off with all countries that are supplying military aid to Albania. Suppose, further, that a reporter asks whether diplomatic relations will be broken off with Russia, and the State Department official replies "Russia is supplying military aid to Albania, isn't she?" The unstated, but obvious, conclusion is that diplomatic relations will be broken off with Russia.

EXERCISES

XI

Supply the missing premise or conclusion in each of the following enthymemes, express the resulting argument in syllogistic form, and test for validity using the traditional rules.

1. Green apples shouldn't be eaten because they give one a stomachache.
2. Handling toads causes warts, and Jack has warts.
3. It couldn't have been a brown recluse spider because they have a violin-shaped marking on their backs.
4. Some Scotsmen are not stingy because McTaggart is a Scotsman.
5. You know Thales was impractical for he was a philosopher.
6. Only those wearing ties were admitted and John was wearing a tie.
7. Our ideas reach no farther than our experience: we have no experience of divine attributes and operations: I need not conclude my syllogism: you can draw the inference yourself. (David Hume, *Dialogues Concerning Natural Religion*)

SORITES

Syllogisms have been defined as arguments containing only three categorical propositions. However, it is obvious that it is possible for valid arguments to contain more than three categorical propositions. For instance

> All Quakers are pacifists.
> All pacifists believe war morally unjustifiable.
> All who believe war morally unjustifiable are social protesters.
> All Quakers are social protesters.

An argument of this type, which is composed of four or more categorical propositions, is called a **sorites.** Traditional logicians treat sorites as chain arguments composed of two or more incompletely expressed syllogisms. For example, the following argument can be constructed from the first two premises of the above sorites:

> All Quakers are pacifists.
> All pacifists believe war morally unjustifiable.
> All Quakers believe war morally unjustifiable.

And from the conclusion of this argument and the third premise of the sorites, the following argument can be constructed:

> All Quakers believe war morally unjustifiable.
> All who believe war morally unjustifiable are social protesters.
> All Quakers are social protesters.

Since the conclusion of this argument is the same as the conclusion of the sorites, the sorites has been shown to be valid.

A number of interesting sorites in which the reader is left to draw the conclusion were formulated by Lewis Carroll in *Symbolic Logic*. For example:

> No ducks waltz.
> No officer ever declines to waltz.
> All my poultry are ducks.

From the first and third of these propositions, the following argument can be formulated:

No ducks waltz.	*No D is W*
All my poultry are ducks.	*All P is D*
None of my poultry waltz.	*No P is W*

And from the conclusion of this argument and the remaining premise of the sorites, the following argument may be constructed:

None of my poultry waltz.	*No P is W*
No officer ever declines to waltz.	*All O is W*
None of my poultry is an officer.	*No P is O*

EXERCISES

XII

What conclusions can be drawn from the following sorites?*

1. (1) Some babies are illogical.
    (2) Nobody is despised who can manage a crocodile.
    (3) Illogical persons are despised.

2. (1) Everyone who is sane can do logic.
    (2) No lunatics are fit to serve on a jury.
    (3) None of your sons can do logic.

3. (1) There are no pencils of mine in this box.
    (2) No sugarplums of mine are cigars.
    (3) The whole of my property that is not in this box consists of sugarplums.

4. (1) No terriers wander among the signs of the Zodiac.
    (2) Nothing that does not wander among the signs of the Zodiac is a comet.
    (3) Nothing but a terrier has a curly tail.

5. (1) All the old articles in this cupboard are cracked.
    (2) No jug in this cupboard is new.
    (3) Nothing in this cupboard that is cracked will hold water.

---

*The above sorites were adapted from Lewis Carroll's (Charles Dodgson) *Symbolic Logic*.

OTHER METHODS OF SYMBOLIZING
CATEGORICAL PROPOSITIONS

Stating categorical propositions in standard form is not the only way they may be symbolized. Although standard form has the obvious advantage of being similar to ordinary language, other methods are more useful in exhibiting the relationships which hold between the classes in categorical propositions.

Venn Diagrams

One method, invented by the nineteenth century logician, John Venn, and known as *Venn diagrams,* uses two intersecting circles to represent the relationships between two classes

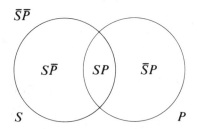

The area within the circle on the left, labeled $S\bar{P}$, represents the class of things that are *S*'s but not *P*'s. The area within the circle on the right, labeled $\bar{S}P$, represents the class of things that are *P*'s but not *S*'s. The area lying within both circles, and which is labeled *SP*, represents the class of things that are both *S*'s and *P*'s. The area outside both circles, which is labeled $\bar{S}\bar{P}$, represents the complements of *S* and *P*, that is, the class of things that are neither *S*'s nor *P*'s.

The following diagrams are used to represent the four standard types of categorical propositions:

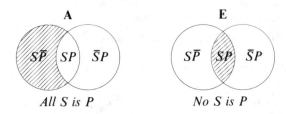

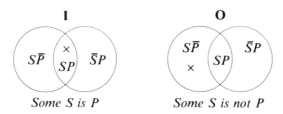

Shaded areas represent classes that have no members. In the diagram for an **A** proposition, the area $S\bar{P}$ is shaded to indicate that anything that is an S is also a P, or to say the same thing differently, nothing is an S and not a P. Since **E** propositions assert that nothing is both an S and a P, the area SP which is common to the two classes is shaded to indicate that this class has no members. An **I** proposition asserts that there is at least one S that is a P. This is diagrammed by placing an x in the area SP, which is common to the two classes. An **O** proposition asserts that there is at least one S that is not a P. Thus, it is diagrammed by placing an x in the area $S\bar{P}$.

Venn Diagrams and Existential Import

There is an important difference in the interpretation of **A** and **E** propositions by traditional rules and their interpretation in accordance with Venn diagrams. This difference is that, in the application of traditional rules, one assumes that **A** and **E** propositions have existential import while, in the application of Venn diagrams, one does not make this assumption. To assume that a proposition has **existential import** is to assume that some of the classes mentioned in it have members. Thus, in applying traditional rules, one assumes that **A** and **E** propositions are assertions about classes which have members, whereas in applying Venn diagrams one does not assume this. For example, the proposition 'All angels enjoy playing the harp', interpreted in accordance with traditional rules, is construed as asserting that there are angels and that all of them enjoy playing the harp. But the same proposition symbolized by Venn diagrams

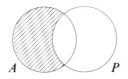

is understood as asserting only that *if* there are angels, then they enjoy playing the harp. Consequently, the diagram for this proposition does not contain an area in which there is a symbol to show that there is an angel.

Both application of traditional rules and use of Venn diagrams presuppose that **I** and **O** propositions have existential import. Thus, a Venn diagram for the **I** proposition 'Some angels hate playing the harp' contains an *x* to show that there is at least one angel who hates playing the harp.

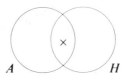

At first sight the interpretation of **A** and **E** propositions as having existential import might seem more useful. And it is true that, as a rule, existential import is assumed when **A** and **E** propositions are asserted in everyday discourse. Thus if someone were to say 'All pacifists are socialists', we would normally assume that he believes that there are pacifists. But existential import is not always assumed in everyday discourse. For example, if someone were to say 'All people who trespass on this property will be prosecuted', we would not necessarily interpret this as claiming that someone will trespass, but only as claiming that *if* anyone trespasses he will be prosecuted.

If we interpret **A** and **E** propositions as asserting existence, then only those propositions in ordinary discourse which have existential import can be symbolized. On the other hand, if we do not interpret **A** and **E** propositions as asserting existence, then both those propositions in ordinary discourse that do, and those that do not, have existential import can be symbolized. For example, to symbolize an **A** proposition which asserts existence, we simply symbolize it as stating *both* an **A** and an **I** proposition. And to symbolize an **E** proposition which asserts existence, we simply symbolize it as stating *both* an **E** and an **O** proposition. Thus, the interpretation of **A** and **E** propositions as not having existential import is in fact more useful.

Algebraic Notation

Another method of symbolizing categorical propositions, often called **algebraic notation,** makes use of the symbols: S, $\bar{S}$, P, $\bar{P}$, etc., to stand for classes; the symbol $=$ for equality; the symbol $\neq$ for inequality; and the symbol 0 to stand for the empty class, or the class having no members. The four standard types of categorical propositions are symbolized in this notation as:

A $S\bar{P} = 0$ **I** $SP \neq 0$

E $SP = 0$ **O** $S\bar{P} \neq 0$

The formula $S\overline{P} = 0$ describes the shaded area of a Venn diagram for an **A** proposition; similarly the formula $SP = 0$ describes the shaded area of a Venn diagram for an **E** proposition. And since the Venn diagram for an **I** has an x in the area represented by SP to show that it is not empty, the formula $SP \neq 0$ represents that area. (The inequality symbol, $\neq$, is read as 'is not equal to'.) Venn diagrams for **O** propositions have an x in the area $S\overline{P}$, so the formula $S\overline{P} \neq 0$ describes that area. One advantage of the algebraic notation is that it makes explicit the difference in existential import between **A** and **E**, **I** and **O** propositions.

EXERCISES

XIII

Symbolize the following using: (a) standard forms, (b) Venn diagrams, and (c) algebraic notation.
1. Oysters are out of season.
2. Some Indians do not weave baskets.
3. Some chickens crossed the road.
4. None of the oysters contained pearls.
5. Some winner was not present.
6. A few congressmen will abstain on this issue.
7. Charities are tax-exempt organizations.
8. Some accounts are uninsured.
9. Any person who works for the United States government is eligible for membership.
10. Negligence will not be tolerated.

XIV

Symbolize the first ten propositions in exercise II on page 152 using: (a) Venn diagrams and (b) algebraic notation.

VENN DIAGRAMS AS A TEST FOR VALIDITY

Venn diagrams can be used to show the validity or invalidity of categorical syllogisms. Three intersecting circles are needed to diagram a categorical syllogism, one for each class term. To diagram the syllogism:

> All scarey movies are aired late at night.
> All horror movies are scarey.
> _____
> All horror movies are aired late at night.

we need a circle representing scarey movies, S, one representing programs aired late at night, A, and one representing horror movies, H.

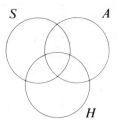

The first premise is an **A** proposition asserting that $S\overline{A} = 0$. Since H is not mentioned in this premise, we ignore the circle representing H and diagram $S\overline{A} = 0$.

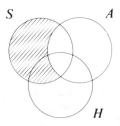

The second premise is also an **A** proposition; it asserts that $H\overline{S} = 0$. So we disregard the circle for A and diagram $H\overline{S} = 0$.

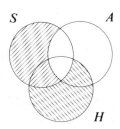

The conclusion asserts that $H\overline{A} = 0$. This conclusion follows from the premises because the relation asserted by the conclusion has been diagrammed in diagramming the premises. The area $H\overline{A}$ has been shaded in diagramming the premises, so the syllogism is valid.

Let us use a Venn diagram to show that the following syllogism is invalid:

All steamboats have paddle wheels.
No steamboats are vessels having radar equipment.
No vessels having radar equipment have paddle wheels.

Again, we diagram the first premise, $S\overline{P} = 0$, disregarding R.

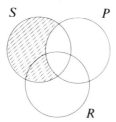

Then, we diagram the second premise, which is an **E** proposition, asserting $SR = 0$.

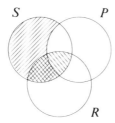

On inspection of the diagram, we see that the conclusion $RP = 0$ has not been diagrammed because only part of the area RP has been shaded. Since not all of RP is shaded, this syllogism has been shown to be invalid.

When categorical syllogisms contain one universal and one particular premise, it is necessary to diagram the universal premise first, regardless of the order of the premises in the syllogism. To see why this procedure is necessary for an adequate test of validity, consider the syllogism:

> Some mushrooms are poisonous.
> All mushrooms are tasty.
> Some things which are tasty are poisonous.

If the universal premise is diagrammed first, part of the area referred to by the particular premise (area MP) is shaded. So we know that if $MP \neq 0$, the area which contains at least one member must be the area common to M, P, and T because the area common to M and P, but excluded from T, is empty.

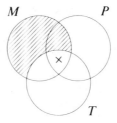

The diagram shows this syllogism to be valid. Its conclusion is $TP \neq 0$, and there is an x in TP. If the universal premise had not been diagrammed first, we would not have known in which part of MP to place the x, because we could not have determined whether there were any members common to all three classes, or whether there were only members common to M and P. Thus, we would not have known whether the syllogism was valid or invalid.

Sometimes we are forced to place x's on boundaries. For example, in the case of the syllogism:

> Some Athenians were philosophers.
> Some dramatists were not Athenians.
> Some dramatists were not philosophers.

Since both premises are particular, it does not matter which is diagrammed first. But if the major premise, $AP \neq 0$, is diagrammed first, the result is

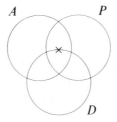

The major premise tells us that there is at least one member of the class represented by the area AP, but we do not know whether that member is included in D, so the x is placed *on* the line. Putting the x on one side or the other of the line would assume information that we do not have. When the minor premise is diagrammed, we face the same situation. The minor premise, $D\overline{A} \neq 0$, tells us that there is at least one member of the class represented by $D\overline{A}$. But, again, when we inspect the diagram, we see that

$D\overline{A}$ is divided by the boundary of P, and we cannot assume that the x is either included in, or excluded from, P, so we must put the x on the line

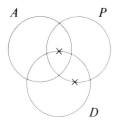

The argument is seen to be invalid because $D\overline{P} \neq 0$ has not been diagrammed. There is an x on the boundary of P, but there is no x in the area which is contained in D but not in P.

EXERCISES

XV

Show whether the following syllogisms are valid or invalid by means of Venn diagrams:

1. All kumquats are citrus fruits.
    All citrus fruits are suitable for making jelly.
    All kumquats are suitable for making jelly.

2. No respectable persons are public drunks.
    All sots are public drunks.
    No sots are respectable persons.

3. Only fools rush in where angels fear to tread.
    All people who drive without fastening their seat belts are fools.
    Only people who rush in where angels fear to tread are people
      who drive without fastening their seat belts.

4. All mares cause bad dreams.
    There are no things that cause bad dreams which are not evil.
    Some mares are evil.

5. All cows moo.
    Some things which moo, bite.
    Some things which bite are cows.

6. No neurotic can be trusted with an important position.
    All generals can be trusted with important positions.
    Some generals are not neurotic.

7. Committee chairmen are not elected officials.
   Committee members are not elected officials.
   No committee members are committee chairmen.

8. No single-minded individual is indecisive.
   Some indecisive people hold authoritative positions.
   Not all people in authoritative positions are single-minded.

9. At least one entity at the tea party was a rabbit.
   Some things that go down rabbit holes are not rabbits.
   Some things that go down rabbit holes were not among the
   entities at the tea party.

10. Some steamboats are powered by diesels.
    Some things powered by diesels operate on land.
    Some steamboats operate on land.

ANTILOGISMS

Use of algebraic notation makes available another test of validity for categorical syllogisms. This test is a type of indirect proof in which the conclusion of the syllogism to be tested is replaced by its contradictory. The resulting argument is known as an **antilogism.** The antilogism of a valid syllogism must meet three requirements:

1. It must contain two propositions which are equalities
   and one which is an inequality.

2. One term in each equality must be the complement
   of a term in the other equality.

3. The inequality must contain the two terms which
   are not common to the equalities.

To test the syllogism

All magazine salesmen are working their way through college.
All people working their way through college are students.
All magazine salesmen are students.

first, symbolize it in algebraic notation

$$M\overline{W} = 0$$
$$W\overline{S} = 0$$
$$\overline{M\overline{S}} = 0$$

Next, construct its antilogism by replacing the conclusion by its contradictory. The contradictory of a proposition in algebraic form is easily formulated by changing an inequality to an equality, or an equality to an inequality. Thus, the antilogism of the example above is:

$$M\overline{W} = 0$$
$$W\overline{S} = 0$$
$$\overline{MS} \neq 0$$

Now, check to see if the antilogism meets the requirements for antilogisms of valid syllogisms. This antilogism meets the first requirement since two of the propositions (the premises) are equalities, and one (the conclusion) is an inequality. It also meets the second requirement because the equalities contain terms which are complements (W and $\overline{W}$). And it meets the third requirement because the inequality (the conclusion) contains both M and $\overline{S}$, the two terms which are not common to the equalities. Since the antilogism meets all three requirements, the syllogism is valid.

Another Example

All professionals are former amateurs.
Some former amateurs are wealthy.
Some wealthy persons are nonprofessionals.

Syllogism	*Antilogism*
$P\overline{F} = 0$	$P\overline{F} = 0$
$FW \neq 0$	$FW \neq 0$
$W\overline{P} \neq 0$	$W\overline{P} = 0$

The first requirement is met: Only the first premise and the conclusion are equalities. The second requirement is also met: The equalities contain terms which are complements (P and $\overline{P}$). But, the third requirement, that the inequality must contain the two terms not common to the equalities, is not fulfilled. (It contains F and W, but the terms not common to the equalities are $\overline{F}$ and W.) Thus, the syllogism is invalid.

EXERCISES

XVI

Use antilogisms to test the syllogisms in exercise XV on page 175 for validity.

EXISTENTIAL IMPORT AND VALIDITY

Since traditional logicians interpret all categorical propositions as having existential import, while modern logicians interpret only particular propositions as having existential import, some syllogisms that are valid according to traditional rules are invalid according to Venn diagrams and antilogisms. Syllogisms of which this is true have universal premises and particular conclusions. For example, since a syllogism of the form

All S is P
All P is R
Some S is R

has universal premises, diagramming its premises cannot result in an *x* being placed anywhere in the diagram. Therefore, the conclusion, which is a particular proposition, cannot be diagrammed in diagramming the premises.

The fact that some arguments are valid according to traditional methods, but invalid according to modern methods, does not mean that modern logicians are right and traditional logicians wrong, or vice versa. For, as long as one is working with classes which have members, traditional logic is an appropriate means of dealing with them. But modern logic is more useful because, as pointed out above, it can be used to symbolize both those propositions which have existential import and those which do not. Thus, it is possible to state all arguments which are valid by traditional methods in such a way that they are also valid by modern techniques.

EXERCISES

XVII

1. Use Venn diagrams or antilogisms to determine whether any of the syllogisms in exercises IX, page 162, which are valid by traditional rules are invalid by Venn diagrams or antilogisms.

2. Use traditional rules to determine whether any of the syllogisms in exercises XV, page 175, which are invalid by Venn diagrams and antilogisms are valid by traditional rules.

SUGGESTED READINGS

BIRD, OTTO, *Syllogistic and Its Extensions.* Fundamentals of Logic Series. Ed. Ernan McMullin. Englewood Cliffs, N.J.: Prentice-Hall, Inc., 1964.

COHEN, MORRIS R. and ERNEST NAGEL, *An Introduction to Logic and Scientific Method.* New York: Harcourt, Brace & World, Inc., 1934.

EHLERS, HENRY, *Logic By Way of Set Theory.* New York: Holt, Rinehart and Winston, Inc., 1968.

LEE, HAROLD NEWTON, *Symbolic Logic.* New York: Random House, 1961.

10

INDUCTION

The previous chapters dealt wholly with deductive logic. However, any survey of the patterns of reasoning in science and ordinary affairs shows that inductive arguments are used as often, if not more often, than deductive arguments. In fact, we proceed for the most part by combining these two kinds of arguments. Deductive arguments were defined in chapter I as arguments in which it is claimed that if the premises are true, then the conclusion must be true. Inductive arguments were defined as arguments in which it is claimed that if the premises are true, then it is probable that the conclusion is true. A valid deductive argument was defined as an argument in which it is impossible for the premises to be true and the conclusion false. It follows from this definition of validity that an inductive argument can never be valid. This does not mean that inductive arguments are to be condemned; it means only that they are of a fundamentally different character from deductive arguments. Since inductive arguments have a different character, different techniques are needed to evaluate them. In this chapter we will examine the basic character of inductive arguments, state criteria for their evaluation, and examine some misuses of inductive reasoning.

BASIC CHARACTER
OF INDUCTIVE ARGUMENTS

Although the conclusion of an inductive argument does not follow *necessarily* from its premises, there are innumerable cases in which we are very confident that the conclusion *does* follow. For instance, if one sees a small yellow bird in a cage and the bird is producing sounds characteristic of canaries, one is likely to conclude that the small yellow bird is a canary. Although it is possible that one might encounter a small yellow caged bird which sounded like a canary but was not one, we would normally rather confidently infer in this situation that we had encountered a canary. We make inferences of this type continually—when we expect the white liquid in a carton labeled 'milk' to be milk, when we expect floors to support our weight, alarm clocks to ring, fire to cook our food, the sky to darken at sunset, etc.

One important characteristic of inductive arguments is that our confidence in the truth of their conclusions can be increased or decreased by adding other premises. Suppose that the person encountering the small yellow caged bird which sounded like a canary were in the home of a friend who had previously mentioned that he owned a canary. This additional information would obviously increase one's confidence in the truth of 'This bird is a canary'. But suppose instead one knew that the owner of the bird was extremely interested in some group of finches, many of which are yellow. The addition of this information to the original premises would obviously decrease one's confidence in the truth of 'This bird is a canary'.

In these three cases we have three distinct arguments:

(1) There is a small yellow bird in this cage.
     This bird sounds like a canary.
     This bird is a canary.

(2) There is a small yellow bird in this cage.
     This bird sounds like a canary.
     The owner of this bird owns a canary.
     This bird is a canary.

(3) There is a small yellow bird in this cage.
     This bird sounds like a canary.
     The owner of this bird is extremely interested
       in finches, many of which are yellow.
     This bird is a canary.

Although none of these three sets of premises could establish the truth of its conclusion with certainty, the premises of argument (2) offer the strongest evidence for its conclusion and those of (3), the weakest. In other words we can say that 'This bird is a canary' is most probable given the premises of (2), and least probable given the premises of (3).

The possibility of assessing inductive arguments in terms of probability is one of their fundamental characteristics. However, the word 'probability' has more than one meaning, and several different types of arguments can be referred to as "probability arguments." Exploration of some of these meanings will help us become clearer about the nature of inductive arguments.

PROBABILITY

A Priori Probability

One type of probability, known as *a priori* probability, involves the use of mathematical formulae. Since mathematical operations are deductive rather than inductive in nature, it might seem that discussion of *a priori* probability is out of place in a chapter on induction. (If 2 is multiplied by 3, the result is not probably 6, but necessarily 6.) However, mathematical operations often enter as steps in inductive arguments and illustrate one of the ways in which deductive and inductive inferences are combined to gain information.

Suppose one had a "true" as opposed to a "fixed" coin. By a "true" coin we mean one such that if it were tossed, there would be two equally possible outcomes—heads or tails. The *a priori* probability that such a coin will land heads up is determined by the ratio of the number of possibilities resulting in heads to the total number of possible outcomes. In a single toss of the coin there are two possible outcomes, one of which is heads, so the probability of getting heads is *1/2*. Similarly, the probability of getting tails on a single toss is *1/2*. The reason these are called *a priori* probabilities is that they are not determined by actually flipping the coin, but by considering possible outcomes *prior* to actual flipping.

To determine the *a priori* probability that a die will land with a **6** up, the same ratio—possible outcomes resulting in a **6** being up to total number of possible outcomes—is needed. Hence, the probability of a **6** coming up on a single roll of a die is one out of six, or *1/6*.

Probabilities are always determined on the basis of particular information. In the case of the probability of getting a **6** on a single roll of a die, the relevant information is that a die has six faces and that on a single roll there is an equal likelihood of any one of six sides landing on top. Notationally, probabilities are represented by the form

$$p(b/a)$$

which is read as : the probability of *b* given that *a*. To represent the above example in this notation, we would let *b* be 'getting a **6** on a single roll of a die', and *a* be 'dice have six faces, each of which has an equal chance of being on top after the roll'.

There is only one numerical value for $p(b/a)$ on any given interpretation of *b* and *a*. The probability that some statement is true, or that some state of affairs will obtain, may have different numerical values given different "background information;" but with respect to any particular set of information, it can have only one value.

Since the numerical value of $p(b/a)$ is a ratio of some of a set of possibilities to all of the possibilities included in that set, it is always a fraction lying between 0 and 1. In the case of two mutually exclusive events one or the other of which must occur—such as getting either heads or tails on a single toss of a coin—the sum of the probabilities is equal to 1. Let $p(h/s)$ be the probability of getting heads on a single toss, and let $p(t/s)$ be the probability of getting tails on a single toss. Then

$$p(h/s) + p(t/s) = 1$$

or numerically expressed

$$1/2 + 1/2 = 1$$

From this we also know that the probability of getting either heads or tails is 1

$$p((h \lor t)/s) = 1$$

And, therefore

$$p((h \lor t)/s) = p(h/s) + p(t/s)$$

Since the probability of getting heads is the same as the probability of *not* getting tails, i.e.,

$$p(h/s) = p(\sim t/s)$$

the probability of getting tails or not getting tails is 1

$$p((t \lor \sim t)/s) = 1$$

and

$$p(t/s) + p(\sim t/s) = 1$$

or, again

$$1/2 + 1/2 = 1$$

Hence, if b and c are mutually exclusive, and either b or c must obtain given a, we have the following general formulae:

$$p((b \lor c)/a) = p(b/a) + p(c/a)$$
$$p(b/a) + p(c/a) = 1$$

If a set of possibilities includes more than two outcomes and each of them is mutually exclusive of the others, this method of calculating their probabilities is still applicable. In the example above in which we determined that the probability of getting a **6** on a single roll of a die is *1/6*, we were able to use this method because the roll of a die has six equally possible mutually exclusive results. Hence, if we wish to determine the probability of rolling either a **1** or a **6**, then

$$p((1 \oslash 6)/s) = p(1/s) + p(6/s)$$
$$1/6 + 1/6 = 1/3$$

It is customary to simplify this notation whenever the same set of conditions is referred to in every expression in a formula. For instance, in the example just used *s* represents the condition that an ordinary die is to be rolled once and appears in every term of $p((1 \oslash 6)/s) = p(1/s) + p(6/s)$. Thus, for the sake of simplicity we may take $p(1 \oslash 6) = p(1) + p(6)$ to mean the same as the original formula. We will use the simpler notation in all cases in which it is appropriate.

If we wish to determine the probability of rolling an odd number, then

$$p(1 \oslash 3 \oslash 5) = p(1) + p(3) + p(5)$$
$$1/6 + 1/6 + 1/6 = 1/2$$

It is useful to note that from

$$p(b/a) + p(c/a) = 1$$

it follows that

$$p(b/a) = 1 - p(c/a)$$

There are many instances in which the latter formula affords a much shorter way of calculating probability. To see why, compare the two following methods for calculating the probability of *not* rolling a **1** on a single roll of a die:

(1) $p(\sim 1) = p(2) + p(3) + p(4) + p(5) + p(6)$
     $= 1/6 + 1/6 + 1/6 + 1/6 + 1/6$
     $= 5/6$

(2) $p(\sim 1) = 1 - p(1)$
     $= 1 - 1/6$
     $= 5/6$

Another principle is required for the calculation of *a priori* probability for independent occurrences. For example, if two coins are tossed, or one coin is tossed twice, the results of the two tosses are independent, i.e., neither toss affects the other. The probability of getting tails on two tosses, $p(t/2)$, can be determined by multiplying the probability of getting tails on the first toss, $p(t/f)$, by the probability of getting tails on the second toss, $p(t/s)$:

$$p(t/2) = p(t/f) \times p(t/s)$$
$$= \quad 1/2 \quad \times \quad 1/2 \quad = \quad 1/4$$

Similarly, the probability of rolling a pair of 1s on a pair of dice (or by rolling one die twice) can be determined:

$$p((1/f) \quad \text{and} \quad (1/s)) = p(1/f) \times p(1/s)$$
$$= \quad 1/6 \quad \times \quad 1/6 = 1/36$$

The situation is only slightly more complicated if we wish to determine the probability of rolling a 7. In each of the cases we have considered so far, the numerical value of the probability has been a ratio of the possible cases yielding a particular result to all of the possible cases. This ratio is seen straightforwardly when we note that there is a one-out-of-six chance of rolling a 1 on a single die. A little reflection makes it clear that the same ratio is being obtained when we calculate the probability of rolling a pair of 1s—since we are considering two dice, each having six faces, there are *36* possible results, and only one of these *36* is a pair of 1s. Thus the probability of rolling a 7 is the ratio of the possibilities resulting in a 7 to the *36* possible results. Six possibilities result in a 7: (1) **1** on the first die and **6** on the second, (2) **6** on the first die and **1** on the second, (3) **2** on the first die and **5** on the second, (4) **5** on the first die and **2** on the second, (5) **3** on the first die and **4** on the second, (6) **4** on the first die and **3** on the second. Using the formula above for the conjunction of two independent possibilities, we know that the probability of getting any *one* of these six pairs is *1/36*. For example

$$p((1/f) \quad \text{and} \quad (6/s)) = p(1/f) \times p(6/s) = 1/6 \times 1/6 = 1/36$$
$$\text{and} \quad p((5/f) \quad \text{and} \quad (2/s)) = p(5/f) \times p(2/s) = 1/6 \times 1/6 = 1/36$$

The probability of getting any one of these six mutually exclusive possibilities follows from the principle for disjunction discussed earlier

$$p(7) = p(1 \cdot 6) + p(6 \cdot 1) + p(2 \cdot 5) + p(5 \cdot 2) + p(3 \cdot 4) + p(4 \cdot 3)$$
$$= 1/36 + 1/36 + 1/36 + 1/36 + 1/36 + 1/36$$
$$= 1/6$$

EXERCISES

I

1. Calculate the probability of rolling either a **5** or a **6** on a single roll of a die.
2. Calculate the probability of rolling an even number on a single roll of a die.
3. Calculate the probability of getting three heads in three consecutive tosses of a coin.
4. Calculate the probability of getting either two heads or two tails on two consecutive tosses of a coin.
5. On a single roll of a pair of dice, calculate the probability of rolling: (a) a **9**, (b) a **10**, (c) a **12**, (d) any pair in which both dice have the same numerical value.

Generalized Principles for Calculating
A *Priori* Probabilities

The principles introduced in the previous section are effective only when certain restrictions are placed on them. The principle for calculating the probability of a disjunction is effective only when the disjuncts are mutually exclusive, while the principle for calculating the probability of a conjunction is effective only when the conjuncts are independent. However, both of these principles can be generalized so that they are effective in other cases as well.

The principle for calculating the probability of a mutually exclusive disjunction, $p((b \oslash c)/a) = p(b/a) + p(c/a)$ can be stated more generally for any a, b, and c as

$$p((b \lor c)/a) = p(b/a) + p(c/a) - p((b \cdot c)/a)$$

The general disjunction rule also covers the special case of mutually exclusive disjunction because in that case $p((b \cdot c)/a) = 0$.

To illustrate use of the generalized disjunction rule, let us calculate the probability that at least one **6** will turn up when a die is rolled twice. The probability of getting a **6** on either the first or second roll is given by

$$
\begin{aligned}
p((6/f) \lor p(6/s)) &= p(6/f) + p(6/s) - p((6 \cdot 6)/2) \\
&= 1/6 \quad\;\; + 1/6 \quad\; - 1/36 \\
&= 11/36
\end{aligned}
$$

Similarly, the principle for calculating the probability of a conjunction in which the conjuncts are independent, $p((b \cdot c)/a) = p(b/a) \times p(c/a)$, can be generalized for any a, b, and c as:

$$p((b \cdot c)/a) = p(b/a) \times p(c/b)$$

To illustrate use of the generalized conjunction rule, let us calculate the probability of drawing two spades in two consecutive draws from a deck of cards. To determine this probability we must know whether the card drawn first will be returned to the deck. Since a deck contains *52* cards, *13* of which are spades, the probability of getting a spade on the first draw is *13/52*, or *1/4*. Since we are only concerned with the case in which both drawings yield spades, there will be *12* spades in addition to the one drawn first. If the spade drawn first is returned to the deck, then the first drawing will have no effect on the second. When the two drawings are independent, the probability of getting a spade each time is the same, *13/52* or *1/4*. Hence, when the card from the first drawing is returned to the deck, the probability of turning up two spades can be obtained by using the specialized conjunction rule: *1/4* × *1/4* = *1/16*. *But*, if a spade obtained on the first drawing is not replaced, then the two drawings are not independent. In this case *51* cards will remain in the deck, *12* of them spades. Thus use of the generalized conjunction rule

$$p((s \cdot s)/2) = p(s_1/d_1) \times p(s_2/d_2)$$
$$= 13/52 \quad \times 12/51$$
$$= 1/17$$

where s_1/d_1 represents getting a spade on the first draw and s_2/d_2 represents getting a second spade on the second draw, yields the probability of drawing two spades on two draws.

EXERCISES

II

1. What is the probability of drawing five cards of the same suit consecutively, if the cards drawn are not returned to the deck?
2. What is the probability that either a **7** or an **11** will come up in three rolls of a pair of dice?
3. A player in a game of draw poker holds the **5** of hearts, and the **6, 7, 8,** and queen of clubs. For what should he draw?
4. Suppose a player in a game of draw poker holds the **6, 7,** and **9** of diamonds; the **10** of spades; and the **10** of clubs. Which of the following options should he favor: (a) discarding one of the **10s** and drawing for a straight, (b) discarding both of the **10s** and drawing for a flush, or (c) discarding the three diamonds and drawing for a third **10**?
5. Suppose that you have discovered an old diary in the attic of a decaying mansion. From the diary you learn that on the property there is a buried treasure lying under a lane *46* paces from a gate. There are seven gates on the property. There

is a single lane through the main gate. There are only three other outside gates; in each case the lane through the gate goes in three directions within *46* paces inside the gate. There are two lanes leading to the swimming pool gate, but *30* paces inside the pool area the lane ends. Through the garden gate there is a single lane, which does not divide for at least *60* paces in either direction. There is a single lane to the gate to the kennels, and it goes in two directions *15* paces inside the gate. What is the probability you will dig in the right place first?

Relative Frequency

All the probabilities we have considered so far are *a priori* probabilities. To calculate *a priori* probabilities, one needs to consider only a set of initial conditions (for example, that a deck contains *52* cards and a certain number of drawings will be made) and a principle (or formula) which yields the ratio of possibilities favoring a particular outcome to the total number of possibilities. Actual outcomes are not taken into consideration. If one were to toss a true coin ten times, and heads came up eight times, that would not alter the *a priori* probability of expected outcomes. The *a priori* probability that heads will turn up on any given toss would still be *1/2*.

Whenever past outcomes *are* taken into consideration in determining expected outcomes, the probability of a particular outcome is calculated by ascertaining its relative frequency with respect to previous outcomes in similar situations. The numerical value of the probability is the ratio of cases in which that particular outcome was obtained to all previous outcomes. For example, suppose that a series of tests has been performed on *100* cars of the same make and model and three of these have been found to have faulty brakes. Thus three of these *100* cars, or *3* percent, have been observed to have faulty brakes. This figure can be used to estimate the frequency with which cars of this make and model can be expected to have brake failures in circumstances sufficiently similar to the test conditions.

Even the most cursory survey of the information we encounter daily will show that a large portion of that data is obtained by establishing relative frequencies. The reason for this is that most of the things we are interested in having information about are members of large classes—the class of human beings, the class of consumer products, etc. Since these classes have so many members it is practically impossible to get information about every member of a class. Hence, estimates about the characteristics of classes are made on the basis of observation of some of their members. When information is obtained in this way, the whole class, or group, about which the information is obtained is called a **population,** and the portion of the group which is actually observed is called a **sample.**

We also use relative frequencies to characterize comparatively large groups when it *is* possible to observe every member of the group. Employing relative frequencies in these cases allows us to describe the group as a whole, and makes use of the information about the group more convenient. For example, suppose that we wish to describe scores on an intelligence test taken by *2000* students. One way of offering a description would be simply to list the *2000* scores. Although this procedure would constitute a complete description, we are seldom satisfied with information in this form. One way of putting this information into a more useful form would be to state the **arithmetic mean,** i.e., the score obtained by adding up all the individual scores and dividing by the total number of individuals. Or, we might wish to state the **median:** the score which is in the middle, having the same number of scores above and below it. Or, we might wish to state the **mode:** the score made by the largest number of individuals.

Use of statistical data to describe groups of individuals by giving information about the relative frequency of properties which characterize those groups is known as **descriptive statistics.** Use of statistical data to predict the relative frequency of properties characterizing groups is known as **projective statistics.** An example of projective statistics is provided by the situation described above in which it was predicted that *3* percent of cars of a particular make and model *would* have brake failure under conditions similar to test conditions.

A great deal of scientific investigation involves acquiring accurate descriptive statistical data about samples and then projecting these results so that they apply to populations. To acquire accurate descriptive data, it is often necessary to select two samples from the population under investigation. One of these is designated as the **experimental group;** the other, the **control group.** The researcher then attempts to see that all the relevant factors except the one being tested are similar for the experimental and control groups. For example, suppose that a drug company were testing a new drug on rats. Two groups of rats would be kept as nearly as possible under the same conditions, except that the experimental group would be administered the new drug while the control group would receive a placebo (an ineffective substance administered in the same way the drug is). There are a great many instances of this sort in which the use of control groups is necessary to make sure that the data obtained is a measure of the condition being tested. This is especially true in cases where humans are the subject of investigation.

To correctly interpret statistical data, it is also often necessary to know the range and standard deviation of the values obtained. The **range** is simply the maximum difference between the two extreme numerical values. For example, suppose that a *10*-point quiz is taken by ten students, and that their scores are *4, 2, 3, 9, 4, 9, 5, 8, 6,* and *10*. The range for this set of scores is *9*—the number of possible scores between, and including, *10* (the highest score), and *2* (the lowest).

Standard deviation is a measure of dispersion within a range and is determined by calculating the square root of the arithmetical average of the squares of deviation from the mean. Calculation of standard deviation is not as difficult as it sounds. Consider again the ten scores above. The mean of these scores is *6*—the sum of all the scores, *60*, divided by the number of scores, *10*. Now we need to know how far each of these scores deviates from the mean. This is shown in the second column below.

Score	Deviation from Mean	Square of Deviation
4	−2	4
2	−4	16
9	+3	9
3	−3	9
4	−2	4
9	+3	9
5	−1	1
8	+2	4
6	0	0
10	+4	16

The first score, *4*, is two less than the mean, *6;* the second score, *2*, is four less than the mean; the third score, *9*, is three more than the mean, etc. The column on the right contains the squares of the deviations: *4* is −*2* squared, *16* is −*4* squared, *9* is +*3* squared, etc. The sum of the squares of the deviation is *72*. If *72* is divided by *10* (the number of scores), the result is *7.2*. The square root of *7.2* is *2.68*, which is the standard deviation for this set of scores. That is to say, the average deviation of the individual scores from the mean is *2.68*.

Another use for statistics in describing data, one frequently used in evaluating individual scores on examinations taken by a large number of people, is to determine percentile ranks. The **percentile rank** of a score is the percentage of scores which are less than or equal to that score. The following table lists in increasing order the scores we considered above. The second column shows the number of people making each score, or stated alternatively, the frequency of the occurrence of the score. The third column shows the cumulative frequency of scores in the order in which they are listed.

Score	Frequency	Cumulative Frequency
2	1	1
3	1	2
4	2	4
5	1	5
6	1	6
8	1	7
9	2	9
10	1	10

From the table we can see that the person making a score of *8* has done better than six other people taking the exam, and that there are *7* scores less than, or equal to, this person's score. To obtain the percentile rank of *8* in this set of scores, divide its cumulative frequency by the total number of scores and multiply the result by *100* (7 divided by *10* is *.7*, and *.7* multiplied by *100* is *70*). A percentile rank of 70 means that the person making a score of *8* did as well, or better than, 70 percent of those taking the exam. The percentile rank of a score enables one to tell at a glance the relationship of one score to others, whereas simply knowing an individual score gives one very little information. Consider how little one would know about the score of *8* in our example if he did not know any of the other scores or did not know the possible number of points on the test.

EXERCISES

III

1. Given the following set of numerical values, find (a) the mean, (b) the median, (c) the mode, (d) the range, and (e) the standard deviation.

2	*5*	*7*	*10*
2	*6*	*7*	*25*
2	*6*	*8*	*60*
4	*7*	*8*	*80*
4	*7*	*10*	*100*

2. Suppose that the numberical values above represent the salaries in thousands of dollars per year of people in a particular community: (a) What conclusions about the distribution of wealth in this community will these data support? (b) How would one's expectations regarding the distribution of wealth vary if he considered *only* the arithmetic mean? Only the median? Only the mode? (c) What is the percentile rank of *$7000* in this community?

Epistemic Probability

In addition to *a priori* probability and relative frequency, a third type of probability, epistemic probability, is sometimes recognized. For example, consider the remark 'Susan will probably be late'. A person who makes this kind of remark can usually offer only very rough estimates of the number of occasions Susan is on time and the number of occasions she is late. Consequently, the evidence this person has for believing that Susan will be late is different from evidence showing that in the last two months Susan has attended *40* events scheduled to begin at a specific time and has been late to *30* of them; hence the probability that she will be late on this occasion is *0.75*. It is also quite different from the evidence on which *a priori* probabilities are based. However, the conclusion that Susan will be late may nevertheless rest on evidence, viz., the knowledge of Susan's behavior possessed by the person making the assertion. Since the word 'epistemic' is used to refer to knowledge, some philosophers call this kind of evidence *epistemic probability*. Because different people possess different knowledge, the epistemic probability of a statement can vary from person to person. Furthermore, because we are capable of acquiring new information and of forgetting, the epistemic probability of a statement can vary for the same person at different times.

One should note, however, that it is still the case that a particular body of information, whoever possesses it, will offer a fixed amount of support for a particular conclusion. It may be reasonable for Tom, given his relevant information, to believe that the price of a particular stock will go up; while it is reasonable for Dick, given his relevant information, to believe that the stock will go down. But if the belief is reasonable for Tom, then it is reasonable for *anyone* having the *same* information as he; and the same is true of Dick's belief. To be able to say which beliefs are reasonable on the basis of the information available for use as inductive premises is to have criteria for evaluating inductive arguments, and we will turn to these criteria in the next section.

The Meaning of 'Probability'

We have seen that there are at least three ways to interpret the meaning of 'probability': (1) as *a priori* probability, (2) as relative frequency, and (3) as epistemic probability. Philosophers have not reached general agreement on whether these are the only meanings the word has. Other meanings have been proposed. Some philosophers have argued that all of the meanings of 'probability' are reducible to *a priori* probability, while others have maintained that all are reducible to relative frequency. We will not attempt to resolve any of these disputes here, or even to delineate the positions which have been taken. We wish only to point out that this fundamental issue concerning the philosophical theory of inductive logic is not yet settled to everyone's satisfaction. However, the fact that there is such controversy does not affect the development of criteria for evaluation of inductive arguments.

TYPES OF INDUCTIVE INFERENCES
AND THEIR MISUSES

Thus far we have examined the character of inductive arguments in terms of the meaning of 'probability' in statements such as 'The probability of drawing a king is *1/13*', 'The probability that this tire will be safe for *25,000* miles is *0.87*', and 'I will probably forget my umbrella'. Another means of classifying inductive arguments, suggested by Rudolf Carnap, is with respect to whether an inference is made from sample to population, from population to sample, or from sample to sample.

Inferences from Sample to Population

One of the most common types of inference from sample to population is induction by simple enumeration. The argument form of simple enumeration can be represented as follows:

> a is an F and a is a G
> b is an F and b is a G
> c is an F and c is a G
> . . . .
> n is an F and n is a G
> ————————————————
> For all x, if x is an F, then x is a G.

A shorter representation of this argument scheme is

> All instances of F's observed so far have been G's.
> ————————————————
> All F's are G's.

Arguments of this sort are used to establish such conclusions as the boiling or freezing points of chemical compounds, that acid turns blue litmus paper red, etc. For example

> Sample a is water and boils at 100°C. at sea level.
> Sample b is water and boils at 100°C. at sea level.
> Sample c is water and boils at 100°C. at sea level.
> . . . .
> Sample n is water and boils at 100°C. at sea level.
> ————————————————
> All water boils at 100°C. at sea level.

Or
> In all observed instances, water has boiled at 100°C. at sea level.
> ————————————————
> Water boils at 100°C. at sea level.

Induction by simple enumeration need not have a conclusion of the form *All F's are G's*. For instance, arguments such as

> 90% of the seeds in Burrpea Company's Package A germinated.
> 90% of the seeds in Burrpea Company's Package B germinated.
> 90% of the seeds in Burrpea Company's Package C germinated.
> . . . .
> 90% of the seeds in Burrpea Company's Package N germinated.
> ————————————————
> 90% of the seeds packaged by Burrpea Company will germinate.

are inductions by enumeration. The similarity of the form of this argument to the form of those above is obvious. The most apparent difference is that the conclusion of the first argument has the form *All F is G* while the conclusion of the second argument has the form *x percent of F is G*. Statements of the form *All F is G* are sometimes called **inductive generalizations** and those of the form *x percent of F is G* are sometimes called **statistical generalizations.** Since the inductive generalization *All F is G* might also be written as the statistical generalization *100 percent of F is G*, the form of the conclusion does not affect the form of the argument.

There are cases in which we should be suspicious of conclusions reached by simple enumeration. Consider

> In all observed instances the price of Product *X* has been 25 cents.
> All Product *X*'s will cost 25 cents.

Since we have no guarantee that inflation is about to cease permanently, we do not have much confidence in this conclusion. Our mistrust of this inference comes from knowing that the argument neglects relevant information. This is to say that one of the criteria for a good inductive argument is that it take into account *all* of the available *relevant* information. But specifying precisely what counts as relevant information is an extremely difficult task.

We know that information is relevant to establishing a particular conclusion when the statements involved contain assertions about causally connected events. If we wish to conclude something about the speed of automobiles, the size of their engines is a relevant consideration, because engine size is causally connected with speed. But if we wish to conclude something about the color of automobile upholstery, engine size is irrelevant since it is not causally related to upholstery color. However, the fact that causal connections indicate *relevant* considerations does not help us specify a *criterion* for relevance, for the situations in which we need a criterion for relevance are likely to be precisely those where we do not know what the causal connections are. And since inductive arguments, such as simple enumeration, are quite often the means by which causal connections are established, a criterion for relevance in terms of causal relations would involve a vicious circularity. Hence, instead of attempting to specify a causal criterion for relevance which applies to arguments in which an inference is made from sample to population, we will specify other criteria for their evaluation. If these other criteria are selected appropriately, they should go some way toward ensuring that such arguments rely on relevant considerations. One way of arriving at such criteria is to make explicit the considerations involved in selecting samples.

There are numerous notorious examples of erroneous conclusions based on biased samples. A **biased sample** is one which does not accurately represent the entire population. Such a sample can result from observing too few instances, and the likelihood that a small sample will be biased increases in proportion to the diversity of the population. For example, suppose that six people in a trade organization with one hundred members were interviewed, and the result showed that five of these six were satisfied with current trade regulations, while the sixth was dissatisfied with them. On the basis of this sample, one could conclude that *83* percent of the membership of this organization are content with current trade regulations. This estimate *might* be accurate, but it *could* easily be the case that, in interviewing all one hundred members, we would find that sixty were satisfied with the current regulations, while forty were dissatisfied; hence, *83* percent would have been much too high and would have misled us about the opinions of the membership. It is also possible that the five people in the original sample could have been the only members who were satisfied.

An advertising campaign based on a very small sample recently resulted in a lawsuit against a manufacturing company. The promotion was built around the claim that two out of three members of a profession, the membership of which numbered in the thousands, preferred a particular product over all of its competitors. The company manufacturing one of its competitors initiated legal proceedings when they discovered that the sample surveyed was comprised of only six members of the profession.

Increasing sample size obviously tends to decrease the probability of an erroneous conclusion, but in some cases even a sample which includes a high percentage of the population may nevertheless be biased. However, we can increase our confidence in estimates made from relatively small samples if we take into account the kind of sample being used.

For most purposes it is important to have a **random sample.** There are several means by which random samples can be obtained, and the method employed varies according to the subject matter being investigated. For instance, a botanist who attempts to characterize accurately the flora of a flat area might select samples by walking diagonally across the area and tossing hoops to his right and left alternately every eight steps, then classifying and counting the plants within each hoop. In many cases it is extremely difficult for the investigator to select samples at random, because his choice may be influenced by factors of which he is unaware. If our botanist set out without a particular procedure and simply placed hoops at what he thought to be randomly selected spots, in his zeal to get data he might choose (even without realizing it) to place his hoops only in places where the vegetation appeared to be more lush. Or, if he were more lazy than zealous, he might choose areas where the vegetation appeared to be more sparse.

To avoid biased samples, botanists might assign numbers to the samples they wish to consider and then select from the numbers. For example, in describing the flora of an area they might map it, then divide the map into sections of equal size and assign numbers to each section. The investigator could then choose among the numbers, taking as his samples the land areas corresponding to the numbers chosen. But it has also been shown that humans frequently do not avoid bias in their selection of numbers. However, the effect of our aesthetic tastes for particular numbers can be nullified by using random number tables. These tables contain numbers selected by chance by a computer.

The problem of biased sampling becomes especially critical when surveying a stratified population. A population is said to be **stratified** when it has distinguishable subclasses. For example, the total population of the United States contains a great variety of subclasses differing in occupation, religious affiliation, educational and economic level, political opinion, etc. To get an unbiased sample from such a population, one attempts to obtain a random sample from each relevant subclass, or stratum. Political pollsters who have failed to do this have often met with disaster. One of the best known examples of this is the *Literary Digest* poll for the 1936 presidential election. The *Literary Digest* had previously held a very good record for accuracy in political polls, but their prediction of a substantial victory for Landon over Roosevelt resulted in the demise of the magazine. The major difficulty with this particular poll was that the sample was obtained from the magazine's own subscribers and from persons listed in city telephone directories all of whom were relatively prosperous. During the Depression years such a questionnaire would have reached very few economic strata, not to mention its neglect of the rural population; hence the poll actually sampled the opinions of only a particular sort of voter, not the entire population of voters.

Another case where sampling is likely to characterize a population inaccurately is one in which the population is constantly changing. For instance, one obviously could not determine the growth rate of an organism by taking all of one's samples during one period of its development. What is needed in such situations is a series of samples with appropriate lapses of time between them. The length of time lapse needed is obviously dependent on the subject matter under investigation, but, generally speaking, if the rate of change is rapid, time lapses between samples should be shorter than the time lapses between samples when the rate of change is slow.

Apart from these difficulties, which must be overcome to obtain reliable information about populations on the basis of samples, it is also useful to note how even carefully selected samples can be used to mislead. One case of this type was mentioned earlier as an instance of a sample which was too small. In that case description of the sample—two out of three members of a particular profession prefer product X to all of its competitors—was misleading because part of the information, that the sample included only six persons, was left out. When statistical information is used to influence opinion, sample size is seldom mentioned. Leaving out information is the simplest method of misleading others with arguments involving statistics.

Since many people think of graphs as neutral mathematical representations of information, they have often been used successfully to conceal the omission of important information. The graph below (taken from Darrell Huff, *How to Lie with Statistics*) was used by an advertising company to promote its own wares.

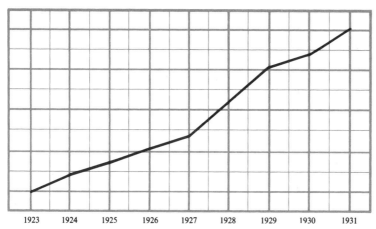

Note that there are no figures to indicate the values on the vertical scale. Thus, as Huff points out, this graph "could have represented a tremendous growth, with business doubling or increasing by millions of dollars a year, or the snail-like progress of a static concern adding only a dollar or two to its annual billings."*

The same effect can be created without omitting the values on the vertical scale. Suppose that we are given the annual sales record of a particular company for a four-year period: first year, *$4.01* million; second year, *$4.08* million; third year, *$4.09* million; fourth year, *$4.11* million. There is an increase in the amount of sales of this company over the period sampled. Compare the two following graphs of this increase:

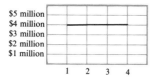 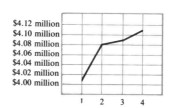

*Darrell Huff, *How to Lie with Statistics*. (New York: W. W. Norton & Co., Inc., 1954), p. 51.

No prospective stock speculator is likely to be impressed by (1), but (2) might get his attention. No mathematical error is made in representing these data by either of these graphs. But a cursory examination of (2) seems to support generalizations about large sales *increases,* while a cursory examination of (1) would be more likely to lead to generalizations about sales being *stable.* Graphs are often very useful in analyzing data and representing the results of analysis, but in cases like the above, more information than is represented by either graph is needed.

The fact that the word 'average' can refer to median, mode, or arithmetic mean is often used to suggest inappropriate generalizations. If one simply speaks of an average without including the data from which the "average" is obtained, his hearer or reader has no way of knowing which of these three is meant. Suppose that a congressman who favors a particular bill to increase taxes argues that the taxpayer will hardly notice paying the higher rate, because the average increase in tax on the items covered by the bill would be only *$.02.* With no opportunity to inspect the figures which yield this "average," many voters would interpret the congressman's claim as meaning that *$.02* was the arithmetic mean or, more loosely, that among the items specified on the bill the increase in tax on a few items would be less than *$.02,* a few would be more than *$.02,* while most would increase exactly *$.02.* Those who took this interpretation for granted might later be surprised to see a table such as this:

	Amount of Tax Increase
Items in Group 1	$ .02
Items in Group 2	.02
Items in Group 3	.02
Items in Group 4	.04
Items in Group 5	.08
Items in Group 6	.10
Items in Group 7	.11
Items in Group 8	.11
Items in Group 9	.12
Items in Group 10	.14
Items in Group 11	.16
Items in Group 12	.16

Since *$.02* occurs three times, it is the mode for these increases, and since the word 'average' may be used to refer to mode, the proponent of the bill could argue that he was not disseminating incorrect information. He has simply produced a descriptive statistic which seems to support his claims about the relatively low amount of the proposed tax increase. Opponents of the bill could argue similarly that the increase would be relatively high because the average (arithmetic mean) is *$.09,* or because the average (median) is *$.105.* In this particular case the arithmetic mean and median yield a more accurate picture than the mode, but this will not always be the case. Therefore, to know which generalizations are supportable, one usually must know which "average" is given.

Regardless of which "average" is cited in support of generalizations, there are obvious advantages in also knowing the range. Consider the difference between the above set of values for which the median is $10\frac{1}{2}$ and the range is 15, and a set of values having a median of $10\frac{1}{2}$ and a range of 55. The set having a range of 55 would include a larger number of relatively low values than relatively high ones since there would be as many below $10\frac{1}{2}$ as above it. The dispersion of values within this range would be quite different from those in the range in the example; hence the generalizations supported by two such sets of data are apt to be quite different.

Leaving out the range and/or standard deviation for presented data can not only suggest inappropriate generalizations, but can also make generalizations appear to be more accurate than they are. Generalizations supported by a set of data having a wide range and a low standard deviation and those supported by a set of data with a narrow range and a high standard deviation are obviously not the same. If one wishes to suggest that a population is homogeneous, it is not to his advantage to mention a high standard deviation; and likewise, if he wishes to make claims implying diversity within a population, it is not to his advantage to mention a low standard deviation.

Paradigm Case Arguments: We have stated that an important requirement of arguments involving generalizations about populations on the basis of information about samples is that the sample be large enough to support the generalization reliably. The weakness of a generalization based on only one instance hardly needs to be pointed out. However, it is sometimes possible to construct satisfactory arguments on the basis of only one case provided that special care is taken to show that the selected case is an ideal representative, or paradigm, of the class covered by the generalization. A **paradigm** is an example which has all of the necessary and typical features of members of that class. Another way of saying this is to say that a paradigm is a *good* example, or an example which exemplifies everything meant by the class concept.

A commonly used form of paradigm case argument reaches a conclusion about what can be said to be true of a class on the basis of what can be said to be true of a paradigm for that class. For example, many philosophical arguments regarding free will begin by arguing that a particular type of action must be free if *any* actions are free, and go on to show that something which is true of this type of action is true of all free actions. In this context it has been argued that I can choose to raise my arm and that this act is free if any acts are free, and since a necessary and salient feature of this act is that I *choose* to do it, therefore all free actions come about in situations in which the agent is able to make a choice.

Notice that the argument used in this example does not claim that there *are* free actions; instead, it arrives at a conclusion about a feature which accompanies free actions if there are any. Thus, whether the argument is satisfactory depends heavily on whether the case chosen *is* a paradigm.

Inferences from Population to Sample

Arguments of the form *All F's are G's,* therefore, *This F is a G* are deductive arguments; but arguments of the form

> All *F*'s observed so far are *G*'s.
> The next *F* observed will be a *G*.

are inductive. The special case in which *all F's* have in fact been observed makes the second form equivalent to the first and, therefore, a deductive argument form. Hence, this type of argument need not be considered here.

The conclusion of the inductive form above can be viewed as constituting a prediction. In the argument

> All eggs in this nest tested so far have been fertile.
> The next egg in this nest which is tested will be fertile.

there can be only a finite number of eggs in a particular nest at a particular time, so the conclusion of this argument makes a prediction about a part of the population which has not been observed (or tested for fertility). On the other hand, the conclusion of the argument

> All of Victoria Holt's novels are romantic mysteries.
> The next novel written by Victoria Holt will be a romantic mystery.

makes a prediction about a *future* part of the population.

It should be obvious that the truth of the premise of each of these arguments fails to guarantee the truth of the conclusion, and that many of the considerations regarding the strength of arguments involving inferences from sample to population are also relevant to those involving inferences from population to sample. Inferences from population to sample, like those from sample to population, frequently make use of descriptive and projective statistics. For example, consider

> Nine out of every ten employees contacted have
>   contributed to the United Fund.
> The probability that the next employee contacted
>   will contribute to the United Fund is 0.9.

The premise contains a descriptive statistic, the conclusion, a projective statistic. Furthermore, conclusions of the form *The next F will be a G* follow from both inductive and statistical generalizations.

As we pointed out above, relevance of the premises to establishing the conclusion is the most important requirement for the strength of all inductive arguments. In the previous section we attempted to ensure that the requirement of relevance would be met by specifying criteria for the selection of samples. Similarly, now we must attempt to ensure that the requirement of relevance will be met by specifying criteria with regard to claims about populations.

We have seen that one of the requirements for samples is that they must be of sufficient size to make generalizations reliable. For precisely the same reasons, generalizations about populations which are used as premises must cover a sufficient number of cases. If *All F's observed so far are G's* is true, but only two out of twenty F's have been observed, our confidence in the likelihood of *The next F observed will be a G* should obviously be less than in a case in which eighteen out of twenty F's have been observed. Leaving out information which is pertinent to evaluation of the strength of claims about populations also allows for misuse of inductive arguments in the same way as omitting information about sample size.

In general we can say that an inductive argument containing an inference about a sample on the basis of a generalization about a population cannot be a strong inductive argument if the generalization itself results from a biased sample. This is to say that one of our concerns in successfully arguing from population to sample is that the argument start from premises which are themselves conclusions of strong inductive arguments containing inferences from sample to population.

Inferences from population to sample often fail because people do not take into account the fact that averages (whether mean, mode, or median) are characteristics of groups, not of individuals. Consider the following argument:

> The average income of persons in the profession
> I am entering is *$15,000* a year.
> _____
> I will make *$15,000* a year.

If the average referred to here is an arithmetic mean, then a few individuals with very high incomes could make this figure too large to represent adequately the income of members of the profession. If the average referred to is the median, then the fact that half of the members of the profession make less than *$15,000* should reduce one's confidence in the conclusion. If the average of *$15,000* is the mode, then a higher degree of confidence is warranted; but the evidence is still far from compelling, for it could be that *200* members of the profession make *$15,000*, while *195* make only

$7,000. Obviously, part of the difficulty in this example is that relevant information has been omitted. But even when all pertinent information has been supplied, any argument in which terms that are only appropriate to the description of a population as a whole are applied to samples will be fallacious. Arguments of this type are a special case of the linguistic fallacy of division discussed in chapter XIII.

The most common failure of inferences from population to sample results from the sample not being sufficiently similar to the population. For example, suppose a sales director made use of the following argument.

> A survey has shown that *46%* of United States homemakers do not own ice-makers but would consider buying one.
> Past sales records for similar products indicate that a reasonable quota for sales personnel in a given area is one half the potential market percentage times the number of households in the area.
> _____
> A reasonable quota for Jack Bunyan, whose territory is northern Alaska, is *23%* of the number of households in northern Alaska.

Our confidence in the truth of the conclusion of this argument is certainly diminished by the fact that it seems likely that homemakers in northern Alaska will be less interested in ice-makers than are homemakers in other areas of the United States. Thus we do not expect the sample (homemakers in northern Alaska) to be sufficiently similar to the population to warrant the sales director's inference. (This error is known as the Fallacy of Accident, see p. 265.)

In this case it is easy to see that a difference in climate is a relevant consideration which has not been taken into account. The instances in which we are apt to be misled by this type of argument are those in which it is difficult to tell whether the population and sample are sufficiently similar. The best precaution against this kind of error is extensive statistical analysis of as many aspects of the data as possible. In the example we have used, a check of the standard deviation for as many aspects of the data as possible would probably show an absence of homogeneity in the population. However, the difficulty in determining whether complex inductive arguments of this sort are weak or strong still remains: There is usually no way of knowing whether one has considered *all* of the relevant aspects. If there were some method for determining whether all relevant aspects had been taken into account, conclusions reached in the natural and social sciences would be much more closely akin to those reached in mathematics.

Inferences from Sample to Sample

Inferences from sample to sample are subject to the same kind of difficulties as those discussed in the preceding paragraph. Arguments involving this kind of inference are a type of analogical argument having the form

$$a \text{ is } F, G, H, \ldots, M$$
$$b \text{ is } F, G, H, \ldots, M$$
$$\underline{a \text{ is } N}$$
$$b \text{ is } N$$

where capital letters represent properties or characteristics of objects, and a and b represent objects or types of objects. In strong arguments of this kind the properties, or characteristics, cited offer good evidence that a and b, or objects of types a and b, are sufficiently similar in relevant respects to conclude that something which is known to be true of one is also true of the other.

> Apple a is small, green, hard, and came from the tree in the southeast corner of Mr. MacGregor's garden.
> Apple b is small, green, hard, and came from the tree in the southeast corner of Mr. MacGregor's garden.
> Eating Apple a gave me a stomachache.
> Eating Apple b would give me a stomachache.

The argument above is a strong inductive argument. Its strength results from the degree of relevant similarity shown between objects a and b.

The following argument is a strong analogical argument from sample to sample in which the samples are objects of particular types rather than individual objects.

> Eagles are birds whose diet consists mainly of fish and whose habitat is trees and cliffs near streams.
> Ospreys are birds whose diet consists mainly of fish and whose habitat is trees and cliffs near streams.
> Eagles are endangered as a species as a result of the use of pesticides.
> Ospreys will be endangered as a species as a result of the use of pesticides.

Just as in the case of all inductive arguments the strength of which depends on there being sufficient similarity among objects or groups of objects, it is often very difficult to know whether arguments from sample to sample have made use of characteristics with sufficient similarity. Many arguments of this type have been the subject of lengthy controversies. For example, various formulations of the Design Argument for the existence of God have occupied the attention of a large number of philosophers and theologians. David Hume presents the Design Argument in the following form:

. . . Look around the world: contemplate the whole and every part of it:
you will find it to be nothing but one great machine, subdivided into an
infinite number of lesser machines, which again admit of subdivisions,
to a degree beyond what human senses and faculties can trace and
explain. All these various machines, and even their most minute parts,
are adjusted to each other with an accuracy, which ravishes into
admiration all men, who have ever contemplated them. The curious
adapting of means to ends, throughout all nature, resembles exactly,
though it much exceeds, the productions of human contrivance;
of human design, thought, wisdom, and intelligence. Since therefore
the effects resemble each other we are led to infer, by all the rules of
analogy, that the causes also resemble; and that the Author of Nature is
somewhat similar to the mind of men; though possessed of much larger
faculties, proportioned to the grandeur of the work, which he has
executed. By this argument . . . , do we prove the existence of a Diety,
and his similarity to human mind and intelligence. (*Dialogue Concerning
Natural Religion*)

Many critics of the Design Argument, including Hume himself, have argued that the argument is ineffective because human contrivances, such as
machines, and the universe cannot be known to be sufficiently similar to
support this analogy.

An important consideration in analogical arguments is the number and
kind of disanalogies between the objects, or types of objects, included in
the argument. It should be obvious that an argument based on two things
with only one similar characteristic and many dissimilar ones must be a
weak analogy. The weakness of the following argument is obviously the
result of this kind of error.

Garlic and chalk are both white.
Garlic is frequently used as a seasoning.
Chalk will frequently be used as a seasoning.

The weakness of arguments which results from their objects being dis-
analogous in a large *number* of respects is generally more easily detectable
than is the weakness of arguments which results from the *kind* of disanal-
ogous characteristics of their objects. As in the case of other forms of
inductive arguments, here again we must consider whether the characteristics cited are relevant or irrelevant to establishing the conclusion. In the
following argument a number of similar characteristics are cited, but they
do not establish the conclusion.

Clyde and Robert can both play chess, type
out messages, answer questions, work
mathematics problems, recite the

> Gettysburg Address, and detect changes
> in the temperature of their surroundings.
> Robert can experience pain.
> _____
> Clyde can also experience pain.

This argument does not initially appear to be exceptionally weak, but suppose that we discover that Clyde and Robert are dissimilar in a very important respect: Clyde is a robot and Robert a human. When we know of this dissimilarity it is much easier to see that this argument would be strengthened considerably if characteristics of a different *kind* were cited in its premises. For instance, if we knew that Clyde, like Robert, was capable of *experiencing* other characteristics ordinarily attributed to humans, such as joy, sorrow, comfort, distrust, and fear, then we would have greater confidence in the truth of the conclusion.

In the last two examples, the dissimilar characteristics are not mentioned in the formulation of the analogies. This is not always the case; such characteristics are often mentioned in analogical arguments. But in strong analogies, the reasons for dissimilarities not decreasing the probability of the conclusion are usually pointed out. When evaluating analogies a good procedure is always to try to discover whether there are relevant dissimilarities which affect the argument. (For further discussion of analogical arguments, see the section on faulty analogies, p.265.)

CONCLUDING REMARKS

In explaining and appraising inductive arguments we have classified them two ways. Since inductive arguments are those in which it is claimed that if the premises are true then it is probable that the conclusion is true, we first classified them as to whether the probability involved is *a priori,* relative frequency, or epistemic probability. Although calculations of *a priori* probabilities are mathematical operations and mathematical operations are deductive rather than inductive, they serve as steps in inductive arguments. The reason for classifying this type of argument as inductive rather than deductive is seen by viewing the argument as a whole. The second way we classified inductive arguments was in terms of whether the inferences involved were from sample to population, from population to sample, or from sample to sample. Any of the three types of probability discussed might be involved in any of these three types of inferences. For example, an inference from sample to population might involve either *a priori* probability, relative frequency, or epistemic probability. (This presupposes acceptance of the position that there are three distinct types of probability.)

The most important consideration in the appraisal of any inductive argument is whether the premises are relevant to establishing the conclusion. Several methods which one may use to help ensure that premises are relevant to establishing a conclusion have been discussed. For example, if there are significant differences in the subclasses of a population, one should obtain stratified samples. An awareness of the methods of attempting to ensure relevance which have been discussed in this chapter can serve as a useful guide in appraising inductive arguments, but in the last analysis the persons who are best able to appraise inductive arguments are those who have the most information at their disposal. Any addition to one's "store of knowledge" increases the probability that he will be successful in evaluating information which is important to him.

SUGGESTED READINGS

KAHANE, HOWARD, *Logic and Philosophy*. 2nd ed. Belmont, Calif.: Wadsworth, 1973.

LUCKENBACH, SIDNEY A., ed., *Probabilities, Problems, and Paradoxes: Readings In Inductive Logic*. Encino, Calif.: Dickenson Publishing Co., Inc., 1972.

SCHEFFLER, ISRAEL, *The Anatomy of Inquiry*. New York: Alfred A. Knopf, 1963.

SKYRMS, BRIAN, *Choice and Chance: An Introduction to Inductive Logic*. Belmont, Calif.: Dickenson Publishing Co., Inc., 1966. 2nd ed., 1975.

II

LANGUAGE

If one is successful in appraising arguments and in arguing effectively, he must not only be concerned with the validity, soundness, and inductive strength of arguments, but also with the language in which they are expressed. For if arguments are inadequately expressed, they will not satisfy these other criteria. In this chapter we discuss some of the basic functions of language, a number of distinctions and concepts which are useful in the formulation and expression of arguments, types of agreement and disagreement, and the role which language plays in agreement and disagreement.

SIX BASIC FUNCTIONS OF LANGUAGE

Almost every human endeavor involves the use of language. Indeed, it is the use of language which most markedly sets human beings apart from other animals. Since language is used for so many purposes, we will not attempt to list all of its functions, but will discuss only six of its more basic and important functions. These are the **informative, directive, emotive, evaluative, operative,** and **ceremonial** functions.

Informative Language

Language is used informatively when it is used in an attempt to state facts, offer explanations, and make predictions. Our goal in using informative language, then, is to inform others of our beliefs and theories about the world. Of course, language may also be used to *mis*inform others. But the factor which determines whether language is being used informatively is not whether what is said is actually true or false, but only whether it can be significantly appraised as true or false. This is the most essential feature of informative language. Some examples of this kind of language are:

> Aaron Copland wrote the ballet *Appalachian Spring*.
> The haploid nucleus of neurospora contains seven chromosomes.
> The eclipse will occur at 11:10 tomorrow.

Directive Language

Language is used directively when it is used in an attempt to tell someone what to do or how to do it. Commands, recipes, directions for assembling something, and rules for filling out tax forms are all instances of directive language. Directive language cannot be significantly appraised as true or false, but it can sometimes be appraised as appropriate or inappropriate. For example, if someone were to say "Close the window, please" when the window was already closed, his remark would be inappropriate in that situation. Directive language also may be appraised as legitimate or illegitimate. For example, a military order given by a sergeant might be legitimate, but the same order given by a corporal might be illegitimate.

Emotive Language

Language is used emotively when it is used in an attempt to express one's feelings and emotions, or to arouse feelings and emotions in others. 'Ouch', 'boo', 'damn', 'whew', and 'alas' are instances of emotive language. However, emotive language is not limited to such simple expressions as these. It ranges all the way from terms of abuse and invective, such as 'wop' or 'nigger', to expressions of religious awe or wonder such as the *Twenty-third Psalm* or Dante's *Divine Comedy*. Most poetic language is emotive in nature; in fact, Wordsworth even defined poetry as "emotion recollected in tranquility." Like directive language, emotive language cannot be significantly appraised as true or false; it can only be appraised as more or less adequately expressing or arousing emotion. Thus, to criticize poetry because what it states is not true is to miss the point.

Evaluative Language

Language is used evaluatively when it is used in an attempt to evaluate things as good or bad, right or wrong, or to prescribe what ought, or ought not, to be done. Examples of evaluative language are:

> Murder is wrong.
> His explanations were inadequate.
> It was a wise and successful plan.
> This is priced too high.

Despite the *prima facie* difference between evaluative language and the other types we have discussed, some philosophers have attempted to reduce it to one or more of those types. However, such attempts now seem to be generally discredited. Stating what ought to be done, or justifying one course of action as better than another, is not the same as stating a fact or expressing emotion, although it may involve both of these. Nor is stating what ought to be done the same as telling someone to do something. To state that a patient has white spots on his tongue is to describe his condition; to tell him to take some aspirin and go to bed is to issue a directive; to become angry and curse him if he does not follow your orders is to express emotion; but to state that being healthy is a worthwhile goal which ought to be pursued is different from each of these and is an instance of evaluative language. Although most philosophers today would deny that evaluative language is reducible to other types, there is still widespread disagreement as to whether it is appropriate to speak of it as true or false, or whether it can only be described as correct or incorrect in some other sense.

Operative Language

Language is used operatively when it is used to promise to do something, or to enter into contracts and agreements.* As in the case of evaluative language, there are philosophers who would attempt to reduce operative language to one of the other functions we have discussed. But, once again, there is a *prima facie* difference between it and the other types. Promising is not the same as expressing or arousing emotion, evaluating, or issuing a

---

*The term 'operative' is borrowed from J. L. Austin and designates a subclass of what he referred to as 'performatives'. Since our aim here is only to list some of the more important functions of language, Austin's more generalized theory of speech acts is not discussed. Students who are interested in the philosophy of language should consult the suggested readings at the end of the chapter.

directive. Nor is promising the same as informing someone of your intentions. For example, to promise to return a book tomorrow is not to predict that you will return it.

As in the case of evaluative language, there is also disagreement regarding the sense in which operative language may be said to be correct or incorrect. But whatever the outcome of this debate, it is obvious from the role promises, contracts, and agreements play in social life that the operative use of language is one of its more important functions.

Ceremonial Language

Language is used ceremonially when it is used to perform some ceremony or ritual. Examples of ceremonial language are:

> I christen this ship the *Good Ship Lollipop.*
> I hereby baptize you.
> I now pronounce you man and wife.

Other examples of ceremonial language are words of greeting or parting, social chitchat, and government proclamations and declarations. Like operative language, ceremonial language obviously plays an important role in social life.

LANGUAGE SERVING MULTIPLE FUNCTIONS

It is rarely possible to describe a human activity in terms of one category alone. Therefore, there is no reason to suppose that a given assertion can serve only one linguistic function at a time. For example, if a wife says to her husband "John, do you realize that we are late for the party?" she may be both stating a fact and urging her husband to hurry. Similarly, the pronouncement "Hear ye, hear ye, the court is now in session" is both directive and ceremonial. It both directs the audience to quiet down and begins the ceremony. And, a remark such as "It was an excellent play" may function both emotively and evaluatively.

One reason for the belief that language can serve only one function at a time is that grammatical form has often been confused with linguistic function. Grammarians have traditionally classified sentences into four types: declarative, imperative, interrogative, and exclamatory. So it has seemed to many people that form could be identified with function, i.e., that only declaratives function informatively, only imperatives function directively, and so forth. But this is not the case. The wife's remark to her husband cited above is interrogative in form, but informative and directive in function. The remark "Goodbye. I had a nice time at your party," on the other hand, is declarative in form but emotive and ceremonial in function.

Not only is it a mistake to think that there is an invariant connection between form and function, but to do so is to overlook important distinctions. For instance, to think that because '*x* is good' and '*x* is yellow' are both declarative in form, they must both function to state facts is to ignore the distinction between describing and prescribing. That is to say, it is to ignore the difference between stating what is or is not the case and stating what ought or ought not to be the case. Finally, some linguistic functions have no special forms; for example, there is no special form for the operative use of language.

EXERCISES

I

1. Explain how the six basic functions of language discussed above differ from one another.
2. Explain why grammatical form and linguistic function cannot be equated.
3. What linguistic function do the following passages perform? If more than one function is performed, specify which function you believe to be primary.
   (a) "Torpedoes! Torpedoes! Damn the torpedoes! Full speed ahead!" (Admiral Farragut)
   (b) "The history of all hitherto existing society is the history of class struggles." (Marx and Engels, *Communist Manifesto*)
   (c) "Double, double toil and trouble; Fire burn, and caldron bubble." (Shakespeare, *Macbeth*)
   (d) "Death, therefore, the most awful of evils, is nothing to us, seeing that when we are, death is not come, and, when death is come, we are not." (Epicurus)
   (e) I promise to tell the truth, the whole truth, and nothing but the truth.
   (f) "But I say unto you, That ye resist not evil: but whosoever shall smite thee on they right cheek, turn to him the other also." (Matthew)
   (g) "There is more to heredity than mutation. The genetical contribution to evolutionary theory is much more extensive and subtle than the mere sudden origin of new characteristics." (George Gaylord Simpson, *Horses*)
   (h) "Nothing in the whole world, or even outside of the world, can possibly be regarded as good without limitation, except a *good will*." (Kant, *Fundamental Principles of the Metaphysics of Morals*)
   (i) The party of the first part hereby agrees to pay the party of the second part, $1,000 (one thousand dollars) in equal installments.
   (j) My heart leaps up when I behold
       A rainbow in the sky.
       So was it when my life began;
       So is it now I am a man,
       So be it when I shall grow old,
       Or let me die! (Wordsworth, *My Heart Leaps Up*)

SIGNS

Logicians are concerned with language as a means of conveying evidence. Thus they are interested primarily in its informative use. We may define **language** for our purpose here, then, as a set of signs adopted for the purpose of conveying information and governed by rules correlating the signs with one another and with their subject matter. A **sign** is an object or event taken by some interpreter as indicating something else. The thing indicated may be of any type whatever—physical or nonphysical. Moreover, there are various ways in which signs may indicate. It is customary to speak of whatever a sign indicates as its **referent.** Although this word is misleading because it suggests that there is only one way in which a sign can indicate, it is still the best single term for talking about the things indicated by signs.

The philosophical study of signs, sometimes called **semiotic,** is divided into three branches: **semantics,** the study of the relations of signs to their referents; **syntactics,** the study of the relations of signs to one another; and **pragmatics,** the study of the relations of signs to those who create and use them.

Signs may be classified as natural or conventional. A **natural sign** is one that stands in a natural relation to its referent. Examples of natural signs are clouds taken to indicate rain and smoke taken to indicate fire. Not only humans, but other animals respond to natural signs. For example, a doe may interpret a noise or an odor as a sign of danger for her offspring. Natural signs, therefore, often function merely as behavorial signals. But it is important to note that even at this level, nothing is a sign apart from some interpreter. Although smoke is causally connected with fire, it is not a sign of fire unless it is taken to be so by some interpreter. A **conventional sign** is one that has been arbitrarily adopted by two or more common interpreters. By 'arbitrary' is meant only that there need be no natural or causal relation between the sign and its referent. For instance, the word 'smoke' has been taken by users of the English language to refer to smoke, but some other sequence of letters could have served this purpose equally well.

SYMBOLS

Conventional signs are often referred to as **symbols.** Symbols are much more complicated than natural signs and, as a rule, cannot be interpreted as merely behavorial signals. They involve conception, and to conceive of something is not the same as reacting in a stimulus-response fashion. The use of symbols allows us to refer to, and talk about, objects and events far removed from immediate experience. Although both humans and other animals respond to natural signs, only humans have developed the capacity to use symbols to any significant extent.

Symbols may be either **linguistic** or **nonlinguistic.** Examples of non-linguistic symbols are the Cross, the Star of David, the Swastika, maps, road signs, one's arm placed in a particular way to indicate a traffic maneuver, etc. Natural languages such as French and German are the primary examples of linguistic symbols, but there are other kinds, for example, mathematical and musical notations.

EXERCISES

II

1. Which function of language is of most interest to logicians?
2. How is 'language' defined above?
3. What is a sign?
4. What is a referent?
5. What is Semiotic? What are its divisions?
6. How do natural and conventional signs (symbols) differ?
7. State whether the signs mentioned in the following examples (taken from William P. Alston, *Philosophy of Language*) are natural or conventional. If conventional, state whether they are linguistic or nonlinguistic.

   (a) Boulders of this sort are a sign of glacial activity.
   (b) This is a diagram of an 80-watt power amplifier.
   (c) 'Equiangular' means the property of having all angles equal to each other.
   (d) When the umpire moves his hands horizontally, palm down, that means safe.
   (e) That expression on his face means trouble.
   (f) 'Pinochle' is the name of a game.
   (g) Four bells indicate fire.

TERMS

One important group of linguistic symbols is called terms. Although the notion of a term is rather easily grasped, it is not easily defined. The following working definition serves our purpose here: **Terms** are the smallest linguistic expressions which serve as units in expressing meaning. This definition distinguishes terms from both letters of the alphabet, which are combined to create terms, and from sentences, which are composed of terms. Of course, some terms may contain other terms as parts. For example, not only the expression 'man', but also the expression 'fat man', is a term.

Terms may be classified as follows: **Syntactical terms** are those such as 'if . . . then', 'either . . . or', 'but', 'some', and 'all', which state relations between other terms or propositions. **Nonsyntactical terms** are either semantic or nonsemantic. **Semantic terms** are those which function referentially. By 'function referentially' is meant naming, denoting, designating, etc. (See the discussion of denoting and designating below.) **Nonsemantic terms** are those which do not function referentially. For example, although such words as 'ouch', 'damn', and 'alas' may be taken as indicating the presence of emotion, unlike words such as 'fear', 'anxiety', and 'hope' they do not refer to emotions.

Semantic terms are of two types: individual and property, or class, terms. As the word suggests, **individual terms** are those that are used to refer to individuals. By an *individual* we mean here, anything that can be regarded as a unit for the purpose of discourse. Thus, not only a single stone, but also a pile of stones, can be regarded as an individual. Similarly, not only a single person, but also a group of people such as an army regiment, can be considered an individual. **Property** or **class terms,** on the other hand, are those that are used to refer to qualities, attributes, and relations of individuals.

Property terms can be classified as one-place, two-place, three-place terms, and so on, depending on the number of individuals they relate. **One-place terms** are those which are applicable to single individuals. For example, 'blue' and 'snub-nosed', in 'This pencil is blue' and 'Socrates was snub-nosed', are one-place terms. **Two-place terms** are those which relate two individuals. For instance, in 'The door is below the staircase' and 'The window is to the right of the door', the terms 'below' and 'to the right of' are two-place terms. 'Between' and 'gives' are examples of three-place terms. 'Sold' is an example of a four-place term, as in 'The Indians sold Manhattan to the settlers for twenty-four dollars'.

Some terms seem at first sight to be one-place, but in fact are more than one, or **many-place terms.** 'Father' in 'x is a father' seems to be one-place, but since a more complete statement of what is meant involves a proposition of the form 'x is the father of y', it is a two-place term. Similarly, a term such as 'sold' mentioned above as an example of a four-place term might be interpreted as a five-place term, 'x sold y to z for w at time t'. For rather obvious reasons, many-place terms are also referred to as *relational terms.*

Individual terms can be classified as follows: (1) **Nondescriptive names** such as 'Fido', 'Bessie', 'George', 'Africa', and 'Rome'. Our reason for calling these words "nondescriptive" is that their assignment is arbitrary; that is to say, one may use a word such as 'Bessie' to refer to anything he wishes, for instance, his pet cow, his automobile, or his wife. (For further discussion concerning why such words do not describe, see the discussion of designation, denotation, and connotation below.) Since most names are nondescriptive, it often happens that more than one thing has the same name. For example, there are many cities named 'Rome'. Furthermore, since more than one thing may have the same name, words of this type provide us with information only if we are acquainted with the things to which they refer.

(2) **Definite descriptions** such as 'the current president of the United States', 'the author of *Waverly*', and 'the man in the third seat from the left in the second row'. Expressions of this type consist of one or more property or class terms which describe the thing referred to, plus words such as 'the' and 'third' which particularize the reference. Since they contain property terms, definite descriptions can provide us with some information about their referents without our being acquainted with them. Thus, although they do not name any individual, they may be used to describe particular individuals.

(3) **Descriptive names** such as 'The Nile River', 'The Chrysler Building', and 'The French Revolution'. Like definite descriptions, expressions such as these contain property or class words and thus give us some information about their referents. But, unlike definite descriptions they do not just describe, they also name. Consequently, they may be thought of as sharing some of the logical features of both definite descriptions and nondescriptive names.

(4) **Indefinite descriptions** or terms such as 'an object', 'a man', or 'someone' may also be used to refer to individuals. However, since they do not particularize the reference in the way that definite descriptions do, they do not give us as much information about their referents. For example, sentences such as 'An object was left by my door' and 'Someone has been eating my porridge' provide only a minimum description of the objects to which they refer.

(5) Finally, there are words such as 'I', 'me', 'you', 'this', 'here', and 'now' which may be called **demonstratives**. Words of this type are distinguished by the fact that their referents change almost every time that the words are used. Like nondescriptive names and indefinite descriptions, they supply us with only minimum information unless we are acquainted with the objects to which they refer.

EXERCISES

III

1. What is a term?
2. How do syntactical terms differ from nonsyntactical terms?
3. Into what two types may nonsyntactical terms be divided?
4. How do semantic and nonsemantic terms differ?
5. Into what two types may semantic terms be divided?

6. How do individual and property or class terms differ?

7. What five types of individual terms were discussed and how do they differ?

8. Classify the following property terms as one-place, two-place, etc.:

    (a) Dimitri is *handsome*.

    (b) The cat is *on top of* the house.

    (c) Dimitri is *drving* the Bentley.

    (d) George *sent* Dick a letter.

    (e) Harry *sold* Bob the goat for twenty-six cents.

USE AND MENTION

If one is to think clearly and communicate successfully, it is necessary to avoid confusion between terms and their referents. At first sight the propositions

Space has no beginning.
Space begins with S.

seem to contradict one another; but they do not, because in the first proposition the word 'space' is *used* to talk about its referent, whereas in the second the word 'space' is *mentioned,* i.e., the word 'space', not its referent, is being talked about. To indicate that a term and not its referent is being talked about, we will enclose the term in single quotes. Thus the second proposition above is written as

'Space' begins with S.

Although this distinction may seem rather simple, failure to make it has resulted in a great deal of confusion in Western thought.

EXERCISES

IV

Which of the italicized words in the following sentences are used and which mentioned?

1. *The Beatles* is the name of a group.

2. *The beetles* were swarming the lamp.

3. *Mississippi* has three pairs of double letters.

4. The *Mississippi* is the longest river in the United States.

5. *Muskogee* is a place where Okies live.

6. The word *cat* names *cats;* and the name for the word *cat* is *cat.*

7. What is the *meaning* of *meaning?*

TYPES AND TOKENS

The distinction between linguistic types and linguistic tokens is also useful for avoiding confusion of thought and achieving successful communication. If we were speaking of linguistic tokens, we would say that there are three words printed below; but if we were speaking of linguistic types, we would say that there is only one:

Dog   Dog   Dog

A **linguistic token** may be defined as an instance of a set of symbols all of which either look or sound alike. Linguistic tokens are physical objects: ink marks on paper, chalk marks on a blackboard, particular sounds, etc. The three words printed above are examples of written tokens. The same words when spoken aloud are examples of spoken tokens. Not only words, but also letters of the alphabet, sentences, and so on, can be linguistic tokens.

A **linguistic type** may be defined as a set of linguistic tokens all of which have the same meaning. Two points need to be noted with regard to this definition. First, since linguistic types are defined in terms of the concept of meaning, they are not physical objects. Second, it is possible for the same linguistic token to belong to more than one linguistic type. For example, the word 'hide' may be taken to mean either: (1) to conceal something, or (2) the skin or fur of an animal. Although these meanings are related, they are nevertheless distinct; and in the former case, the word belongs to one linguistic type, in the latter to another.

EXERCISES

V

1. What is a linguistic token?
2. What is a linguistic type?
3. Which of the following sentences are about linguistic types and which are about linguistic tokens?
   (a) He bought five copies of yesterday's *Times*.
   (b) Stanley had to write 'I am a bad boy' on the blackboard forty times.
   (c) The average novel contains more than 60,000 words.
   (d) Shakespeare had the largest vocabulary of any English writer; he used more than 14,000 words.

AMBIGUITY

Whenever a linguistic token belongs to one and only one linguistic type, it has a single meaning and is said to be **univocal;** whenever a linguistic token belongs to more than one linguistic type, it has more than one meaning and is said to be **equivocal.** Some tokens are equivocal when spoken, but not when written; some are equivocal when written, but not when spoken; and some are equivocal both when written and spoken. Examples of tokens that are equivocal when spoken, but not when written are: (1) 'bear' and 'bare', (2) 'hear' and 'here', and (3) 'rain' and 'reign'. Examples of tokens that are equivocal when written, but not when spoken are: (1) 'tear', which means to rip or pull apart when pronounced one way, but which means moisture from the eye when pronounced another way, (2) 'lead', which means to guide or conduct someone when pronounced one way, but means a metallic element when pronounced another way. Finally, examples of tokens that are equivocal both when written and spoken are: (1) 'hide', mentioned above, (2) 'last', which may mean either something which follows all other items in a series or an instrument on which a cobbler works on shoes, and (3) 'bank', some of the meanings of which are: a hill, the boundary of a stream, and a financial institution.

The fact that linguistic expressions may be equivocal can be both an advantage and a disadvantage in communicating information. One obvious benefit is that it allows us to reduce the number of words required for communication. Another, more important advantage, is that it provides us with a convenient way of expressing different but related meanings. The word 'hide', mentioned above, is an example of a word which does this, the word 'game', another example. (Look up the latter word in an unabridged dictionary and note the different but related meanings it expresses.)

The major disadvantage of equivocal expressions is that they may be used in such a way that it is impossible to tell which of two or more possible meanings is intended. An expression used in this way is said to be **ambiguous.** For example, consider the sentence 'He is a Chinese historian'. This sentence may be taken to mean either that the person described is a student of Chinese history, or that he is a historian who is of Chinese nationality, or both. Consider also the sentence 'The Bible prohibits swearing'. Since the word 'swearing' may mean either taking an oath or speaking irreverently, one is not sure what is being prohibited. Because the ambiguity of these expressions arises from the difficulty of determining who or what is being referred to, they are examples of **referential** or **semantic ambiguity.**

Ambiguity may also result from faulty construction or lack of punctuation and is then known as **syntactical ambiguity.** Expressions which are syntactically ambiguous are called **amphibolies.** For example, consider the following sentences, the first of which is an amphiboly.

(1) The Democrats say the Republicans are sure to win.
(2) The Democrats, say the Republicans, are sure to win.

Two points in particular need to be kept in mind regarding ambiguity. First, ambiguity is dependent on context, i.e., expressions are equivocal when they have more than one meaning, but they are not ambiguous unless they are used in such a way that it is impossible to determine which meaning is intended. Second, ambiguity is a defect only if we are considering language as a means of communicating information. Ambiguity may be quite harmless. For example, puns and *double entrendres* depend upon ambiguity for their humor.

EXERCISES

VI

1. What is meant by saying that a linguistic token is univocal? What is meant by saying that one is equivocal?
2. Find examples of linguistic tokens that are equivocal:
   (a) when spoken, but not when written;
   (b) when written, but not when spoken;
   (c) when both spoken and written.
3. Are there any advantages in using equivocal expressions? Are there any disadvantages?
4. What is meant by saying that a linguistic expression is ambiguous? How does ambiguity differ from equivocation? Is ambiguity always a defect of language?
5. How do semantic and syntactical ambiguity differ? What is an amphiboly?
6. Rewrite the following amphibolies by either changing the word order or inserting commas so that they admit of only one interpretation:
   (a) The huge airplane was landed at midnight by an audacious pilot without running lights or radio contact.
   (b) The first venus fly trap was discovered in North Carolina.
   (c) Do not break your bread or roll in your soup.
   (d) Lord Cavendish, the world famous explorer, described his trip through the jungle in our social problems class.
   (e) He said she was rather angry.
7. Rewrite the following examples of semantic ambiguity so that they admit of only one interpretation.
   (a) "And he spake to his sons, saying, Saddle me the ass. And they saddled *him*." (*Kings I*)
   (b) The partnership between Smith and MacIntyre ended when he drew the firm's money from the bank and fled to Brazil.
   (c) College students are revolting.
   (d) As soon as the students left the classrooms the custodian cleaned them.
   (e) Thanks for the complimentary copy of your new book. I shall waste no time reading it.

VAGUENESS

An expression is **vague** when there are situations in which it cannot be determined whether the expression is applicable, and this indeterminacy of application is not due to lack of knowledge, but to uncertainty of meaning. Examples of vague words are: 'wealthy', 'middle-aged', and 'obscene'. Their use leads to such questions as "How much money does one need to be wealthy?" "At what age does one become middle-aged?" and "Do all, or only some, members of a community have to be offended by a work of art for it to be obscene?" Note that it is not lack of information but lack of definition that prevents these questions from being answered. Of course, one could answer them by an act of arbitrary definition, but there seems to be no good reason for drawing a line at one point rather than another. The folly of arbitrary definition is illustrated by the Soviets, who, when faced with the problem of whether farmers were capitalists, decreed that any farmer who owned three or more cows, even if he owned nothing else, was a capitalist.

The opposite of vagueness is preciseness. An expression is **precise** if we can determine whether or not it applies to anything of which we have sufficient knowledge. Examples of relatively precise terms are 'four', 'mammal', and 'inertia'. Although these are taken from science, scientific terms may also be vague. For instance, because they have not been able to define precisely the terms 'living' and 'nonliving', biologists have been unable to say whether certain viruses are, or are not, alive.

Vagueness should not be confused with generality. 'Vertebrate' is a more general term than 'mammal', but it is not more vague. Nor should it be assumed that vagueness is always an impediment to communication. Science and practical affairs often require that we eliminate vagueness; but, if used intelligently, vague words are adequate for many purposes. In fact, vagueness may at times be preferable to arbitrary definition.

EXERCISES

VII

1. When is an expression vague?
2. How can expressions be made less vague?
3. What is wrong with arbitrary definition as a means of eliminating vagueness?
4. Are general terms necessarily more vague than those which are not as general?
5. Is vagueness always an impediment to communication?
6. With respect to each word in the following list, describe a situation in which:
    (a) There is something to which the word clearly applies; (b) there is something

to which the word clearly does not apply; and (c) there is something about which we would be hesitant to say whether the word does or does not apply.

(1) offensive weapon

(2) luxury

(3) accident

CLASSES

A **class** is the collection of all things which can be correctly referred to by a property term. Thus every property term may be taken as defining a class. However, most classes have more than one defining characteristic. A **defining characteristic** is one that must be present before a property term can be correctly used to refer to some individual. For example, nothing can be a triangle unless it has three sides. Similarly, nothing can be a mammal unless its skin is covered with hair. Defining characteristics must be distinguished from **accompanying characteristics.** It might have been the case, e.g., that most or even all philosophers were more than five feet one inch tall, but that would not have been a defining characteristic of the class *philosophers.* The test as to whether some characteristic is a defining, or only an accompanying, characteristic is whether anything could be a member of the class in question even if it did not have that characteristic. If it could not be a member of that class unless it had that characteristic, then the characteristic is a defining characteristic. If the object could belong to that class without having that characteristic, then the characteristic is only an accompanying characteristic.

DESIGNATION

The set of defining characteristics that must be present for a term to apply correctly to some individual is known as the **designation** of the term, and the term is said to *designate* those characteristics.* All class terms designate. For example, the term 'triangle' designates the properties of being a three-sided, closed, two-dimensional figure. And the term 'mammal' designates the properties of being warm-blooded, hairy, and suckling offspring. Some, but not all, individual terms designate. Descriptive names, definite descriptions and indefinite descriptions designate; nondescriptive names and demonstratives do not. (Some names may seem at first sight to be nondescriptive when in fact they are descriptive. For example, the word

---

*Some authors use the term 'objective connotation' to mean what we mean by the term 'designation', and the term 'subjective connotation' to mean what we mean below by the term 'connotation'. The term 'signification' is also used by some authors to mean what we mean by the term 'designation'.

'God' has been used in Western theology to designate the properties of being omnipotent, omniscient, benevolent, etc., and thus is a descriptive name.)

DENOTATION

The set of individuals to which a term correctly applies is known as the **denotation** of the term, and the term is said to *denote* those individuals. Both individual and class terms may denote. By definition, however, individual terms are those that denote only one individual. Class terms, on the other hand, may denote any number of individuals. Consider the term 'movie star'. Some of the individuals denoted by this term are Doris Day, Raquel Welch, and Peter O'Toole. These individuals are part of the *present* denotation of this term. But, if we were to list its *total* denotation, we would have to include such people as Mary Pickford, W. C. Fields, and Clark Gable. These individuals are part of the *past* denotation of the term 'movie star'. Analogously, those people who are not now, but who become movie stars, constitute the *future denotation* of the term.

It is possible for terms to designate but not denote. For instance, the word 'unicorn' designates the properties of being a one-horned horse-like animal, but since there are no such animals it does not denote. Similarly, the term 'the person in the second seat from the left in the third row' designates certain properties, but it will not denote unless there is someone occupying that seat.

It is also possible for terms to denote, but not designate. This is the case whenever there are no defining characteristics that must be present for the term to refer correctly to some individual. This is true of both nondescriptive names and demonstratives. For example, as pointed out previously, there are certain conditions which must be met for something to be correctly referred to by the word 'cow'; but there are no conditions that must be met in order for a particular cow to be referred to as 'Bessie'. It follows that all things correctly referred to by class terms such as 'cow' have certain properties in common, whereas things referred to by demonstratives or nondescriptive names, such as 'Bessie', do not necessarily have any properties in common.

Any two terms that designate the same properties, provided that they denote at all, necessarily denote the same individuals. Thus the terms 'planetoid' and 'asteroid', which have the same designation, also have the same denotation. But two terms that denote the same individuals need not, and usually do not, designate the same properties. Thus the terms 'equiangular triangle' and 'equilateral triangle' have the same denotation, but they do not have the same designation.

EXERCISES

VIII

1. What is a class?
2. What is a defining characteristic of a class? What is an accompanying characteristic?
3. Which of the following sentences are statements about defining characteristics and which are statements about accompanying characteristics? (Consult a dictionary if needed.)
   (a) All quadrupeds have four legs.
   (b) Koalas are native to Australia.
   (c) Koalas are marsupials.
   (d) All Model T Fords were originally painted black.
   (e) Margarine is a substitute for butter.
   (f) Valid arguments cannot have true premises and a false conclusion.
   (g) Most swans are white.
4. What is the designation of a term? What kinds of terms designate and what kinds do not?
5. What is the denotation of a term? What kinds of terms denote and what kinds do not?
6. What are the possible relations between the designation and denotation of a term?

CONNOTATION

Terms may not only designate and denote but may also *connote*. The **connotation** of a term is the associations and reactions which it produces in those who use it. Two kinds of connotation are of special interest to us here: pictorial and emotive connotation.

The **pictorial connotation** of a term is the images or "pictures" associated with it. Pictorial connotation varies from person to person. For instance, when one person hears the word 'dog' he may picture a small Pekinese, whereas when another person hears this word he may picture a large German shepherd. Contrary to what one might think at first, very few terms have pictorial connotation. (Ask yourself what images or pictures you associate with the words in the foregoing sentence.) Most of the words that have pictorial connotation are proper names or class terms which occur frequently in everyday discourse. Abstract and scientific terms rarely have pictorial connotation.

The **emotive connotation** of a term is the attitudes of favor or disfavor which the term arouses. For example, the word 'snake' produces a feeling of revulsion in many people. Like pictorial connotation, emotive connotation varies from person to person. Nevertheless, the attitudes elicited by a particular term may be similar enough that we may speak of it as having a conventional emotive connotation. Most people who speak English would consider such words as 'fool', 'bungler', and 'jerk' terms of derision, and words such as 'great', 'brilliant', and 'hero' terms of praise.

It is important to note that the same situation can be described by words having radically different emotive connotations. Consider the sentences:

> Smith has reconsidered his conclusion.
> Smith has changed his mind.
> Smith has gone back on his word.

The first sentence portrays Smith as a person who carefully considers all available evidence in order to find the best solution for a problem and thus creates a favorable attitude toward him. The last sentence portrays him as a person who fails to keep his promises and thus creates an unfavorable attitude toward him. The second sentence is relatively neutral in emotive connotation, and thus creates neither a favorable nor an unfavorable attitude toward him.

AGREEMENT AND DISAGREEMENT

Agreement and Disagreement in Belief

If two people agree or disagree regarding the truth or falsity of a proposition, they may be said to **agree or disagree in belief.** For instance, if one person asserts that it is Tuesday and another that it is Wednesday, then they disagree in belief. But if both assert that it is Tuesday, or both assert that it is Wednesday, then they agree in belief. When two people agree or disagree in belief, it does not follow that either is correct. Hence, if it were some day other than Tuesday or Wednesday, then neither of the above individuals' beliefs would be correct.

The foregoing disagreement in belief could be settled rather easily, but some disagreements in belief may take years to settle, and others may never be settled. For example, unless some new evidence is found, people will probably continue to debate whether Lee Harvey Oswald acted alone, or with others, in assassinating John Kennedy. Note, however, that disagreement in belief on this point presupposes agreement in belief that it was Lee Harvey Oswald who assassinated John Kennedy.

Although it may be difficult, or even impossible, to settle some disagreements in belief, the general procedure required to settle disagreement in belief is evident. Only appeal to experience, e.g., to observation and experiment, is capable of settling disagreement in belief.

Agreement and Disagreement in Attitude

If two people favor or disfavor the same thing, then they may be said to **agree in attitude;** whereas if one person favors something and another disfavors it, then they **disagree in attitude.** For example, if two people desire either the election or the defeat of a political candidate, then they agree in attitude; but if one person desires the candidate's election and the other his defeat, then they disagree in attitude.

It is possible for people to: (1) agree in both belief and attitude; (2) agree in belief, but disagree in attitude; (3) disagree in belief, but agree in attitude; (4) disagree in both belief and attitude. The following situation, in which a man and his wife are discussing the tie that his mother-in-law gave him for Christmas, illustrates these four possibilities: Both might think that the tie is an ugly blue; both might think it is blue, but one think that it is ugly and the other think that it is pretty; both might think that it is ugly, but one believe it to be blue and the other think that it is green; one might think that it is an ugly blue, the other that it is a pretty green.

People may agree in attitude even though the reasons for their having that attitude are quite different. For instance, one person might desire the defeat of a candidate for national office because he is prejudiced against the candidate's race, while another might desire his defeat because he is convinced that the candidate is not qualified and consequently his election would not be in the national interest. If this were the case, we could expect the first person's disapproval to be expressed in emotive language and the second person's in evaluative language.

It should be obvious that there are also many reasons for disagreement in attitude. This is one of the reasons that agreement in attitude is often difficult to obtain. Agreement in attitude can sometimes be obtained if agreement in belief can be obtained. If I can convince you that a certain man is a thief, then you may come to share my disapproval of him. However, people who differ radically in attitude are not likely to reach agreement in belief. For example, people who disagree as to which, if any, participant in a war is in the right are not apt to agree concerning the causes of the war. Similarly, people who differ radically in belief are not likely to reach agreement in attitude. People who disagree concerning the causes of a war are not apt to agree as to which, if any, participant is in the right.

EXERCISES

IX

Classify the following pairs of sentences according to the kinds of agreement and disagreement involved:

1. A. Smith has reconsidered his conclusion.
   B. Smith has gone back on his word.

2. A. My doctor says that I am slightly overweight.
   B. I think that you are too fat also.

3. A. Did you see the stunning red dress Mary was wearing?
   B. Yes, it was quite attractive; however, it was purple, not red.

4. A. Did you see the red dress Mary was wearing? It was absolutely obscene.
   B. I thought that it was quite nice; she looks good in red.

5. A. That was a good performance of a Rachmaninoff prelude.
   B. You are wrong; it was a mediocre performance of a Bach fugue.

6. A. North Carolina trounced Duke 42 to 40.
   B. North Carolina squeaked by Duke 42 to 40.

7. A. Yes sir, this is a fine automobile. It has everything—air conditioning, power brakes, power steering, tinted windshield, etc. And it's quite a bargain too.
   B. It is a fine automobile. However, I don't see an air conditioner and it seems overpriced to me.

8. A. I thought the president's speech was articulate, informing, and inspiring.
   B. He spoke well, but it seemed like the same old stuff to me. He just used a lot of big words to say what everybody already knew anyhow.

Verbal Agreement and Disagreement

Suppose two people are arguing and one maintains that the national unemployment rate is 17 percent while the other maintains that it is only $5\frac{1}{2}$ percent. At first sight this appears to be disagreement in belief, but further investigation may show that it is not. For suppose by the word 'unemployed' the first person means 'anyone who does not currently have a job', whereas the second means 'people who are seeking but cannot find a job'. It follows that the first person includes among the unemployed: seasonal workers who are between jobs, people so wealthy that they do not need jobs, and retired people. The second person, however, excludes these from the unemployed. In order to settle the disagreement no additional appeal to observation may be required. All that may be needed is for the word 'unemployed' to be defined.

A disagreement such as the foregoing, in which a key word is used in more than one sense and which can be settled by definition, is known as a **verbal disagreement.** Another example of a verbal disagreement is the well-known dispute whether there is sound when a tree falls in the forest and no one is present. To settle this disagreement, we need only decide whether we wish to define 'sound' in terms of the experience of hearing or in terms of the displacement of air which can be measured by a mechanical device.

We may say, then, given one sense of the word 'sound', no sound is present; but given another sense, sound is present.

Not only merely verbal disagreement, but also merely verbal agreement, is possible. And just as verbal disagreement may mask agreement in belief, verbal agreement may mask disagreement in belief. Thus two people who believe in the existence of a deity may think that they share the same belief until they attempt to define what they mean by the word 'God'.

Verbal disagreement may also hide disagreement in attitude. Consider the following dispute:

>   A.   Dimitri is a true Christian. He has deep respect
>   for spiritual values, high regard for human life,
>   and is never too busy to aid the unfortunate.
>
>   B.   I don't think that Dimitri is a Christian at all.
>   He never reads the Bible, has spoken out against
>   missionaries, and never goes to church on Sundays.

The disputants in this argument are obviously using the word 'Christian' in more than one sense. But it is doubtful whether the dispute could be settled by definition alone. For even if the disputants were to agree on a definition for the term 'Christian', they would still disagree in their attitudes toward Dimitri.

EXERCISES

X

State the different meanings attached to the key words in the following verbal disagreements; and if the disagreements involve underlying disagreement in attitude, state this disagreement also:

1. A.   You cannot step into the same river twice.

   B.   What do you mean? Just yesterday I waded into the Mississippi for the second time this week.

   A.   But that wasn't the same river. The water that was there the first time you entered the river was gone the second time you entered it.

   B.   That's true, but it was still the same river. In fact I entered it at the same place both times.

   A.   Not exactly the same place. For the river is constantly changing its banks, and though you may not have been able to see it, the place at which you entered the river had changed slightly.

   B.   It may have changed slightly, but it was still the same place.

   A.   If it had changed then it could not be the same place. It was a new place. Furthermore, you were not the same person the second time you entered the river. You too had undergone gradual change. In five years you will not look at all like you do now.

2. A. Don't ask me to vote for Senator Black. I believe that we have had enough socialism in this country.
    B. Are you implying that Senator Black is a socialist?
    A. I certainly am. He has consistently voted for Social Security, Medicare, increased welfare, and other governmental giveaways.
    B. That doesn't prove that he is a socialist. Many conservatives have voted for those things.
    A. That is true, but unlike Senator Black, conservatives do not believe in a government-controlled economy.
    B. What do you mean? Conservatives approve of and support such agencies as the S.E.C. and the Federal Reserve System, don't they?
    A. Yes, but Senator Black is in favor of additional and more powerful agencies of this type. Just recently he advocated establishment of a Bureau of Consumer Affairs.
    B. Now you have shown just how silly your argument really is. It is utter nonsense to say that someone is a socialist because he desires to see consumers protected from hidden interest rates, deceptive packaging, and so forth. In fact, you have no reason at all for calling Senator Black a socialist. He does not believe in state ownership of the basic means of production.
    A. So what? Socialists today don't believe in governmental ownership, just in governmental control.
    B. That puts us back where we began. You have already admitted that conservatives favor such agencies as the S.E.C. and Federal Reserve System. Are conservatives to be called socialists then?
    A. Yes, to a certain extent. In fact, this just shows how far this country has gone down the road toward socialism.

3. A. The execution of the Nazi leaders by the Allied Powers was just as much an act of deliberate and premeditated murder as the Nazis' execution of the Jews.
    B. You are wrong. The word 'murder' does not mean simply the taking of human life, but the unjustified taking of human life. For example, if the state takes the life of someone found guilty of a crime legally punishable by death, that is not murder.
    A. What legally punishable act did the Nazis commit? An act is legally punishable only if it breaks some previously existing law.
    B. It is true that the Nazis did not break the laws of a particular state. They were not tried for breaking the laws of a particular state, but for disregard of international law.
    A. There is no such thing as international law. Law can exist only if there is a governing authority that has control over the people in its jurisdiction. Since there is no international government, there is no international law.

SUGGESTED READINGS

ALSTON, WILLIAM P., *Philosophy of Language.* Foundations of Philosophy Series. Edited by Elizabeth and Monroe Beardsley. Englewood Cliffs, N.J.: Prentice-Hall, Inc., 1964.

AUSTIN, J. L., *How To Do Things With Words.* New York: Oxford University Press, Galaxy Book, 1965.

HOSPERS, JOHN, *An Introduction to Philosophical Analysis.* 2nd ed. Englewood Cliffs, N.J.: Prentice-Hall, Inc., 1967.

ROSENBERG, JAY F. and CHARLES TRAVIS, eds., *Readings in the Philosophy of Language.* Englewood Cliffs, N.J.: Prentice-Hall, Inc., 1971.

SEARLE, JOHN R., *Speech Acts: An Essay in The Philosophy of Language.* Cambridge: Cambridge University Press, 1970.

DEFINITION

The best way to avoid vagueness, ambiguity, and verbal disagreement is to define one's terms. *To define a term is to explain its meaning or meanings.* Every definition, then, involves reference to words, but may or may not involve reference to other things. Thus, in defining we are primarily concerned with words and only secondarily, if at all, concerned with other things.

Since people have many different reasons for defining terms and proceed in many ways, it is useful to classify definitions according to both the purpose to be achieved and the method used to achieve this purpose. The first six types of definition we discuss are classified according to purpose; the remaining types, according to method. However, since we are employing a dual classification, any definition we consider will exemplify at least two different types of definition.

DEFINITIONS CLASSIFIED ACCORDING TO PURPOSE

Reportive Definitions

If the purpose of a definition is to report the conventional meaning or meanings of a term, the definition is a **reportive** or lexical definition. Almost all definitions given in dictionaries are reportive. On occasion dictionaries make recommendations regarding the use of terms, but as a rule they simply report how people in fact use terms. Since such reports may be accurate or inaccurate, it is possible to evaluate reportive definitions as true or false.

Stipulative Definitions

If the purpose of a definition is to introduce a term having no previous meaning, the definition is a **stipulative** definition. For example, Madame Curie, needing a word for the metallic element she discovered, called it 'radium'. And Auguste Comte, needing a word for his envisioned science of man, called it 'sociology'. Stipulative definitions are not reports of the way in which terms are used, but are statements of intent or resolves to use a term in a certain way. Thus, stipulative definitions cannot be evaluated as true or false, but only as more or less useful. In general, stipulative definitions are useful only if they do not deceive, confuse, or cause one's audience needless effort.

Precising Definitions

People usually stipulate definitions when there is no existing term to express what they wish to say. However, even if terms do exist, they may be too vague, or too equivocal for one's purposes. As a result, scientists and other thinkers constantly borrow words with conventional meaning and give them a more precise meaning. For example, most people use the word 'city' in a vague way, but census takers attach a precise meaning to the term. Definitions which give a more precise meaning to conventional terms are called **precising definitions.** Precising definitions share some of the logical features of both reportive and stipulative definitions. To the extent that they overlap with conventional meaning, they are reportive and may be evaluated as true or false; but to the extent that they clarify or extend conventional meaning, they are stipulative and can only be evaluated as more or less useful.

Theoretical Definitions

Whenever stipulatve or precising definitions are given for the purpose of stating a theory, they are also **theoretical definitions.** Examples of theoretical definitions are Plato's definition of 'justice', Frege's definition of 'number', and Einstein's definition of 'simultaneity'. Although definitions such as these take some account of previous usage, their aim is not reportive but is to aid in solving theoretical problems and to bring about an increase and systematization of knowledge. Their status, then, is that of an hypothesis which may have to be abandoned or revised as our knowledge increases.

Abbreviative Definitions

An **abbreviative definition** is one that introduces a shorter, more convenient expression to replace a longer, more cumbersome one. Although they neither eliminate vagueness and ambiguity nor increase our knowledge, abbreviative definitions do aid in systematizing thought by making it more economical. Consider the effort saved in writing 'UNICEF' rather than 'United Nations International Children's Emergency Fund'. Or consider the effort saved in using an exponent to write '4^6' rather than '$4 \times 4 \times 4 \times 4 \times 4 \times 4$'.

Persuasive Definitions

Definitions given to change attitudes are called **persuasive definitions.** There are several ways of giving such definitions. Recall the disagreement mentioned above in which A attempts to convince B that Dimitri is a "true Christian." The reasons given are that Dimitri has deep respect for spiritual values, high regard for human life, and is never too busy to aid the unfortunate. Suppose that when challenged, A defends his remarks by arguing that possession of these characteristics constitutes a *definition* of the word 'Christian', and since Dimitri possesses them, it follows by definition that he is a Christian. Because it is possible for people other than Christians to possess these characteristics and since B is favorably disposed toward Christians, A's action can be described as an attempt to use the favorable connotation which B attaches to the word 'Christian' to win his approval of Dimitri. Put more technically, A is attempting to define a term in such a way as to retain its favorable connotation while changing its denotation and designation. One may also define a term so as to retain its unfavorable connotation while changing its denotation and designation. For example, a politician might define the term 'demagogue' so as to make it applicable to a political opponent to whom the term would not normally be applicable.

In addition to defining terms so as to retain a favorable or unfavorable connotation while changing their denotation and designation, one may define them so as to retain their denotation and designation while changing their connotation. For example, a Russian and an American might agree as to the denotation and designation of the term 'capitalist', but the former define it so as to produce an unfavorable connotation and the latter, to produce a favorable connotation.

DEFINITIONS CLASSIFIED ACCORDING TO METHOD

The foregoing types of definition are classified according to the purpose the definition is intended to serve. However, as mentioned above, definitions may also be classified according to the method used to explain the meaning of the term being defined. Definitions classified according to method may be further classified into those in which a term's denotation is cited, and those in which a term's designation is cited.

Denotative Definitions

One of the simplest methods of explaining the meaning of a term is to name, describe, or otherwise indicate examples of things it denotes. A definition arrived at in this way is known as a **denotative definition.** For example, one might define the term 'existentialist novel' by naming such works as *The Brothers Karamazov, The Magic Mountain,* and *The Stranger.* Or one might define a term which refers to a psychiatric disorder by describing several case histories of the illness. We will discuss three types of denotative definitions: enumerative, paradigmatic, and ostensive.

Enumerative definitions. An **enumerative definition** is one in which a term is defined by giving a complete list of the objects denoted by it. For instance, the term 'member of NATO' is defined by the following list: Belgium, Britain, Canada, Denmark, France, West Germany, Greece, Iceland, Italy, Luxembourg, Netherlands, Norway, Portugal, Turkey, and the United States. All denotative definitions have the obvious limitation that they cannot be used to define terms which do not denote. Enumerative definitions have the further limitation that it is often impractical, or impossible, to list everything denoted by a term. Consider, e.g., the difficulties involved in attempting to give an enumerative definition of the term 'star'.

Paradigmatic definitions. Since it is often impractical, or impossible, to give a complete list of the objects denoted by a term, it is important to choose representative examples in giving denotative definitions. A representative example, or **paradigm,** is one that exemplifies both the necessary and typical features of a class. Unfortunately, it is frequently very difficult to find paradigms. Even the best examples may be atypical in one or more ways. For instance, an otherwise good example of a case history of a disease may exhibit some characteristic to a greater or lesser degree than is normally present. Or a case history that is typical of the disease at one stage of development may not be typical at another. In addition to the problem of finding representative examples, one may encounter several other difficulties in giving paradigmatic definitions. Once again, there is the general limitation that denotative definitions can only be applied to terms which have a denotation. More specifically, however, there is the problem that the same objects may serve as examples for more than one term. For instance, the same set of triangles will illustrate either of the terms 'equiangular triangle' or 'equilateral triangle'. Thus it may be unclear what term one is defining.

Ostensive definitions. If the example used to define a term is not named or described, but only indicated by some means such as pointing or nodding one's head, the term is said to be **ostensively defined** (from the Latin word, *ostendere,* which means to point or show). For instance, one might explain the meaning of the word 'dog' to a child by uttering it and pointing at a dog. Or at a more sophisticated level, one might attempt to answer a friend's question, "What does the word 'soul music' mean?," by playing certain records.

Since only the word being defined needs to be stated in an ostensive definition, it is a *nonlinguistic* method of defining. If all definitions were linguistic, i.e., if words could only be explained by using other words, then we would never be able to explain the meaning of any word. There is a sense, then, in which ostensive definition is the most fundamental type of definition. But, despite its importance at an elementary level of experience, ostensive definition has all the shortcomings of other paradigmatic definitions: the general limitation that it is only applicable to terms that denote, and the more specific limitations that the objects chosen may not be representative and that they may serve as examples for more than one term. The last limitation is especially characteristic of ostensive definitions because of the ambiguity of pointing. A classic example of this ambiguity is described by J. H. Weeks in *Among Congo Cannibals:*

> I remember on one occasion wanting the word for Table. There were five
> or six boys standing round, and, tapping the table with my forefinger,
> I asked, "What is this?" One boy said that it was a *dodela,* another that
> it was an *etanda,* a third stated that it was a *bohali,* a fourth that it was
> *elamba,* and the fifth said it was *meza.* These various words we wrote in
> our note-book, and congratulated ourselves that we were working among
> a people who possessed so rich a language that they had five words for
> one article.*

But later Weeks discovered that

> one had thought we wanted the word for tapping; another . . . the word
> for the material of which the table was made; another . . . that we
> required the word for hardness; another thought we wished a name for
> that which covered the table; and the last, not being able, perhaps, to
> think of anything else, gave us the word *meza,* table—the very word we
> were seeking.†

---

*Quoted by Lionel Ruby, *The Art of Making Sense,* 2nd ed., (Philadelphia: J. B. Lippincott Company, 1954), p. 50.
†*Ibid.*

Designative Definitions

A definition given by specifying another term or terms having the same designation—and therefore the same denotation, if there is one—as the term defined is a **designative definition.** It is useful in discussing designative definitions to refer to the term being defined as the **definiendum** and the term or terms used to do the defining as the **definiens.** Since designative definitions assert that their definiendum and definiens are equivalent in designation, and in denotation, if any, logicians often write them by connecting the definiendum and definiens with the symbol '= df.', which is read as 'equals by definition'. Definitions written in this way are called **explicit definitions.**

Synonymous definitions. The term 'synonymous definition' has been used in several different ways. We will use it here to refer to a designative definition in which the definiendum and definiens not only have the same designation, and the same denotation if there is one, but also the *same connotation.* The definiendum and definiens of a synonymous definition, then, are *exact equivalents in every respect* and may replace one another in any context without loss of meaning.

Synonymous definitions sometimes consist of a single word given as an exact equivalent for another single word. This type of definition occurs frequently in bilingual dictionaries. Thus an English-French dictionary will define 'red' as 'rouge' and 'cat' as 'chat'. Definitions of this type also are frequently found in other dictionaries, especially smaller unabridged dictionaries. For example, 'afraid' may be defined as 'frightened'. However, it is often difficult to find a single word that is an exact equivalent of another single word. One reason for this is economy—there is little point in having two words with exactly the same meaning. Moreover, if the definiens consists of several words, it may be even more difficult to find an exact equivalent for the definiendum. For even when words have the same designation and same denotation, they rarely have the same connotation.

Analytic definitions. All designative definitions state that their definiendum and definiens have the same designation, but not all designative definitions state what this designation is. An **analytic definition** is a designative definition, either synonymous or nonsynonymous, in which it is not only claimed that the definiendum and definiens have the same designation, but is also claimed that the definiens provides an analysis of the meaning of the definiendum by stating its designation. Compare the following, the first of which is a nonanalytic, the second, an analytic definition:

'Circle' = df. 'round'

> 'Circle' = df. 'A closed plane curve such that
> all of its points are equidistant
> from a central point'

Types of Analytic Definitions

Definition by genus and difference. One type of analytic definition, definition by genus and difference, has played such an important role in Western thought that some people have considered it the only legitimate type of definition. Definitions by genus and difference are given by stating a general class which contains as a subclass the class to be defined, and then stating the specific manner in which members of the subclass differ from other members of the general class. The general class is called the **genus** (plural: *genera*), its subclasses are called **species** and the characteristic which differentiates the species being defined from other species is called the **differentia** (plural: *differentiae*). Consider the following definition:

> 'Triangle' =df. 'a polygon having three sides'

The term 'polygon' refers to a general class which contains triangles as a subclass, and the term 'having three sides' refers to the specific manner in which triangles differ from other polygons. In this definition, then, *polygon* is the genus, *triangle* the species, and *having three sides* the differentia. Another example of a definition by genus and difference is:

> 'Man' =df. 'rational animal'

We may interpret this definition so that 'animal' refers to a general class which contains man as a subclass, and 'rational' refers to the specific manner in which man differs from other animals. However, we may also interpret it so that 'rational' refers to a general class containing man as a subclass and 'animal' refers to the specific manner in which man differs from other rational beings. In the former case *animal* is the genus and *rational,* the differentia; in the latter, *rational* is the genus and *animal,* the differentia. The fact that either *animal* or *rational* can be taken as the genus in this definition illustrates that, unlike biologists who use the terms 'genus' and 'species' to refer to specific classes, logicians use the term 'genus' to refer to any class divided into subclasses and the term 'species' to refer to any subclass.

Definition by classification. Definitions in which more than one genus and species are cited are sometimes called **definitions by classification.** For example, consider the definition of 'man' given by the logician Porphyry in the third century A.D.:

'Man' =df. 'a mortal, rational, sensitive,
animate, corporeal substance'

Porphyry illustrated this definition with the following "tree":

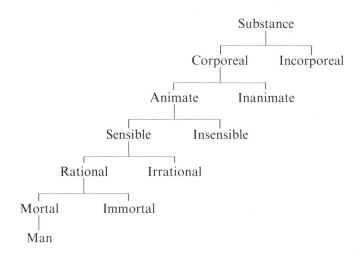

The classification Porphyry used in giving the above definition is based on the **principle of dichotomous division.** That is to say, each genus is divided into two mutually exclusive classes, the differentia and its contradictory or complement. Other classifications based on different principles of division are also possible. For example, the classification of human actions as moral, immoral, and amoral is based on division into three mutually exclusive classes. Although we do not have the space to pursue the matter here, attention to principles of classification can be of tremendous assistance in the organization and presentation of one's ideas. (For further information on this topic, see the suggested readings at the end of the chapter.)

Genetic definitions. A genetic definition is one in which a term is defined by describing the origin, or development, of the class being defined. For example:

'Mule' =df.   'a hybrid between a horse and an ass, usually
the offspring of a male ass and a mare'
'Cousin' =df.   'a son or daughter of one's aunt or uncle'

Causal definitions. A causal definition defines a term by describing the cause, or causes, of the class of objects being defined. (It should be obvious that there is considerable overlap in genetic and causal definitions.)

'Mirage' = df. 'an optical phenomenon produced by a stratum
of hot air of varying density across which the
observer sees reflections, usually inverted, of
some distant object or objects'

Functional definitions. A definition which specifies the meaning of a term by citing purposes or functions served by the class of objects being defined is known as a functional definition. For instance:

'Axe' = df. 'a tool used for chopping, splitting and hewing
wood, especially for felling trees'

Analogical definitions. An analogical definition is one in which a term is defined by stating similarities and/or dissimilarities of two or more things. For example:

'Lute' = df. 'a musical instrument similar to a guitar
but with a bent neck, pear-shaped box,
and more strings than a guitar'

Antonymous definitions. Antonymous definitions are those in which opposition is used as the basis for defining a term. For example, 'impartiality' can be defined as 'freedom from favoritism or bias'. It should be obvious that the utility of defining a term by antonymous definition is dependent on the extent to which its opposite is already understood or defined. Hence, there are many cases in which this method of defining is not applicable.

Operational definitions. Any of the analytic definitions we have discussed can be used as a means of stating a theory. Another method of giving a theoretical definition, one that has been widely utilized and discussed in recent years, is known as operational definition. An **operational definition** specifies a set of procedures or operations for determining whether a term can be correctly applied. For example, an operational definition of the term 'acid' might require that blue litmus paper turn red when brought into contact with an acid solution. And, an operational definition of the term 'gold' would indicate physical and chemical tests for determining whether a substance is gold.

Since operational definitions equate a term's meaning with a description of the tests that must be performed before the term can be correctly applied, one may consider operational definition a type of analytic definition. But since they also require that nonverbal operations be performed to determine the term's denotation, one might also consider them a type of denotative definition.

Although operational definitions are especially useful in science, they are often too complicated for use in everyday affairs. Thus a jeweler might require an operational definition of gold, but he is not likely to need one for 'salt'. (For further information regarding theoretical and operational definitions, see the suggested readings at the end of the chapter.)

CRITERIA FOR EVALUATING DEFINITIONS

If the purpose of definition is to explain the meaning or meanings of a term, then what criteria should we adopt to arrive at acceptable definitions? An adequate answer will take into account both general considerations and the particular type of definition involved.

First, one should *consider the knowledge and experience of those for whom the definition is intended.* For example, if the purpose of a definition is to report the meaning of a word used in everyday discourse, then it should be phrased in language that an average person is likely to understand. Definitions that do not satisfy this criterion are said to be *obscure.* Samuel Johnson's definition of 'net' as 'a reticulated fabric decussated at regular intervals with interstices at the intersections' is a famous example of an obscure definition. On the other hand, if the purpose of a definition is theoretical, rather than reportive, then it is unimportant that it be phrased in language that an average person is likely to understand.

Second, one should *avoid vagueness and ambiguity whenever possible.* For example, in giving nonlinguistic definitions care should be taken in selecting examples. And in giving linguistic definitions care should be taken in wording and punctuation. However, it is not always possible to eliminate vagueness and ambiguity from definitions. An abbreviative definition, for instance, cannot be used to eliminate vagueness or ambiguity. And if one is giving a reportive definition of a vague word, then it is difficult, if not impossible, to report is meaning accurately without using vague language. Failure to note this is one of the reasons that attempts to give reportive definitions often result in stipulative or precising definitions.

Third, one should *avoid emotive language whenever possible.* Of course, this is not always possible—for example, when one is giving a synonymous definition of a term with emotive connotation. But if one's purpose is to inform rather than to arouse emotion, then it is better to give a reportive definition, pointing out that the term has emotive connotation but without directly conveying it. And if one wishes to inform rather than to change attitudes or issue propaganda, then one should also avoid persuasive definition. This consideration has led some philosophers to deny that persuasive definition can legitimately be called definition at all. But since persuasive definition does function to inform people of the meaning of words, there seems no good reason for not calling it 'definition'. On the other hand, because the informative function is subordinate to other aims, persuasive definition is not a very effective means of defining.

Fourth, one should *avoid facetious and figurative language*. A definition such as '*Discretion* is something which a person acquires after he is too old for it to do him any good' may be humorous, but it does not explain the meaning of 'discretion'. And a definition such as 'A *monarch* is the captain of a ship of state' not only fails to explain the meaning of 'monarch' but also may be misleading because it suggests that a monarch can plot the affairs of a state the way a captain plots the course of a ship.

Fifth, *definitions should not be viciously circular*. A definition is circular when the definiendum or some term that is merely a grammatical variation of the definiendum occurs in the definiens, as in the following:

'Art' =df. 'what one finds in art museums'
'Line' =df. 'a linear path'

Most circular definitions give one little or no information and should be avoided for that reason. It is sometimes said that all circular definitions should be avoided, but this is not the case. For instance, a definition such as 'An *artist* is a person who creates art' may be perfectly acceptable *provided that* the word 'art' has already been adequately defined. But, suppose that 'art' has been previously defined as 'whatever is created or produced by an artist'. In that case the definitions given are mutually, or viciously, circular so that the meaning of neither term has been explained. It is not so much circularity then, but mutual or vicious circularity that should be avoided.

Sixth, *definitions should be consistent with definitions already given*. For example, although the definition

'Buddhism' =df. 'a religion based on the teachings of
Gautama Buddha, characterized by
lack of belief in a supernatural being
and by the doctrine of Nirvana that
escape from suffering mortality is the
highest goal of human aspiration'

may seem perfectly acceptable standing by itself, it would not be acceptable if the term 'religion' had been previously defined as 'belief in a supernatural being'.

Seventh, *definitions should not be needlessly negative*. Although antonymous definition is a legitimate procedure, as a rule, opposition is not an adequate way of defining terms. Defining 'bachelor' as 'a man who is not married' is useful, but defining 'bus' as 'a vehicle that is not a car' is not very useful. Similarly, defining 'senior' as 'a student who is neither a freshman, nor a sophomore, nor a junior' is not very useful. A definition of 'senior' as 'a student who is in his final year of study' is much more informative and helpful. Definitions, then, should not be negative when they could be affirmative.

Eighth, *definitions should not be too narrow or too broad.* A definition is too narrow if it prevents us from applying a term to all of the things to which we wish to apply it; a definition is too broad if it allows us to apply a term to things to which we do not wish to apply it. For example, if the definition of 'religion' stated above were put forth as a reportive definition, it would be too narrow since it prevents us from applying the term to Buddhism, which is generally recognized as a religion. On the other hand, the definition of 'bus' given above is too broad, since it allows us to refer to motor-bikes, scooters, and children's wagons as buses.

Finally, *definitions should be adequate to serve the purpose for which they are intended.* It should be apparent, if one considers the many different purposes for which definitions may be given, that there are many considerations we have not discussed that must be taken into account in giving adequate definitions. Stating adequate definitions is not something that can be reduced to a set of mechanical rules, but is rather an art requiring intelligence and judgment. The ultimate test of a definition, then, is simply whether it does the job for which it was intended.

POSTSCRIPT

At the beginning of the chapter, we stated that to define a term is to explain its meaning or meanings. There are few, if any, logicians who would quarrel with this remark. But is every explanation of the meaning of a term a definition? This is a question about which logicians have quarreled. For example, Susan Stebbing writes:

> Definition is only one of the means through which we come to understand words. We must be careful not to use "definition" so widely that it comes to stand for any process enabling us to learn the application of words. These processes are so different that to call them by the same name leads to confusion.*

Stebbing, and those who agree with her, maintain that neither the teaching of proper names, nor explanation of the meaning of a term by citing examples, constitutes definition. They object, in particular, to treating what we have called "ostensive definition" as a type of definition.

Richard Robinson rejects both of these theses. In reply to the first he states:

> Proper names and general names both have meanings that have to be learnt. When Mill said that proper names could not be defined because they had no meaning he was using 'meaning' in a narrow sense; for

---

*L. Susan Stebbing, *A Modern Introduction to Logic,* (New York: Harper Torchbooks, Harper & Brothers, 1961), p. 422. For similar views see John Stuart Mill, *A System of Logic,* I, viii; Morris R. Cohen and Ernest Nagel, *An Introduction to Logic,* (New York: Harcourt, Brace & World, Inc., Harbinger Edition, 1962), p. 229; and Monroe C. Beardsley, *Thinking Straight,* (New Jersey: Prentice-Hall, Inc., 1966), pp. 235–38.

obviously those who come into a new district or a new society have to learn the meaning of proper names.*

Robinson concludes that explanation of the meaning of proper names, like explanation of the meaning of other terms, is a type of definition.

In reply to the second thesis, he writes:

> Teaching the use of a word by means of other words, and teaching the use of a word without the use of other words, are distinct as regards their methods, and therefore shall be given distinct names when we distinguish methods. But they are also identical in their fundamental purpose, which is to teach the use of a word; and there ought to be a name that embraces both of them in virtue of their identity. What more suitable name than 'definition'?[†]

With whom shall we side? It should be clear that to take one side rather than the other is in part to define the term 'definition'. Our view concerning the second point, as the reader can probably infer, is that Robinson has shown sufficient reason for considering "ostensive definition" a legitimate type of definition. On the other hand, we do not find convincing his reasons for treating the teaching of proper names as a type of definition. It does not seem in keeping with the current use of the word 'definition' to treat a remark such as 'Her name is Helen' as defining the word 'Helen'. One reason for this may be, as pointed out earlier, that words of this type can be used in an entirely arbitrary fashion. It was apparently this consideration which led Mill to state erroneously that proper names have no meaning.

SUGGESTED READINGS

BEARDSLEY, MONROE C., *Thinking Straight*. 3rd ed. Englewood Cliffs, N.J.: Prentice-Hall, Inc., 1966.

RESCHER, NICHOLAS, *Introduction to Logic*. New York: St. Martin's Press, 1964.

ROBINSON, RICHARD, *Definition*. Oxford: Oxford Clarendon Press, 1965.

SEARLES, HERBERT L., *Logic and Scientific Methods: An Introductory Course*. 3rd ed. New York: The Ronald Press Co., 1968.

STEBBING, L. SUSAN, *A Modern Introduction to Logic*. New York: Harper Torchbooks, Harper & Brothers, 1961.

---

*Richard Robinson, *Definition*. (Oxford: The Clarendon Press, 1965), pp. 23–24.
[†]*Ibid.*, p. 26.

13

FALLACIES

Logicians use the word **fallacy** to refer to errors of reasoning or arguing. They also use it to refer to arguments which fail to provide adequate evidence for their conclusions. However, as a rule they do not refer to an argument as a fallacy unless it is plausible enough to *appear* to provide adequate evidence for its conclusion. (The word 'fallacy' comes from the Latin *fallere,* to deceive.)

The most obvious reason for an argument failing to provide adequate evidence for its conclusion is that it is invalid. Since the validity or invalidity of an argument depends upon its form, arguments which are fallacious because they are invalid are called **formal fallacies.** The fallacies of denying the antecedent and affirming the consequent discussed in chapter IV are examples of formal fallacies. We have already discussed a number of tests for determining whether arguments are valid or invalid and will not discuss formal fallacies here.

Arguments which are fallacious for reasons other than invalidity are called **informal fallacies.** We will divide informal fallacies into five types: (1) linguistic fallacies, (2) fallacies of begging the question, (3) fallacies of unwarranted assumption, (4) fallacies of relevance, and (5) fallacies of insufficient evidence. Since it is possible for an argument to exemplify more than one type of informal fallacy, this classification is not exclusive. It is also possible for an argument to be both a formal and an informal fallacy.

LINGUISTIC FALLACIES

A linguistic fallacy is one that comes about because of a misuse of language. The following linguistic fallacies are among those that occur most frequently:

Equivocation. The fallacy of equivocation occurs when a key term in an argument is used ambiguously. For example, the argument

> All contemporary philosophers should take account of
> recent advances in symbolic logic.
> Plato and Parmenides were contemporary philosophers.
> Plato and Parmenides should take account of recent
> advances in symbolic logic.

would be valid if we were to interpret the term 'contemporary philosophers' as having the same meaning in both propositions. However, we would normally interpret the first occurrence as meaning 'philosophers living today' and the second as 'philosophers living at the same time'. Consequently, the argument is fallacious. This particular type of equivocation is known as the *fallacy of four terms.* (See page 161.)

Amphiboly. The fallacy of amphiboly occurs when a phrase or sentence in an argument is syntactically ambiguous. (See page 218 for a definition of the term 'syntactically ambiguous'.) Consider the argument

> He said she was crying.
> If he said she was crying, then she was unhappy.
> She was unhappy.

Note that the sentence 'He said she was crying' is ambiguous and may mean either 'He said, she was crying' or 'He, said she, was crying'. If this sentence is interpreted in the same way in both premises, then the argument is valid; but if it is interpreted in different ways, then it is invalid. Note further, that if interpreted as meaning 'He, said she, was crying', then the conclusion 'She was unhappy' seems less plausible than the conclusion 'He was unhappy'. Hence, though the argument interpreted this way is valid, it is not very convincing.

Another example of the fallacy of amphiboly is provided by the nephew who infers from the statement in his uncle's will

> I hereby bequeath one hundred dollars to
> my nephews George and Harry.

that he will receive one hundred dollars. He is interpreting this as meaning that *each* nephew will receive one hundred dollars, whereas context may make it clear that *together* they are to receive one hundred dollars. (This argument can also be interpreted as an instance of the linguistic fallacy of division.)

Accent. The fallacy of accent is the result of improper emphasis of a word or phrase in an argument. For example, suppose someone were to argue that Thomas Jefferson's statement "All men are created equal with respect to certain rights. . . ." implies that Jefferson believed that men were created equal, but not that he believed that men actually are or should be equal with respect to rights. In short, emphasizing the word 'created' makes it appear that Jefferson believed that men are only created equal and after birth are unequal. An examination of the Declaration of Independence, from which this quote is taken, and Jefferson's other writings makes it clear that this is not the case and that he has been quoted out of context. Quoting out of context is, in fact, a frequent source of the fallacy of accent.

A similar fallacy would also occur if someone were to infer from Jefferson's statement that he believed only men and not women should have equal rights. In this case, however, the fallacy could also be interpreted as an instance of the fallacy of equivocation.

Division. Two different but related fallacies have been called "the fallacy of division." One of these will be discussed here; the other will be discussed in the section on fallacies of unwarranted assumption. The **linguistic fallacy of division** occurs when an argument contains a premise in which a term is used collectively and a conclusion in which it is used distributively. A term is used collectively when it is used to refer to a class as a whole; a term is used distributively when it is used to refer to each member of a class. For example, in saying 'Whooping cranes are almost extinct', one is asserting that the species *whooping crane* is almost extinct, not that individual whooping cranes are almost extinct. But in saying 'Whooping cranes are white', one is asserting that individual whooping cranes are white. The term 'almost extinct', then, is being used collectively, whereas the term 'white' is being used distributively. Thus the argument

> Whooping cranes are white.
> Myra is a whooping crane.
> Myra is white.

is valid, but the argument

> Whooping cranes are almost extinct.
> Myra is a whooping crane.
> Myra is almost extinct.

commits the fallacy of division.

Although useful for illustrating the fallacy of division, the second argument is not apt to deceive anyone because it is apparent that the first premise should be taken as making a collective assertion and, therefore, that a conclusion about an individual cannot be deduced. A more problematic situation arises when a premise is amphibolous so that one cannot tell whether it is to be taken in a collective or a distributive sense. Consider the argument

> All the books on the top shelf cost over fifty dollars.
> This book which is on the top shelf cost over fifty dollars.

Does the premise assert distributively that each and every book on the top shelf cost over fifty dollars? Or does it assert collectively that the books on the top shelf taken as a group cost over fifty dollars? If it is interpreted in the former way, then the argument is valid; but if it is interpreted in the latter way, then it is an instance of the fallacy of division.

Composition. Two different but related fallacies have also been referred to as "the fallacy of composition." Once again, one will be discussed here and the other discussed in the section on fallacies of unwarranted assumption. The **linguistic fallacy of composition** is committed when an argument contains a premise in which a term is used distributively and a conclusion in which it is used collectively. Hence, it may be thought of as the "reverse" of the linguistic fallacy of division. Some examples are:

> All men die at some time.
> There will come a time when no men are living.

> Assistant professors at Hogwash College make
>   less money than full professors.
> Hogwash College pays less money to assistant
>   professors than to full professors.

As far as we know, each and every man will die at some time or other. But it does not follow that there will come a time when the species *man* will have ceased to exist. Similarly, since assistant professors at an institution usually make less money than full professors at that institution, we may assume that this is true of Hogwash College. But it does not follow that Hogwash pays less money to assistant than to full professors. This is because the phrase 'pays less money to assistant professors than to full professors' is ambiguous. Taken distributively, assistant professors may be paid less, but, taken collectively, they may be paid more since there may be *more* assistant professors than full professors. Both of these arguments, then, are invalid; moreover they are invalid for the same reason. Each contains a premise which is true if interpreted distributively and a conclusion which is false if interpreted collectively. However, the second argument differs from the first, because it is possible for its conclusion to be interpreted distributively, and therefore possible to give it an interpretation which would make it valid.

EXERCISES

I

Name the fallacy, or fallacies, committed in each of the following examples:

1. 'Impartiality' means not taking sides in a dispute; and I had hoped that the judge would be impartial, but he ruled against me.

2. Newspaper headline: After two nights of looting and rioting, the mayor called a curfew for the next night.
   Newspaper reader: I wouldn't think that the voters would elect a mayor who engaged in such violence.

3. The average beginning salary of college graduates with a major in business is $8700 per year. So, if I major in business, I can expect to begin at $8700.

4. Frank beat both Steve and Fred in the Golden Gloves Tournament. So, Frank must be a terrific boxer because he can beat two people at the same time.

5. "Do you have a large family?"
   "Well, my mother is a size 34 . . ."

6. Alexander Bryant, literary critic: Philip Quinton's new book is a good example of the trash currently found on the market. It is original only in the sense that it has a different title from similar mindless exercises in pornography.
   Advertisement for Quinton's book: Alexander Bryant calls this book both good and original.

7. The man who is walking away from me does not grow smaller. But what I see grows smaller. Therefore, what I see is not the man. (From Henry Ehlers, *Logic by Way of Set Theory.*)

8. You are quite right that it would be a mistake for *this* committee to undertake this work. Since I agree entirely, I have delegated the task to a subcommittee.

9. Jack: Why do you always use the service elevator, Henry, instead of coming and going by the front door the way other employees do?
   Henry: Because the sign over the service elevator reads, "Employees only may use the service elevator."

10. All the angles of a triangle are less than 180°. Therefore angles ABC, BCA, and CAB, which compose this triangle, are less than 180°.

FALLACIES OF BEGGING
THE QUESTION

Fallacies of begging the question take several different forms. In each case, however, the fallacy consists of assuming as proven what one is attempting to prove.

Circular argument. The fallacy of arguing in a circle, or *petitio principii,* is committed when it is argued that a proposition is true because it is true. As thus described, it may be difficult to understand how such an argument could be plausible enough to deceive anyone. However, circular arguments often appear plausible because: (1) the premise and conclusion are worded differently, or (2) other premises intervene between a premise and its reaffirmation in the conclusion.

Suppose someone argues that Jones is insane, and when asked why he believes this, replies that the reason is that Jones is crazy. Or suppose someone argues that the cause of unemployment is that people are out of work. Although the premises of these arguments are worded differently from their conclusions, they are verbally equivalent to their conclusions. All that has occurred, then, is that the same proposition has been asserted twice. Of course, it is usually more difficult to determine that a premise and conclusion are verbally equivalent. Consider the following example given by the nineteenth century logician Richard Whately:

> To allow every man an unbounded freedom of speech must always be,
> on the whole, advantageous to the State; for it is highly conducive to the
> interests of the Community, that each individual should enjoy a liberty
> perfectly unlimited, of expressing his sentiments.*

An example of a circular argument in which several premises intervene between a premise and its reaffirmation in the conclusion is provided by the following argument attributed to Joseph Smith, founder of the Mormon Church. Smith allegedly argued that people could believe what he said because he was God's prophet. When asked for proof that he was God's prophet, he cited the Book of Mormon which states that he is God's prophet. When asked for proof that one can believe what is stated in the Book of Mormon, he argued that this was the case because it was God's word. Finally, when asked how one can know that the Book of Mormon is God's word, Smith replied that one could know this because he (Smith) assures us that it is the case; and whatever he assures us is the case is in fact the case, because he is God's prophet.

Note that all circular arguments are valid. For if their premises are true,

---

*Richard Whately, *Elements of Logic* (London: John W. Parker, 1850), p. 134.

then their conclusions must be true also. But since all that has occurred is that the same proposition has been affirmed twice, no proof has been given that the conclusion is true. Thus circular arguments are not formally fallacious but are informally fallacious.

Question-Begging Expressions. Arguing in a circle is not the only way one can beg the question. Use of question-begging expressions also presupposes that what is to be proven has already been proven. For example, to argue that a certain proposal should be rejected because it is "un-American" is to assume both that the vague expression "un-American" has determinate meaning and that anything that is "un-American" is undesirable. This begs the question because the point to be established is precisely that the proposal is undesirable. Similarly, to argue that any "right-thinking person" would agree that a certain conclusion is justified, or that a conclusion is "clearly" or "obviously" true may be to beg the question. No doubt a "right-thinking person" would accept only justified conclusions, but this in no way proves that the conclusion in question is justified. Nor does claiming that a conclusion is "clearly" or "obviously" true show that the conclusion is in fact true.

Complex Question. The fallacy of complex question occurs when a question is asked that presupposes an answer to another question that has not been asked. For example, the question "How much longer are we going to allow mismanagement of our state government?" presupposes that the question "Is there mismanagement of our state government?" has been answered in the affirmative. Similarly, asking a jury "Are you to let the defendant go free when your wife or child might be his next victim?" presupposes that the defendant has been proven guilty—the very thing it is intended to prove. A classic, though perhaps apocryphal, example of complex question occurred when Charles II asked the members of the Royal Society to explain why putting a live fish in a bowl of water would not cause it to overflow while putting a dead fish in it would. A number of ingenious answers were given before one member of the Society put the question to test and discovered that the alleged phenomenon did not in fact occur.

Repeated Assertion. Adolf Hitler once claimed that if one tells a big enough lie and tells it often enough, then people will come to believe it. Thus, the Nazis continually maintained that the Jews were the cause of Germany's problems, that the Aryan race is superior to all other races, that *der Führer* is never wrong, etc. Similar techniques of repeated assertion are often used in advertising campaigns. If one can just mention one's product often enough, the public will come to buy it. Obviously, as pointed out above, repeating a proposition more than once in no way provides proof for the claim being made.

EXERCISES

II

Name the fallacy, or fallacies, committed in each of the following examples:

1. Why are Americans so much more frustrated and unhappy than citizens of other nations? There are various answers to this question, but the one I believe that most nearly hits the nail on the head is that the family no longer has any importance. Our divorce rate is astounding. And even when families are living together, each member of the family has his own interests and goes in a different direction from the other members.

2. The first book on our reading list contains a statement of outmoded, establishment policies. So, I won't read it because it couldn't possibly contain any useful information.

3. Bob: Why do you waste your time listening to that trash the Rolling Stones play?
    Jim: Why do you call it trash?
    Bob: Because that's what it is. Anyone with a proper musical education would know that right away.
    Jim: Well, I like it. Besides, how do you know whether or not a person has a proper musical education?
    Bob: Only those people who can distinguish good music from bad have a proper musical education.
    Jim: But how can you recognize people who can distinguish good music from bad?
    Bob: That's easy. They are people who prefer old masters like Brahms and Beethoven to trash like rock and roll.

4. A person's strongest motives always determine his actions. For if we wish to determine which of a person's motives are strongest, we need only examine which of the alternative courses of action available to him he chooses to perform.

5. Since this has been called a brilliant and inspired work, and since it was produced by a man of genius, you must realize that you are surely mistaken if you think you have found flaws in it.

6. Ladies and gentlemen of the jury, the prosecution has tried to make out a case that my client is a murderer. But you have heard her say on six different occasions that she did not murder her husband. Her mother and brother have also said that she did not commit the crime, and I'll tell you here and now that my client is not a murderer! I've come to know her pretty well during this trial, and I simply do not believe that she could commit murder. The very idea is absurd. There is only one possible decision that you can reach, then, and that is that my client is innocent.

7. I can see that you are impressed by the efficiency with which the Calibrated Food Chopper works and the marvelous way in which it saves on time and labor in the home. Shall I charge it to your account or do you want to pay cash?

FALLACIES OF UNWARRANTED ASSUMPTION

Logicians usually do not refer to an argument as a fallacy simply because it contains a false premise or rests on a false assumption. This is particularly true if the reasoning involved is correct, i.e., if the argument is valid or the conclusion probable given the premises. However, if an argument contains a false premise or rests on a false assumption which is widely held and often leads to unsound arguments, then such arguments are sometimes spoken of as fallacies. We will refer to arguments of this type as fallacies of unwarranted assumption.

Bifurcation. The fallacy of bifurcation, also known as black-white thinking, occurs when it is assumed that only two alternatives are possible in a given situation when, in fact, more than two are possible. This fallacy is committed, for example, when it is argued that those who are not with us are against us, or that an action that is not moral is immoral. The first argument is fallacious because it is possible for people to be neutral—neither for nor against us. The second argument is fallacious because an action that is not moral need not be immoral; it may be amoral, i.e., such that moral distinctions do not apply at all.

The fallacy of bifurcation often arises because people confuse *contraries* and *contradictories*. Contradictory propositions such as '*X* is black' and '*X* is nonblack', are related such that if one is true the other is false. Contrary propositions such as '*X* is black' and '*X* is white', on the other hand, are so related that both could not be true but both could be false. Thus, given that '*X* is black' is false, we can infer that '*X* is nonblack' is true, but we cannot infer that '*X* is white' is true, for *X* could be *any* color other than black.

False Dilemma. The fallacy of bifurcation also contributes to another fallacy known as false dilemma. For example, suppose that it is argued

If the books in the library agree with the Koran, then they
   should be destroyed because they are useless.
If the books in the library disagree with the Koran, then
   they should be destroyed because they are pernicious.
The books in the library must either agree or disagree
   with the Koran.

Either the books in the library should be destroyed because
   they are useless or they should be destroyed because
   they are pernicious.

Although this argument is valid, it fails to provide adequate evidence for its conclusion. The source of its fallaciousness is the false assumption that the books in the library must either agree or disagree with the Koran. Since they may discuss topics completely different from those discussed in the Koran, they may neither agree nor disagree with the Koran. Pointing out that an argument involving a dilemma need not be accepted by citing an alternative other than those in the disjunctive premise is known as *going between the horns of the dilemma.*

Even if the alternatives cited in the disjunctive premise of a dilemma are exhaustive, one may still attempt to escape its conclusion by denying that one or both of the conditional premises is true. Given the above argument, e.g., one may deny that books which agree with the Koran should be destroyed because they are useless or deny that books which disagree with the Koran should be destroyed because they are pernicious. This way of escaping the conclusion of a dilemma is known as *taking it by the horns.*

One may also rebut a dilemma by *constructing a counterdilemma.* The classic example of such rebuttal occurred in ancient Greece. According to legend, Protagoras, a fifth century rhetorician, agreed to teach a young man named Eulathus the art of winning cases before juries. Protagoras also agreed to wait for his fee until Eulathus won his first case. However, after taking the course Eulathus decided not to go into practice. As a result Protagoras brought suit to force Eulathus to pay him. Protagoras argued in the following way:

> If Eulathus wins this case then he must pay me
>   (by earlier agreement).
> If Eulathus loses this case then he must pay me
>   (by court order).
> Eulathus must either win or lose this case.
> Therefore, Eulathus must pay me.

Eulathus was not dismayed by this argument for he had been a good pupil and learned well. He argued in return

> If I win this case then I need not pay Protagoras
>   (by court order).
> If I lose this case then I need not pay Protagoras
>   (by earlier agreement).
> I must either win or lose this case.
> Therefore, I need not pay Protagoras.

There is no record as to how the court decided.

Slippery Slope. One form of the slippery slope fallacy occurs when it is assumed without warrant that slight differences or differences of degree are unimportant. Thus, some people argue that there is no need for them to vote in elections because their vote could not make a difference in the outcome. Yet if no one were to vote, there could not be an election; and if there were a tie, then one vote would decide the election. The driver who argues that one more drink could not possibly do any harm also commits this fallacy. And, of course, there is the proverbial straw that broke the camel's back.

In a second form of this fallacy, it is argued that because slight differences or differences of degree are unimportant, there is therefore no significant or important difference between things that differ in degree only. For example, it may be argued that if one provides medical care for the aged, then one might as well provide it for the entire population. This is like arguing that if you let the camel get his nose in the tent, then eventually the whole camel will be in the tent. That might be true, but on the other hand it might not. Similarly, there may be good reasons for providing medical care for the aged but not for the entire population.

It has even been argued that there is *no* difference between things that differ in degree only. Thus, some people have argued that there is no difference between sleeping and waking, hot and cold, or good and bad. Arguments of this type rest on the unwarranted assumption that because it is impossible to draw sharp distinctions with regard to a subject matter, no distinction can be drawn at all.

Finally, the slippery slope fallacy may be committed when it is assumed that slight differences or differences of degree are *always* important. The difference between making 69 or 70 on a final examination may be important because it determines whether one receives a *D* or *C* for the course. But the difference between making 98 or 99 on a final examination may not be important because either grade is sufficient for one to receive an *A* for the course.

Composition. One form of the fallacy of composition, the linguistic fallacy of composition which arises from using a term distributively in a premise and collectively in a conclusion, has been discussed. A second type occurs when it is assumed that what is true of a part is necessarily true of the whole. For example, because every tuft in a bale of cotton would make no audible noise if it were dropped, it does not follow that the bale of cotton would make no audible noise if it were dropped. Similarly, because a doctor says that none of the injuries a patient received is sufficient by itself to cause death, it does not follow that all the injuries taken together will not be fatal.

Division. One form of the fallacy of division, the linguistic fallacy of division, has also been discussed. A second type occurs when it is assumed that what is true of a whole is necessarily true of its parts. This fallacy is committed, e.g., when it is argued that a certain object is very heavy, so parts of it will also be very heavy. Another instance is the argument that since a certain proposal would be good for the country as a whole, it will therefore be good for each and every citizen.

Inconsistency. The last fallacy of unwarranted assumption that we will discuss is inconsistency, or assuming contradictory premises. As pointed out in chapter II, arguments with inconsistent premises are valid but worthless because *any* conclusion can be deduced from them. Similarly, any action can be justified by appeal to inconsistent premises. For example, consider the case of a school administrator who dismisses one teacher on the grounds that he is active, and another on the grounds that he is inactive, in politics. As long as such an administrator's reasoning goes undetected or unchallenged, he is able to do whatever he pleases.

Assuming contradictory premises—or propositions such that it is logically impossible for them to all be true—must be distinguished from assuming premises which as a matter of fact are not all true. For example, the politician who promises both to increase governmental services and to reduce taxes has probably promised something which cannot be brought about, but he has not contradicted himself.

EXERCISES

III

Name the fallacy, or fallacies, committed in each of the following examples:

1. If anything is good for an outstanding and crucial industry, such as the automobile industry, then it will be good for the country as a whole.

2. Local Number 176 of the United Mine Workers voted to endorse the Republican candidate. Therefore, Tom Jones, who is a member of this group, is in favor of the Republican candidate.

3. It is unreasonable to inquire either about that which one knows or about that which one does not know. For if one knows then one has no need to inquire, and if one does not know, then he cannot inquire for he does not know what to inquire about. (Adapted from Plato, *The Meno*)

4. I know that you have missed only one class this semester but I am giving you an F anyway. It doesn't matter that you have passed all the tests. If students were interested in a subject, then they would attend the lectures. I simply cannot have students missing most of my lectures and then thinking that they can pass the course.

5. I'm sure that Smythe is a competent biologist. After all, he is a member of the

biology department at Sweetwater College and it is known to have an outstanding biology department.

6. Since every atom is completely determined with regard to its motion and position, and since man's body is composed of atoms, it follows that he too must be completely determined with regard to motion and position.

7. I know that everyone is in favor of individual freedom. Unfortunately, individual freedom leads to social anarchy. This is amply proven by recent events in this country. We must choose then between individual freedom and law and order. I, for one, choose law and order.

8. As a freshman at this institution, you must realize that you can either have a good time during your college years or you can acquire a prestigious academic record. Whichever course you choose, you should begin to concentrate all your energy toward your goal before this orientation week has ended.

9. Everything that is in motion must be moved by something else. If therefore the thing which causes it to move be in motion, this too must be moved by something else, and so on. But we cannot proceed to infinity in this way, because in that case there would be no first mover, and in consequence neither would there be any other mover; for secondary movers do not cause movement except they be moved by a first mover, as, for example, a stick cannot cause movement unless it is moved by the hand. Therefore it is necessary to stop at some first mover which is moved by nothing else. And this is what we all understand God to be.   (St. Thomas Aquinas, *Summa Theologica*)

10. How can you oppose the manufacture of napalm? You spank your children when they don't behave, don't you? And you believe in punishing criminals, don't you?

FALLACIES OF RELEVANCE

Arguments in which the truth of the premises is irrelevant to establishing the conclusions are known as fallacies of relevance. They are also known traditionally as *ignoratio elenchi* (ignorance of what is required to establish or refute a conclusion). The premises of an argument are irrelevant to establishing the conclusion when knowledge that the premises are true in no way provides knowledge that the conclusion is true. For example, consider the argument

> When President Higginson took over the reins at Sweetwater University, the enrollment was less than 3,500 and the faculty numbered less than 100. Now, thirteen years later, the enrollment is over 20,000 and the faculty is in excess of 500. This shows how Sweetwater has grown to be one of the best colleges in the country.

The premises of this argument are irrelevant to establishing the conclusion because knowledge of the size of an institution yields no knowledge whatever regarding its quality. Some of the worst schools in the country are very large and some of the best schools very small.

The premises of an argument may be irrelevant to establishing the conclusion even though the argument is valid. Consider the following argument taken from the preface to a logic text:

> Some say that the purpose of logic books is to teach people "how to think." Now logic books are usually written by logicians, and if it were true that logic teaches people how to think, one would suppose that logicians themselves would be expert thinkers and would make no mistakes (or at least very few). And if *this* were so, all logicians would be rich men. But, alas, that is not the case.*

This argument is intended to show that "logic cannot teach people how to think." In asserting this the author apparently means that logic cannot improve one's reasoning ability or teach one how to think more effectively by avoiding mistakes. According to him, then, logic cannot make one more expert in thinking than one is already. His argument for this thesis may be set out as follows:

> If logic could teach people how to think, then all, or most, logicians would be expert thinkers.
> If all, or most, logicians were expert thinkers, then they would make few mistakes.
> If all, or most, logicians made few mistakes, then they would be rich.
> It is not the case that all, or most, logicians are rich.
> _____
> Logic cannot teach people how to think.

Although this argument is valid, it is fallacious because the premises are irrelevant to establishing the conclusion. It could very well be true both that logic can teach people how to think (improve their reasoning ability) and that logicians are expert thinkers (make few mistakes in reasoning), without being true that all or most logicians are rich. For logicians might have no, or little, interest in applying their reasoning ability to acquire wealth. The considerations that the author advances to prove his conclusion, therefore, are simply "beside the point."

As the foregoing indicates, it is often difficult to determine whether premises are relevant to establishing a conclusion. In fact, fallacies of relevance are probably committed more frequently than any other type of fallacy. Moreover, since there are so many ways to argue irrelevantly, only a few fallacies of relevance have been singled out and given names. Discussions of some of the more frequently encountered fallacies of relevance follow.

_____

*Joseph G. Brennan, *A Handbook of Logic,* 2nd ed. (New York: Harper & Row, 1961).

Argumentum Ad Hominem. The fallacy of *argumentum ad hominem* is committed when, instead of proving or disproving the conclusion of an argument, the person who presents the argument is attacked. There are several different types:

An *argumentum ad hominem* **abusive** occurs when an attack is made on the character of the person presenting the argument. This fallacy is committed, e.g., when it is argued that a legislative proposal could not possibly be adequate because its sponsor is a well-known philanderer who was recently involved in a scandal. It is also committed when it is argued that a particular theory could not be adequate because the individual who stated it has been found to be insane.

An *argumentum ad hominem* **circumstantial** results when it is argued that a person's circumstances make it impossible for him to be sincere or to tell the truth. For example, it might be argued that a particular person's proposal for an increase in spending for higher education is not to be given serious consideration because he is a college professor and would benefit financially from such a policy. Or it might be argued that a proposal for regulating the insurance industry could not possibly be adequate because its author is in the insurance business. Marxists commit this fallacy when they argue that objections to Marxist theory from a member of the bourgeoisie are necessarily biased and therefore need not be answered.

An *argumentum ad hominem* of the type known as **tu quoque** (you also) occurs whenever one *ad hominem* is used to rebut another. For example, suppose that *A* is giving a speech in which he is trying to prove that continuation of the draft is in the best interest of the country and *B* objects to his position saying, "The only reason you favor the draft is that you're too old to be drafted yourself." If *A* were to reply, "The only reason you oppose the draft is that you're afraid of being drafted" then his counter-argument would be an instance of a *tu quoque*. Although this type of argument can serve as an effective debating tactic, it does nothing to prove the truth of one's position.

It is important to note that not every *argumentum ad hominem* is fallacious. For in some cases assessment of a person's character or circumstances is relevant to determining whether the reasons he gives for his opinions are adequate or inadequate. For example, if one has reason to believe that a witness at a trial is biased, or guilty of perjury, then one would be justified in not accepting his claims unless there was corroborating evidence. And while the fact that a proponent of a legislative proposal will benefit financially from its adoption does not show that the proposal is inadequate, it does give one reason to examine it carefully.

One type of *argumentum ad hominem* circumstantial deserves special mention in this connection. This is the argument that a person's actions are inconsistent with his beliefs. While such an argument does not necessarily show that the person's beliefs are false, it does give us some warrant for doubting his commitment to them. And if his beliefs were to constitute a theory about human actions, it might even show them to be false.

Argumentum Ad Ignorantiam. The fallacy of *argumentum ad ignorantiam,* or appeal to ignorance, has two different forms: (1) the argument that a proposition is true because no one has proven that it is false, and (2) the argument that a proposition is false because no one has proven that it is true. The theist's argument that God must exist because no one has shown that he does not, commits the first fallacy. The atheist's argument that God cannot exist because no one has shown that he does, commits the second.

The second of these two forms of argument is much more complicated than the first. For while arguments of type (1) are always fallacious, those of type (2) may or may not be. The reason for this is that in some cases failure to find evidence for a proposition must be counted as evidence that the proposition is false. Suppose, e.g., someone were to claim that a tenth planet, Kryptos, exists and can be found at a certain place in the heavens. If astronomers were to look for this planet with their telescopes and were unable to see it, and were unable to detect its presence in any way, then this would give us warrant for concluding that it did not exist. In this case, however, our rejection of the theory in question would not be based on ignorance but on a positive search for evidence.

Argumentum Ad Verecundiam. All of us constantly appeal to the testimony of others whom we think in a better position than ourselves to ascertain the evidence for some proposition. Most of these appeals are justified, but some are not. When is an appeal to others more knowledgeable than ourselves, to experts in a given field, justified, and when not? If any of the following criteria are violated, then the fallacy of *argumentum ad verecundiam,* or illegitimate appeal to authority, is committed: (1) The authority should be *personally reliable,* that is, there should be no reason to believe that he is biased. (2) He should be *clearly identified.* Vague expressions such as 'experts believe' or 'an authoritative source indicates' should be regarded with suspicion. (3) He should have *professional standing.* The qualifications of an expert are best judged by fellow experts. For example, the opinions of other physicians regarding the competence of a fellow physician are a better guide than the opinions of laymen. (4) The area under discussion should be within the authority's *special field of competence.* An appeal to the opinions of a physician on political matters, or an appeal to the opinions of a politician on medicine, should be given no more credence than those of any other layman. (5) The evidence upon which the authority bases his opinion should be *open to verification and check by other authorities.* (6) *If authorities disagree regarding the matter in question, this should be indicated.* (7) Care should be taken to see that the authority is *not misquoted or misrepresented.*

Argumentum Ad Populum. The fallacy of *argumentum ad populum* is committed whenever anyone appeals to the opinions or passions of the multitude to establish a conclusion.

One form of the fallacy involves the argument that a proposition must be true because all, or most, people believe that it is true. Obviously, however, a proposition can be believed by everyone and yet not be true. If everyone were to believe that the earth is flat, that would not make it flat.

A second form of the fallacy involves the argument that one should approve, or disapprove, something because most people do. This type of argument is the basis for much advertising, e.g., the claim that a certain product is better than its rivals because more people buy it than rival products.

A type of indirect *argumentum ad populum* is frequently encountered in advertising. In this case appeal is not made to popular approval but to the approval of some special group or clique. Thus if a merchant cannot sell his product by claiming that everyone uses it, he may claim that "those in the know" use it. The psychology of this appeal is similar to that found in a more straightforward *ad populum* appeal. In both cases the desire of human beings to gain social acceptance, or to fit into a group, is being exploited.

Argumentum ad populum appeals are also frequently encountered in politics. For example, there is the "plain folks" argument in which a politician claims that he is "just one of the people," an "ordinary fellow like you and me," and, therefore, better qualified to represent us than anyone else. There is also the "bandwagon" argument in which it is argued that one should vote a certain way because "everybody else" is voting that way. *Argumentum ad populum* appeals are a favorite device of demagogues and rabble-rousers. Shakespeare's version of Marc Antony's funeral oration and Hitler's speeches provide examples.

Argumentum Ad Misercordiam. The fallacy of *argumentum ad misercordiam* is committed whenever an appeal to pity is substituted for an appeal to evidence. This fallacy is frequently encountered in courtrooms. For example, rather than argue that his client is innocent, a defense attorney may try to win acquittal by obtaining the jury's sympathy. The following argument taken from Clarence Darrow's defense of Thomas I. Kidd, an officer of the Amalgamated Woodworkers Union being tried for criminal conspiracy, is a classic example:

> I appeal to you not for Thomas Kidd, but I appeal to you for the long
> line—the long, long line reaching back through the ages and forward to
> the years to come—the long line of despoiled and downtrodden people
> of the earth. I appeal to you for those men who rise in the morning
> before daylight comes and who go home at night when the light has
> faded from the sky and give their life, their strength, their toil to make

others rich and great. I appeal to you in . . . the name of those little
children, the living and the unborn.*

Argumentum Ad Baculum. The phrase *argumentum ad baculum* is usually
translated as "appeal to force," but it is more in keeping with current
usage to translate it as "appeal to fear." The fallacy of *argumentum ad
baculum,* then, is committed whenever an appeal to fear or intimidation is
substituted for an appeal to evidence. The argument that a belief could not
be true because "folks around here could get pretty upset if they thought
you believed that" provides an example. A diplomat who argues in the
following way provides another:

> Mr. Ambassador, I'm sure you will agree that your country does not
> have a legitimate claim to the disputed territory along our borders.
> After all, we have twelve divisions of troops ready to protect our
> interest at all times.

Diversion. The fallacy of diversion occurs when instead of trying to prove
or disprove a conclusion, someone attempts to change the subject. Fallacies
of this type are frequent in debates. For as Schopenhauer pointed out in
The Art of Controversy,

> If you find that you are being worsted, you can make a *diversion*—that
> is, you can suddenly begin to talk of something else, as though it had a
> bearing on the matter in dispute, and afforded an argument against your
> opponent. This may be done without presumption if the diversion has,
> in fact, some general bearing on the matter; but it is a piece of
> impudence if it has nothing to do with the case. . . .†

Diversion sometimes takes the form of an **appeal to humor.** A celebrated
example of this type of diversion occurred in the debates of 1860 between
Bishop Wilberforce and Thomas Huxley regarding the Darwinian theory
of evolution. Wilberforce is said to have asked Huxley, "From which side
are you descended from a monkey, your mother's or your father's?" Huxley
replied that Darwin did not maintain that man was descended from a
monkey, but that he had rather be descended from a monkey than to be
descended from a man who would use his intellect to distract an audience
from the real point at issue by irrelevant appeals to humor and prejudice.
(There are various accounts of this debate, none of which perhaps is completely accurate.)

---

*Irving Stone, *Clarence Darrow for the Defense* (Garden City, N.Y.: Doubleday, Doran &
Co., Inc., 1941), p. 112.

†Arthur Schopenhauer, *The Art of Controversy,* trans. T. Bailey Saunders (New York:
Macmillan and Company, 1896), p. 34.

Diversion may also take the form of **quibbling,** or arguing about insignificant details. For example, someone may argue about the meaning of a word when there is no reasonable doubt as to what the word means. Or, he may insist on making fine distinctions which have no immediate bearing on the issue at hand. Or, he may wrangle about details and trivial points in such a way as to avoid or obscure more important issues.

Strawman. The fallacy of attacking a strawman occurs when an implausible, easily attacked, theory is substituted for one that is more plausible and less easily attacked. Its two most common forms are:

Oversimplification: In the fallacy of oversimplification, an oversimplified theory that omits significant details and important qualifications is substituted for the theory being attacked. For example, one frequently encounters people who claim to have refuted Freud by showing that "sex is not everything," or to have refuted Darwin by showing that "men did not descend from monkeys." This fallacy is often unintentionally committed by beginning philosophy students who substitute what they *think* a philosopher said for what he actually said.

Extension: The fallacy of extension occurs when a theory is extended in such a way as to make it apply to areas which it was never intended to cover. For example, suppose *A* argues that *some* public school teachers are not well trained and are not very dedicated to their profession, and *B* responds by attacking the statement that *all* public school teachers are not well trained and not very dedicated. Or suppose that *A* sets forth an economic proposal to solve certain specific economic ills and *B* replies that the proposal must be rejected "because it will not solve all our economic problems overnight."

Non Sequitur. The term *non sequitur* has become part of the vocabulary of most educated people, so perhaps a word needs to be said about it. The literal meaning of the term is 'it does not follow'. Thus, it is used to refer to formal fallacies only. However, the premises of some formal fallacies appear more relevant to their conclusions than the premises of others. So, usually the term *non sequitur* is applied only to those formal fallacies in which there appears to be no relevant connection whatever between the premises and conclusion. A *non sequitur,* therefore, is a wildly implausible argument.

EXERCISES

IV

Name the fallacy, or fallacies, committed in each of the following examples:

1. The Inquisition must have been justified and beneficial, if whole peoples invoked

and defended it, if men of the loftiest souls founded and created it severally and impartially, and its very adversaries applied it on their own account, pyre answering to pyre. (Croce, *Philosophy of the Practical*)

2. Why do you say that there are no such things as witches? No one has ever been able to prove that there aren't.

3. Although the data we acquired from the questionnaire seems to offer strong evidence for your position, your position is not tenable because it would offend some very powerful people in this community. And when those people are offended, there is always a sudden turnover in a number of jobs.

4. Those who say that astrology is not a science are mistaken. The wisest men of history have all been interested in astrology, and kings and queens of all ages have believed in it and have guided the affairs of their nations by it.

5. School board member running for reelection: The new reading program initiated by the city public schools has been an unqualified success. Those children who formerly could not keep up with their peers because of an inability to read at their grade level are now performing much better; in fact, they are doing better than the national average.
    Opposing candidate: Don't let my opponent mislead you. The reading program is not a success. There are still countless people in this city who are unable to read.

6. George: You can't believe what the foreman says. Everyone knows he is a troublemaker and he is just sore about being fired.
    Harry: Of course he is sore about being fired. But he is not a troublemaker. That's the trouble with you guys in management; you think that everyone active in the union is a troublemaker.

7. The witness' statement cannot be reliable, for the record shows that he participated in protest demonstrations against administrative policy in Viet Nam when he was in college.

8. The Health Department should not close down Mr. Mitchell's restaurant, for if they do he is too old to take up another profession and his family will be hurt by the reduction in income.

9. It was his fault, officer. You can tell by the kind of car I'm driving and by the kind of clothing I am wearing that I am a good citizen and would not lie. Look at that rattletrap he is driving, and look how he is dressed. You can't believe anything that a dirty, long-haired hippie like that might tell you. Search his car; he probably has pot in it.

10. My opponent's proposal may be a very good one, but I just can't take it seriously. Whenever he gives a speech he reminds me of a Mississippi riverboat I once heard of. It had enough steam to turn the paddle wheel, or enough to blow the whistle, but not enough to do both. Similarly, he seems to have enough brain power either to talk or to think, but not enough to do both at the same time.

FALLACIES OF INSUFFICIENT
EVIDENCE

Fallacies of relevance occur when the premises of an argument are irrelevant to establishing the conclusion. Fallacies of insufficient evidence, on the other hand, occur when the premises of an argument are relevant but are not themselves sufficient to establish the conclusion. Put differently: Fallacies of insufficient evidence occur when only part of the evidence relevant to establishing a conclusion is taken into consideration. Thus, fallacies of insufficient evidence are also sometimes spoken of as fallacies of neglected aspect. Consider the argument

> Vaccination for smallpox is both useless and undesirable. For more children die each year from vaccination for smallpox than from otherwise contracting the disease.

Although it may be true that more children die each year from vaccination for smallpox than from otherwise contracting the disease, it does not follow that vaccination for smallpox is useless or undesirable. For while more children may die from vaccination than from otherwise contracting the disease, it is not true that more die from vaccination than would die if no one were vaccinated. The evidence on which this argument rests, then, is insufficient.

A second example of a fallacy of insufficient evidence is provided by the businessman who buys a motel because its record of earnings from past years indicates that it would be a good investment. Yet, within a year of his purchase the motel has ceased to show a profit because a long-planned superhighway has been opened causing a change in traffic patterns.

As in the case of fallacies of relevance, it is impossible to list all the different kinds of fallacies of insufficient evidence which one might encounter. The following are some of those more frequently encountered:

Hasty Generalization. The fallacy of hasty generalization or, "jumping to conclusions," is committed whenever anyone generalizes about an entire class on the basis of examples that are either not representative of the class, or are too few in number to support the conclusion. Consequently there are two forms of hasty generalization: The fallacy of unrepresentative examples and the fallacy of insufficient examples.

The fallacy of **insufficient examples** is illustrated by the case of a young man who dates three coeds from a large university and, finding them dull and uninteresting, concludes that all the coeds at that school are dull and uninteresting. Another illustration is the instance in which a public health official examines four cups of wheat from a shipload and, finding that 3 percent of the wheat examined is diseased, concludes that no more than 3 percent of the entire shipload is diseased.

Although the premises of arguments such as these are inadequate to support their conclusions, they do offer *some* evidence for their truth. And since the evidence that inductive arguments provide for their conclusions is a matter of degree, increasing or decreasing the number of examples examined would increase or decrease the probability that their conclusions are true. It would be desirable if we could state some criterion by which we could determine in all cases how many examples have to be examined before one has a sufficient number to support the conclusion. Unfortunately, there seems no way to do this. This does not mean, however, that we lack criteria for evaluating inductive arguments. Some of these criteria are discussed below, while a more extended discussion can be found in the chapter on inductive arguments.

The fallacy of **unrepresentative examples** is also known as the fallacy of converse accident and the fallacy of biased statistics. It is illustrated by the student who, overhearing a group of classmates all say that they did well in a particular course without reading the textbook, concludes that he can do the same. In some circumstances the fact that a group of students had done well in a course without reading the textbook would make it probable that some other student could do likewise. But suppose that the students who were talking are all members of Phi Beta Kappa and that the one who overhears them is not. In fact, suppose that his quality point average is barely adequate to keep him in school. In that case, his conclusion that he, too, can do well in the course without reading the textbook is an instance of the fallacy of unrepresentative examples.

A classic example, mentioned previously, of the fallacy of unrepresentative examples is provided by the *Literary Digest's* prediction that Alfred Landon would defeat Franklin Roosevelt by 370 to 161 electoral votes in the 1936 presidential election. Although the *Digest* polled a large number of people, they selected them from their own subscribers and from telephone directories. Thus, they disregarded the fact that people who could afford to subscribe to the *Digest* or have telephone service in 1936, a period of economic depression, were not a representative cross section of voters. Roosevelt won the election by a landslide (523 to 8) and the *Literary Digest* went out of business.

One way to obtain representative examples is to choose from all segments of the area under consideration (known as the population). For example, in the situation described above, in which one is taking samples from a shipload of wheat, one would select from all areas of the cargo, not just from the most accessible. Similarly, if one were taking samples from a population which exhibits qualitative variations, then one would select so as to obtain representation of significant differences. For instance, in polling voters one would take care to include people of various religious, ethnic, and economic backgrounds. Finally, if one were dealing with a population in which temporal change is important, then one would take samples at several times. In polling voters one would not stop six months, or even three months, before an election, but would continue to poll as long as it was feasible to do so. (For further discussion on these points see the chapter on induction.)

Accident. The fallacy of accident is committed when anyone argues that what is true as a general rule is also true in some special situation. For example, one commits this fallacy if he argues that strenuous exercise is good for most people, so it will be good for John Jones, who is a heart patient. Note that this fallacy does not consist in arguing from a generalization to a specific instance of that generalization, but in arguing from a generalization to some *special or exceptional case* which the generalization is not intended to cover. Thus the argument 'All men are mortal', so 'Socrates who is a man is also mortal', is valid; but the argument 'All people have a right to express political opinions', so 'A person who is a judge should have the right to express his political opinions in the courtroom' commits the fallacy of accident.

Faulty Analogy. An argument by analogy is one in which it is argued that because two or more things or types of things are similar in some respects, they are also similar in another respect or respects. The two most common forms of argument by analogy are:

> Object X has the properties A, B, C, and D.
> Object Y has the properties A, B, C.
> Object Y also has the property D.

> All objects of type X have the properties A, B, C, and D.
> All objects of type Y have the properties A, B, C.
> All objects of type Y also have the property D.

Analogical arguments, like other inductive arguments, are evaluated with respect to the degree of probability that they offer for their conclusions. The most important considerations in evaluating analogical arguments are: (1) the extent to which the properties cited as shared are relevant to establishing that another property is also shared, and (2) the extent to which relevant differences in the objects have been taken into consideration. To the degree that the properties cited as shared are relevant to establishing that the other property is shared, the probability that the conclusion is true is strengthened. To the extent that relevant differences have been overlooked, the probability that the conclusion is true is weakened. For example, suppose that X's and

Y's houses: (a) are approximately the same size, (b) are both of brick veneer construction, and (c) were recently insulated. Suppose, further, that X's fuel bill has dropped by over twenty-five dollars per month. There is then some probability that Y's fuel bill will also drop by over twenty-five dollars per month. Suppose, however, that: (d) Y's furnace is old and worn out, whereas X's is new and efficient, and (e) X's house is in a warmer climatic zone than Y's. The probability that Y's fuel bill will be reduced by over twenty-five dollars per month is then greatly reduced. Suppose once more, though, that X's and Y's furnaces are similar and that their houses are in the same climatic zones. In that case the probability that Y's fuel bill will be reduced by twenty-five dollars per month is considerably increased. Finally, suppose that we weaken the conclusion, i.e., suppose that we conclude only that Y's bill will be reduced by ten dollars or over, not by twenty-five. In that case the probability is once again increased.

All the factors cited in the foregoing example are *relevant* to establishing the conclusion. In general, the presence of one property is relevant to establishing the presence of another only if the two are causally related. Thus the size of a house, type of construction, amount of insulation, type and efficiency of the heating plant, and climatic zone are relevant to the amount of fuel consumed. On the other hand, size of the door knobs, pattern of the wallpaper, and amount of mortgage due are not relevant to the amount of fuel consumed. It should be obvious that the presence of a single relevant property renders an argument more probable than the presence of any number of irrelevant properties. If the properties cited are not relevant, or if relevant differences have been overlooked, then the fallacy of faulty analogy has been committed.

False Cause. The fallacy of false cause has several different forms:

Post hoc ergo propter hoc: (After this, therefore, because of this.) This fallacy is committed when it is argued that A is a cause of B simply because A occurs earlier than B. Reasoning of this type is the source of many superstitions, e.g., that dancing or tom-tom beating can cause rain. The way to show that A is not a cause of B, of course, is to demonstrate that A can be present without B occurring.

Chance Variation: This fallacy occurs when a statistical correlation is taken without further evidence as a causal correlation. Although there may be a statistical correlation between the price of eggs in China and the crime rate in New York City, we are not entitled to conclude that one of these is the cause of the other. Similarly, suppose that 0.08 percent of people taking a particular drug are found to have some disorder such as blood clots or a skin rash. This in no way demonstrates that the drug is the cause of the problem, for further investigation may show that 0.08 percent or more of people who do not take the drug also have the same disorder.

Common Effects: This fallacy comes about when two phenomena, both of which are the result of some third phenomenon, are taken as cause and effect. For example, a patient may have both a skin rash and a fever, but it does not follow that one is the cause of the other, for both may be caused by some third condition.

Reciprocal Effects: It does not follow from the fact that *A* is a cause of *B*, that *B* cannot be a cause of *A*. Yet reciprocal effects, or phenomena that mutually influence one another, are often taken as though the relation held in only one direction. Thus some Marxists have argued that changes in economic production and exchange bring about changes in political ideology, but that changes in political ideology cannot bring about changes in economic production and exchange. Other Marxists admit that changes in political ideology can bring about changes in economic production and exchange but insist that changes in economic production and exchange are more basic and far-reaching. Still other thinkers are equally insistent that changes in political ideology are more basic and far-reaching. To find empirical evidence to settle such a dispute seems difficult.

Confusion of Cause and Condition: Every effect presupposes a set of conditions without which that effect would not have occurred. Sometimes we speak of *some* of these conditions as the cause of the effect, sometimes we speak of the *entire set* of conditions as its cause. If we are trying to understand how a particular effect comes about, then we are apt to speak of the entire set of conditions as its cause. But if we are only trying to bring about or prevent a particular effect, we are apt to speak of one or more conditions which, when added to or subtracted from those already present, would produce that outcome. For example, although many conditions have to be present for a disease to occur, we frequently speak of a particular germ as the cause of a disease. Fallacious arguments often occur because one or more conditions are singled out as *the* cause of an effect, other conditions being ignored. For instance, it is sometimes argued that heredity alone or environment alone must be the cause of the development of personality. Fallacious arguments also often result from failure to note that more than one set of conditions can produce the same effect. For instance, it is sometimes argued that poverty alone is the cause of crime. That this is not the case is shown by the fact that people from wealthy backgrounds sometimes turn out to be criminals. Thus while it may be the case that poverty is *a* cause of crime, it cannot be *the* cause of crime.

Confusion of Cause and Effect: It is also possible to confuse cause and effect—to think that an effect is a cause, or a cause an effect. For example, someone might argue that the cause of John's lack of interest in school is the poor grades he has received when, in fact, the poor grades are not a cause, but a result of, his lack of interest in school. Similarly, one might argue that John smokes because he is nervous when, in fact, he is nervous because he smokes.

Special Pleading. Fallacies of insufficient evidence, especially the type illustrated at the beginning of the section, sometimes lead to another fallacy known as special pleading. This fallacy is committed whenever anyone presents evidence in support of one conclusion, or one side, of an issue while ignoring or withholding evidence that would support another conclusion, or another side, of the issue. This may be done either intentionally or unintentionally. It may be done intentionally, e.g., by an appliance salesman who tells you that the brand of air conditioner he is selling costs less to purchase and to operate, but fails to mention that it costs more to maintain and repair than other brands. It may also be done intentionally by a politician who tells one group of people one thing and another group of people another thing.

A number of statistical devices which someone deliberately engaged in special pleading might use are pointed out in the chapter on induction. For example, biased samples may be used, the significance of slight differences may be exaggerated, averages may be referred to without the kind of average involved being mentioned, and graphs and charts may be constructed so as to give misleading impressions. Moreover, any of the fallacies discussed in the present chapter might be deliberately committed or encouraged as a means of deceiving others. Hopefully, the student who has read this text will neither misuse these techniques in this fashion nor allow their misuse by others to go undetected and unchallenged.

EXERCISES

V

Name the fallacy, or fallacies, committed in each of the following examples:

1. All good soldiers obey their superiors' orders. So what gave you the right to not obey the captain just because you thought he was exceeding his authority?

2. Seventy-five percent of the women in this city are neurotic. I know that this is the case because I am a psychiatrist and seventy-five percent of the women who come to see me are neurotic.

3. "The real problem with the economy is all of you union people who keep forcing wages up. Your higher wages are the cause of higher prices."

   "No, you are making a mistake. The cause of higher wages is that prices increase."

4. In families where the average number of children is two or fewer, the standard of living is higher than in those families having more than two children. The standard is appreciably lower on the average in those families with five or more children. Hence, birth control seems to lead to a higher standard of living. (Manicas and Kruger, *Workbook for Essentials of Logic*)

5. Puerto Rican workers are all shiftless and lazy. I hired two of them last spring and all they did was drink and talk.

6. It is generally conceded that the government is justified in condemning and purchasing property for the construction of roads, schools, and so on. Therefore, the government is justified in depriving its citizens of their property whenever it wants to.

7. Say what you will. I'm not going to let a black cat cross my path. John let one cross his path and shortly thereafter his house caught on fire.

8. If a family consistently spends more than it takes in, it will sooner or later end up bankrupt. Similarly, if our government continues to spend more than it takes in, it too will end up bankrupt. Therefore, the present governmental policy of deficit spending can only end in national disaster.

9. "I am the father of two daughters. When I hear this argument that we can't protect freedom in Europe, in Asia, or in our own hemisphere and still meet our domestic problems, I think it is a phony argument. It is just like saying that I can't take care of Luci because I have Lynda Bird. We have to take care of both of them and we have to meet them head on." (Lyndon Johnson, *The New York Times*, February 3, 1968. Quoted by Robert G. Olson in *Meaning and Argument*.)

10. This washing machine has a larger load capacity than any on the market. It also has controls that enable you to start the cycle anywhere you wish. The motor and working parts are guaranteed for one year. Installation is free, and easy financing is available. What more is there to say?

SUGGESTED READINGS

KAHANE, HOWARD, *Logic and Contemporary Rhetoric: The Use of Reason in Everyday Life*. Belmont, Calif.: Wadsworth, 1971.

ORGAN, TROY WILSON, *The Art of Critical Thinking*. Boston: Houghton Mifflin Company, 1965.

RUBY, LIONEL, *The Art of Making Sense: A Guide to Logical Thinking*. 2nd ed. Philadelphia, Pa.: J. B. Lippincott Company, 1968.

STEBBING, L. SUSAN, *Thinking to Some Purpose*. Harmondsworth, Middlesex, England: Penguin Books, 1939.

SELECTED ANSWERS

CHAPTER 2

Exercises II
Page 7

1. F
3. T
6. F
9. T
12. T
16. F
22. F

Exercises IV
Page 9

2. F
5. T
9. T
11. T
16. F
21. F
23. T

Exercises V
Page 13

1. $F \cdot E$
3. $F \oslash E$
5. $\sim F \cdot E$
8. $R \lor \sim S$
13. $\sim R \cdot \sim S$
18. $C \lor S$
19. $G \oslash B$

23. ambiguous:
    $\sim (F \cdot E)$ or
    $\sim F \cdot \sim E$
31. $(P \lor \sim I) \cdot \sim S$
34. $(\sim P \lor \sim I) \cdot \sim S$
38. $\sim (K \lor L) \cdot (S \cdot J)$
42. ambiguous:
    $(\sim M \cdot \sim W) \lor (\sim \sim S \cdot W)$
    or $(\sim M \cdot \sim W) \lor \sim (\sim S \cdot W)$

Exercises VI
Page 16

2. F
4. T
8. F
16. T
20. T
22. T
24. F

Exercises VII
Page 18

1. $U \supset D$
3. $D \supset U$
8. $C \supset F$
11. $C \supset R$
16. $T \supset (P \cdot S)$
18. $(\sim H \supset S) \cdot \sim F$
21. $G \supset (E \lor F)$

22. $(G \supset E) \lor F$
28. $\sim (K \lor N) \supset (T \oslash C)$
30. $[(\sim D \cdot \sim B) \lor \sim T] \supset C$
32. $(E \supset P) \cdot [(R \cdot S) \lor \sim E]$

Exercises VIII
Page 21

3. T
7. F
10. F
12. T
17. F
19. T

Exercises IX
Page 21

3. $\sim H \equiv \sim S$
5. $\sim H \equiv S$
6. $\sim (W \equiv A)$
9. $(E \supset W) \cdot (E \equiv P)$
11. $[\sim (W \equiv S) \supset O] \cdot (O \supset W)$

Exercises X
Page 25

1. Contingent
2. Tautology
4. Contingent
8. Contradiction

CHAPTER 3

Exercises I
Page 29

1. Valid
4. Invalid
8. Valid
9. Invalid

Exercises II
Page 30

1. $P \supset U$ Invalid
   $\dfrac{U}{P}$

6. $(B \lor M) \supset I$ Valid
   $A \supset (B \cdot M)$
   $\dfrac{A}{I}$

4. $\sim L \supset A$ Invalid
   $\dfrac{\sim A}{\sim L}$

9. $\sim(S \equiv \sim B)$ Valid
   $\dfrac{L \supset (S \equiv \sim B)}{\sim L}$

Exercises III
Page 33

1. Invalid
2. Valid
4. Invalid
9. Invalid
11. Valid

Exercises V
Page 36

1. Consistent, Invalid
4. Inconsistent (therefore, valid)
6. Consistent, Valid
9. Consistent, Valid

CHAPTER 4

Exercises I
Page 39

4. $T \supset W$ Invalid,
   $\dfrac{\sim W}{T}$ No name

7. $F \supset E$ Invalid,
   $\dfrac{\sim F}{\sim E}$ Fallacy of Denying
        the Antecedent

5. $R \supset C$ Invalid,
   $\dfrac{C}{R}$ Fallacy of Affirming
        the Consequent

10. $C \supset T$ Valid,
    $\dfrac{\sim T}{\sim C}$ *Modus tollens*

Exercises II
Page 41

1. *Modus ponens*
3. Fallacy of Denying the Antecedent
5. *Modus tollens*
7. Fallacy of Affirming the Consequent

Exercises III
Page 43

2. (3) ~p 1, 2 *M.T.*

5. (4) ~q 2, 3 *M.T.*
   (5) ~p 1, 4 *M.T.*

7. (5) ~$(t \lor w)$ 3, 4 *M.T.*
   (6) $p \oslash q$ 2, 5 *M.P.*
   (7) ~s 1, 6 *M.P.*

4. (1) $(P \cdot F) \supset (M \cdot H)$
   (2) $T \supset (P \cdot F)$ $\underline{\lfloor M \cdot H}$
   (3) $(E \equiv C) \supset T$
   (4) $E \equiv C$
   (5) T 3, 4 *M.P.*
   (6) $P \cdot F$ 2, 5 *M.P.*
   (7) $M \cdot H$ 1, 6 *M.P.*

Exercises IV
Page 44

2. (1) $A \supset \sim C$ $\lfloor L$
   (2) $\sim\sim C$
   (3) $S \supset A$
   (4) $\sim S \supset L$
   (5) $\sim A$ 1, 2 *M.T.*
   (6) $\sim S$ 3, 5 *M.T.*
   (7) L 4, 6 *M.P.*

Exercises V
Page 45

Question 2

4. (1) $p \supset q$
   (2) $q \supset r$ $\lfloor t$
   (3) $\sim p \supset s$
   (4) $s \supset t$
   (5) $\sim r$
   (6) $p \supset r$ 1, 2 H.S.
   (7) $\sim p \supset t$ 3, 4 H.S.
   (8) $\sim p$ 5, 6 *M.T.*
   (9) t 7, 8 *M.P.*

Exercises VI
Page 46

2. (1) $D \supset P$ $\lfloor D \supset \sim T$
   (2) $P \supset \sim T$
   (3) $D \supset \sim T$ 1, 2 H.S.

3. (1) $E \supset O$ $\lfloor E \supset M$
   (2) $O \supset S$
   (3) $S \supset D$
   (4) $D \supset M$
   (5) $E \supset S$ 1, 2 H.S.
   (6) $E \supset D$ 3, 5 H.S.
   (7) $E \supset M$ 4, 6 H.S.

6. (1) $R \supset C$ $\lfloor \sim R$
   (2) $C \supset H$
   (3) $H \supset (W \lor \sim A)$
   (4) $(S \cdot I) \supset \sim(W \lor \sim A)$
   (5) $S \cdot I$
   (6) $R \supset H$ 1, 2 H.S.
   (7) $R \supset (W \lor \sim A)$ 3, 6 H.S.
   (8) $\sim(W \lor \sim A)$ 4, 5 *M.P.*
   (9) $\sim R$ 7, 8 *M.T.*

9. (1) $(M \lor P) \supset B$ $\lfloor A$
   (2) $B \supset (L \lor C)$
   (3) $(L \lor C) \supset \sim W$
   (4) $\sim\sim W$
   (5) $\sim(M \lor P) \supset (S \cdot G)$
   (6) $(S \cdot G) \supset K$
   (7) $K \supset A$
   (8) $(M \lor P) \supset (L \lor C)$ 1, 2 H.S.
   (9) $(M \lor P) \supset \sim W$ 3, 8 H.S.
   (10) $\sim(M \lor P)$ 4, 9 *M.T.*
   (11) $\sim(M \lor P) \supset K$ 5, 6 H.S.
   (12) $\sim(M \lor P) \supset A$ 7, 11 H.S.
   (13) A 10, 12 *M.P.*

Exercises VIII
Page 49

2. (1) $W \supset (E \vee P)$
   (2) $P \supset H$ |E
   (3) $\sim H$
   (4) W
   ───────
   (5) $E \vee P$ 1, 4 *M.P.*
   (6) $\sim P$ 2, 3 *M.T.*
   (7) E 5, 6 D.S.

4. (1) $E \supset F$
   (2) $F \supset T$ |$\sim E$
   (3) $S \vee \sim T$
   (4) $S \supset D$
   (5) $\sim D$
   ───────
   (6) $E \supset T$ 1, 2 H.S.
   (7) $\sim S$ 4, 5 *M.T.*
   (8) $\sim T$ 3, 7 D.S.
   (9) $\sim E$ 6, 8 *M.T.*

7. (1) $(S \supset T) \vee (L \supset C)$ |$\sim S$
   (2) $\sim(L \supset C)$
   (3) $M \supset (P \cdot B)$
   (4) $D \otimes \sim(P \cdot B)$
   (5) $\sim D$
   (6) $M \vee \sim T$
   ───────
   (7) $S \supset T$ 1, 2 D.S.
   (8) $\sim(P \cdot B)$ 4, 5 D.S.
   (9) $\sim M$ 3, 8 *M.T.*
   (10) $\sim T$ 6, 9 D.S.
   (11) $\sim S$ 7, 10 *M.T.*

9. (1) $(S \supset R) \vee (\sim S \supset H)$ |$S \supset R$
   (2) $(\sim S \supset H) \supset V$
   (3) $V \supset (P \cdot G)$
   (4) $(P \cdot G) \supset N$
   (5) $N \supset (C \cdot L)$
   (6) $O \supset \sim(C \cdot L)$
   (7) O
   ───────
   (8) $\sim(C \cdot L)$ 6, 7 *M.P.*
   (9) $(\sim S \supset H) \supset (P \cdot G)$ 2, 3 H.S.
   (10) $(\sim S \supset H) \supset N$ 4, 9 H.S.
   (11) $(\sim S \supset H) \supset (C \cdot L)$ 5, 10 H.S.
   (12) $\sim(\sim S \supset H)$ 8, 11 *M.T.*
   (13) $S \supset R$ 1, 12 D.S.

Exercises X
Page 52

1. (1) $(S \supset T) \cdot (\sim S \supset F)$ |$T \vee F$
   (2) $S \otimes \sim S$
   ───────
   (3) $T \vee F$ 1, 2 C.D.

5. (1) $(I \supset B) \cdot (\sim B \supset F)$
   (2) $C \supset (\sim B \vee \sim F)$ |$\sim I \vee \sim\sim B$
   (3) C
   ───────
   (4) $\sim B \vee \sim F$ 2, 3 *M.P.*
   (5) $\sim I \vee \sim\sim B$ 1, 4 D.D.

8. (1) $(H \supset \sim S) \cdot (P \supset S)$ |$\sim P$
   (2) $\sim\sim S \otimes \sim S$
   (3) $\sim\sim H$
   ───────
   (4) $\sim H \vee \sim P$ 1, 2 D.D.
   (5) $\sim P$ 3, 4 D.S.

12. (1) $R \vee N$ |S
    (2) $(R \supset \sim A) \cdot (N \supset S)$
    (3) $(R \supset F) \cdot (N \supset M)$
    (4) $(F \vee M) \supset L$
    (5) $L \supset W$
    (6) $W \supset \sim\sim A$
    ───────
    (7) $\sim A \vee S$ 1, 2 C.D.
    (8) $F \vee M$ 1, 3 C.D.
    (9) L 4, 8 *M.P.*
    (10) $L \supset \sim\sim A$ 5, 6 H.S.
    (11) $\sim\sim A$ 9, 10 *M.P.*
    (12) S 7, 11 D.S.

Exercises XI
Page 55

2. (1) $(A \supset H) \cdot {\sim}S$ $\vert {\sim}A$
   (2) $S \vee {\sim}H$
   (3) ${\sim}S$ 1, Simp.
   (4) ${\sim}H$ 2, 3 D.S.
   (5) $A \supset H$ 1, Simp.
   (6) ${\sim}A$ 4, 5 *M.T.*

3. (1) $C \cdot U$ $\vert F$
   (2) N
   (3) $[(C \cdot U) \cdot N] \supset F$
   (4) $(C \cdot U) \cdot N$ 1, 2 Conj.
   (5) F 3, 4 *M.P.*

5. (1) $W \supset {\sim}R$ $\vert F \vee {\sim}C$
   (2) $({\sim}R \supset F) \cdot (P \supset {\sim}C)$
   (3) $W \vee P$
   (4) ${\sim}R \supset F$ 2, Simp.
   (5) $W \supset F$ 1, 4 H.S.
   (6) $P \supset {\sim}C$ 2, Simp.
   (7) $(W \supset F) \cdot (P \supset {\sim}C)$ 5, 6 Conj.
   (8) $F \vee {\sim}C$ 3, 7 C.D.

7. (1) $(P \supset D) \cdot (U \supset {\sim}D)$ $\vert C$
   (2) $(F \supset N) \cdot (G \supset {\sim}N)$
   (3) $\{[(P \supset D) \cdot (F \supset N)] \cdot [(U \supset {\sim}D) \cdot (G \supset {\sim}N)]\} \supset S$
   (4) $(S \cdot I) \supset C$
   (5) I
   (6) $P \supset D$ 1, Simp.
   (7) $F \supset N$ 2, Simp.
   (8) $(P \supset D) \cdot (F \supset N)$ 6, 7 Conj.
   (9) $U \supset {\sim}D$ 1, Simp.
   (10) $G \supset {\sim}N$ 2, Simp.
   (11) $(U \supset {\sim}D) \cdot (G \supset {\sim}N)$ 9, 10 Conj.
   (12) $[(P \supset D) \cdot (F \supset N)] \cdot [(U \supset {\sim}D) \cdot (G \supset {\sim}N)]$ 8, 11 Conj.
   (13) S 3, 12 *M.P.*
   (14) $S \cdot I$ 5, 13 Conj.
   (15) C 4, 14 *M.P.*

9. (1) $(A \vee D) \supset C$ $\vert {\sim}U$
   (2) $(N \cdot V) \supset {\sim}C$
   (3) ${\sim}(A \vee D) \supset {\sim}U$
   (4) $P \supset N$
   (5) $I \vee V$
   (6) $P \cdot {\sim}I$
   (7) P 6, Simp.
   (8) N 4, 7 *M.P.*
   (9) ${\sim}I$ 6, Simp.
   (10) V 5, 9 D.S.
   (11) $N \cdot V$ 8, 10 Conj.
   (12) ${\sim}C$ 2, 11 *M.P.*
   (13) ${\sim}(A \vee D)$ 1, 12 *M.T.*
   (14) ${\sim}U$ 3, 13 *M.P.*

Exercises XII
Page 58

1. (1) $(B \lor C) \supset \sim M$ $\qquad \boxed{\sim M}$
    (2) B
    (3) $B \lor C$ $\qquad$ 2, Add.
    (4) $\sim M$ $\qquad$ 1, 3 M.P.

2. (1) $C \supset P$ $\qquad \boxed{C \supset F}$
    (2) $(C \cdot P) \supset F$
    (3) $C \supset (C \cdot P)$ $\qquad$ 1, Abs.
    (4) $C \supset F$ $\qquad$ 2, 3 H.S.

5. (1) $T \supset L$ $\qquad \boxed{\sim T \lor \sim M}$
    (2) $M \supset C$
    (3) $L \supset G$
    (4) $\sim G$
    (5) $\sim L$ $\qquad$ 3, 4 M.T.
    (6) $\sim L \lor \sim C$ $\qquad$ 5, Add. $\qquad$ or
    (7) $(T \supset L) \cdot (M \supset C)$ $\qquad$ 1, 2 Conj.
    (8) $\sim T \lor \sim M$ $\qquad$ 6, 7 D.D.

    (6) $\sim T$ $\qquad$ 1, 5 M.T.
    (7) $\sim T \lor \sim M$ $\qquad$ 6, Add.

8. (1) $H \supset \sim P$ $\qquad \boxed{\sim H}$
    (2) $(H \cdot \sim P) \supset M$
    (3) $\sim (H \cdot M)$
    (4) $H \supset (H \cdot \sim P)$ $\qquad$ 1, Abs.
    (5) $H \supset M$ $\qquad$ 2, 4 H.S.
    (6) $H \supset (H \cdot M)$ $\qquad$ 5, Abs.
    (7) $\sim H$ $\qquad$ 3, 6 M.T.

10. (1) $D \supset E$ $\qquad \boxed{\sim D}$
    (2) $[(D \cdot E) \supset U] \cdot (M \supset I)$
    (3) $\sim U \lor \sim I$
    (4) $\sim \sim M$
    (5) $\sim (D \cdot E) \lor \sim M$ $\qquad$ 2, 3 D.D.
    (6) $\sim (D \cdot E)$ $\qquad$ 4, 5 D.S.
    (7) $D \supset (D \cdot E)$ $\qquad$ 1, Abs.
    (8) $\sim D$ $\qquad$ 6, 7 M.T.

13. (1) $(N \equiv C) \supset (C \equiv A)$ $\qquad \boxed{\sim (N \equiv C)}$
    (2) $[(N \equiv C) \cdot (C \equiv A)] \supset (N \equiv A)$
    (3) $\sim (N \equiv A)$
    (4) $\sim [(N \equiv C) \cdot (C \equiv A)]$ $\qquad$ 2, 3 M.T.
    (5) $(N \equiv C) \supset [(N \equiv C) \cdot (C \equiv A)]$ $\qquad$ 1, Abs.
    (6) $\sim (N \equiv C)$ $\qquad$ 4, 5 M.T.

CHAPTER 5

Exercises I
Page 64

1. Truth-functionally equivalent
3. Not truth-functionally equivalent
6. Not truth-functionally equivalent
8. Truth-functionally equivalent

Exercises II
Page 64

1. (1) $\sim F \supset \sim C$ | M
   (2) $F \supset M$
   (3) C
   (4) $\sim \sim C$ 3, D.N.
   (5) $\sim \sim F$ 1, 4 *M.T.*
   (6) F 5, D.N.
   (7) M 2, 6 *M.P.*

2. (1) $L \vee (S \vee P)$ | $\sim E$
   (2) $(L \vee P) \supset \sim E$
   (3) $\sim S$
   (4) $L \vee (P \vee S)$ 1, Comm.
   (5) $(L \vee P) \vee S$ 4, Assoc.
   (6) $L \vee P$ 3, 5 D.S.
   (7) $\sim E$ 2, 6 *M.P.*

5. (1) $F \supset \sim N$ | $\sim F$
   (2) $(N \vee A) \vee \sim E$
   (3) $(I \vee K) \supset \sim (A \vee \sim E)$
   (4) $P \supset (K \vee I)$
   (5) P
   (6) $K \vee I$ 4, 5 M.P.
   (7) $I \vee K$ 6, Comm.
   (8) $\sim (A \vee \sim E)$ 3, 7 M.P.
   (9) $N \vee (A \vee \sim E)$ 2, Assoc.
   (10) N 8, 9 D.S.
   (11) $\sim \sim N$ 10, D.N.
   (12) $\sim F$ 1, 11 *M.T.*

9. (1) $P \cdot (N \cdot B)$ | $\sim C$
   (2) $[(W \vee N) \cdot T] \supset D$
   (3) $(C \supset \sim D) \cdot T$
   (4) $C \supset \sim D$ 3, Simp.
   (5) $P \cdot (B \cdot N)$ 1, Comm.
   (6) $(P \cdot B) \cdot N$ 5, Assoc.
   (7) N 6, Simp.
   (8) $N \vee W$ 7, Add.
   (9) $W \vee N$ 8, Comm.
   (10) T 3, Simp.
   (11) $(W \vee N) \cdot T$ 9, 10 Conj.
   (12) D 2, 11 *M.P.*
   (13) $\sim \sim D$ 12, D.N.
   (14) $\sim C$ 4, 13 *M.T.*

11. (1) $[I \supset (C \supset W)] \cdot [(\sim S \cdot \sim D) \supset I]$ | $C \supset (C \cdot W)$
    (2) $(\sim S \vee O) \cdot (\sim D \vee V)$
    (3) $(B \supset \sim O) \cdot (\sim B \supset T)$
    (4) $B \otimes \sim B$
    (5) $\sim T \cdot (P \cdot \sim V)$
    (6) $\sim O \vee T$ 3, 4 C.D.
    (7) $\sim T$ 5, Simp.
    (8) $\sim O$ 6, 7 D.S.
    (9) $\sim S \vee O$ 2, Simp.
    (10) $\sim S$ 8, 9 D.S.
    (11) $\sim D \vee V$ 2, Simp.
    (12) $(\sim T \cdot P) \cdot \sim V$ 5, Assoc.
    (13) $\sim V$ 12, Simp.
    (14) $\sim D$ 11, 13 D.S.
    (15) $\sim S \cdot \sim D$ 10, 14 Conj.
    (16) $(\sim S \cdot \sim D) \supset I$ 1, Simp.
    (17) I 15, 16 *M.P.*
    (18) $I \supset (C \supset W)$ 1, Simp.
    (19) $C \supset W$ 17, 18 *M.P.*
    (20) $C \supset (C \cdot W)$ 19, Abs.

13. (1) $(L \supset C) \cdot (L \supset F)$ $\lfloor C \vee V$
   (2) $L \vee (F \vee W)$
   (3) $[F \supset (M \vee I)] \cdot (O \supset F)$
   (4) $(\sim A \vee \sim W) \cdot A$
   (5) $(M \vee I) \supset V$
   (6) $\sim A \vee \sim W$ 4, Simp.
   (7) A 4, Simp.
   (8) $\sim \sim A$ 7, D.N.
   (9) $\sim W$ 6, 8 D.S.
  (10) $(L \vee F) \vee W$ 2, Assoc.
  (11) $L \vee F$ 9, 10 D.S.
  (12) $L \supset C$ 1, Simp.
  (13) $F \supset (M \vee I)$ 3, Simp.
  (14) $F \supset V$ 5, 13 H.S.
  (15) $(L \supset C) \cdot (F \supset V)$ 12, 14 Conj.
  (16) $C \vee V$ 11, 15 C.D.

Exercises III
Page 68

1. (1) $(P \cdot I) \supset L$ $\lfloor W$
  (2) $(\sim P \vee \sim I) \supset W$
  (3) $\sim L$
  (4) $\sim(P \cdot I)$ 1, 3 M.T.
  (5) $\sim P \vee \sim I$ 4, D.M.
  (6) W 2, 5 M.P.

4. (1) $(T \vee P) \supset W$ $\lfloor \sim(T \vee P)$
  (2) $\sim W \vee (S \cdot I)$
  (3) $\sim(\sim S \vee \sim I) \supset \sim E$
  (4) $\sim V \supset E$
  (5) $\sim V$
  (6) E 4, 5 M.P.
  (7) $\sim \sim E$ 6, D.N.
  (8) $\sim \sim(\sim S \vee \sim I)$ 3, 7 M.T.
  (9) $\sim S \vee \sim I$ 8, D.N.
 (10) $\sim(S \cdot I)$ 9, D.M.
 (11) $\sim W$ 2, 10 D.S.
 (12) $\sim(T \vee P)$ 1, 11 M.T.

6. (1) $\sim(\sim E \cdot \sim P) \supset (U \supset C)$ $\lfloor H$
  (2) $E \cdot (A \supset P)$
  (3) $\sim(U \cdot C)$
  (4) $(\sim U \vee T) \supset H$
  (5) E 2, Simp.
  (6) $E \vee P$ 5, Add.
  (7) $\sim(\sim E \cdot \sim P)$ 6, D.M.
  (8) $U \supset C$ 1, 7 M.P.
  (9) $U \supset (U \cdot C)$ 8, Abs.
 (10) $\sim U$ 3, 9 M.T.
 (11) $\sim U \vee T$ 10, Add.
 (12) H 4, 11 M.P.

9. (1) $(S \supset N) \cdot (R \supset G)$ $\lfloor \sim R$
  (2) $\sim(N \cdot G)$
  (3) $(L \cdot \sim I) \supset S$
  (4) $(\sim L \vee I) \supset M$
  (5) $(\sim M \cdot W) \vee \sim C$
  (6) C
  (7) $\sim \sim C$ 6, D.N.
  (8) $\sim M \cdot W$ 5, 7 D.S.
  (9) $\sim N \vee \sim G$ 2, D.M.
 (10) $\sim S \vee \sim R$ 1, 9 D.D.
 (11) $\sim M$ 8, Simp.
 (12) $\sim(\sim L \vee I)$ 4, 11 M.T.
 (13) $L \cdot \sim I$ 12, D.M.
 (14) S 3, 13 M.P.
 (15) $\sim \sim S$ 14, D.N.
 (16) $\sim R$ 10, 15 D.S.

Exercises IV
Page 70

1. (1) $\sim B \lor F$ $\lfloor \sim(B \cdot \sim R)$
    (2) $F \supset R$
    (3) $B \supset F$ 1, M.I.
    (4) $B \supset R$ 2, 3 H.S.
    (5) $\sim B \lor R$ 4, M.I.
    (6) $\sim(B \cdot \sim R)$ 5, D.M.

2. (1) $\sim U \lor P$
    (2) $P \supset R$ $\lfloor \sim R \supset \sim U$
    (3) $U \supset P$ 1, M.I.
    (4) $U \supset R$ 2, 3 H.S.
    (5) $\sim R \supset \sim U$ 4, Trans.

5. (1) $M \supset E$ $\lfloor C \supset J$
    (2) $(\sim N \lor \sim R) \supset \sim E$
    (3) $C \supset \sim(N \cdot R)$
    (4) $M \lor J$
    (5) $E \supset \sim(\sim N \lor \sim R)$ 2, Trans.
    (6) $E \supset (N \cdot R)$ 5, D.M.
    (7) $M \supset (N \cdot R)$ 1, 6 H.S.
    (8) $(N \cdot R) \supset \sim C$ 3, Trans.
    (9) $M \supset \sim C$ 7, 8 H.S.
    (10) $\sim M \supset J$ 4, M.I.
    (11) $\sim J \supset M$ 10, Trans.
    (12) $\sim J \supset \sim C$ 9, 11 H.S.
    (13) $C \supset J$ 12, Trans.

7. (1) $T \supset M$ $\lfloor L \supset H$
    (2) $(\sim F \supset \sim M) \cdot (\sim F \lor S)$
    (3) $(\sim S \supset \sim T) \supset \sim(L \cdot \sim H)$
    (4) $\sim F \supset \sim M$ 2, Simp.
    (5) $\sim F \lor S$ 2, Simp.
    (6) $M \supset F$ 4, Trans.
    (7) $T \supset F$ 1, 6 H.S.
    (8) $F \supset S$ 5, M.I.
    (9) $T \supset S$ 7, 8 H.S.
    (10) $\sim S \supset \sim T$ 9, Trans.
    (11) $\sim(L \cdot \sim H)$ 3, 10 *M.P.*
    (12) $\sim L \lor H$ 11, D.M.
    (13) $L \supset H$ 12, M.I.

10. (1) $N \supset B$ $\lfloor H$
    (2) $(M \supset S) \cdot (S \supset \sim B)$
    (3) $\sim(N \cdot M) \supset H$
    (4) $M \supset S$ 2, Simp.
    (5) $S \supset \sim B$ 2, Simp.
    (6) $\sim S \lor \sim B$ 5, M.I.
    (7) $(M \supset S) \cdot (N \supset B)$ 1, 4 Conj.
    (8) $\sim M \lor \sim N$ 6, 7 D.D.
    (9) $\sim(M \cdot N)$ 8, D.M.
    (10) $\sim(N \cdot M)$ 9, Comm.
    (11) H 3, 10 *M.P.*

13. (1) $(O \lor E) \lor (L \cdot S)$ $\lfloor L \cdot S$
    (2) $\sim(O \cdot \sim I)$
    (3) $I \supset \sim O$
    (4) $P \lor \sim E$
    (5) $\sim P \cdot R$
    (6) $\sim P$ 5, Simp.
    (7) $\sim E$ 4, 6 D.S.
    (8) $O \supset \sim I$ 3, Trans.
    (9) $O \supset (O \cdot \sim I)$ 8, Abs.
    (10) $\sim O$ 2, 9 *M.T.*
    (11) $\sim O \cdot \sim E$ 7, 10 Conj.
    (12) $\sim(O \lor E)$ 11, D.M.
    (13) $L \cdot S$ 1, 12 D.S.

15. (1) $R \supset F$ $\lfloor \sim T \supset \sim A$
    (2) $\sim(F \lor \sim R) \lor P$
    (3) $(P \cdot \sim T) \supset \sim A$
    (4) $\sim R \lor F$ 1, M.I.
    (5) $F \lor \sim R$ 4, Comm.
    (6) $\sim\sim(F \lor \sim R)$ 5, D.N.
    (7) P 2, 6 D.S.
    (8) $\sim(P \cdot \sim T) \lor \sim A$ 3, M.I.
    (9) $(\sim P \lor T) \lor \sim A$ 8, D.M.
    (10) $\sim P \lor (T \lor \sim A)$ 9, Assoc.
    (11) $\sim\sim P$ 7, D.N.
    (12) $T \lor \sim A$ 10, 11 D.S.
    (13) $\sim T \supset \sim A$ 12, M.I.

Exercises V
Page 73

1. (1) $A \cdot (M \vee H)$ $\lfloor P$
    (2) $\sim(A \cdot M)$
    (3) $(A \cdot H) \supset P$
    (4) $(A \cdot M) \vee (A \cdot H)$ 1, Dist.
    (5) $A \cdot H$ 2, 4 D.S.
    (6) P 3, 5 *M.P.*

4. (1) $(M \cdot \sim I) \vee (M \cdot \sim E)$ $\lfloor T$
    (2) $M \supset (P \vee T)$
    (3) $\sim(P \vee A)$
    (4) $M \cdot (\sim I \vee \sim E)$ 1, Dist.
    (5) M 4, Simp.
    (6) $P \vee T$ 2, 5 M.P.
    (7) $\sim P \cdot \sim A$ 3, D.M.
    (8) $\sim P$ 7, Simp.
    (9) T 6, 8 D.S.

7. (1) $(N \vee W) \cdot (\sim N \supset \sim P)$ $\lfloor \sim T$
    (2) $H \supset \sim N$
    (3) $\sim(W \cdot \sim P)$
    (4) $T \supset (H \cdot \sim P)$
    (5) $N \vee W$ 1, Simp.
    (6) $\sim N \supset W$ 5, M.I.
    (7) $\sim W \vee P$ 3, D.M.
    (8) $W \supset P$ 7, M.I.
    (9) $\sim N \supset P$ 6, 8 H.S.
    (10) $H \supset P$ 2, 9 H.S.
    (11) $\sim H \vee P$ 10, M.I.
    (12) $\sim(H \cdot \sim P)$ 11, D.M.
    (13) $\sim T$ 4, 12 *M.T.*

9. (1) $G \supset [W \supset (B \cdot T)]$ $\lfloor G \supset (W \supset \sim E)$
    (2) $[G \cdot (W \cdot T)] \supset (U \cdot \sim E)$
    (3) $\sim G \vee [W \supset (B \cdot T)]$ 1, M.I.
    (4) $\sim G \vee [\sim W \vee (B \cdot T)]$ 3, M.I.
    (5) $(\sim G \vee \sim W) \vee (B \cdot T)$ 4, Assoc.
    (6) $[(\sim G \vee \sim W) \vee B] \cdot [(\sim G \vee \sim W) \vee T]$ 5, Dist.
    (7) $(\sim G \vee \sim W) \vee T$ 6, Simp.
    (8) $\sim(G \cdot W) \vee T$ 7, D.M.
    (9) $(G \cdot W) \supset T$ 8, M.I.
    (10) $(G \cdot W) \supset [(G \cdot W) \cdot T]$ 9, Abs.
    (11) $[(G \cdot W) \cdot T] \supset (U \cdot \sim E)$ 2, Assoc.
    (12) $(G \cdot W) \supset (U \cdot \sim E)$ 10, 11 H.S.
    (13) $\sim(G \cdot W) \vee (U \cdot \sim E)$ 12, M.I.
    (14) $[\sim(G \cdot W) \vee U] \cdot [\sim(G \cdot W) \vee \sim E]$ 13, Dist.
    (15) $\sim(G \cdot W) \vee \sim E$ 14, Simp.
    (16) $(\sim G \vee \sim W) \vee \sim E$ 15, D.M.
    (17) $\sim G \vee (\sim W \vee \sim E)$ 16, Assoc.
    (18) $G \supset (\sim W \vee \sim E)$ 17, M.I.
    (19) $G \supset (W \supset \sim E)$ 18, M.I.

Exercises VI
Page 75

1. (1) $\sim C \vee P$ $\lfloor C \equiv P$ 4. (1) $S \equiv \sim P$ $\lfloor \sim S$
   (2) $P \supset G$ (2) $\sim S \vee P$
   (3) $\sim G \vee C$ (3) $(S \cdot \sim P) \vee (\sim S \cdot \sim\sim P)$ 1, M.E.
   (4) $C \supset P$ 1, M.I.   (4) $\sim(S \cdot \sim P)$ 2, D.M.
   (5) $G \supset C$ 3, M.I.   (5) $\sim S \cdot \sim\sim P$ 3, 4 D.S.
   (6) $P \supset C$ 2, 5 H.S.   (6) $\sim S$ 5, Simp.
   (7) $(C \supset P) \cdot (P \supset C)$ 4, 6 Conj.
   (8) $C \equiv P$ 7, M.E.

7. (1) $S \equiv (T \cdot O)$ $\lfloor R \supset \sim S$
   (2) $(T \cdot O) \equiv (E \cdot P)$
   (3) $\sim(E \cdot P) \vee (F \vee M)$
   (4) $(F \vee M) \supset A$
   (5) $\sim A \vee \sim(W \cdot R)$
   (6) $R \supset W$
   (7) $[S \supset (T \cdot O)] \cdot [(T \cdot O) \supset S]$ 1, M.E.
   (8) $[(T \cdot O) \supset (E \cdot P)] \cdot [(E \cdot P) \supset (T \cdot O)]$ 2, M.E.
   (9) $S \supset (T \cdot O)$ 7, Simp.
   (10) $(T \cdot O) \supset (E \cdot P)$ 8, Simp.
   (11) $S \supset (E \cdot P)$ 9, 10 H.S.
   (12) $(E \cdot P) \supset (F \vee M)$ 3, M.I.
   (13) $S \supset (F \vee M)$ 11, 12 H.S.
   (14) $S \supset A$ 4, 13 H.S.
   (15) $A \supset \sim(W \cdot R)$ 5, M.I.
   (16) $S \supset \sim(W \cdot R)$ 14, 15 H.S.
   (17) $R \supset (R \cdot W)$ 6, Abs.
   (18) $R \supset (W \cdot R)$ 17, Comm.
   (19) $\sim(W \cdot R) \supset \sim R$ 18, Trans.
   (20) $S \supset \sim R$ 16, 19 H.S.
   (21) $R \supset \sim S$ 20, Trans.

10. (1) $P \cdot (B \vee T)$ $\lfloor L \equiv N$
    (2) $(P \cdot T) \supset \sim(L \vee N)$
    (3) $(\sim L \vee \sim N) \supset \sim(P \cdot B)$
    (4) $(P \cdot B) \vee (P \cdot T)$ 1, Dist.
    (5) $\sim(P \cdot B) \supset (P \cdot T)$ 4, M.I.
    (6) $\sim(P \cdot B) \supset \sim(L \vee N)$ 2, 5 H.S.
    (7) $(\sim L \vee \sim N) \supset \sim(L \vee N)$ 3, 6 H.S.
    (8) $\sim(\sim L \vee \sim N) \vee \sim(L \vee N)$ 7, M.I.
    (9) $(L \cdot N) \vee (\sim L \cdot \sim N)$ 8, D.M.
    (10) $L \equiv N$ 9, M.E.

Exercises VII
Page 78

1. (1) $J \supset (P \supset E)$ $\underline{\lvert (J \cdot P) \supset S}$
   (2) $E \supset S$
   ___
   (3) $(J \cdot P) \supset E$ 1, Exp.
   (4) $(J \cdot P) \supset S$ 2, 3 H.S.

3. (1) $E \supset P$ $\underline{\lvert \sim E}$
   (2) $E \supset \sim C$
   (3) $\sim P \vee C$
   ___
   (4) $P \supset C$ 3, M.I.
   (5) $E \supset C$ 1, 4 H.S.
   (6) $C \supset \sim E$ 2, Trans.
   (7) $E \supset \sim E$ 5, 6 H.S.
   (8) $\sim E \vee \sim E$ 7, M.I.
   (9) $\sim E$ 8, Taut.

6. (1) $[(A \cdot D) \supset W] \supset (P \cdot R)$ $\underline{\lvert A \cdot D}$
   (2) $P \supset (K \supset \sim R)$
   (3) $K \cdot W$
   ___
   (4) $P \supset (R \supset \sim K)$ 2, Trans.
   (5) $(P \cdot R) \supset \sim K$ 4, Exp.
   (6) $[(A \cdot D) \supset W] \supset \sim K$ 1, 5 H.S.
   (7) K 3, Simp.
   (8) $\sim \sim K$ 7, D.N.
   (9) $\sim [(A \cdot D) \supset W]$ 6, 8 *M.T.*
   (10) $\sim [\sim (A \cdot D) \vee W]$ 9, M.I.
   (11) $(A \cdot D) \cdot \sim W$ 10, D.M.
   (12) $A \cdot D$ 11, Simp.

9. (1) $B \supset (B \supset \sim R)$ $\underline{\lvert \sim B \cdot \sim R}$
   (2) $B \equiv R$
   ___
   (3) $(B \cdot R) \vee (\sim B \cdot \sim R)$ 2, M.E.
   (4) $\sim B \vee (B \supset \sim R)$ 1, M.I.
   (5) $\sim B \vee (\sim B \vee \sim R)$ 4, M.I.
   (6) $(\sim B \vee \sim B) \vee \sim R$ 5, Assoc.
   (7) $\sim B \vee \sim R$ 6, Taut.
   (8) $\sim (B \cdot R)$ 7, D.M.
   (9) $\sim B \cdot \sim R$ 3, 8 D.S.

12. (1) $[E \supset (P \supset L)] \cdot [(L \cdot D) \supset F]$ $\underline{\lvert S}$
    (2) $(T \supset D) \cdot (V \supset \sim F)$
    (3) $T \cdot V$
    (4) $(E \cdot P) \vee \sim [V \cdot (\sim S \vee N)]$
    ___
    (5) $E \supset (P \supset L)$ 1, Simp.
    (6) $(E \cdot P) \supset L$ 5, Exp.
    (7) $V \supset \sim F$ 2, Simp.
    (8) V 3, Simp.
    (9) $\sim F$ 7, 8 *M.P.*
    (10) $(L \cdot D) \supset F$ 1, Simp.
    (11) $\sim (L \cdot D)$ 9, 10 *M.T.*
    (12) $\sim L \vee \sim D$ 11, D.M.
    (13) $T \supset D$ 2, Simp.
    (14) T 3, Simp.

(15) D 13, 14 *M.P.*
(16) $\sim\sim D$ 15 D.N.
(17) $\sim L$ 12, 16 D.S.
(18) $\sim(E \cdot P)$ 6, 17 *M.T.*
(19) $\sim[V \cdot (\sim S \vee N)]$ 4, 18 D.S.
(20) $\sim V \vee \sim(\sim S \vee N)$ 19, D.M.
(21) $\sim\sim V$ 8, D.N.
(22) $\sim(\sim S \vee N)$ 20, 21 D.S.
(23) $S \cdot \sim N$ 22, D.M.
(24) S 23, Simp.

14. (1) $(P \supset U) \cdot (U \supset I)$ $\mid \sim S$
    (2) $(\sim L \vee I) \supset (T \equiv S)$
    (3) $\sim T \vee (T \supset \sim S)$
    (4) $(A \cdot O) \supset (\sim I \supset P)$
    (5) $A \cdot O$
    _____
    (6) $\sim I \supset P$ 4, 5 M.P.
    (7) $P \supset U$ 1, Simp.
    (8) $\sim I \supset U$ 6, 7 H.S.
    (9) $U \supset I$ 1, Simp.
    (10) $\sim I \supset I$ 8, 9 H.S.
    (11) $I \vee I$ 10, M.I.
    (12) I 11, Taut.
    (13) $I \vee \sim L$ 12, Add.
    (14) $\sim L \vee I$ 13, Comm.
    (15) $T \equiv S$ 2, 14 *M.P.*
    (16) $\sim T \vee (\sim T \vee \sim S)$ 3, M.I.
    (17) $(\sim T \vee \sim T) \vee \sim S$ 16, Assoc.
    (18) $\sim T \vee \sim S$ 17, Taut.
    (19) $\sim(T \cdot S)$ 18, D.M.
    (20) $(T \cdot S) \vee (\sim T \cdot \sim S)$ 15, M.E.
    (21) $\sim T \cdot \sim S$ 19, 20 D.S.
    (22) $\sim S$ 21, Simp.

Exercises VIII
Page 81

(1) $p \oslash q = $ df. $\sim[\sim(p \vee q) \vee \sim(\sim p \vee \sim q)]$
(2) $p \equiv q = $ df. $(p \supset \sim q) \supset \sim(\sim p \supset q)$
(3c) $\sim(p \cdot q) \cdot \sim(\sim q \cdot \sim p)$
(4e) $[\sim(\sim p \vee q) \vee \sim(\sim q \vee r)] \vee (\sim p \vee r)$
(5b) $\sim\{p \supset [(\sim q \supset r) \supset \sim(q \supset \sim r)]\}$

CHAPTER 6

Since most of the answers to the problems in Chapter 6 are given there, no selected answers are provided.

CHAPTER 7

Exercises I
Page 107

1. (1) $(p \cdot q) \supset (r \cdot s)$ $\underline{\; p \supset \sim t \;}$
   (2) $q \cdot (r \supset \sim t)$
   (3) | p C.P.
   (4) | q 2, Simp.
   (5) | $p \cdot q$ 3, 4 Conj.
   (6) | $r \cdot s$ 1, 5 *M.P.*
   (7) | r 6, Simp.
   (8) | $r \supset \sim t$ 2, Simp.
   (9) | $\sim t$ 7, 8 *M.P.*
   (10) $p \supset \sim t$ 3–9 C.P.

3. (1) $q \supset (\sim r \vee s)$ $\underline{\; p \supset (q \supset \sim r) \;}$
   (2) $\sim p \vee \sim s$
   (3) | p C.P.
   (4) || q C.P.
   (5) || $\sim r \vee s$ 1, 4 *M.P.*
   (6) || $\sim \sim p$ 3, D.N.
   (7) || $\sim s$ 2, 6 D.S.
   (8) || $\sim r$ 5, 7 D.S.
   (9) | $q \supset \sim r$ 4–8 C.P.
   (10) $p \supset (q \supset \sim r)$ 3–9 C.P.

5. (1) $s \supset [\sim t \supset (u \cdot v)]$ $\underline{\; s \equiv u \;}$
   (2) $\sim t \cdot \sim r$
   (3) $(u \vee p) \supset [\sim r \supset (s \cdot p)]$
   (4) | s C.P.
   (5) | $\sim t \supset (u \cdot v)$ 1, 4 *M.P.*
   (6) | $\sim t$ 2, Simp.
   (7) | $u \cdot v$ 5, 6 *M.P.*
   (8) | u 7, Simp.
   (9) $s \supset u$ 4–8 C.P.
   (10) | u C.P.
   (11) | $u \vee p$ 10, Add.
   (12) | $\sim r \supset (s \cdot p)$ 3, 11 *M.P.*
   (13) | $\sim r$ 2, Simp.
   (14) | $s \cdot p$ 12, 13 *M.P.*
   (15) | s 14, Simp.
   (16) $u \supset s$ 10–15 C.P.
   (17) $(s \supset u) \cdot (u \supset s)$ 9, 16 Conj.
   (18) $s \equiv u$ 17, M.E.

9. (1) $G \supset [W \supset (B \cdot T)]$ $\underline{\; G \supset (W \supset \sim E) \;}$
   (2) $[G \cdot (W \cdot T)] \supset (U \cdot \sim E)$
   (3) | G C.P.
   (4) || W C.P.
   (5) || $W \supset (B \cdot T)$ 1, 3 *M.P.*
   (6) || $B \cdot T$ 4, 5 *M.P.*
   (7) || T 6, Simp.
   (8) || $W \cdot T$ 4, 7 Conj.
   (9) || $G \cdot (W \cdot T)$ 3, 8 Conj.
   (10) || $U \cdot \sim E$ 2, 9 *M.P.*
   (11) || $\sim E$ 10, Simp.
   (12) | $W \supset \sim E$ 4–11 C.P.
   (13) $G \supset (W \supset \sim E)$ 3–12 C.P.

Exercises II
Page 109

1. (1) $(p \supset q) \cdot (r \supset s)$ $\lfloor \sim(p \vee r)$
  (2) $(q \vee s) \supset t$
  (3) $\sim t$
  (4) $\sim\sim(p \vee r)$ I.P.
  (5) $p \vee r$ 4, D.N.
  (6) $q \vee s$ 1, 5 C.D.
  (7) t 2, 6 $M.P.$
  (8) $t \cdot \sim t$ 3, 7 Conj.

6. (1) $(p \supset \sim r) \cdot (q \supset s)$ $\lfloor \sim x \cdot y$
  (2) $(\sim r \supset t) \cdot (s \supset \sim u)$
  (3) $(t \supset \sim x) \cdot (\sim u \supset y)$
  (4) $p \cdot q$
  (5) $\sim(\sim x \cdot y)$ I.P.
  (6) $x \vee \sim y$ 5, D.M.
  (7) $\sim\sim x \vee \sim y$ 6, D.N.
  (8) $\sim t \vee \sim\sim u$ 3, 7 D.D.
  (9) $\sim\sim r \vee \sim s$ 2, 8 D.D.
  (10) $\sim p \vee \sim q$ 1, 9 D.D.
  (11) $\sim(p \cdot q)$ 10, D.M.
  (12) $(p \cdot q) \cdot \sim(p \cdot q)$ 4, 11 Conj.

9. (1) $(N \vee W) \cdot (\sim N \supset \sim P)$ $\lfloor \sim T$
  (2) $H \supset \sim N$
  (3) $\sim(W \cdot \sim P)$
  (4) $T \supset (H \cdot \sim P)$
  (5) $\sim\sim P$ I.P.
  (6) T 5, D.N.
  (7) $H \cdot \sim P$ 4, 6 $M.P.$
  (8) $\sim W \vee P$ 3, D.M.
  (9) $\sim P$ 7, Simp.
  (10) $\sim W$ 8, 9 D.S.
  (11) $N \vee W$ 1, Simp.
  (12) N 10, 11 D.S.
  (13) $\sim\sim N$ 12, D.N.
  (14) $\sim H$ 2, 13 $M.T.$
  (15) H 7, Simp.
  (16) $H \cdot \sim H$ 14, 15 Conj.

Exercises III
Page 110

1. (1) $\lfloor \sim(p \vee q)$ C.P. $\lfloor \sim(p \vee q) \supset (\sim p \cdot \sim q)$
  (2) $\lfloor \sim p \cdot \sim q$ 1, D.M.
  (3) $\sim(p \vee q) \supset (\sim p \cdot \sim q)$ 1–2 C.P.

4. (1) $\sim[\sim(p \cdot \sim p) \vee (q \cdot \sim q)]$ 1.P. $\lfloor \sim(p \cdot \sim p) \vee (q \cdot \sim q)$
  (2) $(p \cdot \sim p) \cdot \sim(q \cdot \sim q)$ 1, D.M.
  (3) $p \cdot \sim p$ 2, Simp.

6. $\lfloor [p \supset (q \supset r)] \supset [(p \supset q) \supset (p \supset r)]$
  (1) $\lfloor p \supset (q \supset r)$ C.P.
  (2) $\lfloor\lfloor p \supset q$ C.P.
  (3) $\lfloor\lfloor\lfloor p$ C.P.
  (4) $\lfloor\lfloor\lfloor q \supset r$ 1, 3 $M.P.$
  (5) $\lfloor\lfloor\lfloor q$ 2, 3 $M.P.$
  (6) $\lfloor\lfloor\lfloor r$ 4, 5 $M.P.$

(7) $\big|\,\big|\,p \supset r$ 3–6 C.P.

(8) $\big|\,(p \supset q) \supset (p \supset r)$ 2–7 C.P.

(9) $\big[p \supset (q \supset r)\big] \supset \big[(p \supset q) \supset (p \supset r)\big]$ 1–8 C.P.

Exercises IV
Page 111

   1. *KNpr*
   4. *NCpNq*
   7. *ANpAqNr*
  10. *ANKpNqNKqNp*

Exercises V
Page 113

   1. $\sim . p \supset \sim q$
   4. $p \lor q : r \equiv s . \sim q$

CHAPTER 8

Exercises I
Page 122

   1. *Cr*
   5. $Pn \equiv \sim Pp$
   7. $(Hd \supset Ge) \cdot (He \supset Le)$
   9. $(x)(Cx \supset Bx)$
  11. $(\exists x)(Cx \cdot Hx)$
  14. $(x)(Mx \lor Rx)$
  19. $(\exists x)[Px \cdot \sim(Cx \lor Lx)]$
  26. $(x)\{Px \supset [Rx \equiv Ex \lor Ix)]\}$
  30. $(x)\{[(Hx \cdot Bx) \supset Ax] \cdot [(Ox \cdot Sx) \supset (\sim Mx \lor Lx)]\}$

Exercises II
Page 124

   1. All bound.
   3. First two bound, third free.

Exercises III
Page 132

   1. (3) Every instance of x in ϕx must be replaced by a corresponding a in ϕa or
      (4) E.I. cannot be used to infer ϕy from $(\exists x)\phi x$ if y (x in this case) has a previous
   5.   free occurrence (step 3).
      (6) Every instance of x in ϕx must be replaced by a single variable or single
          constant in inferring ϕa or ϕy from $(x)\phi x$ by U.I.
      (7) E.I. cannot be used to infer ϕy from $(\exists x)\phi x$ if y has a previous free occur-
          rence (step 6).

(10) U.G cannot be used to generalize a line containing a variable obtained by E.I.

9. (5) Quantifier rules apply to whole lines only.

   (9) Only instances of a single variable or single constant can be bound by E.G.

12. (5) Every instance of x in ϕx must be replaced by a single variable or single constant in inferring ϕa or ϕy from $(x)\phi x$ by U.I.

   (11) Only instances of a single variable can be bound by U.G.

   (15) Every instance of a in ϕa or y in ϕy must be replaced by a corresponding x in ϕx in inferring $(\exists x)\phi x$ from ϕa or ϕy by E.G.

Exercises IV
Page 135

1. (1) $(x)(Hx \lor Jx)$ $\underline{\mid Ja}$
   (2) $\sim Ha$
   (3) $Ha \lor Ja$ 1, U.I.
   (4) Ja 2, 3 D.S.

4. (1) $(x)[(\sim Ax \cdot Bx) \lor Cx]$ $\underline{\mid (x)(Ax \supset Cx)}$
   (2) $(\sim Ax \cdot Bx) \lor Cx$ 1, U.I.
   (3) $Cx \lor (\sim Ax \cdot Bx)$ 2, Comm.
   (4) $(Cx \lor \sim Ax) \cdot (Cx \lor Bx)$ 3, Dist.
   (5) $Cx \lor \sim Ax$ 4, Simp.
   (6) $\sim Ax \lor Cx$ 5, Comm.
   (7) $Ax \supset Cx$ 6, M.I.
   (8) $(x)(Ax \supset Cx)$ 7, U.G.

7. (1) $(x)\{Dx \supset [Fx \supset (Gx \cdot Hx)]\}$ $\underline{\mid (\exists x)(Fx \supset Hx)}$
   (2) $(\exists x)Dx$
   (3) Dx 2, E.I.
   (4) $Dx \supset [Fx \supset (Gx \cdot Hx)]$ 1, U.I.
   (5) $Fx \supset (Gx \cdot Hx)$ 3, 4 *M.P.*
   (6) $\sim Fx \lor (Gx \cdot Hx)$ 5, M.I.
   (7) $(\sim Fx \lor Gx) \cdot (\sim Fx \lor Hx)$ 6, Dist.
   (8) $\sim Fx \lor Hx$ 7, Simp.
   (9) $Fx \supset Hx$ 8, M.I.
   (10) $(\exists x)(Fx \supset Hx)$ 9, E.G.

10. (1) $(x)[(Lx \lor Nx) \supset Kx]$ $\underline{\mid (x)(Sx \cdot Tx)}$
   (2) $(x)(\sim Kx \cdot Mx)$
   (3) $(x)\{\sim Lx \supset [\sim Nx \supset (Sx \cdot Tx)]\}$
   (4) $(Lx \lor Nx) \supset Kx$ 1, U.I.
   (5) $\sim Kx \cdot Mx$ 2, U.I.
   (6) $\sim Kx$ 5, Simp.
   (7) $\sim (Lx \lor Nx)$ 4, 6 *M.T.*
   (8) $\sim Lx \cdot \sim Nx$ 7, D.M.
   (9) $\sim Lx \supset [\sim Nx \supset (Sx \cdot Tx)]$ 3, U.I.
   (10) $(\sim Lx \cdot \sim Nx) \supset (Sx \cdot Tx)$ 9, Exp.
   (11) $Sx \cdot Tx$ 8, 10 *M.P.*
   (12) $(x)(Sx \cdot Tx)$ 11, U.G.

Exercises V
Page 136

3. (1) $(x)[(Bx \cdot Vx) \supset Tx]$ $\lfloor (\exists x)(Vx \cdot \sim Bx)$
    (2) $(\exists x)(Vx \cdot \sim Tx)$
    (3) $Vx \cdot \sim Tx$ 2, E.I.
    (4) Vx 3, Simp.
    (5) $(Bx \cdot Vx) \supset Tx$ 1, U.I.
    (6) $\sim Tx$ 3, Simp.
    (7) $\sim(Bx \cdot Vx)$ 5, 6 *M.T.*
    {8) $\sim Bx \vee \sim Vx$ 7, D.M.
    (9) $\sim\sim Vx$ 4, D.N.
    (10) $\sim Bx$ 8, 9 D.S.
    (11) $Vx \cdot \sim Bx$ 4, 10 Conj.
    (12) $(\exists x)(Vx \cdot \sim Bx)$ 11, E.G.

6. (1) $(x)[Px \supset (Ix \vee Wx)]$ $\lfloor (Jc \cdot Kc) \cdot Sc$
    (2) $(x)[(Px \cdot Ix) \supset Kx]$
    (3) $(x)[(Px \cdot Wx) \supset Jx]$
    (4) $(x)(Jx \supset Sx)$
    (5) $(x)\{[Jx \cdot Sx] \vee Ox] \supset Kx\}$
    (6) $Wc \cdot Pc$
    (7) $(Pc \cdot Wc) \supset Jc$ 3, U.I.
    (8) $Pc \cdot Wc$ 6, Comm.
    (9) Jc 7, 8 *M.P.*
    (10) $[(Jc \cdot Sc) \vee Oc] \supset Kc$ 5, U.I.
    (11) $Jc \supset Sc$ 4, U.I.
    (12) Sc 9, 11 *M.P.*
    (13) $Jc \cdot Sc$ 9, 12 Conj.
    (14) $(Jc \cdot Sc) \vee Oc$ 13, Add.
    (15) Kc 10, 14 *M.P.*
    (16) $Jc \cdot Kc$ 9, 15 Conj.
    (17) $(Jc \cdot Kc) \cdot Sc$ 12, 16 Conj.

8. (1) $(x)[(Ox \vee \sim Lx) \supset Dx]$ $\lfloor (x)\{Sx \supset [(Rx \cdot \sim Lx) \supset Dx]\}$
    (2) $(Ox \vee \sim Lx) \supset Dx$ 1, U.I.
    (3) $\sim(Ox \vee \sim Lx) \vee Dx$ 2, M.I.
    (4) $Dx \vee \sim(Ox \vee \sim Lx)$ 3, Comm.
    (5) $Dx \vee (\sim Ox \cdot Lx)$ 4, D.M.
    (6) $(Dx \vee \sim Ox) \cdot (Dx \vee Lx)$ 5, Dist.
    (7) $Dx \vee Lx$ 6, Simp.
    (8) $(Dx \vee Lx) \vee (\sim Sx \vee \sim Rx)$ 7, Add.
    (9) $Dx \vee [Lx \vee (\sim Sx \vee \sim Rx)]$ 8, Assoc.
    (10) $[Lx \vee (\sim Sx \vee \sim Rx)] \vee Dx$ 9, Comm.
    (11) $[(\sim Sx \vee \sim Rx) \vee Lx] \vee Dx$ 10, Comm.
    (12) $[\sim Sx \vee (\sim Rx \vee Lx)] \vee Dx$ 11, Assoc.
    (13) $\sim Sx \vee [(\sim Rx \vee Lx) \vee Dx]$ 12, Assoc.
    (14) $\sim Sx \vee [\sim(Rx \cdot \sim Lx) \vee Dx]$ 13, D.M.
    (15) $Sx \supset [(Rx \cdot \sim Lx) \supset Dx]$ 14, M.I.
    (16) $(x)\{Sx \supset [(Rx \cdot \sim Lx) \supset Dx]\}$ 15, U.G.

Exercises VI
Page 138

1. $(x)Cx$, $\sim(\exists x) \sim Cx$
5. $\sim(x)(Px \supset Fx)$, $(\exists x)(Px \cdot \sim Fx)$

3. $(\exists x)(Lx \cdot Px)$, $\sim(x)(Lx \supset \sim Px)$
5. $(\exists x)(Ex \cdot \sim Dx)$, $\sim(x)(Ex \supset Dx)$

Exercises VII
Page 138

3. (1) $(x)[(Fx \vee Gx) \supset Hx]$ $\vert\ (\exists x)Hz$
  (2) $\sim(y)(Jy \vee \sim Fy)$
  —————————————
  (3) $(\exists y) \sim (Jy \vee \sim Fy)$ 2, Q.N.
  (4) $\sim(Jy \vee \sim Fy)$ 3, E.I.
  (5) $\sim Jy \cdot Fy$ 4, D.M.
  (6) Fy 5, Simp.
  (7) $(Fy \vee Gy) \supset Hy$ 1, U.I.
  (8) $Fy \vee Gy$ 6, Add.
  (9) Hy 7, 8 *M.P.*
 (10) $(\exists z)Hz$ 9, E.G.

5. (1) $\sim(x)(Gx \supset Jx)$ $\vert\ (\exists y)(\sim Fy \vee Jy)$
  (2) $\sim(y)[Fy \cdot (Gy \vee Hy)]$
  (3) $\sim(\exists x)[(Fx \cdot \sim Gx) \cdot \sim Jx]$
  —————————————————
  (4) $(\exists y) \sim [Fy \cdot (Gy \vee Hy)]$ 2, Q.N.
  (5) $\sim[Fy \cdot (Gy \vee Hy)]$ 4, E.I.
  (6) $(x) \sim [(Fx \cdot \sim Gx) \cdot \sim Jx]$ 3, Q.N.
  (7) $\sim[(Fy \cdot \sim Gy) \cdot \sim Jy]$ 6, U.I.
  (8) $\sim Fy \vee \sim(Gy \vee Hy)$ 5, D.M.
  (9) $\sim Fy \vee (\sim Gy \cdot \sim Hy)$ 8, D.M.
 (10) $(\sim Fy \vee \sim Gy) \cdot (\sim Fy \vee \sim Hy)$ 9, Dist.
 (11) $\sim Fy \vee \sim Gy$ 10, Simp.
 (12) $Fy \supset \sim Gy$ 11, M.I.
 (13) $Fy \supset (Fy \cdot \sim Gy)$ 12, Abs.
 (14) $\sim(Fy \cdot \sim Gy) \vee Jy$ 7, D.M.
 (15) $(Fy \cdot \sim Gy) \supset Jy$ 14, M.I.
 (16) $Fy \supset Jy$ 13, 15 H.S.
 (17) $\sim Fy \vee Jy$ 16, M.I.
 (18) $(\exists y)(\sim Fy \vee Jy)$ 17, E.G.

7. (1) $(x)(Px \supset Lx)$ $\vert\ Cc$
  (2) $\sim(\exists x)[Lx \cdot (Bx \cdot \sim Cx)]$
  (3) $(x)(Ux \supset Bx)$
  (4) $Pc \cdot Uc$
  —————————
  (5) $(x) \sim [Lx \cdot (Bx \cdot \sim Cx)]$ 2, Q.N.
  (6) $\sim[Lc \cdot (Bc \cdot \sim Cc)]$ 5, U.I.
  (7) $\sim Lc \vee \sim(Bc \cdot \sim Cc)$ 6, D.M.
  (8) $Pc \supset Lc$ 1, U.I.

(9) Pc	4, Simp.
(10) Lc	8, 9 $M.P.$
(11) $\sim\sim Lc$	10, D.N.
(12) $\sim(Bc \cdot \sim Cc)$	7, 11 D.S.
(13) $\sim Bc \vee Cc$	12, D.M.
(14) $Uc \supset Bc$	3, U.I.
(15) Uc	4, Simp.
(16) Bc	14, 15 $M.P.$
(17) $\sim\sim Bc$	16, D.N.
(18) Cc	13, 17 D.S.

10. (1) $\sim(\exists x)(Gx \cdot \sim Fx)$ $\mid (\exists x)(Wx \cdot Ax)$
   (2) $\sim(x)(Fx \cdot Gx)$
   (3) $(x)[\sim Gx \supset (Px \equiv Tx)]$
   (4) $\underline{\sim(\exists x)[(Px \equiv Tx) \cdot \sim(Wx \cdot Ax)]}$

(5) $(\exists x) \sim (Fx \cdot Gx)$	2, Q.N.
(6) $\sim(Fx \cdot Gx)$	5, E.I.
(7) $(x) \sim (Gx \cdot \sim Fx)$	1, Q.N.
(8) $\sim(Gx \cdot \sim Fx)$	7, U.I.
(9) $\sim Gx \vee Fx$	8, D.M.
(10) $Gx \supset Fx$	9, M.I.
(11) $Gx \supset (Gx \cdot Fx)$	10, Abs.
(12) $\sim(Gx \cdot Fx)$	6, Comm.
(13) $\sim Gx$	11, 12 $M.T.$
(14) $\sim Gx \supset (Px \equiv Tx)$	3, U.I.
(15) $Px \equiv Tx$	13, 14 $M.P.$
(16) $(x) \sim [(Px \equiv Tx) \cdot \sim(Wx \cdot Ax)]$	4, Q.N.
(17) $\sim[(Px \equiv Tx) \cdot \sim(Wx \cdot Ax)]$	16, U.I.
(18) $\sim(Px \equiv Tx) \vee (Wx \cdot Ax)$	17, D.M.
(19) $\sim\sim(Px \equiv Tx)$	15, D.N.
(20) $Wx \cdot Ax$	18, 19 D.S.
(21) $(\exists x)(Wx \cdot Ax)$	20, E.G.

Exercises VIII
Page 141

8. (from Exercises IV, page 135)

(1) $(x)[Ax \supset (Bx \cdot Lx)]$		$\mid (x)\{Ax \supset [Kx \supset (Lx \vee Mx)]\}$
(2)	Ay	C.P.
(3)	Ky	C.P.
(4)	$Ay \supset (By \cdot Ly)$	1, U.I.
(5)	$By \cdot Ly$	2, 4 $M.P.$
(6)	Ly	5, Simp.
(7)	$Ly \vee My$	6, Add.
(8)	$Ky \supset (Ly \vee My)$	3–7 C.P.
(9)	$Ay \supset [Ky \supset (Ly \vee My)]$	2–8 C.P.
(10)	$(x)\{Ax \supset [Kx \supset (Lx \vee Mx)]\}$	9, U.G.

10.   (from Exercises V, page 136)
      (1) $(x)(Mx \supset Ax)$ $\vert (x)[Mx \supset (\sim Hx \supset Lx)]$
      (2) $(x)[(Mx \cdot Ax) \supset (Fx \cdot Lx)]$
      (3) $(x)[(Mx \cdot Lx) \supset Ox]$
      (4) $(x)[(Mx \cdot Fx) \supset Tx]$
      (5) $(x)\{[(Mx \cdot Ox) \cdot Tx] \supset (\sim Hx \supset Bx)\}$
      (6) $(x)[(Mx \cdot Bx) \supset Lx]$
      (7) | My C.P.
      (8) | | $\sim Hy$ C.P.
      (9) | | $My \supset Ay$ 1, U.I.
      (10) | | Ay 7, 9 M.P.
      (11) | | $(My \cdot Ay) \supset (Fy \cdot Ly)$ 2, U.I.
      (12) | | $My \cdot Ay$ 7, 10 Conj.
      (13) | | $Fy \cdot Ly$ 11, 12 M.P.
      (14) | | Ly 13, Simp.
      (15) | $\sim Hy \supset Ly$ 8–14 C.P.
      (16) $My \supset (\sim Hy \supset Ly)$ 7–15 C.P.
      (17) $(x)[Mx \supset (\sim Hx \supset Lx)]$ 16, U.G.

5.   (from Exercises V, page 136)
      (1) $(x)(Kx \equiv Ex)$ $\vert (\exists x)Ax$
      (2) $(\exists x)(Kx \lor Ex)$
      (3) $(x)[(Kx \cdot Ex) \supset Ax]$
      (4) $Kx \lor Ex$ 2, E.I.
      (5) $\sim (\exists x)Ax$ I.P.
      (6) $(x) \sim Ax$ 5, Q.N.
      (7) $\sim Ax$ 6, U.I.
      (8) $(Kx \cdot Ex) \supset Ax$ 3, U.I.
      (9) $\sim (Kx \cdot Ex)$ 7, 8 M.T.
      (10) $Kx \equiv Ex$ 1, U.I.
      (11) $(Kx \cdot Ex) \lor (\sim Kx \cdot \sim Ex)$ 10, M.E.
      (12) $\sim Kx \cdot \sim Ex$ 9, 11 D.S.
      (13) $\sim (Kx \lor Ex)$ 12, D.M.
      (14) $(Kx \lor Ex) \cdot \sim (Kx \lor Ex)$ 4, 13 Conj.

Exercises IX
Page 143

2.   Valid
     1-member universe:

$Fa \lor Ga$ $(\sim Fa \equiv Ga) \cdot (Fa \equiv \sim Ga)$ $\vert \sim Fa \lor \sim Ga$
 T   T T   F   T   T   T   T   F   F   T   T   F
   T   F   F   F F   F   F
                           F
                             F

     2-member universe:

$(Fa \lor Ga) \lor (Fb \lor Gb)$
 T   T T   T   T   T
   T   T   T
     T

$[(\sim Fa \equiv Ga) \cdot (Fa \equiv \sim Ga)] \vee [(\sim Fb \equiv Gb) \cdot (Fb \equiv \sim Gb)]$

F T T T F T F T T T T F T
    F   F   F   F   F   F
       F   F
          F
             F

$\vert (\sim Fa \vee \sim Ga) \vee (\sim Fb \vee \sim Gb)$

F T F T F T F T
   F   F   F   F
        F

3-member universe:

$[(Fa \vee Ga) \vee (Fb \vee Gb)] \vee (Fc \vee Gc)$

T T T T T T T T T
  T   T   T
     T   T

$\{[(\sim Fa \equiv Ga) \cdot (Fa \equiv \sim Ga)] \vee [(\sim Fb \equiv Gb) \cdot (Fb \equiv \sim Gb)]\} \vee$

F T T T F T F T T T T F T
   F   F   F   F   F   F   F
      F   F
                 F   F

$[(\sim Fc \equiv Gc) \cdot (Fc \equiv \sim Gc)]$

F T T T F T
   F   F
      F

$\vert [(\sim Fa \vee \sim Ga) \vee (\sim Fb \vee \sim Gb)] \vee (\sim Fc \vee \sim Gc)$

F T F T F T F T F T F T
   F   F   F   F   F   F
         F   F

5. Invalid in 3-member universe
    1-member universe:

$Pa \cdot Qa$ $Pa \cdot \sim Qa$ $\vert Ra \supset Pa$
F F   F F   T F
   F   F   F

2-member universe:

$(Pa \cdot Qa) \vee (Pb \cdot Qb)$ $(Pa \cdot \sim Qa) \vee (Pb \cdot \sim Qb)$
F   T T   F   F T
   F   T   F   F   F
        T   F

$\vert (Ra \supset Pa) \cdot (Rb \supset Pb)$
T F   T T
   F   F
      F

3-member universe:

$[(Pa \cdot Qa) \vee (Pb \cdot Qb)] \vee (Pc \cdot Qc)$
T T T   F F
   T   T   F
      T   T

$$[(Pa \cdot \sim Qa) \vee (Pb \cdot \sim Qb)] \vee (Pc \cdot \sim Qc)$$
$$\quad\ \text{T}\ \ \ \text{F}\qquad\ \text{T}\ \ \ \text{F}\qquad\ \text{F}$$
$$\qquad \text{F}\qquad\qquad \text{T}^{\text{T}}\quad\ \ \text{F}$$
$$\qquad\quad \text{T}\qquad \text{T}\qquad\quad \text{T}\qquad \text{F}$$

$$\underline{\ \big|\ [(Ra \supset Pa) \cdot (Rb \supset Pb)] \cdot (Rc \supset Pc)}$$
$$\qquad\quad \text{T}^{\ \text{T}}\qquad \text{T}^{\ \text{T}}\qquad \text{T}^{\ \text{T}}\ \text{F}\ \ \text{F}$$
$$\qquad\qquad\quad \text{T}\qquad\qquad \text{F}$$

10. Invalid in 1-member universe:

$$Pa \supset (Fa \vee Ga)$$
$$\text{T}\quad\ \text{T}\ \ _{\text{T}}\ \text{F}$$
$$\qquad\ \text{T}$$

$$Ga \supset [Ha \supset (Ia \equiv Ja)]$$
$$\text{F}\qquad \text{F}\ \ _{\text{T}}\ \text{T}\quad\ \text{T}$$
$$\qquad\qquad \text{T}$$

$$Pa \vee (Ha \cdot Ia)$$
$$\text{T}\qquad \text{T}\ _{\text{T}}\ \text{T}$$
$$\qquad\quad \text{T}$$

$$Ia$$
$$\text{T}$$

$$Ra \supset (Pa \cdot Ha)$$
$$\text{T}\quad\ \text{T}\ _{\text{T}}\ \text{T}$$
$$\qquad\ \text{T}$$

$$\underline{\ \big|\ \sim Ra}$$
$$\text{F}^{\ \text{T}}$$

CHAPTER 9

Exercises II
Page 152

1. No D is T
4. All K is A
8. All W is R

12. Some P is D,   Some P is not D
19. All E is C
31. All S is T
38. All G is E

Exercises VI
Page 159

Original	1. All W is G	5. Some F is not non-V
Converse	Some G is W (by limitation)	
Obverse	No W is non-G	Some F is V
Contrapositive	All non-G is non-W	Some V is not non-F

Original	8. Some non-R is A
Converse	Some A is non-R
Obverse	Some non-R is not non-A
Contrapositive	

Exercises VII
Page 159

If 'All O is S' is true, then: (1) T, (5) Ind., (7) F, (10) T.
If 'All O is S' is false, then: (1) F, (5) Ind., (7) Ind., (10) F.

Exercises VIII
Page 159

If 'No *E* is *O*' is true, then: (1) F, (5) F, (7) F, (9) T.
If 'No *E* is *O*' is false, then: (1) Ind., (5) Ind., (7) Ind., (9) F.

Exercises IX
Page 162

1. Invalid.   Violates Rule 3. Undistributed middle.
4. Invalid.   Violates Rule 5. Illicit exclusion.
9. Valid.

Exercises X
Page 164

1. All *C* is *S*   Valid   5. Some *C* is not *A*   Invalid
   All *U* is *C*   All *A* is non-*S*   (illicit major)
   ──────────   ────────────────
   All *U* is *S*   Some non-*S* is not *C*

Exercises XI
Page 165

1. No things which give one a stomachache are things which
   should be eaten.
   All green apples are things which give one a stomachache.
   ───
   No green apples are things which should be eaten.

   No *S* is *E*   Valid
   All *G* is *S*
   ─────────
   No *G* is *E*

6. All those people who were admitted were people who were wearing ties.
   All members of the class containing only John are people who were
      wearing ties.
   ───
   All members of the class containing only John were people who were
      admitted.

   All *A* is *W*   Invalid
   All *J* is *W*   (undistributed middle)
   ─────────
   All *J* is *A*

Exercises XII
Page 167

1. (1) Some *B* is *I*   (2) No *D* is *M*   (4) No *I* is *M*
   (2) No *D* is *M*   (3) All *I* is *D*   (1) Some *B* is *I*
   (3) All *I* is *D*   (4) No *I* is *M*   (5) Some *B* is not *M*

4. (1) No *T* is *W*   (1) No *T* is *W*   (4′) All *H* is non-*W*
   (2) No non-*W* is *C*   (3) All *H* is *T*   (2) No non-*W* is *C*
   (3) All *H* is *T*   (4) No *H* is *W*   (5) No *H* is *C*

Exercises XIII
Page 171

	Standard Form	Venn Diagrams	Algebraic Notation
1.	All O is S	O ⬰ S	$O\bar{S} = 0$
5.	Some W is not P	W ⬰ P	$W\bar{P} \neq 0$
6.	Some C is A,	C ⬰ A	$CA \neq 0$ and
	Some C is not A	and ⬰	$C\bar{A} \neq 0$
10.	No N is T	N ⬰ T	$NT = 0$

Exercises XIV
Page 171

1. D ⬰ T $DT = 0$

7. D ⬰ P $D\bar{P} = 0$

10. S ⬰ T $ST \neq 0$

Exercises XV
Page 175

1. All K is C
   All C is S
   ――――――――
   All K is S

   K ⬰ C / S Valid

5. All C is M
   Some M is B
   ――――――――
   Some B is C

   C ⬰ M / B Invalid

9. Some E is R
   Some G is not R
   ――――――――
   Some G is not E

   E ⬰ R / G Invalid

Exercises XVI
Page 177

1.	$K\bar{C} = 0$	Valid		5.	$C\bar{M} = 0$	Invalid
	$C\bar{S} = 0$				$MB \neq 0$	(violates rule 2
	$K\bar{S} \neq 0$				$BC = 0$	and rule 3)
7.	$CE = 0$			9.	$ER \neq 0$	
	$ME = 0$	Invalid			$G\bar{R} \neq 0$	Invalid
	$MC \neq 0$	(violates rule 2)			$G\bar{E} = 0$	(violates rule 1)

Exercises XVII
Page 178

1. Number 3 is valid by traditional rules but invalid by Venn diagrams and Antilogisms.

CHAPTER 10

Exercises I
Page 186

1. $p(5 \oslash 6) = p(5) + p(6) = 1/6 + 1/6 = 1/3$

5. (a) $p(9) = p(6 \cdot 3) + p(5 \cdot 4) + p(4 \cdot 5) + p(3 \cdot 6)$
   $\quad\quad = 1/36 \quad\ + 1/36 \quad\ + 1/36 \quad\ + 1/36$
   $\quad\quad = 1/9$

   (d) $p(\text{pair}) = p(1 \cdot 1) + p(2 \cdot 2) + p(3 \cdot 3) + p(4 \cdot 4)$
   $\quad\quad\quad\quad\quad\quad\quad\quad\quad\quad + p(5 \cdot 5) + p(6 \cdot 6)$
   $\quad\quad\quad\quad = 1/6$

Exercises II
Page 187

3. The Flush. The probability that he will draw another club is 9/47, while the probability that he will complete the straight by drawing a four or a nine is $4/47 + 4/47 = 8/47$.

4. (a) Discard one 10. Draw for an inside straight. The probability of drawing an 8 (4/47) is greater than the probability of drawing 2 diamonds (90/2162) or of drawing another 10 (2/47).

Exercises III
Page 191

1. (a) 18
   (b) 7
   (c) 7
   (d) 99
   (e) 27.919

CHAPTER 11

Exercises I
Page 211

3. A. Directive; Emotive
   C. Ceremonial
   E. Operative; Ceremonial
   H. Evaluative
   J. Emotive

Exercises II
Page 213

7. A. Natural
   D. Conventional; Non-linguistic
   F. Conventional; Linguistic

Exercises III
Page 215

8. A. One-place
   C. Two-place
   E. Four-place

Exercises IV
Page 216

1. Mentioned
4. Used
7. Used; Mentioned

Exercises V
Page 217

  3. A. Tokens
       D. Types

Exercises VI
Page 219

  6. b. The venus fly trap was first discovered
         in North Carolina.
  7. c. College students are in rebellion.
  7. e. Thanks for the complimentary copy of
         your new book. I shall read it
         right away.

Exercises VIII
Page 223

  3. A. Defining
       D. Accompanying
       G. Accompanying

Exercises IX
Page 225

  1. A. Agreement in belief
       B. Disagreement in attitude
  7. A. Disagreement in belief
       B. Both agreement and disagreement
         in attitude

CHAPTER 12

No selected answers provided.

CHAPTER 13

Exercises I
Page 247

  1. Equivocation
  3. Division (linguistic)
  8. Accent
 10. Composition (linguistic)

Exercises II
Page 250

  1. Complex question
  4. Circular argument
  5. Question-begging expression

Exercises III
Page 254

  1. Composition
  3. False dilemma
  7. Bifurcation
 10. Slippery slope

Exercises IV
Page 261

  1. *Ad Populum*
  5. Strawman: Extention
  6. *Ad Hominem* Circumstantial
      and *Tu Quoque*
 10. Diversion: Appeal to Humor

Exercises V
Page 268

  1. Accident
  3. False Cause: Common effects and reciprocal effects
  8. Faulty Analogy

INDEX